YOUNG MEN AND THE SEA

DANIEL VICKERS WITH VINCE WALSH

Young Men and the Sea

YANKEE SEAFARERS IN THE AGE OF SAIL

YALE UNIVERSITY PRESS   NEW HAVEN & LONDON

Published with assistance from the Annie Burr Lewis Fund.
Published with assistance from the Kingsley Trust Association Publication Fund established
by the Scroll and Key Society of Yale College.

Set in Scala and Scala Sans type by Duke & Company, Devon, Pennsylvania.
Printed in the United States of America by Edwards Brothers, Ann Arbor, Michigan.

Library of Congress Cataloging-in-Publication Data
Vickers, Daniel.
Young men and the sea : yankee seafarers in the age of sail / Daniel Vickers with Vince Walsh.
    p.   cm.
Includes bibliographical references and index.
ISBN 0-300-10067-1 (cloth : alk. paper)
1. Seafaring life—New England—History. 2. Seafaring life—Massachusetts—Salem—History.
3. Sailors—New England—History. 4. Sailors—Massachusetts—Salem—History. 5. Salem
(Mass.)—History, Naval. 6. New England—History, Naval. I. Walsh, Vince. II. Title.
F4.V53 2005
387.5'09744'5—dc22

2004024094

A catalogue record for this book is available from the British Library.

The paper in this book meets the guidelines for permanence and durability of the Committee
on Production Guidelines for Book Longevity of the Council on Library Resources.

10 9 8 7 6 5 4 3 2 1

To Christine

CONTENTS

DURING THE NINETEENTH CENTURY, the sea and the people who made their living upon it became something to write about. James Fenimore Cooper, Richard Henry Dana, and Herman Melville were only the best known of many writers who felt moved to tell the story of men whose habits seemed increasingly at variance with modern ways. In a world where mechanism, routine, and calculation dominated more and more of life, the sea seemed to be one place still ruled by forces that humans could not pretend to control, a place where the Gradgrinds and Bounderbys were not to be found, where friendship and heroism, as well as evil and terror, still governed human life, and where the sublime ruled over the mundane. During the middle decades of the nineteenth century, the sea acquired a romantic aura—to which Dana, Melville, and the others partly responded and partly contributed—that it has essentially never shed.

Students of American maritime life have been sailing on this tack for most of the past century. Although they may disagree about many things, they all have been captivated by the distinctiveness of seafaring life, and much of their work is designed to explain why anyone would undertake it. Even my own early work—written in a rooming house in Toronto a quarter-century ago, when the only maritime society I knew was one I had created in my head—made a great deal of the border between land and sea and invested a lot of energy in explaining why people ever crossed it.

This book, however, was conceived and researched during the fifteen years I spent teaching history in Newfoundland. Living among people who had almost all grown up beside the sea changed many of my ideas about what maritime labor meant to those who did it. From the big-city perspective of Toronto, where I was born, seafaring had always seemed an unusual occupational choice, and I began, like most historians do, possessed of the conventionally romantic notions of its exceptional, bewitching nature. In Newfoundland, however, I met for the first time a large body of people who saw nothing unusual in maritime labor. Both among my neighbors, who until recently had at one time or another either worked on the water or married someone who did, and among my colleagues at Memorial University, who were engaged in exploring their history, the answer to why men went to work on the deep seemed self-evident: what else were they to do?

Although it is dangerous to transport the attitudes of the present day directly into the study of the past, analogy can be a place to begin, and if the experience of one maritime society suggests a new way of looking at another—even if the two are centuries apart—we would be foolish to ignore the opportunity. Whether an account of seafaring in preindustrial New England that emphasizes its ubiquitous and unexceptional character truly fits the evidence readers must decide for themselves. This book, however, was conceived among people who still see things that way, and it was by borrowing their sense of maritime life that this project was first imagined.

ACKNOWLEDGMENTS

MY FIRST BOOK, ON farmers and fishermen in coastal New England, was based on a dissertation and thus a project I researched and wrote myself. This study is quite different. Although the text is still the product of my own hand, the bulk of the research was performed by others—graduate and undergraduate students trained in maritime history by the Maritime Studies Research Unit at Memorial University in Newfoundland, Canada. Although as their supervisor I am responsible for any errors they may have committed, I have been struck, while checking and rechecking their labors over the past fifteen years, by the care with which nearly all of them performed their work. Indeed, some of them were more assiduous and more ingenious than their mentor, and for this I am deeply grateful.

None of them could have been hired or trained without the help of five institutions: the Social Sciences and Humanities Research Council of Canada (SSHRCC), the Memorial University of Newfoundland (MUN), the University of California, San Diego (UCSD); the Peabody-Essex Museum of Salem, Massachusetts (PEM), and the National Archive and Records Administration Regional Office in Waltham, Massachusetts (NARA-Waltham). SSHRCC awarded me three major research grants in support of the project, used mainly for travel to archives and research assistance. MUN provided me with the fine facilities of its Queen Elizabeth II Library, whose holdings in maritime history are ably developed by Michael Lonardo;

the collection of the Maritime History Archive, under the inspired direction of Heather Wareham; the space, computer facilities, and financial support of its Maritime Studies Research Unit; and a long succession of under-graduate research assistantships to make possible the time-consuming process of data collection and input. The James Duncan Phillips Library of the PEM provided me with its wonderful archive of public and private records relating to the maritime history of Salem, and it generously allowed my students and me free accommodation in the Gardner-Pingree House on many occasions to help bring this project to conclusion. The NARA-Waltham provided access to the remarkably rich files of the U.S. First District Court, and its staff cheerfully dealt with several other unusual requests. Finally, UCSD provided me with the time to turn all the research performed by Newfoundlanders into the book before you.

Parts of Chapter 4 were reworked from "Young Men and the Sea: The Sociology of Seafaring in Eighteenth-Century Salem, Massachusetts," *Social History*, 24 (1999), 17–38 (see http://tandf.co.uk/journals); and "An Honest Tar: Ashley Bowen of Marblehead," *New England Quarterly*, 69 (1996), 531–553.

Many scholars have assisted me in formulating the ideas contained in the chapters to follow, but from a long list let me single out Jerry Bannister, Valerie Burton, Sean Cadigan, Judith Fingard, Skip Fischer, Farley Grubb, Michael Jarvis, Michael Meranze, Lisa Norling, and Marcus Rediker. To Jeffrey Bolster and Chris Clark, who read the manuscript in its entirety, I am especially thankful. Let me also acknowledge the many students—graduate and undergraduate—who assisted in the research. They include Penny Biggin, Glenn Brown, Lynn Burke, Andrea Channing, Will Clark, John Cowan, Mike Dove, Mark Eddy, Sara Flaherty, William Howse, Mark Hunter, Kelly Johnson, Sean Kennedy, Kathryn Philpott, Jason Rogers, James Rose, Duane Spracklin, Trudy Stafford, Sarah Vickers, Simon Vickers, Todd Welker, Carla Wheaton, and Michelle White.

Then there is Vince Walsh. Vince joined the Masters program at MUN in 1989, signed on to the *Young Men and the Sea* project a year later, and wrote a superb masters thesis on the shipmasters of Salem from 1630–1720. After graduating, he took a job coordinating the development of the Newfoundland and Labrador Heritage Web site, but he has continued to devote nights, weekends, and summer holidays to the book ever since. Over fifteen years, he developed several key elements of the project's research design, made four extended research trips to Salem, introduced me to the computer databases in which most of the research was recorded, constructed the network by which the different computers in the project were connected, undertook a huge amount of the basic research himself, trained many of the assistants, talked over the problems of maritime history with me endlessly, and finally read and reread all of the manuscript more times than was probably good for him. I actually wrote the book, but in every other respect, the line at which his contributions end and mine begin is impossible to tell. Most important of all—for me anyway —has been his friendship and good humor. To have run into Vince at the inception of this study was an extraordinary stroke of luck.

Finally, I would like to thank my wife, Christine, who has contributed her research, critical, and editorial skills to this project from the beginning. *Young Men and the Sea* has not made her life any easier, and her willingness to share the power of her judgment with me is a wonderful thing. To have had the fortune of completing this book in her company is the greatest blessing I own.

—Daniel Vickers

Introduction

THE OCEAN IS A hostile environment, and the decision to live and work upon it strikes most of us as something that ought to be explained. *Moby-Dick* begins with an apology; Ishmael goes whaling, Melville tells us, penniless and bored, as a way "of driving off the spleen." John Masefield in "Sea Fever" justifies his compulsion to go "down to the seas again" by declaring that "the call of the running tide / Is a wild call and a clear call that may not be denied." In a poem by Rudyard Kipling, laboring men facing the prospect of a winter's unemployment are drawn to sea almost instinctively by "the beat of the off-shore wind."[1] Most historians who study the age of sail have followed Melville, Masefield, Kipling, and dozens of others in believing that the seafaring life must be accounted for in terms of some compulsion—external or internal—that drove men to it. Seamen were, by different interpretations, either drawn by "high wages and the ocean's lure," "forcibly torn from the land," driven by a combination of "desire . . . wish . . . need . . . [and] yearning," or the victims of "forces beyond . . . [their] control."[2] The interpretations have differed, but they share a common belief that men need compelling motives to undertake such extraordinary work.

Most history that is "maritime," especially in the United States, follows one particular meaning of the word by restricting itself to matters "connected, associated, or dealing with shipping, naval matters, navigation, seaborne trade, etc." Such a definition encompasses seaborne commerce, naval power, fisheries, piracy, and life afloat, and it promotes an understanding of the sailor's world as something unique, formed primarily by the social, cultural, and economic relations that oceanic voyaging in the age of sail created. The best new social history of the maritime world has not been insensitive to the landward forces that bore on sailors' lives, but these works define themselves primarily by their acceptance of the distinctiveness of life at sea. Whether class, gender, or race relations are at stake, all of this rich literature rests in varying measure on the exceptionality of seafaring.[3]

Yet the word *maritime* can be used in another sense, denoting "places, 'bordering the sea' or persons 'living near or by the sea.'" In this sense Sir Thomas Herbert could in 1634 define Brittany as a "marittime part of France," and we can still speak of Nova Scotia, New Brunswick, and Prince Edward Island as the Maritime Provinces of Canada. This second definition does not contradict the first, but it emphasizes far more the interrelationship between land and sea. The popular and academic understanding of what it meant to be an American seafarer, however, has usually emphasized the maritime context in the first sense: the sea, the ship, and the social relations that prevailed aboard. The landward origins, portside social connections, and subsequent shore careers of the seafaring population—their maritime context in the second sense—are seldom invoked to explain why sailors act as they do.[4]

There are several good reasons for this. Sources for writing the history of shipboard life abound for mariners—probably more so than for any other early modern laboring occupation. Sea narratives constitute a vivid literary genre that extends back several centuries; court records have described troubles afloat in close and compelling detail for even longer; and the ship's logs that describe the workaday world of the sailor have no real parallel in any other line of early modern employment. The task of tracing mariners' lives ashore, however, before and after their adventures on the deep, is much more difficult. Men who at sea were the heroes of their story were, on land, simply faces in the crowd; tracing their personal stories into port involves daunting problems of evidence. Furthermore, we study sailors *as sailors* precisely because that is what they did for a living. Historians can no sooner ignore the identity that the sea attached to seamen than they can deny that which the soil lent to farmers, the forest to loggers, or the waterfront to shipwrights. Finally, the seafaring life has persistently attracted attention because it provides so much excellent script. Mariners visited exotic places, encountered close shaves, and brushed shoulders with eccentric characters—all frequently enough to provide any good writer with a surfeit of stories. Their home lives, by contrast, could be comfortable or tedious but rarely thrilling.

Yet does this focus on the extraordinary fairly represent them? After all, the majority spent most of their lives—perhaps even most of their working lives—on land. They were born and grew up there; they often worked on the waterfront between voyages; they usually maintained close ties with parents, siblings, wives, children, neighbors, and extended kin at home; they frequented churches, taverns, brothels, and other local institutions in port; and if they were lucky enough to survive their years at sea, they returned to shore to take up other callings or retire. Even the work they performed on the water took place much closer to home, in more routine voyages, than popular imagination assumes. Any portrait of sailors that casts them primarily as adventurers to distant parts distorts the context within which most seafaring actually unfolded.

What defined these men as maritime people was less the distances they traveled than the time they spent upon the water. Modern people, who rarely work on the ocean, have forgotten that during the age of sail most mariners hailed from towns and villages facing the sea, where waterborne activity was from an early age entirely normal and utterly ubiquitous. As little boys they played along the beach, fished from the rocks, punted about in boats, learned about the winds and tides, watched the vessels as they moved in and out of port, and listened to their older brothers talk about their work on the deep. In such communities, nobody would ever have asked why young men went to sea; the greater puzzle would have been why certain individuals decided not to.

This is not to say that everyone became a sailor for life, for even if most youths in maritime societies shipped themselves before the mast several times in their teens and twenties, few remained seamen into middle age. Many died, others were promoted, and most of the remainder slipped into different lines of work on shore. Even those who remained merchant seamen throughout their working careers usually tried their hands from time to time at other forms of maritime labor—fishing, whaling, privateering, or naval service, to name some of the more common choices. Mariners could be apprentices, wage laborers, co-adventurers, ship's officers, or self-employed vessel owners at different points in their lives in various branches of the maritime economy, and the assortment of paths they could negotiate through this maze of alternatives was beyond number. There could never have been a single maritime culture that enveloped and defined these men. They piloted themselves through life as circumstances required, playing the wanderer, settler, rowdyman, churchgoer, overgrown child, or domineering patriarch according to what felt useful or natural at the time. And these sources of identity were rooted as much in the cultural habits and folkways of home as they were in the regimen of life afloat. Indeed, we err when we draw too strict a distinction between the two.

To a point, perhaps, one can generalize about the sailor's lot by placing his experience along a spectrum. In the greater ports that supported long-distance trade in larger vessels where the gulf between capital and labor was considerable, most mariners were wage earners, family was seldom close at hand, the ladder of promotion was steep, and shipboard relations were tense. In smaller ports that focused on coasting and fishing, owner-ship, operation, and command were not as strictly divorced one from an-other, mariners knew their mates as neighbors and kin, sailors might rea-sonably expect to acquire a degree of independence and mastery in their calling, and the discipline of life at sea was less severe. Yet actual mariners seldom sailed their life courses on a single tack. A teenager who had grown up in an outport village and learned the ropes as a fisherman working offshore might well find himself ten years later shipping out of London or New York as a foremast hand on transatlantic voyages of six months or more. Similarly, a seasoned mariner with many footloose years spent criss-crossing the oceans might just as easily choose to marry and settle down on shore, either back home or abroad. Any attempt to classify sailors as adventure-seeking youths, old salts, shipmasters on the make, saltwater mechanics, proletarians, or lumpenproletarians runs into this obstacle: that in the course of their lives most seafaring men fell into several of these roles.

What we already know about mariners is largely defined by such roles; what we have yet to discover is the complicated pattern by which they moved from one role to another. Numerous factors weighed in this process, but none so much as age. Commands at sea were delivered along an axis of seniority; promotion to the quarterdeck and retirement to shore occurred with the passage of years; and the whole run of a sailor's career took place in the shadow and frequent reality of an early death. The history of age has its students, but they are few in number alongside those who focus their attention on race, class, and gender. In one sense this is reasonable, for the latter categories all have important political constituencies in the modern world, while every stage in life is always evanescent, and youth is the only form of dependency we all outgrow. Still, one cannot make sense of early modern society—on land or at sea—without serious attention to the significance of age, seniority, and the course of people's lives.[5]

The seaport of Salem, Massachusetts, is an ideal setting in which to investigate all of these matters. Cities like London, New York, or Boston may have been larger, and villages like Manchester, Ipswich, and Chebacco were certainly more numerous, but Salem combined features of both city and village in a way that allows us to deal with many sorts of questions that would be unanswerable elsewhere. Where did sailors come from and what did they do with their lives? Salem was at different periods in its history both a generator and recipient of maritime labor. As a seaport, it participated at one point or another in many different types of shipping (small- and large-scale, short- and long-haul, coastal and global), and it is possible therefore to compare experiences in different trades. Furthermore, the town was small enough—counting perhaps one thousand inhabitants in 1650, four thousand in 1750, and twenty thousand in 1850—that it is possible to trace large numbers of individual mariners with some confidence through local records, an impossible task in a little village or a larger city. Finally, the Salem waterfront possesses a density of historical documentation probably unmatched by any other seaport in the preindustrial English-speaking world. The experience of one seaport will not answer for all the rest, of course, but to examine maritime society we need a point of entry, and for that purpose this town provides a wealth of the best evidence imaginable.

On top of this, Salem simply matters. The first town founded in the Massachusetts Bay Colony, the last important scene of witchcraft persecution in Western history, the site of the House of Seven Gables, and the birthplace of Nathaniel Hawthorne—this spot represents to Americans much that is significant about their past. Yet the role seafaring played in its history usually passes without notice. How many of us realize that Salem was originally settled by fishermen, that most of the presiding judges in the witch trials of 1692 were shipowners, that Hawthorne's seven-gabled house was constructed out of profits earned in the codfish trade, and that Hawthorne himself was the son, grandson, and great-grandson of sea captains? Salem was first and last a seafaring community, in both the eyes of contemporaries and the experience of its own residents, most of whom from the town's inception through the early republic depended on maritime employment. The character of this dependency is our quarry in this book: the actual relationship between young men and the sea.

CHAPTER ONE

Landsmen on the Water

NEW ENGLAND, 1620–1645

ALL OF THE NORTH AMERICAN colonies were originally maritime colonies. By the nature of things, Europeans had to arrive by water, and invariably they sought out places to settle by nosing around the harbors and estuaries of the new land. They constructed their first rude homes along the coast or by the shores of navigable rivers, not only because these were the first lands they found, but also because they wished to communicate easily with home and with one another. Few of them were trained mariners, but during the hungry years that followed settlement they learned to row and sail the inshore waters, fishing, hunting, and renewing contact with ships from the mother country. Even their early meetings with native Americans—trading, begging, and fighting—as often as not drew them out into salt water.

This was so even in colonies we tend to associate with agriculture and the export of staple crops. Capt. John Smith of Jamestown first learned about the lands and peoples that lived around Chesapeake Bay by sailing its length and breadth in a "strong ribb'd bark."[1] The Dutch West India Company placed its first permanent settlements in New Netherlands at the mouths of the Hudson, Mohawk, Connecticut, and Delaware rivers as garrisons to defend against seaborne attack and to guard the freshwater channels of trade to the interior. The French Acadians settled in farmsteads strung out along the tidal marshlands that ringed the Bay of Fundy, the waters of which connected them to one another and to the harbor at Port-Royal, where they sailed to sell the surplus of their fields. It could not have been otherwise. The first uncontested resource that European settlers met with in North America was the ocean, and the first open highways were the rivers, lakes, and coastal waters. Not every harbor produced a seaport. Not every seaport supported a fleet of three-masted ships. But everywhere it paid to be handy in boats.

Most students of the colonization process in America have missed this truth. In their histories, the ocean has been chiefly an obstacle over which the settlers had to pass in order to play their historical roles as conquerors, planters, or Christians. Once ashore, we are usually told, the planters turned their backs on the water and marched off to found agricultural villages where the sea played no further role in their lives. There they set about dealing with the problems that engage our interest today —transplanting European culture, attacking the wilderness, constructing communities, negotiating gender roles, dealing with native Americans, enslaving Africans, and so forth. Yet all of these activities forced the early colonists out onto the water repeatedly, and to the founders of New England, though landlubbers at the start, the sea rapidly became part of everyday life. Not only had all of them crossed it, but most of them now lived beside it, worked upon it, or dealt with those who did. Although the social historians of New England have tended to rush precociously into the interior, the settlers themselves hung back, preferring town sites by the coast or along navigable waterways as long as they could find room to plant there. They did this because they were practical people who recognized, in spite of their lack of previous seafaring experience, that the water could be useful to those who learned how to sail, row, and paddle upon it. The maritime history of the Puritan colonies was not simply "commerce," or "transport"—an abstract process or a merchant invention that somehow moved goods and people about. It was real activity engaged in by actual New Englanders, and never more generally than at the beginning, when the great majority of colonists were still in regular contact—directly or indirectly —with the ocean.

When the first Pilgrim colonists set foot on Cape Cod in November 1620, after "long beating at sea," William Bradford recalled, they "fell upon their knees and blessed the God of Heaven who had brought them over the vast and furious ocean, and delivered them from all the perils and miseries thereof, again to set their feet on the firm and stable earth, their proper element." There on the beach were "no friends to welcome them nor inns to entertain or refresh their weatherbeaten bodies; no houses or much less towns to repair to, to seek for succour." Already, wrote Bradford, "it was winter, and they that know the winters of that country know them to be sharp and violent, and subject to cruel and fierce storms." "Besides," he continued, "what could they see but a hideous and desolate wilderness, full of beasts and wild men," a country whose "woods and thickets, represented a wild and savage hue." So in this, their hour of crisis, how did they set about rescuing themselves? They built a boat.[2]

As Bradford remembered, the Pilgrims' first significant act as colonists on that lonely stretch of beach was not to construct shelters, find food, or gather fuel but to begin to assemble in the shortened hours of that late autumn day the shallop they had brought with them "in quarters" aboard the *Mayflower*, so that they could find their way around. The colonists themselves were not skilled sailors. They had crossed the ocean not as seafaring adventurers but as rural villagers looking for land on the other side where they could plant their homes, live comfortably, and worship in their own manner far from the persecuting arm of the English church and state. Yet it made little sense to explore the New England coastline for a place to live on foot, so in this little shallop, crewed by seamen from the ship, "ten of their principal men" explored the bay that autumn and decided on Plymouth as a place to settle. By December the Pilgrims had shifted the focus of their energy from sea to land, laying out a street that climbed upward from the beach and constructing a common house by the harbor. As the winter progressed, they added a few small cottages of English design, but many families remained on board ship during the cold weather, and it was not until the first day of spring in 1621 that the last of the Pilgrims came ashore. Throughout these months of famine and sickness, which killed nearly half the colonists, the *Mayflower*'s stores, supplemented by such fish as the healthier members of the community could catch in the bay, saved Plymouth from extinction. Without ship and shallop, nearly all of the settlers would undoubtedly have died.[3]

In 1621, their first full year in America, the surviving Plymouth colonists turned to husbandry in earnest, planting corn in the Indian manner in fields abandoned by the Wampanoags several years before. By autumn they had begun to lay in a "good store" of fish, waterfowl, wild turkeys, and venison, to "gather in the small harvest they had, and to fit up their houses and dwellings against the winter," when without warning another ship, the *Fortune*, arrived with thirty-six more destitute settlers on board—promptly throwing the colony on half-rations again. The following two years brought more of the same. While harvests improved, every new shipload of reinforcements consumed more than could easily be spared, and the struggle to feed themselves drove the Pilgrims continually back to the sea—but now without the help of experienced sailors. Fishing became critical. In the spring of 1623, the last of their seed corn planted and their "victuals . . . spent," the colonists divided themselves into several companies and took turns around the clock, going out in their single poorly fitted boat "with a net they had bought" to seine for bass and other fish. "Neither did they return till they had caught something," recorded Bradford, "though it were five or six days before, for they knew there was nothing at home." Facing chronic hunger, they also cruised the Cape Cod shore bartering for corn from the Indians. On one occasion, a visiting company of fishermen agreed to pilot a Plymouth vessel all the way to the coast of Maine, where the colonists managed to obtain a "present refreshing" of food from the ships that had arrived for the summer fishery. By means of this voyage, they learned "the way to those parts," and in subsequent years, when their farms had grown and they had surplus corn to sell, the Pilgrims reversed the trade imbalance and began shipping Indian meal to the eastward. Much of the fur they obtained to pay their debts in England was also fetched by sea, at first from native villages nearby and later from their own trading posts in Maine. Clapboard was another early export from the colony, and some of that may have been brought by water as well. In this way, necessity taught them both the geography of the coastline and the means of navigating it. By dint of practice, they learned to become seamen of sorts, and for at least a decade their developing ability to pilot small craft up and down the coast proved basic to survival.[4]

Not only Plymouth but all of New England's earliest colonies depended on coastal seafaring of this kind. Throughout the 1620s a thin but persistent network of waterborne traffic connected the Pilgrims at Plymouth, Thomas Weston's outpost at Wessagusset, Thomas Morton's settlement at Mount Wollaston, the Dorchester Company's colony at Cape Ann, a scattering of overwintering fur traders on the coast of Maine, and the still numer-

MAP 1.1 New England coast in the seventeenth century

ous villages of native Americans (Map 1.1). Driven by the fear of hunger and cold, settlers in each of these colonies ventured out in all manner of small craft to fish the ledges offshore, hunt waterfowl in nearby marshlands, and fetch timber for shelter and heat. When their needs could not be answered locally, they loaded their vessels with the produce of the country and struck out across waters whose shoals and tidal currents they barely knew to truck with one another or with visiting fishermen for the things they lacked. None of this trade engendered any considerable wealth, nor did any of these ocean-fronting settlements ever develop into a seaport of note. We remember the Pilgrims today as husbandmen, householders, separatists, and celebrants of thanksgiving, not as coasters or fishermen. Yet in the sense of living beside the ocean and employing it to conduct the ordinary business of life, these earliest European settlers on New England's Atlantic shores had become by necessity a maritime people.[5]

The founding of Massachusetts in 1629, the arrival of the Winthrop fleet in 1630, and the spread of Puritan settlement throughout New England during the 1630s prompted a rapid intensification of economic activity along the Atlantic shore. Those New Englanders who undertook what we now term the Great Migration came in numbers and with money and ambition beyond anything the region had seen before, and within a couple of years the intermittent trickle of coastal shipping that had been typical of the 1620s widened into a steady stream. As early as 1631 traders from the Bay Colony were sailing north to provision fishermen in Maine, south to procure grain from the colonists at Plymouth. Fishing companies set up stations at Marblehead and Dorchester, and Boston developed almost instantly into the principal seaport of the colony. Hundreds of newcomers disembarked every year with cash in their pockets looking for passage to any one of a dozen or so new communities scattered around Massachusetts Bay. There they began clearing woodland, constructing sawmills, building farms, raising cattle, and in short order generating commodities to sell. The evolution of Boston itself into a market town and a center of administration drew the same settlers back again by water in order to transact their public and private affairs. The quantity of business in transporting the settlers and their belongings along the coast, up various rivers to the new town sites, and back again with the fruits of the new economy in tow kept a good number of smaller vessels—chiefly "barks, catches, lighters, [and] shallops" of less than 10 tons' burden—busy the year round.[6]

By 1635 Massachusetts Bay stood at the hub of a coastal shipping network that extended along most of the New England coastline. At the Trelawney plantation on Richmond Island a hundred miles northeast of Boston, manager John Winter traded in livestock, beaver, corn, fish, and European manufactures with the Puritan seaport throughout the 1630s, and many smaller undocumented operations must have done the same. As the Puritan colonists pushed west to the Connecticut Valley and south to Rhode Island, coasters learned to navigate the passage around Cape Cod into Long Island Sound. Commerce with the Dutch had drawn Massachusetts vessels in this direction as early as 1633, but after the founding of Hartford and Springfield in the mid-1630s, this became a regular trade route. Because of the length of these voyages and the need to sail across open water, mariners began to employ barks and pinnaces of 20 tons or more—considerably larger than the boats that answered local needs around

Massachusetts Bay. By 1634 vessels of double or triple this tonnage, some of them constructed in New England, had begun sailing to Virginia. In 1637 the *Desire,* a ship of 120 tons built in Marblehead, journeyed a step farther to the West Indies. Finally, in 1643 the *Trial* of 150 tons sailed across the Atlantic to open a foreign trade with Spain. Although lengthy voyages were still rare enough in this period to be newsworthy, they were plainly not beyond the colonists' reach.[7]

The importance of these expeditions has often been recognized, and rightly so. At a time when the Puritan colonies were chronically short of supplies, they brought home much-needed cattle, goats, corn, cotton, and other provisions. By encouraging the construction of ships, they generated new business inside the colony and demonstrated to prospective immigrants in the old country that there were livings to be made in New England. In the act of trading overseas, the Puritans had learned where their fish, timber, and livestock could be marketed profitably, so that when the colonial economy fell on hard times with the end of the Great Migration in the early 1640s, they could pursue an export-driven strategy of development. Nevertheless, before 1645, foreign commerce employed few colonists directly. For all their economic portent, these voyages were not the means by which most New Englanders first gained their familiarity with the sea.

This fundamental process began not in ships but in boats. Like the Pilgrims at Plymouth, the Puritans discovered immediately that getting about on land, particularly if one had something heavy to carry, was difficult at best. No roads yet existed upon which one could drive a cart; Indian trails were not designed for draft animals; and even travel by foot was frequently interrupted by swamps, rivers, rough terrain, and saltwater inlets. For some time, the geography of the country was not well understood, and the penalty for getting lost in this wilderness could be stiff. Granted, New Englanders struggled continuously to transform the country and make it more traversable. They drove their oxen into the bush to haul out timber and beat out pathways underfoot; they cut back the forest and widened these tracks into cartways; they built bridges across some rivers and found fords across others; and in doing all these things they learned the lay of the land. But they also found out almost overnight that the less of this they had to do, the easier their lives would be. Fishing, hunting, wooding, visiting, hauling, shopping, and trading—first locally and then abroad—were lighter tasks when conducted afloat.

For small cargoes over short distances, the colonists relied upon what they termed canoes. William Wood saw some of these during the early 1630s and described them as "made of whole pine trees, being about two foot and a half over, and twenty foot long." Although none of the English settlers had ever set eyes on dugout craft before they arrived in New England, the Massachusetts Indians used them all the time. Samuel de Champlain encountered such a vessel, manned by five or six natives, when he rounded Cape Ann in the summer of 1605. Apparently, they were fashioned out of "the thickest and tallest" trees, felled with stone hatchets, then gouged out with fire, and finished with stone scrapers. Canoes of this construction may have been "liable to upset" unless one was "well-skilled in managing them," but they were the vessels of choice in these waters when the Puritans arrived, and the English adopted them immediately. Without roads or skilled boatbuilders, the colonists turned to what worked, and the canoe became, in Wood's phrasing, the settler's "water-horse," a basic piece of equipment to be built or purchased, mastered, and maintained like any other tool.[8]

These primitive vessels were especially popular, as one might expect, in towns with extensive shorelines, where even the shortest trip could be complicated by some sort of saltwater barrier. In Salem, for example, with its numerous rivers and bays, a trip to the North Fields could take several hours by foot but only ten minutes by boat. Crossing over to the Bass River Side (modern-day Beverly) could mean either a day of plodding through thicket and swamp or a twenty-minute paddle. Consequently, as William Wood observed, every household in town owned one or two canoes, and local residents used them as they would a horse and cart—fetching wood, traveling to the fields, or transporting produce to market. Only after 1645, in fact, did carts begin to outstrip canoes in importance in the inventoried estates of Essex County, and up to that time the use of these small craft constituted almost half of the maritime activity documented in the records of the county's Quarterly Courts.[9]

For heavier work, New Englanders used bigger craft—boats, skiffs, and shallops. Although varied in appearance, these were larger, keeled vessels—more seaworthy than canoes and generally driven by sail. Though European in design, they were probably built as often by mariners and

FIGURE 1.1 Shallop unloading at a fishing stage. This shallop of French design is unloading cod at a fishing stage in Newfoundland. With a single mast and a crew of three, it is identical to those employed in the fisheries and coastal trades of seventeenth-century New England. Source: Duhamel de Monceau, *Traite des Pesches*, Part 2 (Paris, 1772), detail from plate 18. (Courtesy of the Peabody-Essex Museum)

fishermen themselves as by professional boatbuilders or shipwrights. Evidence for how these vessels were employed in those early years, although scant, does suggest that boats and skiffs were used for longer voyages across greater stretches of open water. During the 1630s, for example, Francis Johnson, Peter Palfray, Anthony Dike, and Roger Conant ran a fur-trading establishment in Casco Bay with a boat, a skiff, and a canoe. When the partnership shipped off its skins to "the Massachusets," they did so in the boat. The largest of these inshore craft were shallops—open-decked, double-ended, possessing one or two masts, and manned by two or three men (Figure 1.1). In 1641 the Essex County Court directed that William Trask of Salem construct a "way or passage" around his mill dam on the North River for shallops to pass on their way to and from the town's fields. These sturdy little vessels were the particular choice of fishermen in these early years, but since they could hold several tons of cargo, other colonists used them for transporting serious loads.[10]

The colonists did not take to the ocean naturally, for hardly any of them were watermen—born or bred. Most came from towns and villages in the southeast of England, where they followed farming or a variety of artisanal trades, and few of them knew anything of boats. Indeed, the early years in Massachusetts were flecked with accidents—many of them fatal—stemming from their inexperience. The first of these involved Henry Winthrop, the governor's son, who drowned in a creek near Salem the day after he arrived in New England. Better documented were the misadventures of Richard Garrett. This middle-aged shoemaker had moved to New England with his wife and family in the Winthrop fleet of 1630. In December of that first year, with the temperature plunging and a frigid wind blowing off the land, he decided one day to travel by water with his daughter, Hannah, and four other passengers to Plymouth, several hours southward along the coast. His friends knew of his inexperience on the water and tried to talk him out of it, but with the courage of innocence and the wind abaft, the party set out into Massachusetts Bay in a little shallop hoping to reach the Pilgrim settlement before nightfall. When darkness and stormy weather overtook them, they had to put into another harbor short of their destination and heave out their killick (a stone-and-branch anchor) to hold them from being driven out to sea. Then, as the little craft pitched about in the dark, the killick fell apart, and taking on water they began to drift with the storm. By good fortune Cape Cod lay in their path, and the wind drove them ashore somewhere near Wellfleet, where, after having cut their legs out of the ice that had gathered in the bilge, they spent a frigid night ashore. The next day, an Indian family came upon the shipwrecked company and attempted to save them by building a wigwam over their heads, "for they were so weak and frozen as they could not stir." Yet there was little that could be done. Garrett soon perished, and although the Indians carried the remainder of the group on their backs fifty miles to Plymouth, most of these frostbitten survivors died as well. Only Hannah Garrett and Henry Harwood made it home alive, and Harwood "lay long under the surgeon's hands," losing several limbs as the price for his foolhardy adventure. The story of this tragedy spread quickly through the colony, almost certainly as a message on human pride and seafaring stupidity. If people like Garrett were going to use the ocean readily, they should treat it with respect.[11]

This was apparently a difficult lesson to learn. Several years after the Garrett tragedy, Henry Sewall, a troublesome individual fresh from England, insisted on sailing "deep laden" from Boston to Ipswich in the face of a November gale and "was cast away upon the rocks" at the head of Cape Ann. Three days later, a member of the Boston church named John Willis, along with three others, was fetching wood from an island in Boston harbor; not "having any skill or experience," they attempted to pilot their laden boat home against the ebb tide in the middle of a northeast storm and were drowned when their boat sank. Again, the next winter, a "great shallop" tried to sail out from a harbor on the north shore of Cape Ann but, "through the unskilfulness of the men, was cast upon the rocks."[12]

Canoes—as given to "tickleness" in those days as now—were particularly dangerous. William Noddle of Salem was drowned in 1632 while paddling a canoe loaded with wood across the sheltered waters of the South River. Commonly the colonists took their little craft "afowling . . . sometimes two leagues to sea," although five of them were lost in 1634 on just such a hunting trip off Kettle Island. By 1636 the traffic in canoes around Salem was dense and dangerous enough that the town decided to require all such craft to be inspected for seaworthiness. To further alleviate the problem, it established regulated ferries across the North River to the farms beyond and from the South River to the fishing settlement at Marblehead. Even so, people loath to wait their turns for a paid passage frequently launched their canoes in the middle of the foulest weather. By 1638 the toll of accidents finally prompted the General Court to forbid the use of dugouts around the ferry routes and for a short period to prohibit the construction of any canoes at all.[13]

It is impossible to know in any precise way how high the incidence of boating mortality really was or when and why it began to diminish. Undoubtedly over time, New Englanders learned about winds, currents, tides, shoals, and the way all of these worked together along the coast. They discovered how to ride out a squall, steer in heavy weather, and adjust for the tides; and they also learned when to stay ashore. Additionally, the colonists began to understand the virtues of keeping a vessel shipshape, stowing cargo safely, and maintaining their craft in good repair. Although hardly seasoned mariners, they were undergoing a rough, practical education in the basics of seafaring. The importance of this knowledge to the maritime history of New England cannot be underestimated. It was not a common cultural inheritance, but at a time when the majority of the settler population lived within an hour's walk of the ocean, it was acquired in some measure by most male New Englanders of the day. This did not of itself generate a community of professional mariners, let alone a shipping industry. If the development of maritime industries had been that simple, every European possession in the New World would have acquired local fleets and resident mariners, which obviously never happened. Nonetheless, when the opportunity to enter the shipping business presented itself with the collapse of English freighting services during the Civil War of the 1640s, New Englanders did not shrink from launching their own voyages overseas. In the process of becoming watermen, they had lost their fear of the sea.

A second branch of maritime activity in early New England was the coasting industry. Coasters were, by definition, professional seamen who had mastered the handling of smaller sailing vessels and now made their business freighting cargo up and down the coast where they lived. On the one hand, they were rarely skilled in navigational technique, experienced in the direction of larger vessels, or very familiar with foreign waters. On the other hand, their seafaring skills might be considerable, and their knowledge of local geography was second to none. Coasters congregated wherever people were freighting goods and passengers over short distances, and between 1620 and 1645 there was enough of this business moving along the shore between Maine and Connecticut to attract a sizable number of these seafaring specialists.

Even when Plymouth was the only permanent settlement in New England, there was traffic enough to support this sort of enterprise. John Oldham had come to the Pilgrim colony in 1623 with no serious intention of joining in the community of religious separatists but every hope of enriching himself in trade. After quarreling with Bradford, he left the colony and moved to the Dorchester Company fishing station at Cape Ann, and he spent the rest of his career in commercial dealings with fishermen and Indians up and down the New England coast between Maine and Connecticut. "Mad Jack" (as Thomas Morton termed him) was a trader and soldier as much as a mariner, and he ranged the coast pursuing countless business schemes with ambition and a hot temper until he died at the hands of the Narragansett Indians in 1636.[14]

With the arrival of the Puritans in 1629 and the new demand for coastal transport, the number of coasters multiplied. One of them was

John Gallop, a fisherman by training who had migrated to New England in 1630 and settled in Boston. By 1632 he had acquired a sound enough reputation for his knowledge of the coast that Governor Winthrop commissioned him to sail eastward and gather information about the pirate Dixy Bull. The following year, Gallop was carrying goods and people between Boston and Ipswich on Massachusetts's North Shore, and by the late 1630s he was trading along the whole New England coastline between Maine and the Connecticut River. Though a church member, Gallop seems to have been like Oldham a tough customer: fond of a drink, ready to fight, and willing to take on all kinds of business.[15]

A few good Puritans took up coasting as well. John Jackson came to Massachusetts to pursue the fishery and was granted a piece of shoreline by the town of Salem for this purpose in 1636. Although he settled there immediately with his wife and child, he soon quit fishing to become a coaster—ferrying troops and prisoners between Boston and Connecticut, for example, during the Pequot War of 1637. Several years later he attracted the favorable notice of Governor Winthrop for his cool response under pressure when the pinnace he skippered sprang a leak on a voyage to New Haven. The passengers and crew had both abandoned ship and were preparing to make for land in an overloaded skiff, but Jackson stayed with his vessel and prevailed upon them to come back. Under his direction they succeeded in "laying the bark upon the contrary side" so that the leaky seam rose out of the water, and after bailing out the craft they returned to Salem "under a fine fresh gale" without loss of life or property. Winthrop called Jackson "a godly man and experienced seaman," language suggesting perhaps that the two did not necessarily go together. Yet even Oldham and Gallop found New England agreeable enough as a place to live, and with each passing year the number of professional coasters resident in the colony multiplied.[16]

So too did their knowledge of the coast—a development that can be charted through the history of the expeditions they undertook. In the summer of 1637, for example, twenty men sailed in a pinnace for Sable Island off the coast of Nova Scotia to hunt walrus but returned again six weeks later in defeat, forced to admit that they could not find the place. Later in the year, reported John Winthrop, "they set forth again with more skilful seamen, with the intent to stay there all winter" and this time succeeded in establishing a station on the island. Late in the winter of 1639 a bark set out to bring them home, "but by foul weather she was wrecked there," and the sealers were forced to construct "of her ruins" a small vessel they called the *Make Shift* in which to return. Something may have been learned from the experience, as Winthrop implied when he concluded that "it was found to be a great error to send thither before the middle of the 2 month [April]." By 1641 the Bay Colonists seem to have mastered the business. That summer, some Boston "adventurers" dispatched a vessel with twelve men to overwinter on the island, and a year later the merchants "fetched off their men and goods all safe." The cargo of "teeth," walrus hides, seal-skins, and black fox pelts that they brought with them sold for £1,500.[17]

The Sable Island adventure was exotic enough to attract Winthrop's attention on several occasions and to allow us to reconstruct a small part of this learning process, but similar stories must have been repeated else-where. For some years, coasters undoubtedly found it difficult to find com-petent help in this colony of landsmen. Of the two vessels that John Old-ham and John Gallop were commanding off the coast of Connecticut in 1636, for instance, one was crewed by "one man more, and two little boys," while the other had "only two English boys, and two Indians."[18] The remark-able thing about coasting in New England, however, was the rapidity with which it developed. It was men like Oldham, Gallop, and Jackson who made possible most of whatever commerce existed inside New England before the advent of roads. Settling, provisioning, marketing, fishing, lumbering, and fur trading would have been all but impossible otherwise.

As vital as watermen and coasters were to the New England settlements in these founding decades, they were not mariners in the fullest sense, and it is plain from the writings of Winthrop and his friends that the sea-faring men whom the Puritan fathers really hoped to attract were skilled and godly shipmasters. The coastal communities of New England would never evolve into real seaports without a community of resident master mariners who knew how to recruit sailors, manage large vessels, navigate the seas, draft financial instruments, conduct commerce, and make them-selves understood in foreign parts. The problem was how to lure men with these qualifications away from large and busy English seaports to settle in a land without ships. No sea captain driven by common sense alone would make such a decision, but the Great Migration was not fueled entirely by common sense. A small number of Puritan sea captains did move to the Bay Colony during the 1630s, driven largely by spiritual purpose.

William Peirce was a London shipmaster who lived in the Thames-side neighborhood of Ratcliffe and had met the Pilgrims at Plymouth, when, as master of the *Anne,* he delivered a cargo of sixty passengers and 60 tons of goods to the colony in 1623. Sympathetic to the planters on religious grounds, he became friends with Governor William Bradford and assisted him in many of the Pilgrims' battles with merchants and creditors in England. He had been sailing the Protestant seaway between Old and New England for the better part of a decade, first in the service of Plymouth and then in the employ of the Massachusetts Bay Company, when in 1632 a ship under his command was cast away near the mouth of Chesapeake Bay. As its cargo, along with most of his personal estate, was "swallowed up in the sea," Peirce began to wonder if in all of this there was not a providential message. "It is time to look about us," he wrote Bradford, "before the wrath of the Lord break forth to utter destruction," and that same year, at forty-one years of age, he uprooted his family and moved them to Boston. "A godly man and most expert mariner," Peirce was welcomed in Massachusetts, admitted to the church immediately, and granted land as well. On shore he served the town and colony repeatedly over the next several years as selectman and member of several provincial committees dealing with trade, and in 1639 he provided New England with its first locally published almanac. None of this forced him to retire from the sea, and during the late 1630s he spent much of his time freighting Pequot captives, African slaves, and English passengers up and down the North American coast between Boston and the West Indian colonies. In the course of the last of these voyages, transporting a shipload of prospective settlers from New England to the Puritan colony of Providence Island off the coast of Nicaragua in 1641, he learned that "a great fleet of Spanish ships was abroad," and he advised the passengers to turn back, volunteering to cover part of their losses himself. When they refused his offer, Peirce replied, "Then I am a dead man"; indeed, as he stood on into the harbor, he ran into cannon fire from the Spanish, who had recently captured the island, and was struck down and killed.[19]

Having lost his life in the Protestant cause, Peirce was a hero to the colonists—almost a martyr of prophetic gifts—and his story was told and retold around the hearths at home. Yet he was not the only talented mariner of Puritan inclination who eventually decided to settle in New England.

Thomas Graves, also from Ratcliffe, was an energetic, young shipmaster in his mid-twenties when in 1629 he began working for the Bay Colony ferrying immigrants to Massachusetts. His Puritan views made a positive impression on John Winthrop, who later termed him "an able and godly man," but although he was plainly sympathetic to the colonists, Graves had no consuming desire to join them. Only in 1638, after a decade of dealings in the Bay Colony, did he, with his wife, Katherine, and several young children, finally decide to move themselves across the Atlantic. Settling in Charlestown, they were granted land and admitted to the church, and for the next fifteen years Graves followed a career at sea, mainly in the employ of Boston merchants. In 1643 he commanded the locally built ship Trial on the first recorded voyage from Massachusetts to Spain, delivering a cargo of fish to Bilbao and then returning from Málaga "laden with wine, fruit, oil, iron, and wool, which was a great advantage to the country, and gave encouragement to trade." No sooner was he back in the country, moreover, than he refitted his vessel and set off to do business with the French Acadians at Port Royal. During the English Civil War years, Graves returned and served in the parliamentary navy, obtaining the rank of rear admiral, yet he kept his home in Massachusetts, and his wife raised their children there. When he died in 1653 at age forty-eight, he had accumulated a sizable estate and founded a prominent New England family.[20]

Thomas Coytmore was yet another shipmaster, drawn to New England in large part by religious preference. As with Peirce and Graves, this "right godly man and . . . expert seaman" visited Massachusetts several times before settling there in 1638, and like the others, he was granted land and church admission almost immediately. In 1642 he was commander of the Trial on her maiden voyage to the Azores and the West Indies. This was one of the first ships ever constructed in Boston, and the colonial leadership entertained great hopes that it might lead the way to a regular commerce with the tropics. The Trial's departure was an occasion of considerable ceremony; John Cotton, the minister of the First Church in Boston, "was desired to preach aboard her," wrote Winthrop, though "upon consideration that the audience would be too great for the ship, the sermon was at the meeting house." The voyage itself succeeded beyond all expectation. In Fayal, Coytmore found "an extraordinary good market for his pipe staves and fish," which he exchanged for a cargo of wine and sugar. At St. Christophers in the West Indies, he "put off some of his wine for cotton and tobacco," and the ship's company also salvaged "50 guns, and anchors, and cables" from a wreck on the ocean floor with the help of a borrowed diving bell. "And so, through the Lord's blessing," concluded Winthrop, "they made a good voyage, which did much encourage the merchants." Two years later, while sailing off the coast of Spain, his ship ran aground in the dark and broke apart, and Coytmore was drowned—again, like Peirce and Graves, in the prime of life.[21]

These three were not the only master mariners to settle in New England before 1645. Thomas Beecher commanded a vessel in the Winthrop fleet of 1630 and then settled permanently himself the following year in Charlestown, where he was admitted to the church, filled numerous offices, and lived until his death in 1637. Nicholas Trerice, another mariner who learned about Massachusetts through involvement in the immigrant trade, decided to move with his wife, Rebecca, to the Bay Colony, where she kept house in Charlestown while he was abroad voyaging around the Atlantic. On balance, however, the number of trained shipmasters who settled in New England before 1645 was not very great—and for good reason, since neither Boston nor any of the smaller coastal towns of New England possessed anything like a shipping industry in which they could find regular employment. Those who did come were counting on God's grace—that it would fall on those who assisted in the construction of the Puritan commonwealth, and that as it fell on New England as a whole they would prosper as individuals within it. To abandon a career in a seaport such as London in order to take one's chances on the New World frontier was a gamble, and indeed, only those with the most compelling motives chose it.[22]

It would be interesting to know something of the seamen who accompanied Captain Peirce and the others on these early voyages, but their story remains a mystery. According to Winthrop, Thomas Coytmore managed to ship a crew of "godly seamen" on his trip to the Azores in 1642, but who they were or where they came from was never mentioned. Indeed, the manner in which Winthrop described them may imply that Massachusetts shipmasters often had to rely on the ungodly to man their vessels; certainly there were enough of these around. Still, young Puritans were not immune to sea fever. Emmanuel and Lucy Downing were at the very center of the Great Migration—Lucy was a Winthrop—and their two boys, Joshua and Robert, were both bent on seafaring careers from a very early age. Even before he had turned thirteen, Joshua was said to be "very eager for sea Imployment," and when his mother learned that William Peirce was taking on apprentices, she considered approaching him. Peirce was killed soon after at Providence Island, and the parents placed their son instead with Capt. Thomas Hawkins of Boston. By 1646 Robert Downing had also begun his seafaring career and was searching about for a ship-master who would take him in hand. What happened to the two of them the records do not reveal, but one gets a sense from their experiences that local boys from committed Puritan families did go to sea, and that New England's first generation of master mariners were prepared to train them. At the same time, however, there is no saying whom else the Peirces, Graveses, and Coytmores hired to round out their crews, and it would be unwise to hazard a guess from these shreds of evidence.[23]

Even if relatively few professional deepwater mariners joined in the Great Migration, it remains true that during the first decades of settlement, New England was a largely maritime society. Few of the colonists may have followed the sea as a lifelong calling, but then only a small minority of men, even in the most maritime sectors of the North Atlantic rim—Brittany, Galicia, Norway, Holland, or Cornwall, for example—did this. Early New England was a maritime society in the same sense as were these other regions: that the majority of people lived near the ocean all the time, that all men and women depended on the ocean some of the time, and that nearly all men actually worked upon the ocean—in vessels large or small —at one time or another. The Puritan immigrants, most of whom hailed from rural backgrounds in the mother country where the sea rarely figured, did not move to New England with this in mind. Once there, however, they found themselves, as it were, tossed in the deep end and compelled to swim—or at least to sail, row, and paddle sufficiently to find their way about and survive in a land without roads.

CHAPTER TWO

Salem's First Mariners, 1645–1690

ON JUNE 24, 1629, after a "long and tedious journey through the great-est sea in the world," Francis Higginson and his companions on board the *Talbot* sailed up the North Shore from Cape Ann and "passed the curi-ous and difficult entrance into the large, spacious harbor of Naimkecke," an Algonkian term meaning comfortable haven. Although none of them could do more than guess at what lay behind the "thick wood and high trees" that lined the shore, the sight of sheltered water must have been a welcome one. Another vessel, the *George,* was already moored in the bay; Governor Endicott's shallop was also there to pilot them to their anchorage; and undoubtedly a number of smaller craft were out on the water to greet them and lend a hand transporting the new arrivals and their possessions ashore. Higginson sensed that this was a seaport, and time would prove him right.[1]

Naimcecke, as Salem was first named, though as yet only a collection of huts and lean-tos scarcely visible from the deck of the *Talbot,* sat on a low neck of land that jutted about two miles out into Massachusetts Bay. The base of this peninsula was actually buried in a coastal indentation, leaving Salem with the estuary of the North River on one side and a larger harbor, into which the South River emptied, on the other (Map 2.1). The second of these, where Higginson's ship had anchored, would continue to be the haven of preference for larger vessels to the end of Salem's maritime

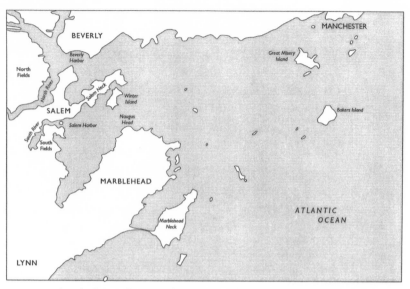

MAP 2.1 Salem harbor and surrounding towns in the seventeenth century

history. Although tidal flats stretched out a couple of hundred feet from shore, rendering the port a little less commodious and convenient than many sailors would have liked, the situation was snug enough, especially for smaller vessels.

The soil the town sat upon was sandy and not particularly fertile, and there was little marshland about for hay, but from the start the English discovered they could pasture livestock, grow corn, and plant gardens there —provided that they did not work the land too intensively. On the mainland across the North and South rivers and beyond the base of the peninsula, the possibilities for agriculture were markedly better, and there most of the settlers cleared their first fields. Although the land about the town was heavily wooded in parts, Francis Higginson claimed there was so "much ground cleared by the Indians," with grass "very thicke, very long, and very high" that wherever farming was possible, it could begin right away. William Wood praised the quality of the timber, the quantity of "diverse springs hard by the seaside," and the rich store of "basses, eels, lobsters, clams, etc.," to be caught in the shallows off shore. Furthermore, Salem had the feel of a central place. Though situated on the coast, it was surrounded on nearly all points of the compass by land, upon which separate settlements would soon be founded. As a town site it possessed no single compelling quality, but in the combination of features it afforded, Salem obviously struck immigrant settlers as a reasonable spot to pitch their homes. As Higginson put it, the prospect of the town was "neither too flat in the plainness, nor too high in hills, but partakes of both in a mediocrity, and fit for pasture or for plough or meadow ground, as men please to employ it."[2]

The first of Salem's European inhabitants were part of a small group of families who under the sponsorship of the Dorchester Company had tried to found a fishing station on Cape Ann in 1624. After two unprofitable years, the company was dissolved, and most of the colonists returned to England, but a few of them stayed on and moved fifteen miles southwest along the coast to settle on the peninsula at Naimcecke. What they saw in the site they never wrote down, but with several years' experience on Massachusetts's North Shore, they could form a considered judgment, and they chose it over other spots. In 1628, they were joined by a shipload of settlers under the direction of John Endicott—the vanguard of the Puritan Great Migration that would colonize New England over the next decade—and the next year these were followed by Higginson and his friends, part of the new Massachusetts Bay Company. With each passing month, the town acquired a more settled flavor, and in the summer of 1629, at Higginson's suggestion, they renamed it Salem, after the Hebrew word for peace. Although John Winthrop and his companions in the fleet of 1630 decided to bypass Endicott's settlement and found the seat of government for the Bay Colony at Boston, Salem continued to grow through the 1630s. Generous land grants, easy proximity to the ocean, and a flourishing church all attracted immigrant Puritan families, including a surprising number of well-to-do gentlemen, and by the end of the decade the town's population stood at close to five hundred souls.[3]

Yet nobody who visited Salem during the early 1640s would have predicted the extraordinary seafaring history it was to enjoy in the decades and centuries to come. The town was still no more than a collection of about two hundred small clapboard cabins with a few larger homes scattered among them. On the waterfront there were no public buildings, no wharves, and merely the barest accommodation for travelers. There was a storehouse on the South River in 1636 and a fish house on Winter Island in 1652, but otherwise the sources mention no warehouses of any kind in Salem before 1660. The local fleet of vessels was still composed only of boats, and the maritime horizons of most settlers were strictly coastal. Salem was, however, surrounded by water, and the habit of using the ocean, as we have seen, was already a matter of practical necessity. Although the town had as yet none of the amenities of a seaport, it was evolving nonetheless into a primitive maritime community.[4]

During the early 1640s, political events overseas set the seafaring economy of New England on a quickened path of development. After decades of bickering, the struggle between king and Parliament in the mother country finally erupted in 1642 into the epochal conflict of the English Civil War. As religious and political radicals openly challenged Charles I and as Parliament began to promise a general reformation of church and state, Puritans in the mother country started to wonder whether it was really necessary or even proper to cross the Atlantic and abandon the struggle at home. Once the New Jerusalem seemed just around the corner in England, the prospect of moving to Massachusetts proved less compelling, and the Great Migration slowed to a trickle. As migration ebbed, the flow of currency carried by these immigrants into the colony dried up as well, and without cash or any obvious commodities that could be exported to England in return for the imports they needed, the Bay Colonists—in Salem and throughout New England—began to cast about for new methods of paying their way. Merchants in particular were pinned most immediately by credit obligations, and it was they who devised a solution to the problem. Recognizing that the plantation colonies to the southward were falling into a pattern of specialized staple production, they saw markets there for conventional English provisions—farm produce, timber, and fish—that New England could generate in surplus. Assembling cargoes composed of these mundane commodities, they sought out markets overseas and resolved to "trye all ports to force a trade." By transporting the produce of a temperate climate to colonists who lived in semitropical or tropical environments, the New England traders constructed a commercial economy so profitable that it lasted relatively intact to the end of the colonial period.[5]

Although the outlines of this tale are well understood, it has generally been rendered as an episode in the history of trade—as the achievement of the New England producers, consumers, and merchants who initiated the system and whose interests it served. In this version of events, commodities are described as moving in stages to market under orders from

farmers, fishermen, artisans, and traders, yet the human agents of transport—the boatmen, coasters, and mariners who performed most of the
work—remain practically invisible. This leaves us with a portrait of a New
England society in the seventeenth century in which the seizure of the
land is central and the employment of the sea peripheral. In fact, the Puritan colonies began as a strip of coastal settlements dependent on the sea,
and as those original settlements grew into permanent towns, the maritime
skills and habits acquired by the founders did not evaporate. No single
sector of the maritime economy of the seventeenth century absorbed a
majority of the local population, and indeed, taken separately, boating,
coasting, and deepwater shipping may seem unimportant—either the
professional activities of a seafaring minority or the casual practices of an
agrarian majority. In their sum, however, they defined directly part of the
life cycle of most men and indirectly the lives of almost everyone else who
dwelled in this ocean-fronting society.

Examined from the air, the coastline north of Boston has a jagged aspect,
and many of the towns founded there during the seventeenth century had
ratios of seaboard to land surface that resembled those of an island. In
1645 Salem was no more than fifteen miles wide at its broadest point, yet
within its boundaries lay nearly fifty miles of coast. Ipswich, Newbury,
and Salisbury also had complicated shorelines, and Gloucester was a maze
of necks and inlets. There is little wonder that William Wood encountered
so many canoes in Salem when he visited there during the 1630s or that
boats were more common than farm carts in all of these towns during
the early decades of settlement. They were simply more practical, and as
the number of people who lived along the coast increased, so the number
of small craft and the uses to which they were put multiplied accordingly.[6]

Much of this activity amounted to nothing more than the extension
onto the ocean of the most humdrum and casual activities of daily life.
Settlers who owned sections of salt marsh, pastureland on islands offshore,
or woodlots up the coast used watercraft to reach their property. When
Thomas Bowen was apprehended for "sailing from Gloster harbor on the
Lord's Day . . . having hay in his boat," he was probably engaged in a task
of this sort. Craftsmen and those involved in heavier lumbering and manufacturing work depended on small vessels as well. During the 1650s, em-
ployees of the Saugus ironworks delivered bar iron and finished wares to

Boston and Salem by boat. Samuel Bennett, a farmer and carpenter in Lynn, transported "plancke, timber and cord wood" around Massachusetts Bay in his lighter during the 1660s. The basic rounds of visiting and shopping could often be undertaken more conveniently by water, as could public business. The town of Bradford arranged in 1681 to have its county taxes, in the form of corn, shipped in the constable's skiff and another man's boat down the Merrimack River and around Cape Ann to Salem.[7]

The development of the cod fisheries and the growth of ocean-borne commerce redoubled people's dependence on boats. In harbors such as Salem, where there were as yet no wharves, all vessels of any draft—from ships to shallops—had to anchor offshore and be serviced by smaller craft from the waterfront. These could be as small as the birchbark canoe that Joshua Rogers, "beeinge sum thinge in drinke," tumbled out of while paddling out to board a Salem fishing ketch in 1668; or it could be as substantial as the "boat" valued at £5 that the merchant Thomas Bishop of Ipswich kept to load and unload his fleet of five vessels trading overseas. By the 1680s there was enough lighterage going on in Salem Harbor to employ twenty or more local boats the year round.[8]

All types of people owned watercraft. Arthur Sanden and his wife, Margaret, kept a tavern in their three-room home by Marblehead harbor from 1640 until his death in 1666 and found a small skiff useful to fetch from Salem barrels of wine and "strong waters," as well as the ingredients for the beer they brewed for sale to local fishermen. One of the first settlers in Gloucester, Walter Tibbot, had three canoes as part of the basic equipment for the two small farms he owned on Cape Ann. Edward Gillman, a sawmill operator in Exeter, owned a "flat-bottomed boat" in the early 1650s that he used for freighting timber down the Piscataqua River and along the coast to Salem and Boston. A well-to-do shipmaster-turned-merchant of Salem, John Hardy, kept a "boat & Cannow" in the harbor, in part to ferry cargo to and from three trading ketches in which he owned shares. Men with some propertied stake in the colony—land and animals especially—were more likely to own boats than those without, and residents of the towns with the most extensive shorelines—Salem, Marblehead, Ipswich, and Gloucester—had more need of them than those from relatively landlocked communities. But any householder who lived beside the sea without a boat might have found himself more dependent on his neighbors than he would prefer.[9]

Heads of households were not, of course, the only ones to use these boats. The actual work of sailing and paddling was often delegated to other family members, though not indiscriminately. Boys short of their mid-teenage years, for one, were not commonly trusted on the water. The lower limit on age is suggested by an expedition undertaken by nine young men of Ipswich who paddled out to Hog Island and Castle Neck "in planting time" during the spring of 1667. This group included several hired men, aged eighteen to twenty-six years, as well as "Goodman Wood's boys," John and Nathaniel—both teenagers—and fifteen-year-old Samuel Dutch with his friend, Jonathan Clark. The same year, while John Kenerick and John Newmarch, Jr., were loading barrel staves into a boat near the mouth of the Chebacco River, they spotted Seth and William Story, aged nineteen and seventeen, respectively, "with three canoes grounded in a little cove" while they gathered thatch. Another witness to this scene was William Woodbury, an eighteen-year-old from Beverly, who had sailed up the coast together with his father to cut hay. We know that boys younger than this worked regularly alongside their fathers and older brothers on shore during this period, but rarely, it seems, did they labor on the water.[10]

Similarly, boating was not an activity of the elderly, or at least not in a way that caught the eyes of their neighbors. By far the oldest boatman on record in seventeenth-century Essex County was William Woodbury's father, Humphrey, aged sixty-one when the two of them sailed from Beverly to Chebacco. Older men had no particular aversion to the water; they were simply retreating from strenuous physical work in general once they had robust sons whom they could send in their stead. When Robert Knight of Marblehead dispatched his teenage boys, John and Robert, to pick up "several parcels of wood . . . standing ready cut at the stumps" at his wood lot in Kettle Cove, he probably felt that, as a father who had just passed sixty, he had earned the privilege of ducking heavy labor, and anyway he had better things to do at home.[11] Boating was mainly the business of men in their physical prime.

Women spent far less time on the water than did men. On one occasion in 1636, Abigail Lord of Salem was said to have borrowed a canoe belonging to Ralph Fogg, and, by failing to beach it properly, allowed it to drift across the harbor to Marblehead, where George Wright, the ferryman, hauled it off the rocks. Thirty years later a jury of inquest reported that Sarah Taylor, a fisherman's wife from the Isle of Shoals, had been sailing in company to Ipswich in the winter of 1666, possibly to pick up supplies, when the boat she was in struck the bar at the mouth of the harbor and dumped her into the sea, where she drowned. These, however, are the only unambiguous references to women using small boats—by themselves, with others, or even as passengers—in fifty years of recorded court testimony in seventeenth-century Essex County. That female colonists would have forgone short-distance water transport entirely, of course, stretches the imagination. At other times and places New England women did use small boats when they had to. Martha Ballard of Hallowell, Maine, could never have functioned as a healer and midwife after the American Revolution had she not been willing to cross the Kennebec River to reach her patients. In seventeenth-century Massachusetts, moreover, it is quite possible to imagine her ancestors paddling across the Merrimack to help out at harvest, rowing from Marblehead to Salem to buy a few yards of cloth, or taking the ferry to Beverly to visit a sister. The fact remains, however, that these court records, which document women's other activities in such detail, make almost no mention of their working or even traveling in small craft, and we can only assume that the domestic tasks that were women's primary responsibility seldom demanded or allowed this sort of coastal travel.[12]

Even among men, boating skills were not entirely universal, and their ubiquity probably diminished slowly over time. By the end of the seventeenth century a rough but serviceable system of roads connected most coastal communities with one another, and people could avoid traveling by sea if they wanted to. In the coastal towns of Essex County, the ratio of carts to boats rose from 1:2 before 1645 to 3:1 in subsequent decades, and in Salem the ratio climbed from 1:3 to 3:2. Nevertheless, certain types of work by their nature continued to draw the men and boys of North Shore communities out onto the water in a way that must have seemed to them entirely normal throughout the colonial period. Wherever there were ocean-bound properties to reach, bays and rivers to cross, or heavy loads to move, the route over water was the one to take. The sense that the sea was there to be used—respectfully but without undue worry—became part of this maritime culture.[13]

Boating became a little less universal during the second half of the seventeenth century, when a growing number of coastal mariners began to take over the business that generated regular freight and to run it for profit. Colonists with something to sell were ready enough to carry their commodities to the tidewater, but if their cargoes were bulky or they were pressed for time, they were often just as happy at that point to pay somebody else to ship their goods to market. Whereas boating was part of everyday working life for most men and boys on the North Shore, coasting was a business and a profession. A more specialized line of work that took the men who followed it away from home for days or weeks at a stretch, it was not to everybody's taste and became the calling of a peculiar minority.

In broad terms, the coasting industry served to connect smaller and more peripheral New England communities with larger towns, where the produce of the land—mainly furs, farm crops, timber, and fish—could find a market, and where imported goods could be purchased in bulk. Although the most important of these towns naturally was Boston—the only place in New England where almost anything could be bought or sold—Salem served a similar function on a lesser, more specialized scale. In comparison to other towns along the North Shore, Salem had a number of small advantages and one major one. To some extent, it benefited from having been settled first. From an early date, Salem attracted more than its share of well-to-do English immigrants—such gentlemen as George Corwin and William Browne, who may have felt that the town already had a feel of permanence suited to people of their stature. Furthermore, geography had favored the town by giving it a decent harbor and placing it within a day's travel, by boat or on foot, of most of Essex County. During the 1650s George Corwin did a lively business with farmers all over the region, selling them a variety of English dry goods and West Indian provisions in return for the grain, butter, cheese, livestock, and barreled meat that they shipped by water or drove overland to his store by the South River.[14] Timber products, such as board lumber, shingles, and barrel staves, could also be ferried to Salem and sold. George's son, Jonathan Corwin, ran a sawmill at Wells along the Maine coast in 1680 that furnished loads of timber to be shipped southward to his warehouse in Salem, and the presence of wood products in the inventories of other merchants in town as well as in the export records of the customshouse, indicates that lumber had a considerable market there.[15] The General Court added to Salem's historical and natural advantages by establishing it as one of two seats for the Essex County Court. Twice a year, people of property and influence from around the county would congregate there to serve as magistrates and jurymen or to settle their own disputes, and in off hours there was plenty of time for them to transact business as well.

As a destination for farm and forest produce, however, Salem had its limits. Any coaster who had troubled himself to sail this far could in a few more hours reach Boston, where the markets were larger and the shopping was undoubtedly better. Even the residents of Essex County freighted more of their surplus farm and forest produce to the provincial capital than they ever did to Salem. Robert and Stephen Cross of Ipswich ran one of the most active coasting operations of the seventeenth century, shipping wheat, pork, pease, rum, Indian corn, oaken staves, and pine boards, as well as human passengers, up and down the length of the New England coast without ever mentioning a stop in Salem.[16] So while it is important to recognize that Salem served as a market town within the rural economy of the North Shore, it is also true that if rural produce had been Massachusetts's only important commodity, Salem would probably never have become a real seaport at all.

The key to Salem's development, and the major reason that local merchants such as the Corwins needed timber and provisions to begin with, was the proximity of the resident cod fishery. Massachusetts's first and largest fishing port was Marblehead—less than a mile by water from the beach on the South River and part of Salem politically until 1649. Most of the capital that financed this fishery during its formative years came through Boston from abroad. The fishermen, however, were local residents, and by settling in New England, where they could provision themselves inexpensively from colonial sources, they created a commercial opportunity for enterprising Salem traders to seize. In order to launch their voyages at the beginning of each season, these fishermen needed boats, timber, nails, salt, bait, bread, cider, lines, leads, and dozens of other commodities. Some of these could be manufactured locally; others had to be imported; but all of them had to be assembled before the season commenced and advanced to the fishermen on the promise of repayment at the end of the year. This was an intricate business, involving the coordination of a great many households in dozens of trades, all operating on delicate lines of credit. To profit within it, one had to know one's customers and clients personally—who was reliable and who was not—and this sort of intimate knowledge could be acquired only at close hand. Boston stood too far away, and so the business of outfitting the industry devolved onto Salem, a town squarely positioned between farmers and fishermen.[17]

From the mid-1640s onward, therefore, it was the fishery that generated most of the coastal traffic in and out of Salem harbor. Early in the year, the fishermen themselves in their single-masted, undecked shallops averaging around twenty-five feet in length, would visit the waterfront stores and warehouses on the South River to stock up on the gear they needed before setting off eastward. Between voyages, they would return to deliver their dried fish and to reprovision themselves, and at the end of the year they would come in with the balance of their catch to settle accounts. When the cod struck, however, the work of fishing was intense, and at such times the men were loath to spend time away from their lines. During the season, therefore, coasters could find plenty of business freighting supplies out to the fishing camps and carrying dry fish back again. Andrew Woodbury of Salem was one of them. In the summer of 1654 he ran into his neighbor, Paul Mansfield, at Monhegan Island on the Maine coast and promised to freight the eighty quintals of cod that Mansfield and his company had caught to John Codner's stage in Marblehead, a hundred miles to the south. Woodbury was busy enough that even though the fish would likely have occupied less than a third of the hold in his bark, Mansfield's cargo had to wait in line until a later voyage. Similarly, Mordecai Cravett of Salem made a business in the early 1660s carrying supplies from William Browne's warehouse in Salem to fishermen at Damariscotta and Matinicus (near Monhegan), where he would load cod for delivery to merchants back in Massachusetts.[18]

Cravett may have been a bigger operator than some. In 1663 he charged £7, 15s. per month for his "men and victuals," implying that his bark, the *Content,* probably carried a crew of three or four. But most coasters probably resembled him, preferring similar, sturdy craft that could carry hefty, paying freights even if they cost more to build and run. Some coasters continued to conduct their business in boats and lighters, but those who could soon acquired shallops, barks, sloops, and even two-masted ketches that could handle any weather. William Carr of Salisbury agreed in 1677 to build for Robert Dutch of Ipswich a ketch of 25 tons' burden, the masted hull of which cost the latter about £80. The contract between them described it as "in length by the keele thirty fower foot, in breadth twelve foot by the beame & six foot deep in the hold." The hull was of two-inch

FIGURE 2.1 Seventeenth-century New England ketch. Source: William A. Baker, "Adventure: A Seventeenth Century Ketch," *American Neptune*, 30 (1970), 91. (Courtesy of the Peabody-Essex Museum)

white oak planking, and the vessel was to have a forecastle raised one foot and a cabin raised two feet above the pine deck "with scuttles & hatches sutable." This was a prime vessel of its kind—identical to many that were sailing to the Caribbean (Figure 2.1)—and some coasters made do with less. But if ketches like this could expect to earn £6 a month, as Dutch's two sons asserted before the courts, one can understand why they were in demand.[19]

Neither the colony nor the coasters themselves kept records sufficient to allow us to reconstruct the size of their coasting fleet or the numbers of people it employed, though these must have been considerable. During the 1680s, Boston and Salem were clearing together more than 10,000 tons of shipping annually. Most of this cargo had been delivered to these seaports by water, and if we can assume a rough proportionality of lading, those goods would have required hundreds of voyages in fair-sized sloops or thousands of typical boatloads to assemble.[20] Moving from this sort of estimate to any more precise judgment is impossible, for there is no way of knowing exactly how large these watercraft were, how often they visited the colony's seaports, how fully loaded they may have been, or how many crew on average they carried. Men followed this line of work, however, in every community along the North Shore, and they were people with whom almost everyone dealt as a matter of course.

The earliest coasters were immigrants—men like John Gallop and John Oldham, drawn to New England for a variety of reasons, not the least of which was to make money. The growing demand for freighting services, however, soon drew native-born New Englanders into the business as well. In certain ways these coasters resembled their neighbors. Their business originated in the towns and villages of coastal New England, and there they generally dwelled among the rural people whose transport needs they understood and served. In age they ranged from their teens to their late forties (the normal lifetime of hard physical work in seventeenth-century New England), and like their neighbors, they usually owned the tools of their trade—in this case, the vessels themselves. Close to two-thirds of them also owned land (though few were wealthy) and the majority were householders with families. The Cross brothers of Ipswich, Robert and Stephen, were in all of these ways typical of their kind. Sons of a town founder, they worked on their father's farm, married local girls, and settled near the mouth of the Ipswich River. By their early twenties, the two had turned to coasting, and from the late 1660s onward they earned their livings freighting fish and timber, often in partnership, along the New England shore. Both became landowners, and Stephen in particular did well enough in life to acquire the Saltonstall estate—a large home on fourteen choice acres by the Ipswich River.[21]

If coasters belonged in certain ways to these communities, however, they also had a deserved reputation for hard living and wildness that set them apart, and in this, too, the Cross brothers of Ipswich were typical. As a young man, Stephen was arraigned for "pulling up bridges at the windmill," throwing sticks and stones at the house of the town clerk, and fighting "upon a lecture day in sermon time," while Robert ran afoul of the law almost as frequently for his drunk and disorderly habits. On one occasion the two of them dug up the grave of an Indian sagamore and carried the skull about town on a pole, and a year later they were both admonished by the court for disparaging several magistrates. Stephen in particular was a turbulent fellow of quick tongue and ready fist. Later in life, he tried to convert the Saltonstall home into a tavern, and in 1691, when the town tried to arrest him for illegally drawing and selling drink, Cross rushed the marshall's party, "tooke his nacked sword," and told the deputy "that he would Run him through if thur was no more dayes in the world," then "clapt the point of his Rapier" to the marshall's breast and bid him "git out of his hous." Throughout their coasting careers, Stephen and Robert spent an enormous amount of time before the courts, not only for their misdemeanors but also in bitter civil litigation over freight contracts and vessel construction. When they died a few years apart around the turn of the century, many of their neighbors in Ipswich must have breathed a little easier.[22]

And the Crosses were not unusual for their kind. Coasters in general had a reputation as a rowdy crew with little use for Puritan standards of social discipline. John Lee, partner with Robert Cross in the sloop *Adventure*, was constantly before the courts for such offenses as "wording it" with constables, shooting off pistols indoors, stealing from a crewmate while he slept, and a sexual dalliance with the wife of a local fisherman. Another pair of brothers with whom the Crosses had dealings were John and Samuel Dutch. Frequently in trouble with the law, the Dutch brothers fell under a cloud of suspicion in 1679, when a piece of kenting cloth they had undertaken to freight to Ipswich disappeared during a warehouse fire on the Boston waterfront. When the kenting surfaced in Ipswich and the two of them suddenly proved able "to pay thare Debts long due & to hire people to work & to pay them in goods & to supply theare familyes with new & good things," the Derby family that owned the cloth sued them and obtained restitution. Even more litigious than the Crosses or the Dutches was Mordicai Cravett, coaster and fisherman of Salem. Battles with creditors punctuated his seafaring career on a nearly annual basis, and when the house that he lost by a defaulted mortgage burned to the ground in 1666, his wife and attorney, Edith—believed by her enemies to be a witch—was accused of setting the fire. Although the evidence against her was only circumstantial and she was acquitted by the Court of Assistants, the Cravetts were undeniably sharp dealers, and the number of those willing to testify against them suggests that the coaster and his wife were not well liked.[23]

The Chubbs of Beverly were another family that seemed to marry coasting with the sort of behavior their neighbors found disruptive. Thomas

Chubb, the son of an early planter, leased a boat in his late twenties and early thirties and ferried fish and timber between Marblehead, Beverly, and Boston. Most of his life he was in and out of trouble. As a teenager, he had assaulted a young maidservant in Beverly, "lifting her up and violently striking her head against the door-sill and joist of the house." Before he married, he had already been convicted of another assault, accompanied by theft, and as a householder, he was charged and imprisoned for stealing fish and taking a horse. His younger brother John assisted him on his coastal voyages and was just as much a rowdyman. A heavy drinker and prone to "threatening words," John had at different times been presented for killing a horse in Ipswich, dressing to excess "beyond that of a man of his degree," and helping to torch a church under construction at Chebacco. Not surprisingly he knew the Crosses from Ipswich, with whom he had a "difference" in 1682. Another one of John Chubb's friends was Thomas Chick, a married man and father, who had just settled in Manchester in 1679 when he was hired by Chubb to assist in freighting boards from Mackrell Cove to Marblehead. Chick made enemies in Beverly almost immediately by "upbraiding John Grover for praying in his family" and by "taking . . . Grover by the neckcloth . . . [and] calling him rogue." Thomas Ives, the owner of Chubb's boat, insisted that Chick be dismissed immediately, and within a year, the Manchester selectmen were petitioning the court to have the newcomer removed since (they argued) he was likely to remain unemployed and become a charge to the town.[24]

Criminal litigation is, of course, a peculiar prism through which to learn about these men. By their nature, legal records describe wrongdoing as defined by the groups of people whose interests the courts serve, and one of the purposes of the judicial system in Massachusetts was to establish on earth a certain brand of Christian order that was much more easily achieved in settled farming villages than in the host of remote islands, bays, and rivers where coasters did a great deal of their business. That so much of the evidence concerning the lives of these men was created by the courts has two consequences. On the one hand, it may well portray them as a rowdier lot than they really were. What struck a Puritan magistrate as abusive language may have felt to a coaster like the only way to negotiate. On the other hand, it systematically overlooks those whose lives were by legal standards above censure. Some of these freighters stayed quite clear of the courts, and a scattered one had spiritual credentials that compared quite favorably with those of their neighbors. Robert Nash, master of a bark that shipped timber out of Piscataqua in 1650, seems to have avoided trouble most of his life, and his wife was a member of the Boston church. Mordicai Cravett, for all the problems with his Salem neighbors, was still granted a prominent seat in the south gallery of the meetinghouse in 1658.[25]

In the eyes of local authorities, however, men of this calling bore an undeniable stigma. As early as 1633 the General Court directed that "common coasters" (along with "unprofittable fowlers & tobacco takers") be placed under special surveillance as being unusually prone to idle behavior. And for every Nash or Cravett who felt more or less comfortable within the spiritual culture of reformed Protestantism, there were many more who did not. Indeed, fewer than 20 percent of these coasters possessed any recorded connection, however faint, to a local church. On balance the life of the professional coaster squared poorly with the social norms of landed New England society.[26]

Why, in fact, so many of these men were so tough and rebellious one can only surmise. On the one hand, the profession often required it. Coasters had to deal with strangers all the time—people who would not be subject to the type of familial and neighborly pressure that set limits to aggressive negotiation within communities. Few coasters had either the riches or the friends in high places that could force their business connections to take them seriously. Especially in the isolated parts of New England where many of them did much of their trade, strong language and personal intimidation might be the only way to make sure that an agreement would be honored. On the other hand, some of those coasters whose personal histories are best documented—the Crosses and Chubbs, for example—began battling the local establishment as teenagers, well before they had begun seafaring at all. For young men temperamentally unsuited to accepting authority, coasting may have provided an arena of profitable activity out of the Puritan line of vision, where an aggressive personality could be an asset.

Although coasters could often be troublesome neighbors, they were clearly part of this seafronting society. As commercial operators and professional seamen, they stood apart from the majority of their neighbors for whom boats were simply another piece of household equipment, yet they were equally necessary to the workings of the maritime economy. The presence of resident coasters did not distinguish Massachusetts from most other North American settlements of the seventeenth century, for these men congregated wherever there were commodities to buy, sell, and transport by water—the business of every colony. In the maritime societies that the English colonists constructed from Newfoundland to Barbados during the seventeenth century, coasters were, indeed, the prime agents of local commerce, and their rowdy and tempestuous ways were undoubtedly well known along the entire Atlantic seaboard.[27]

While every settlement that fronted on the ocean depended from the first on boating and coastal transport, very few colonies in the New World acquired, even in the course of many decades, a true deepwater shipping fleet. In this respect Massachusetts was different. Within a few years of its founding, Boston merchants were dispatching locally built and locally manned vessels of considerable tonnage to Virginia, the Caribbean, the Wine Islands of the Atlantic, and eventually to Europe itself. Had this never happened, the seaboard towns of the colony would have retained their maritime flavor, for the ocean was still there, and coasters would still have conducted their business along the shore assembling cargoes to be shipped overseas by sailors from other parts. But coasters never congregated in large commercial centers; they dwelled in the outports along with the people they served. Only a deepwater shipping industry could generate the economies of scale that encouraged the gathering of merchants, shipmasters, seamen, and all the attendant maritime artisans and service people around central harbors. If we are to understand the development of seaport society in New England, therefore, we need to examine the shipping industry that supported it.

During the first decade or two of settlement, few New Englanders were themselves willing to invest in shipping. Vessels were expensive, exports were scarce, and for some time merchants found a better return on their money and time provisioning incoming settlers. When the Great Migration ended in the 1640s and the flow of immigrants ceased, however, the bottom dropped out of the local provisioning trade, and merchants began to consider new ways of employing their capital. Had Massachusetts possessed a single dominant staple product with an obvious market overseas, most of them would simply have chosen to become agents for the greater London merchants who would have controlled the trade. Indeed,

some of them did this, especially in the early years. The new English colonies in the West Indies and the Chesapeake had grown rapidly since 1630,
and by 1650 they counted together well over 50,000 consumers, hungry
for the sort of northern farm and forest produce they could not or would
not raise themselves. Furthermore, the Civil War at home had crippled
the West Country fishery, and with cod prices at an all-time high, there
was plenty of money to be made exporting fish to the Wine Islands and
Spain. Merchants in Boston, Salem, Ipswich, Newbury, and a few lesser
towns within the Bay Colony exploited these opportunities by importing
dry goods carried in English vessels and selling these manufactures to
their New England customers in return for assorted cartloads and boatloads
of timber products, livestock, garden produce, barreled beef, codfish, and
a variety of other commodities. These products the merchants assembled
into cargoes and delivered largely at first to the same English ships that
had brought the dry goods to the colony in the first place. Most of these
vessels hailed from London and were bound for the Iberian Peninsula,
the Caribbean, or the Wine Islands. There the produce could be sold to
the agents of English merchant houses with whom New Englanders were
dealing in order to repay the debts that were accumulating in the ledgers
of those firms. In such a commercial system, the colonists were dependent
on English credit and clearly the subordinate partners. Yet on the periphery
of the European world-economy, where capital was scarce but resources
plentiful, it made good economic sense; and in the fish trade to Spain,
where markets were large enough, it persisted as the normal form of commerce into the eighteenth century.[28]

Eventually, however, the challenge of marketing this wide range of
exports forced merchants in the Bay Colony to assume control of the business themselves. For a newly settled region, Massachusetts possessed an
unusually complex economy. By 1650, farmers, craftsmen, fishermen,
and housewives were already immersed in a network of local exchange
that had two functions: redistributing resources around the region and
producing small surpluses that could be traded for English manufactures.
Trading Indian meal for oaken barrels for dried fish for woolen cloth and
so forth, farmers, fishermen, craftsmen, and their wives constructed an
internal market that was by the New World standards of the seventeenth
century remarkably dense. Within this network of petty exchange there
were middlemen's profits to be captured, and through hundreds of sepa-

rate dealings inside the system, an astute trader could assemble diversified cargoes for export. The knowledge needed to practice this complex business, however, was considerable and could be obtained only locally. In such single-staple colonies as Newfoundland or Virginia, commercial relations among households existed, but not at the same density. There, more people found it more profitable to fish or raise tobacco and buy their provisions and manufactured goods from elsewhere than to take up smithing, shipbuild-ing, or ropemaking on anything like the scale necessary to produce diversi-fied economies. Though such colonies were deeply engaged in external markets overseas, they did not acquire as rapidly the internal markets that linked one household to another. The more diversified the colony—and Massachusetts was remarkably so from the start—the more local business it generated, and the more quickly a sizable resident merchant community developed on the spot.

To profit effectively from an export system that included such a range of commodities, merchants were well advised to acquire their own ship-ping. This was not the case in the staple colonies, where the volume and simplicity of cargoes attracted a steady flow of English vessels sailing to a small number of relatively predictable markets. The Newfoundland fisheries, for example, were serviced by a fleet of specialist export vessels known as sack ships, and traders on the island interested in shipping their fish to Southern Europe could normally purchase from West Country shippers the freighting they needed. In Massachusetts, by comparison, the cargoes to be picked up were too small and the colonial markets where most of these exports could profitably be sold were too thin to attract many specialist freighters. Picking up cargoes in New England to peddle hogshead by hogshead and seaport by seaport around the West Atlantic was a difficult way for a large English vessel to make money. Indeed, the letters of instruc-tion and charter parties under which they sailed were often too restrictive to make such port-hopping possible. Accordingly, Massachusetts merchants with provisions to sell within these dispersed colonial markets had every incentive to acquire vessels of their own. Such craft could be small enough to profitably service lesser seaports; they could be commanded by ship-masters, whom the New Englanders knew personally; and they could be gov-erned by written instructions that allowed these captains the flexibility they needed to tramp about and hawk their cargo. For all these reasons the logic of Massachusetts's export economy encouraged a local shipping industry.

In a timber-rich colony, this was most easily accomplished by having these vessels built locally. Massachusetts's shipwrights had begun framing coastal vessels during the 1630s, but the scale of their operations multiplied many times over during the several decades that followed the end of the Great Migration. The first flurry of activity occurred during the depression of the early 1640s, partly in response to the developmental efforts of the different seaports and the colonial government, partly because the Civil War had plunged England's fishing and shipping industries into disarray, and partly because the sugar and tobacco booms were generating demand in the plantation colonies for northern provisions. John Winthrop noted with enthusiasm the launching of two sizable ships in 1641 and five more in 1642. At midcentury, a ready market for vessels of all sizes kept shipwrights employed from Scituate to Salisbury, and by 1665, the colony's fleet was said to include about 130 vessels of 20 tons' burden or more. In 1676 Edward Randolph estimated that twenty vessels a year were sliding down the ways in Massachusetts's harbors and that there were now 730 vessels of 6 tons or greater built and owned within the Bay Colony. Half of these, he claimed, were large enough to be engaged in foreign trade, and many of them were eventually sold overseas. These latter figures must be read with caution, for Randolph was trying to persuade the English government that Massachusetts was developing into a major competitor within the North Atlantic, and he probably exaggerated in order to carry his case. Still, he was agitating among broadly informed people who would be hard to fool for long, and his general point—that New Englanders were constructing a sizable shipping fleet—was plain for everyone to see.[29]

Until about 1660, vessels from abroad continued to dominate Massachusetts's overseas commerce. In the smaller towns of Salem and Plymouth, shipping was still confined to fishing and coasting, and few traders there possessed any direct connections abroad. Even in Boston, where some local merchants had become shipowners, the bulk of outward-bound cargoes was carried in vessels from London, Bristol, or the smaller ports in England's West Country. By the early 1660s, however, England's advantage was diminishing visibly. John Hull described the "hundred sail of ships" that came into Boston harbor in 1664 as being both "of our and strangers," and a fragmentary stretch of customs records from the period confirms his judgment. During the fall and winter of 1661–1662, locally owned vessels now accounted for 40 percent of the tonnage and about half the vessels that cleared port. By the 1680s the balance of vessel owner-ship had tipped decisively in Massachusetts's direction. During six months in 1687, a full 76 percent of the vessels departing from Boston for destina-tions around the North Atlantic were locally registered, and in the Caribbean trade, the proportion of New England registries among vessels arriving from those parts probably approached 85 percent.[30]

This was not a fleet of three-masted ships. In 1665 the General Court reported that about 60 percent of locally owned vessels were between 20 and 40 tons' burden; in 1676 Randolph figured similarly that about 70 percent of the Bay Colony's vessels were less than 50 tons; and during the last two decades of the century Massachusetts vessel registries record a mean tonnage for locally owned craft of between 45 and 50 tons. Large ships visited Massachusetts harbors often enough, carrying passengers and dry goods from the mother country, but few New England merchants owned vessels of more than 150 tons, and we can assume that voyages operating on this scale were more profitably managed in larger ports abroad.[31]

Yet even if the world of great ships, large crews, and hefty cargoes lay far in the future—as yet outside the experience of New England shippers—the achievements of the seventeenth century were remarkable enough. By the outbreak of King William's War in 1689, the deepwater fleet based in Boston and Salem resembled in its tonnage profile that of smaller En-glish seaports such as Plymouth or Dartmouth, and by 1702 Boston was, in registration of shipping tonnage, more important than any English sea-port save London and Bristol. Within sixty years of their foundation, Boston and Salem had developed into noteworthy provincial seaports—the com-mercial centers of this *New England* overseas.[32]

Of the two towns, Salem was clearly the junior partner, for while Boston established itself as a market town and port of call at its foundation, the seaport on the North Shore entered the shipping industry only belatedly through its connection to the cod fishery. The shallops that had fished the Gulf of Maine and freighted cargo to and from the grounds in the early decades of settlement were too small to profitably engage in overseas com-merce, but during the 1660s and 1670s, Salem merchants began gradually to withdraw the credit that had underwritten the quasi-independent boat fishery of earlier times and to reinvest their money in larger, two-masted ketches. These seaworthy vessels allowed fishermen, hired now on shares, to follow the cod to any number of the vast offshore banks that could be worked in sequence throughout most of the year. Whether it was the lure of a newer and more productive fishery or the decline of an older and exhausted one that prompted this transition is impossible to judge, but as Salem entered the last quarter of the seventeenth century, local fishing merchants had undoubtedly acquired a more impressive fleet. Even a banks fishery, however, could not operate the year-round; the storms of December, January, and February were too dangerous to permit it. Accordingly, the owners of these new and relatively expensive vessels began to cast about for ways to employ them in the off-season, and the most obvious solution lay in the provisioning trades to Virginia and the West Indies.[33]

There were a number of precedents for this in Salem's early history. Joseph Grafton of Salem coasted as far south as Connecticut in 1637; Walter Price owned a ship, the *True Return,* that sailed from Salem with an unspecified cargo to Barbados in 1648; and Richard More of Salem commanded a ketch that provisioned the English expedition against Jamaica in 1654. It was not, however, until the 1660s and the development of the banks fishery that a local fleet of Salem-based trading vessels came into being. Much of this trade was initially directed toward Maryland and Virginia—little more than an extension of earlier cruises into Long Island Sound. Such voyages could take as little as three months to complete, and a vessel large enough to prosecute the banks fishery could easily sandwich a trip southward into the lull between seasons. Skipper Edward Hilliard of Salem commanded several voyages to Chesapeake Bay during the late 1660s in the fishing ketch *Tryall,* and like other masters in this trade, he crewed his vessel with fishermen. By the late 1660s a fair number of Salem-owned ketches spent part of the year carrying provisions and English dry goods southward to the tobacco colonies.[34]

By the 1670s the surge in Caribbean sugar production enabled by the transition to slavery had created a sizable new market for New England provisions, and by 1680 the number of voyages to St. Kitts, Nevis, Jamaica, and especially Barbados far outnumbered those to the Chesapeake. Nearly all of this travel occurred during the winter in fishing ketches, 20 to 40 tons in burden, carrying mixed cargoes that included timber products, a few horses, some barreled meat and mackerel, and a great quantity—generally more than half their total lading—of dry cod. More than other New

England vessels, those from Salem headed mainly for Barbados, the largest Caribbean market during the seventeenth century, in the hope that their cargoes could there be disposed of with a minimum of fuss and they could make it home in time for the valuable spring fishery. They might have obtained better prices had they visited a wider variety of islands (as did Boston vessels, which were used strictly to carry freight and not under the same seasonal urgencies), but the risk of missing out on the best fishing at home persuaded most of them to dump their cargoes and run.[35]

After 1675 a small but growing number of Salem vessels began to compete with the English in the transatlantic codfish trade to the Azores, Madeira, and ports on the Iberian Peninsula. The first of these on record was a Corwin vessel, commanded by Benjamin Ganson, that sailed to Madeira in 1676 with cod to trade for pipes of wine, and two years later a Salem vessel landed a similar cargo in Bilbao—the premier fish port in all of Spain. The simplicity of this trade, consisting of large cargoes that could easily be discharged in a single port, continued to attract vessels from London and the West Country seaports, which dominated the business until the middle of the eighteenth century. Nevertheless, Salem had begun dispatching perhaps a voyage a month in that direction by the 1680s.[36]

The ownership of this fleet was concentrated from its earliest days in the hands of what John Josselyn described as a class of "very rich Merchants." The first generation of these were gentlemen for the most part, born mainly in England's countryside and possessing little practical knowledge of maritime matters beyond what they had encountered as passengers in the Great Migration. William Browne, George Corwin, and Timothy Lindall—the three wealthiest Salem shipowners of the seventeenth century—all came from rural backgrounds, and when they took up commerce in Salem they did so initially as the most affluent residents of a market town, not as "traders by sea." Some less affluent competitors—Walter Price and John Turner, for example—had mariners among their family connections, and a few members of this class, like Philip English and John Hardy, had as younger men been shipmasters themselves. But serious shipowning and active seafaring cut against each other occupationally. Provisioning merchants of the sort that flourished in Salem acquired most of the information that was vital to their business—concerning the farmers, loggers, and fishermen who generated the cargoes that underwrote their shipping ventures—on the waterfront, around the warehouses, and in the taverns of Salem itself. When shipmasters became managing shipowners in a serious way, they usually quit the deep.[37]

As an elite, the group remained relatively open. The Browns, the Corwins, and the Prices might trace their origins to the Great Migration, but Timothy Lindall (1661), Deliverance Parkman (1673), Philip English (1674), and William Hirst (1674) were all latecomers, and by the end of the century, their wealth rivaled or even exceeded that of founding families. Furthermore, as new shipowning families were added to the roster, others disappeared. When Edward Wharton died in 1678, a fairly substantial merchant with a large inventory of imported manufactured goods and an "old small catch," his name disappeared from the annals of Salem shipping for good. Likewise, John Hardy's descendants included several successful shipmasters but none who could ever be termed a vessel owner and merchant in the way that he could. An aggressive, clever, and fortunate trader could build a fortune by shipping to overseas markets in auspicious times, but shipwreck, disease, piracy, war, or just softening markets could strip those riches away, and over a generation or two they frequently did. Even among families who held on to their estates, the sons and grandsons frequently pulled out of the notoriously risky business of maritime trade to become gentlemen and invested their property in land.[38]

Not everyone with investments in Salem's merchant fleet was quite as well-to-do. Around the fringes of the true merchant elite could be found a number of lesser shipowners—usually shipwrights or master mariners who retained as investments the vessels they constructed or commanded. William Jeggles was a shipbuilder with a little yard on the South River who owned a small ketch worth £50 when his estate was probated in 1659. John Pomeroy agreed in 1673 to become part-owner in a 30-ton ketch that he expected to command in the Barbados trade, and when Capt. Nathaniel Grafton died in 1671, probably in his early thirties, he owned one-eighth of another ketch, the *Dove*. Trustworthy shipmasters and shipwrights could find credit for such purchases and both commonly supplemented their regular earnings and business with investments of this sort.[39]

From the time of its inception, however, Salem's deepwater fleet belonged mainly to a fluid but identifiable merchant class. Although the passage of time added to this group more and more individuals such as English, with real maritime roots and broad social ties within the community, vessel owners were rarely active mariners themselves at any stage in

Salem's history. Rather, they were gentlemen who played prominent roles in the church, dominated the town government and local magistracy, commanded military troops, represented Salem in the General Court, occupied seats on the governor's council, and wished their sons to assume their places when they retired. They lived in larger homes of two and three stories along the main street (Essex Street today) close to the town center, impressively furnished throughout with carpets and curtains of different hues, armchairs and writing desks, great candlesticks and brass andirons, and all the other amenities of a comfortable life. Nathaniel Hawthorne's House of Seven Gables, erected by John Turner in 1668, is the best known of these, but it was only typical of a good many homes that merchants had constructed for themselves during the years of Salem's first shipping boom. The dozen or so local worthies who controlled the local commercial and fishing fleets, by their wealth, power, and gentlemanly stance above the world of manual labor, constituted in the seventeenth century. a distinct, if not closed, resident merchant class.[40]

The size of the trading fleet they owned is impossible to calculate with perfect accuracy. In a private letter written in 1697, John Higginson estimated that in the late 1680s there were sixty fishing ketches based in Salem, and since court and customs records agree that nearly all the port's overseas business was conducted in fishing ketches, we can take this as a benchmark of sorts. Higginson's figure, however, is probably somewhat high for the trading fleet, since it is unlikely that every fishing ketch set off overseas every winter. The customs records in Barbados recorded thirty-six voyages from Salem in twenty-five vessels over a two-year period in 1686–1688. On the assumption that most Salem vessels trading to the Caribbean would have called into Barbados at least once over a twenty-four-month stretch, it is difficult to place the number trading to West Indian ports at much more than thirty. And since the Caribbean trade dominated local commerce, it is hard to imagine that Salem's fleet trading to all ports in the North Atlantic numbered more than fifty.[41]

This is not to belittle their success. For a merchant class in a small town that counted only two thousand souls to have acquired forty to fifty oceangoing vessels within a single generation was no small achievement, and the province recognized this in 1683 by establishing Salem as the lawful port of entry for the entire North Shore of Massachusetts. Taken together the fleet that was based in the North and South rivers could

FIGURE 2.2 John Turner House (constructed ca. 1668). John Turner, a successful mariner-turned-merchant, constructed this house shortly after he arrived in Salem in 1668. When he died in 1680, he owned the house along with several warehouses, a wharf, four oceangoing ketches, and shares in ten other vessels, most of which were engaged in the fish trade to the West Indies. The house passed through several generations of merchants and mariners in the Turner and Ingersoll families, and in the nineteenth century became the subject of Nathaniel Hawthorne's novel *The House of Seven Gables*. This view of the rear of the house facing Turner Street shows the door of the cent-shop that the spinster Hepzibah Pyncheon operated in that story. (Frank Cousins and Phil M. Riley, *The Colonial Architecture of Salem* [Boston, 1919], plate following p. 11)

undoubtedly have employed most of the young men in town. By 1689 Salem was a seaport.[42]

If this was how Salem acquired a fleet, how did local shipowners find the men to sail it? A few mariners may have joined in the Great Migration, but most Puritans were craftsmen and farmers, not seamen. Although they learned swiftly enough the contours of their own coastline and the rudiments of working small craft on relatively short journeys, the art of deepwater seafaring required a specialized knowledge of shiphandling, navigation, geography, and business methods that few of the early colonists possessed or were ready to learn. In time, the town did attract a group of mariners—as all working seaports must. Yet of their origins we know very little: far less than we do of their neighbors—the accused witches, judges, and afflicted girls who were caught up in the whirlwind of 1692. Indeed, so thoroughly has the public imagination focused on this latter story, most of which actually transpired in the far inland precincts of the town, that the sailors who in fact constituted the central cast of characters in the long span of Salem's history have been quite overshadowed.

Unlike the maritime community of Boston, which developed rapidly out of trading connections mainly with London during the 1640s and 1650s, Salem's seafaring population remained for the first few decades rather small and unspecialized. The small number of saltwater mariners who settled alongside the South River during this early period also spent time in the fishery and coasting trades and had property on shore to tend as well. When they sailed abroad, moreover, the vessels and the business they handled were usually based in Boston, to which Salem was still only a satellite. John Marston, a carpenter in his early forties, had originally come over to New England as a servant during the Great Migration, and after working out his term, married locally, acquired land, and joined the church. In the spring of 1658, however, he also commanded the *Return*, a Salem ketch that carried wine and other cargo from Barbados to Boston. Henry True was a farmer, first in Salem and then in Salisbury, but he also served a stretch as the captain of the *Return* on a similar voyage two years later. Neither of these men was a career mariner, though both must have been fairly experienced to have earned the trust of those shipowners who hired them. We can only assume that they picked up their seafaring skills along the shore, became part-time mariners, and from time to time extended themselves on voyages overseas. From our sedentary modern perspective, their gumption may seem a little breathtaking, but remember that the first generation of New England mariners had already taken one terrific gamble in their lives, simply in moving to the New World. Stretching a coastal voyage into tropical latitudes may have struck them as quite an acceptable risk.[43]

One of the few professional mariners who called Salem home in these early years was Capt. Richard More, who assisted in the English conquest of Jamaica in 1655. The son of a broken marriage, he was bound out at age eleven to William Brewster and sailed to New England with the Pilgrims in the *Mayflower*. There he grew up, married, and started out his adult life as a farmer in Duxbury. During the 1640s, however, he took up seafaring, and by 1649, when he moved to Salem, he was calling himself a mariner. Like many shipmasters, he did some trading on the side and eventually acquired a share in a ketch, a warehouse, and "wharf land," as well as several assorted building lots around town, an orchard, and ten acres of farmland in the South Field. After he retired from the sea, he claimed to have been "brought very low" and obtained a license in 1671 to run a tavern to make ends meet, but he was still a man of some property when he died in 1696. More was a professional mariner in a way that True or Marston was not, yet even he was no thoroughgoing specialist. All of these men were products of a frontier maritime society where one had to try one's hand at many things to survive.[44]

After 1660, however, Salem began to acquire a deepwater shipping fleet, and a core of professional mariners began to assemble within the town. The chief agent of this change, as we have seen, was the banks fishery. Cod was the commodity that launched Salem on its seafaring trajectory, and idle fishing ketches were the principal vehicles in which the trade was carried on. The sailors themselves, however, came from a variety of origins. Some, indeed, were fishermen from England's West Country who had signed on as servants for a summer's voyage to Newfoundland and who at the end of the season had taken passage to New England instead of returning home. The English naval officers at Newfoundland believed that they had been deliberately left behind on the island to save cargo space on the trip back to England. Having fallen into debt over the winter, it was argued, they then took ship with Yankee traders and moved on to New England—where provisions were cheaper, employment steadier, and credit easier—to recoup their fortunes. Although this story was probably just one variation on a far more complicated pattern, it was, indeed, well known in Massachusetts that many local fishermen came from Newfoundland.[45]

Once settled in the coastal towns of the Puritan colony, they were free to make their livings as they wished, and many of these immigrant fishermen became merchant seamen on the side. Most probably made their first voyage during the winter months, ferrying the very fish they had caught the previous summer to the West Indies or the Chesapeake. Robert Starr came to Massachusetts from England, probably via Newfoundland, about 1650. Soon after his arrival, he married Susanna Hollingworth, the daughter of a local shipwright, inherited a house and land from his father-in-law, and became a fishing client of the Salem merchant George Corwin. By 1663 he was also a sailor in the ketch *Swallow*, "bound to the north-ward," and three years later he was berthed on a ketch belonging to Corwin, trading to Virginia and Newfoundland. He lived in Salem in a house near the waterfront and shipped from there regularly until he died in 1678. Starr was not alone. On the basis of the fragmentary court and business records surviving from the period, it is possible to connect roughly one-third of those mariners who lived in Salem between 1660 and 1689 to the fishery. If one considers those whose fishing labors were never recorded, the proportion probably rises to well over half. In an important way, fishing and shipping were complementary industries, and throughout the seventeenth century, a good many men moved back and forth between the two.[46]

Yet in certain respects this strategy was less than satisfactory. For one thing, the interval between the end of the fall and the start of the spring fishing season in New England was only three months. Voyages to Virginia could be completed before winter was out, but those to the Caribbean usu-ally lasted five months or more, and a transatlantic crossing could take even longer. Much of the extra money that fishermen earned in extended journeys of that nature they lost again if they missed out on the spring season at home. The merchants who outfitted these voyages and profited from the fishery as much as they did from the fish trade felt much the same way. The spring was the most valuable season, when the "merchant-able" fish of greatest value were landed, and without dry cod to ship, their export business would largely evaporate. Merchants may also have felt ambivalent about employing fishermen as business agents overseas—es-pecially if the voyage in question promised to be at all complicated. Al-though fishermen were skilled sailors, and the skippers among them had often trained themselves in navigation, a professional shipmaster familiar with financial instruments and foreign customs would more likely possess the sort of savoir faire needed in countinghouses abroad.[47]

Fortunately for them, the rapidly growing fishing economy on the North Shore proved a magnet for just this sort of ambitious young mariner. By 1675 cod exports from Massachusetts had risen to more than three thousand metric tonnes annually (worth close to £35,000), and a good portion of this was shipped out of Salem. Opportunity on this scale drew in not only fishermen but also professional mariners lukewarm about the heavy, often brutal, work of catching cod out on the banks but attracted by the wages and profits to be made in marketing it overseas. Although the precise routes by which these men found their way into the employ of Salem merchants can only be guessed at, the general circumstances that attracted them are easy enough to imagine. Massachusetts was one stop on the circuit of transatlantic commerce during the mid-seventeenth century. Dozens of master mariners called into Boston and the lesser ports of New England every year to deliver passengers and dry goods and to pick up fish and timber, and every one of them must have wondered what it was like to live there. The buzz of activity they saw in every shipyard meant that new vessels were rolling down the ways, all of which needed masters. Since merchants in Boston and Salem were ready to advance their captains a share in the vessels they commanded as well as the credit to invest in ventures of their own, any man on the make would have sensed the opportunities that the seaports of the Bay Colony had to offer.[48]

Furthermore, unlike most English colonies of the period, Massachusetts possessed towns where one could easily imagine raising a family. Shipmasters were generally married, and married men who moved to the colonies often discovered that their wives were reluctant to join them and leave behind the network of neighbors and kin that had helped to sustain life at home. This must have been doubly so in the case of mariners and fishermen, who were likely to be away at sea much of the time. In Massachusetts, however, there were churches, schools, markets, shops, and a range of skilled craftspeople that would have struck an Englishwoman as supportive and familiar. Even more important, there were other women with families who could assist them in the ordinary domestic tasks of gardening, home manufacture, and the like, as well as with the extraordinary female burdens of childbirth and infant care. Not all seafaring men were sensitive to their wives' needs, but neither were they anxious to live alone, and Salem must have seemed a place where one might plausibly plant a family.[49]

For every deck officer, the growing fleet needed three or four foremast hands, and fortunately most of what attracted shipmasters to Salem served to recruit ordinary seamen, too. New England had a reputation among sailors for high wages, easy credit, and ready employment, and every year this lured a number of men ashore to try their luck in the labor markets of the colony. Some of them landed in Massachusetts by accident. Job Tookey was a ship's boy who "cutt all the Sinews" of his right hand on a voyage to New England in 1681 and was put ashore in Piscataqua, where he was "forced to lye Lame upwards of Six Months" before making his way up the coast to Marblehead, looking for work as a fisherman and merchant seaman. Of difficult temperament, he eventually settled in Beverly, where ten years later, single and quarrelsome, he fell under suspicion of employing witchcraft to murder several of his neighbors. Another English mariner, Stephen Griggs, arrived in Salem by a similarly accidental process. In 1664 the captain of the *Black Eagle,* in which Griggs had sailed to Massachusetts, announced to the crew a change of plans—that he was taking the vessel on a fishing voyage and they had "three or four Dayes" to consider whether or not they would join him. Griggs and most of his mates declined the offer, saying they would not go "for the wages offered," since they were not "fitted with materials for a fishing voyage." Accordingly, the captain set out for Boston to raise another crew, and after he failed to reappear with the wages he owed them, and "seeing no victuals dressed for them for two or three days," they left the ship "to buy provisions for their natural sustinance." Most of the crew soon left town again, probably shipping out on similar voyages, but Griggs hung on in the Salem area, married locally, and ironically turned eventually to fishing himself.[50]

A good many sailors first set foot in Massachusetts when they deserted the vessels on which they were shipped. In jumping ship, they forfeited their wages and ran the risk of imprisonment or flogging, but given New England's reputation as a place to look for work, Salem probably struck them as a fair spot to take their chances. In 1669 the *Jeremiah* of Bristol was cruising the Massachusetts coast loading fish when the mate, Edward Watkins, the boatswain, Christopher Smith, and the gunner, Edward Woodman, decided to desert the vessel and strike out on their own within the colony. One of their friends on board had heard them plan among themselves to purchase a "ketch or vessel for themselves," sneak ashore at night, and presumably sail off into hiding until the ship had left. Apparently they made it ashore and came within £5 of purchasing a ketch before they were captured and placed under arrest at Christopher Lattimore's premises in Marblehead. By this point, the master of the *Jeremiah* was just as happy to see the last of them and refused to take them back on board. The three of them were "acompani of thefes," he claimed, and

Woodman in particular "was no more mate than a dog." Eventually, the *Jeremiah* weighed anchor with its cargo of fish for the Caribbean, leaving the three mariners behind and thereby granting their wish. What happened to Watkins and Smith the records do not reveal, but Woodman stayed on in Marblehead as a fisherman, married the daughter of the town's leading merchant, moved to Salem, and ended up a shipmaster himself, freighting fish to the West Indies. The court records are not rife with cases of this nature, but that does not by itself prove that such instances were rare. Indeed, most deserters probably vanished ashore and were never pursued.[51]

When a young sailor put down roots in Salem, the decision was obviously personal. For some individuals of Puritan temperament the chance to resettle in a godly commonwealth would have been important; for others the personal autonomy that seemed to go along with life in the New World may have been the main attraction; still others were probably induced to settle for purely material motives. In general, however, these seafaring men, though chiefly still single, recognized that Salem might someday be a good place to make a home. From a professional angle, the growing fleet created a high rate of promotion for younger mariners. Particularly if they were well traveled, were quick in business, and knew something of navigation, they might soon be trusted to replace a local fisherman in command of a vessel on its trading voyage southward in the winter. Such a position on the quarterdeck, which might have been nothing but a pipe dream in the English seaports from which they had sailed, was a stronger possibility in the more fluid society of New England.

For a young bachelor settling down usually meant finding a spouse, and in this regard Massachusetts was also favored, since the colony was widely known for its population of eligible and "well-Riged" young women. What this rigging consisted of may be left to the imagination, but undoubtedly in the seventeenth century, the New England colonies possessed more settled families and hence more single girls than any other English settlement in the New World. More than half of those deckhands who took up residence in Salem between 1660 and 1689 married local women, and it is hard to imagine that for young men this was not a decisive attraction. Of course, there were plenty of girls back home as well, but in Massachusetts, where land was inexpensive and where the common resources of water, forest, and marshland were lightly exploited and generally accessible, the economic prospects for young householders were probably better.[52]

Naturally enough, the most likely to settle permanently in Salem were those with the means to purchase places there. When John Tawley arrived in Salem about 1675, he brought enough capital with him to set himself up rapidly as a trader and shipmaster of consequence and to render himself a suitable mate for Elizabeth Boyden, whom he married in 1676. By the early 1680s he had acquired a wharf and warehouse as well as a share in the ketch *Content,* which he sailed both to Newfoundland and to the West Indies on trading voyages. At his death in 1690, he owned part of a much larger vessel, the bark *Prudent Betty,* held bills of exchange on England, kept a large and well-appointed house, and owned a female slave to assist his wife in running it. Immigrant seamen whose fortunes had not advanced, by contrast, often spent a few years in New England and then moved on. Nicholas Durrell tried his hand at farm labor and soldiering in King Philip's War before shipping with Adam Westgate on a voyage to the West Indies in 1677. Although a few years later he persuaded the town of Salem to give him a plot of land on which to build a house, he never found anyone to marry and never made it to the quarterdeck. In 1690 his taxable wealth placed him among the poorest inhabitants in town, and soon after he disappeared. That 73 percent of all immigrant mariners who sailed on locally owned vessels between 1660 and 1689 chose to settle in Salem speaks to its attractions for working mariners.[53]

Through to the end of the seventeenth century, immigrant fishermen and professional mariners provided most of the labor for Salem's growing fleet. Yet because New England towns were composed mainly of settled families, they were also full of children, and with so many young boys living within a few minutes' walk of the ocean and familiar from childhood with boats, sails, winds, and tides, it was only a matter of time before they would grow up and begin to join the immigrants in the forecastles of Salem's burgeoning fleet. The first native-born seaman on record in Salem was young John Archer, a carpenter's son who sailed twice to the West Indies as a teenager in the late 1650s, and with every passing decade, the number of local boys on board Salem vessels gradually increased. By the 1680s roughly one Salem mariner in three had been born into a Massachusetts family.[54]

What prompted some colonists to follow the running tide and go to sea—for a portion of their lives at least—they never said. As a social group, we know that they were young—most were under thirty years of age—

and that they came from nearly all social ranks and occupational back-grounds. Mariners encouraged their sons to go to sea; but so did craftsmen, farmers, fishermen, and even a few merchants. Although some local sea-men had been born into poverty, many more came from middling families, and some had enjoyed truly comfortable upbringings. Robert Bray, Jr., was the son of a fisherman from Ipswich, England, who arrived in Salem in the late 1660s, never occupied a public office, and remained one of Salem's poorer inhabitants until his death in the 1690s. By contrast, John Ruck, Jr., who sailed to Bilbao in the *John & Elizabeth* in 1678 as a young man of twenty-one years, was the son of one of Salem's most prominent citizens—a merchant and landowner, who held numerous positions of authority within the town and colony throughout the period. When the Brays and the Rucks sailed together, they were undoubtedly sensitive to the social distinctions that separated them, and they knew that in all proba-bility their futures would diverge.[55]

Many of these early seamen were outsiders to the Puritan experiment: immigrant fishermen and mariners, who moved to Salem for practical reasons and initially felt a little out of place. Within a short period of time, however, partly as a consequence of intermarriage to families of the Great Migration and partly because so many sons of Puritan families began to choose the sea themselves, any cultural gap that had once existed between sailors and settlers in Salem itself began to vanish. Away from home, young New England mariners may have sown their wild oats in the water-front dens of foreign ports, but inside the Bay Colony one would have found it progressively harder with each passing decade to distinguish them from the rest of the population.

What sailors shared in common, more than any other feature, was the simple experience of having grown up beside the sea. Remarkably, of all the New England–born mariners who sailed in or out of Salem during this period, not one had grown up more than five miles from salt water. Sailors here as everywhere in the early modern world tended to hail from seaside communities, partly because it was easier for those who had grown up in the company of fishermen, coasters, and mariners to imagine them-selves at sea, partly because like most people who lived in these coastal communities they knew something about seafaring from their experience in small boats, and partly because it was up and down the coast that ship-masters searched for the hands they needed. In 1670 Capt. Richard Hollings-

worth was riding home to Salem when he crossed paths with Timothy
Roberts and his mother on the Boston road. Hollingsworth was about to
depart on a lengthy voyage around the North Atlantic and, needing hands,
enquired as to whether Roberts would join him. The two of them negotiated
terms right there in the middle of the road. Roberts was shipped as a seaman, though he also agreed to bring along his adze and perform some
cooperage on the side, and they settled on a wage of thirty-five shillings
a month. Many factors brought Hollingsworth and Roberts together that
day—supply, demand, and luck, among others—but they also ran into
each other because the two of them lived beside the sea. Proximity to the
coast, more than any other single factor, set the parameters of the maritime
labor market in Massachusetts.[56]

Conversely, the maritime labor market defined much of working life
for men along the coast. In 1665 the General Court reported a total of 132
vessels of greater than 20 tons' burden owned inside the colony, and using
normal manning ratios of the day, these vessels would have employed between 850 and 900 men. Based on the 1675 figures of an Order in Council
and the 1676 figures of Edward Randolph, we can venture an informed,
conservative guess that there were 50 additional three-man shallops, barks,
and sloops of between 6 and 20 tons. In its entirety, therefore, the Massachusetts shipping and coasting fleet of that period probably employed just
over 1,000 men.[57] If we can assume that men aged fifteen to fifty constituted
20 percent of the colony's 25,000 white inhabitants in 1665 and that 45
percent of these individuals lived in communities bordering on the coast,
then we can place the population of working-age males in the maritime
communities of Massachusetts at 2,250, of which these 1,000 mariners
represented close to one-half. If one applies the same arithmetic to Edward
Randolph's higher (though probably exaggerated) estimates of Massachusetts's entire fleet-fishing, coasting, and shipping, in 1676 the colony's
maritime industries would have employed almost every man and boy who
lived along the coast. Certainly, the forty to fifty trading vessels that belonged
to Salem during the 1680s would have employed somewhere between
200 and 250 men—somewhat more than half the men of working age living
in the town at the time. Considering that the crews of all these vessels were
constantly shifting in personnel, remembering that there were scores of
even smaller vessels that escape this calculation, and recognizing that these
calculations ignore the fishery entirely, one cannot avoid the conclusion

that most men in coastal Massachusetts spent a significant portion of their working lives on the water. Few of them were dedicated specialists. Before, during, and after their careers afloat, they spent much of their time on shore gardening, hunting, cutting wood, gathering hay, tending animals, building and repairing their homes, and doing scores of other tasks. Yet for the great majority, maritime labor was a part of life.[58]

It has been estimated that in Louis XIV's France, a continental country with a huge peasant population, mariners accounted for fewer than one in every three hundred inhabitants. In Restoration England, where it was almost impossible to live more than fifty miles from salt water and sea-faring traditions were much stronger, the fraction was somewhat higher at one in sixty. In the Dutch Republic, whose economy was famously rooted in the richest fisheries, the largest commercial fleet, and arguably the most powerful navy in Europe, the ratio stood at one in thirty-four. In Massachusetts, however, the proportion of mariners to total population in 1665 reached one in twenty-five.[59] This colony, whose history is usually represented in agrarian images, was in truth one of the most thoroughly maritime societies to be found during the seventeenth century anywhere around the North Atlantic rim. That society did not extend as yet very far inland, and by the end of the seventeenth century a growing number of New Englanders dwelled outside it—that is, in rural villages where neither boating, nor coasting, nor deepwater shipping was part of everyday life. But for those in Massachusetts who lived by the sea—meaning the majority of colonists through most of the seventeenth century and nearly all of those who lived in Salem—maritime labor was part of life.

CHAPTER THREE

The Eighteenth Century

SAILORS AT SEA

THE IMAGE OF LIFE at sea that has come down to us through literature and popular history is informed overwhelmingly by the experience of the long-distance trades. Lengthy voyages took sailors into distant and exotic climes and made excellent stories. From Richard Hakluyt to Richard Henry Dana and beyond, sailor-journalists and their editors have recognized this and put onto paper and into print the tales of travel and adventure that seafaring to remote parts of the world generated and that the reading public still loves to consume. A great many of these have survived, and today they occupy shelves and shelves of library space. Not only do they still read well, but as historical sources go they are unusually rich. Longer voyages, being stressful, dangerous, and prone to conflict, also produced an enormous body of legal documentation. Court proceedings involved writs, responses, instruments of protest, and court depositions, all of which have survived in archives by the boxful. Though sketchier in detail and harder to read, these accounts have the advantage of being rooted in oral testimony not dependent on the literacy of the participants. Taken all together, those published and unpublished sources not only make ripping yarns; they also allow historians to uncover more about the work culture of mariners than is probably possible for any other preindustrial occupation. It is no wonder they have exercised such a hold on those who seek to describe seafaring in the age of sail.

The problem with this approach, however, is that a great many mariners sailed principally not in the far reaches of distant seas but in waters they knew in routine voyages to ports nearby. Such trips rarely generated good copy; nor, given their short duration and familiarity of working conditions, were they commonly plagued by difficulties, either social or natural. Yet as human experience they mattered just as much, and, indeed, in purely quantitative terms—that is, in man-days afloat—shorter voyages probably counted for most of what early modern mariners understood to be the seafaring life. In eighteenth-century Salem this was certainly the case. Though every mariner who ever shipped out of this seaport periodically ran into the emergencies and disasters that might accompany longer voyages—storms, shipwreck, hard usage, capture, impressment, and the like—the great majority of the voyages they undertook unfolded over a matter of a few months with little fanfare. Seafaring of this sort was hard, demanding labor, and it sometimes placed the men who followed it in extraordinary plights, but most of it took place in a working environment that was, if not predictable, at least generally familiar and governed principally by custom. Like any customary regime, the shipboard world possessed a locus of authority—a master qualified by age and experience who administered direction and correction when the unexpected occurred. The truth remains, however, that on Salem vessels of the eighteenth century, most sailors understood their duty and performed it more or less willingly, because they shared with their captains a common understanding of what a voyage was about.

On the morning of May 25, 1767, young John Hodges, Jr., walked down to the wharf on the South River to assume command of a new topsail schooner, the *General Wolfe*, on a summer's voyage to the Caribbean. Hodges was only eighteen years of age, extremely young for a master, but his father owned the *General Wolfe*, and with parental trust in his pocket, John had climbed to the quarterdeck much faster than most. To help him that morning, he hired two local men, "the nieger Primus Manning" and Frank Silver, a local sailor of Portuguese descent, both of whom he paid in tobacco. Together, over the next few days, they got out the ship's boat, reattached the anchor, unbent the sails, painted the deck with turpentine, blackened the masts, topmasts, booms, and jibbooms with tallow and tar, and began the long task of stowing cargo and provisions for the projected voyage to the West Indies. For several weeks, bundles of shingles, staves, hoops, and boards, hogsheads of fish and water, barrels of pork and bread, and a set of cooper's tools, among many other sundries, were ferried out from the shore and lowered into the hold or fastened down on the main deck. The pace of work was not desperate; one day was lost to rain; another to a New England "Leacktion Day"; and Hodges rested on the Sabbath. Yet the language of the journal implies that the captain was not merely a supervisor. One afternoon, he reported having been "imployd in Making and Tarring 2 tarpolings"; another day he noted "myself and Primus imploy'd in getting som bords out of the hold and stow'd them on deck." There were days when he may have stood aloof from the actual physical labor, but this sort of language implies that much of the time he sweated it shoulder to shoulder with his hired hands.[1]

As the hold filled with cargo and the date of departure drew near, Captain Hodges, like any master, turned his mind to the problem of assembling a crew. In the portledge bills of the day (Figure 3.1), all members of the crew, from the mate on down, usually entered into pay just a few days before the vessel departed. Exactly how Hodges went about shipping his men he never recorded; the process was probably too informal and private to merit it. By the end of the third week, however, negotiations of some sort were clearly under way, for the crew itself had begun to take over the work of preparing the vessel. On June 6 Joseph Neale was helping Hodges carry on board twenty-five hogsheads of fish and forty-five bundles of barrel hoops; four days later, the two of them were joined by Zachariah Burchmore and Samuel Buffum to load more fish; and some time after that Joshua Trask and an anonymous cooper filled out the ship's complement. In all probability these men were paid as casual laborers until just before they sailed, but they had clearly been gathering as a crew for two or three weeks. Drawn from a social network defined chiefly by local residence and the elaborate personal and genealogical web that constituted local society, they were sailing among familiar faces.[2]

On June 25, once the last bundle of staves had been stowed belowdecks and Captain Hodges had shipped his crew of five, the *General Wolfe* weighed anchor and set sail for Dominica. Taking his departure from Cape Ann, Hodges set his course on a southeasterly heading across Georges Bank with the intention of following a long sweeping course far out into the Atlantic in order to catch the trade winds and run down to the West Indies

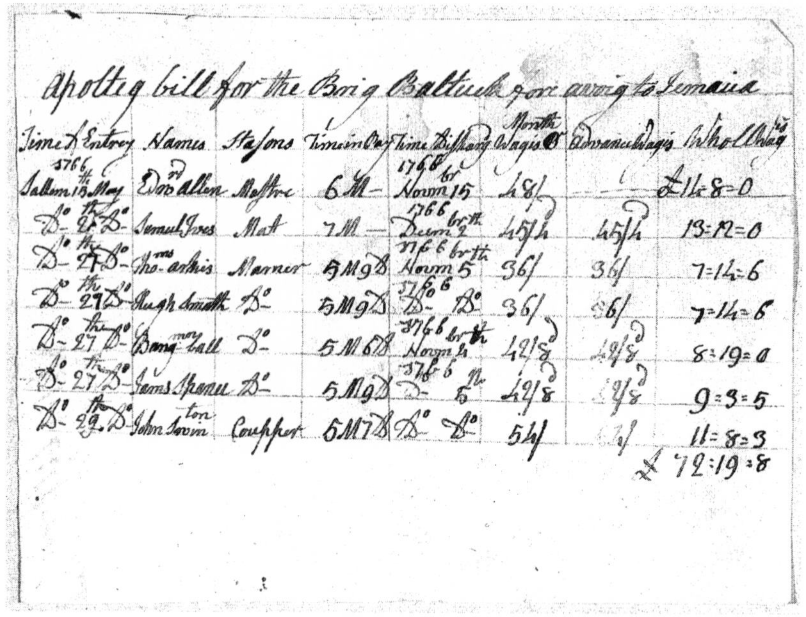

A poltig bill for the Brig Baltick from a voige to Jemaica

Time of Entrey	Names	Stations	Time in Pay	Time Discharg	Month Wages	Advance Wages	Whole Wages
1766 Sallem 13th May	Edwd Allen	Mastre	6 M	1766 Novm 15	48/		£11:8=0
Do 27th Do	Samuel Jones	Mat	7 M	1766 Decm 9th	45/4	45/4	13:12=0
Do 27th Do	Thos archis	Marrner	5 M 9 D	1766 Novm 5th	36/	36/	7:14:6
Do 27th Do	Hugh Smith	Do	5 M 9 D	1766 Do Do	36/	36/	7:14:6
Do 27th Do	Benjm Hall	Do	5 M 6 D	1766 Novm 2th	42/8	42/8	8:19=0
Do 27th Do	James Spence	Do	5 M 9 D	1766 Do 5th	42/8	42/8	9:3=5
Do 29th Do	John Sorton	Couper	5 M 7 D	Do Do	54/	54/	11=8=3
							£72:19=8

FIGURE 3.1 Portledge bill, schooner *Baltick*, 1766. The portledge bill was a record of wages kept by the master and delivered to the managing owner of the vessel after its return. It gives the name and rank of each crew member, his dates of hire and discharge, and the rates of pay. The *Baltick* is the vessel pictured in Figure 3.2. Source: Felt Family Collection, box 3, folder 13, James Duncan Phillips Library. (Courtesy of the Peabody-Essex Museum)

from the northeast. For three weeks the crew sailed southeast with a pleasant quartering breeze until they had reached a point about a thousand miles east of Bermuda. Then, late on the evening of July 14, they encountered the trade winds and wore away to the southwest. Two uneventful weeks after that, on an overcast, squally morning late in July, the *General Wolfe* sailed into the open roadstead at Roseau on the west coast of Dominica.[3]

A recent addition to the British Empire, Dominica had been captured from the French during the Seven Years' War and was still thinly settled, with little to offer by way of markets and produce. Since 1766, however, Roseau had been a free port and rendezvous for vessels from Martinique and Guadeloupe looking for slaves and provisions, and the *General Wolfe* came loaded mainly with hogsheads of fish and bundles of timber to trade with these foreigners. That afternoon, Hodges and three hands rowed ashore through the inclement weather to assess the state of the local market, and the following morning, after the vessel was officially entered with the port officials, the crew of the *General Wolfe* began to off-load its cargo. Some of the merchandise they ferried ashore, but most was transferred directly to other vessels—schooners, sloops, and pettiaugers from neighboring islands—and replaced with ballast hauled from the beach. By August 12 the hold of the *General Wolfe* had been "clear'd out," and the following day Hodges and his crew departed for the Spanish colony of Santo Domingo, where they hoped to take on a cargo of molasses for the trip home to New England.[4]

They arrived in Monte Cristi on a Sunday evening late in August, and the next morning the crew set about constructing an awning over the main deck, in the shelter of which the cooper was to set up hogsheads while Hodges made arrangements to have them filled. Every two or three days over the next six weeks, Spanish boats pulled alongside with several "buckowes" of molasses, which the men of the *General Wolfe* hoisted aboard, emptied into the hogsheads, and returned. The men then stowed the cargo belowdecks and waited for the next delivery. Most of the molasses was earmarked for the owners, but nearly every one of the crew acquired an adventure—usually a hogshead of molasses or a tierce of sugar—on his own account. Many days there was no work about stowage, and Hodges usually put the men to overhauling the vessel: unbending the sails, striking and slushing the topmasts, painting the spars with turpentine, scraping the blocks and deadeyes, and careening and painting the vessel itself. Finally, during the second week of October, the crew packed up the last of the molasses, took on board a supply of bread and water, and bent the sails again. On the eve of their departure for Salem, Hodges discovered that his purse full of gold coins and a silver buckle had been stolen out of his chest. He suspected a Spanish sailor from one of the coasting vessels, but there was nothing to do about the "son of a bitch" except to call on God to "damn and blast him to hell."[5]

The day after the robbery, on October 14, the *General Wolfe* set sail for home, this time on a direct, northerly course for Cape Cod. Well into autumn now, Hodges could not expect the string of "fair and pleasant" days he had enjoyed on the voyage down, and the vessel encountered several nasty blows along the way. A few hundred miles off the Carolinas a "violent gail of wind" struck the vessel, accompanied by a very long sea and some terrible squalls. One huge wave "burried up half the Cabin"; another "Carried away the bow Sprit end." For two days Hodges and his men lay to in the midst of the storm, pumping out the water they had shipped until at last the wind moderated. After some impromptu repairs to the bowsprit, they regained their way, got soundings on Georges Bank on November 3, and came to an anchor in Salem harbor after dark the following night.[6]

The voyage of the *General Wolfe* had its moments. One can be certain that Captain Hodges fulminated to his friends over the papist swine who had stolen his purse, and stories of the wild forty-eight hours spent riding out the October gale were no doubt told and retold for several days after the ship's return. Had any of the crew ever written his memoirs, either of these stories might have merited a paragraph. Yet as far as Hodges's journal reveals, most of the 133 days that these men spent sailing to the West Indies and back passed in a very routine manner. Nobody deserted the *General Wolfe;* no extraordinary discipline occurred worth recording; there were no mutinies on board; and the vessel was neither captured nor chased by pirates or privateers. We can imagine all manner of conflict: pitting officers against men, sailors against sailors, mariners against bureaucrats, English against Spaniards, or the ship and its crew against the sea. There was a huge body of maritime law to cover every one of these possibilities. But on this voyage, as on most others recorded in the journals of Salem mariners from the colonial period, conflict was resolved in unremarkable ways. Most of the time, the crew's energies were occupied by hard, steady, and generally familiar work.

John Hodges's seventeenth-century seafaring ancestors might have found this plain and unremarkable voyage a little peculiar. Like most of the commercial regions in which New Englanders traded, the Caribbean was a far busier place in 1767 than it had been a hundred years before. No New England vessel of the earlier period would have called in at Dominica, which was then still inhabited primarily by Caribs. The *General Wolfe* itself was the product of a new century: its schooner rig would have puzzled sailors of an earlier period for a while at least, and its size would have well outstripped the fishing ketches that dominated Salem's West India trade in the seventeenth century. Yet New Englanders of an earlier age could doubtless have mastered these changes in fairly short order. A schooner was not a ketch, but as a two-masted, mixed rigged vessel, it did not differ radically from its predecessors. The shipping business that these mariners knew, in its core commodities and sailing routes, was a recognizable adaptation of the system established by their ancestors several generations before.

As a business, however, it operated on a larger scale in 1775 than it had a hundred years earlier, for the eighteenth century was an eventful one in the history of the Atlantic world. Rapid growth in population, production, and consumption, and the rising demand for free and unfree labor throughout the New World served to multiply the volume of colonial shipping several times over before the outbreak of the American Revolution. Salem took part in the unfolding history of merchant capital within the British Empire, largely through the expansion of its traditional lines of trade, but the town's overseas trade grew unevenly, and this rocky course of development needs to be charted.

The three decades of prosperity that had first turned Salem into a seaport ended with the outbreak of King William's War in 1689. Within a few months enemy warships and privateers were cruising the coastal waters between the fishing banks of Newfoundland and the trading lanes of the Caribbean, seizing New England vessels at will. Although Massachusetts began recruiting sailors and shipping tonnage for military expeditions against Acadia and New France, outfitting guard vessels to protect its shipping, and raising taxes on everyone to pay the cost, the foreign trade of the colony fell into a rapid tailspin, and the shipping industry slid with it. At Barbados the number of entries from New England ports dropped from more than 100 annually in the late 1680s to just over 50 per year by the mid-1690s; in Jamaica the number fell from 17.5 per annum in the late 1680s to 11 per annum in the late 1690s. These were the shipping lanes that New England had owned in the last years of peace, and the traffic along them plummeted.[7]

No Massachusetts seaport, however, suffered as Salem did. Precise figures are hard to come by, but the trade to Barbados collapsed—from eighteen vessels annually in 1686–1688 to four annually from 1695 through 1697. For the most part, this was a direct consequence of the cod fishery's destruction by French privateers. Since fishing ketches were not the swiftest vessels, carried little sail while at work, fished in waters far from home, and went totally unarmed, the French were able to seize much of the fleet and drive the rest into hiding. The town requested that the province provide a ship of war to protect the fishery off Nova Scotia, but not until 1696 was any action taken sufficient to deter the enemy. By 1697, John Higginson told his brother, there were only six fishing ketches left in town. Without fish, Salem had little to export, so that even surviving vessels saw little activity during the 1690s.[8]

To compound these strictly maritime problems, a wave of witchcraft accusations swept through Salem in 1692, throwing the town into deeper turmoil. In a period of little more than a year, 185 residents were accused of witchcraft, and 19 people were executed. Although most of the trouble occurred in Salem Village, inland from the seaport, there was not a soul anywhere in town who did not know—as a neighbor, employer, debtor, or creditor—several of those involved in the trials. The outbreak began, moreover, just as the seizure of vessels, the burning of outposts, and the killing or capture of colonists by the French and Indian enemy along the coast were reaching their peaks. Salem residents must have started to wonder whether the town was falling victim to cosmic forces beyond anyone's control and whether it was safe to remain there. Indeed, over the two years surrounding the crisis they left in droves, dropping the number of taxpaying householders throughout Salem by 38 percent, and the population of the waterfront ward, where the most mobile individuals lived, by a full 70 percent.[9]

The worries about witchcraft relaxed after 1693, and a brief peace allowed fishing and commerce to rebound a little around the turn of the century. But in 1701 Queen Anne's War broke out, and for another decade Indian raiding to the eastward, French predation at sea, and soaring taxes to pay for the colony's defense reduced Salem's maritime economy to privateering and little more. Alarmed at the losses to colonial shipping, Massachusetts leaders informed the British government in 1709 that without naval engagement with the enemy "this country must be abandoned as to its trade." The Treaty of Utrecht in 1713 brought conflict on the high seas to an end, but the quarter-century of war had stalled the economy and prevented the population of the town from rising at all (see Graph 1, Appendix B). Even in 1716, after three years of peace, only fourteen Salem-owned ships—mostly converted privateers—cleared customs for foreign parts.[10]

In the years between the close of Queen Anne's War in 1713 and the outbreak of King George's War in 1744, Salem regained its commercial feet. Entries and clearances from the harbor returned to and even exceeded the levels of the seventeenth century, and the population of the town inched upward as well. Yet although peace was undoubtedly a boon, these were not wildly prosperous years by any means. Stiff competition in the fisheries from England and France combined with sluggish markets in Spain and the West Indies to dampen business through the 1720s and 1730s, and war with the French and Spanish during the 1740s produced another wave of privateering that forced many fishermen to haul up their vessels and left traders to venture out only at the risk of being seized in transit.[11]

Only after the Treaty of Aix-La-Chapelle in 1748 did the soft markets and wartime dangers that had retarded Salem's commercial development for more than half a century finally lift to usher in another period of real prosperity. Principally this was driven by a deep secular shift within the Atlantic economy, as the stagnant population growth, weak demand, and low prices prevalent throughout Europe and the Americas between 1675 and 1750 finally began to reverse. Falling mortality, larger families, and a quickening economy in western Europe and especially Great Britain drove the prices of almost all commodities within the imperial economy sharply upward in the second half of the century. As colonists everywhere responded by settling new lands and planting new fields, and by importing new laborers—free and slave—to handle much of the work, seaports such as Salem involved in shipping produce and manufactures around the Atlantic enjoyed flush times. Britain's stunning successes on land and sea during the Seven Years' War of 1756–1763 multiplied the protected markets within which New England shipmasters like John Hodges could profitably deal, and the British navy's hegemony on the high seas allowed local vessels like the *General Wolfe* to fish and trade almost anywhere they pleased in the North Atlantic. Between 1690 and 1740, fewer than 120 vessels had cleared Salem's customshouse in any year for which records survive, and only about 15 percent of these were owned in Salem. After 1750, by comparison, clearances almost always topped 200 vessels annually, of which 35 percent were local. The population of the town tracked this pattern of commercial growth and climbed rapidly right up to the outbreak of the American Revolution.[12]

Much of the eighteenth-century expansion occurred within traditional structures, but certain elements of Salem's maritime economy also changed in character. For one thing, the seaport grew a little more specialized. In the first half-century of its history, Salem had competed with Boston in most branches of commerce, including the transatlantic trades. Up until that time, English merchants had conventionally dispatched a few dozen vessels every year to New England laden with manufactures and ready to buy fish, in either Salem or Boston, for delivery to markets in southern Europe. In the course of the eighteenth century, however, Salem ceased to play much of a role in the generalized import business, and it lost its status as the only consequential market town on Massachusetts's North Shore. This process began during the 1720s and 1730s, when control over the Iberian fish trade began to pass from the English shipowners who had dominated it since the seventeenth century into the hands of a new group of New England merchants based principally in the old fishing outport of Marblehead.

For nearly a hundred years, the town on the rocks had served as little more than a satellite of Salem and Boston. As late as 1714, wrote its pastor John Barnard, "there was not so much as one foreign trading vessel belonging to the town," and the residents who caught and dried the cod "left the merchants of Boston, Salem, and Europe, to carry away the gains." In the subsequent decades, however, Marblehead was colonized by a crowd of well-financed newcomers from Boston, who joined with some ambitious local fish dealers to launch several vessels of their own into the direct export of fish. By 1750 Marblehead had grown into a merchant seaport in its own right, and vessels owned there accounted for about half of Massachusetts's fish trade with Spain through the next quarter-century. By the mid-1760s, boasted Barnard, his hometown possessed a fleet of "between thirty and forty ships, brigs, snows, and topsail schooners engaged in foreign trade."[13]

Marblehead did not gain this fleet at Salem's expense, for most of the transatlantic shipping business had previously been owned not in Massachusetts but abroad. Yet when the fish trade departed for Marblehead, English vessels manned by English crews stopped visiting Salem as often, and Salem lost much of its function as a market town and port of call. During the seventeenth century, the direct import of English manufactures had involved Salem merchants as distributors to northern New England through a commercial network independent of Boston; now Salem, like any other town, obtained these items indirectly from dry goods dealers in the provincial capital. Before 1720, moreover, English mariners had been a common sight on the Salem waterfront, and they played a recognizable role in town life, bringing business for local taverns, useful news from the old country, and frequent trouble for the town's constables. By the middle of the eighteenth century, vessels and crews from foreign parts rarely put in to Salem, and the business and information they had brought with them disappeared. Paradoxically, as Salem grew in size and wealth, it also grew in on itself.[14]

No longer quite the market town it once had been, Salem saw the structure of its coasting business alter as well. During the seventeenth century, Salem had served as the commercial hub for a string of coastal communities stretching along Massachusetts's North Shore and for the summer fishing camps on the coast of Maine. By 1740 much of this coastal commerce had vanished. The offshore banks fishery, which had been launched more than fifty years earlier and had almost entirely replaced the inshore shallop fishery, required fewer coasting services, since it provisioned itself and freighted its own fish. Several outports—namely Newbury, Gloucester, and Marblehead—had developed into marketing centers in their own right, and traders there could deal directly with Boston or even in foreign markets without ever calling in to Salem. As the town's role as a port of call for English shipping began to diminish, the shopping there rarely merited the trip.

Yet the logic that made this seaport less of a magnet for its neighbors along the North Shore actually reinforced the coasting business linking it to Boston. As Salem began to depend more on the provincial capital for English imports, merchants and traders discovered a growing need for more regular transport inside Massachusetts Bay. Accordingly, by the middle of the eighteenth century, the short-haul coasting business attracted more Salem residents than ever. George Peele employed a couple of hands on his 20-ton sloop *Mary*, freighting cargoes of fish, molasses, and "English goods" between Boston and Salem for Timothy Orne, Richard Derby, and Miles Ward between 1755 and 1767. Similarly, Jonathan Archer shipped horses, shingles, "damnified flax," and a host of other commodities for Timothy Orne on the same run between 1745 and 1758. Some of these coasters occasionally trekked farther afield—to Nova Scotia, Philadelphia, the Carolinas, and even as far as the West Indies—but the bulk of their business remained inside Massachusetts.[15]

How many coasters were in business at any given time is difficult to estimate, for none of their personal papers have survived, and no officials kept track of their travels. During the Seven Years' War, coasting vessels were required to pay a shipping duty to cover the cost of guard vessels that the province had equipped and sent to sea, and between 1758 and 1762, about a half-dozen Salem coasters were assessed every year for the privilege of carrying on their business. This was in time of war, however, when shipping was at a low ebb. A better measurement of the relative importance of coasting within the Salem fleet is the impact coasters made in the business records of the merchants who employed them through peace *and* war. During the period 1738–1768, Timothy Orne kept a series of account books in which he recorded his dealings with forty-two shipmasters employed in foreign trades and fifteen coasters employed along the Massachusetts shore. In Richard Derby's accounts, stretching from 1756 to 1770, the equivalent ratio was twenty-two shipmasters to eight coasters. If it can be assumed that this proportion of roughly 3:1 applied to the vessels of the Salem fleet as generally as it did to their masters, then it can be estimated that for every three vessels dispatched in foreign trades, there was one employed along the coast. In 1765, for example, when fifty-one Salem-owned vessels cleared the harbor for distant parts, there probably were between fifteen and twenty locally owned coasting sloops handling the collection and distribution of cargoes along the shore.[16]

The busiest branch of Salem's shipping industry in the eighteenth century, however, was still the provisioning trade to the plantation colonies, pursued with more energy than ever, though by now on an entirely familiar plan. Every year, at the onset of winter, most of Salem's seafaring population, mainly in coasting sloops and fishing schooners of under 50 tons, set sail for the southern colonies laden with fish, timber, farm produce, and a variety of manufactured goods. In April or May they returned with barrels of beef, pork, and grain from Pennsylvania and the Chesapeake or hogsheads of molasses, rum, and salt from the West Indies. As summer approached, some of them launched a second voyage southward carrying fish that had just arrived from the spring fishery off Cape Sable while others headed for the Nova Scotia fishing banks to land next year's cargo. Eleazar Moses was one of many who followed this sort of pattern. Each winter between 1715 and 1717, Moses set sail from Salem as master of the 35-ton sloop *Dolphin*, with a crew of four and a cargo of mixed New England produce for a different plantation colony—Barbados in 1715, Surinam in

1716, and the Bahamas in 1717—and every spring, after five months away, he returned with a lading of tropical produce—molasses and rum from Barbados and Surinam and lignum vitae from the Bahamas. Then, in the summer and fall between these Caribbean voyages, Moses usually went fishing as a common sharesman on another sloop, the *Speedwell*.[17]

A smaller number of Salem vessels, generally ships and brigantines, were dedicated traders that conducted their business throughout most of the year around the North Atlantic. Primarily they dealt in fish and salt, especially the higher grades of spring cod that were dispatched to southern Europe or the Wine Islands during the summer months and the finest quality salt from the Bay of Biscay. A few of these purely merchant vessels, however, sought other destinations: Ireland, where New England timber could be traded for barreled beef, hard bread, and linens; Connecticut, where farm produce could be picked up for delivery to the West Indies; or the Caribbean Islands themselves, where refuse fish always found a market. The men and ships who pursued these trades worked a more varied routine than did Eleazar Moses and the *Dolphin*. During a thirty-month period extending from December 1714 to June 1717, the sloop *Beginning*, with John Green as master, sailed on five voyages—two to Barbados, one to the Leeward Islands, one to the Tortugas, and one to North Carolina. Between the summer of 1711 and the fall of 1712, Philip English's sloop *Mary,* commanded by his son William, made three trips—one to Canada, another to Virginia, and a third to Surinam. The following year, Philip English placed his son in command of the brigantine *William and Susanna* with instructions to sail for Connecticut "to Load with Staves or what else may be proper for Ireland" and then make his way "to Corke & Lymrick or Either of them or what other Place or Port thare which you by advice may think Best." In Ireland he was to abide by the Navigation Acts, remain in compliance with his charter party, purchase a cargo of "Goods & Marchandise," and return. As in the previous century, therefore, some of these New England traders continued to "trye all ports to force a trade."[18]

The voyage of the *William and Susanna,* however, was an unusual one, for Salem vessels more frequently followed straightforward shuttle routes. Although some had to spend weeks crisscrossing Chesapeake Bay or island-hopping in the Caribbean in order to empty their holds and assemble reasonable return cargoes, most trips had in essence only two main legs—there and back. The longest ventures were those to Europe, which normally lasted five or six months; those to the West Indies usually took three to five months; a Chesapeake cruise could occupy two to four months; and voyages within the northern colonies between Philadelphia and Newfoundland seldom required longer than six or eight weeks. Shipmasters from Boston might occasionally undertake triangular or polygonal routes—say, from Massachusetts to Newfoundland to Spain and home again. The larger seaport was a center for the distribution of English dry goods, and vessels based there earned considerable freight delivering these to other ports, chiefly on the North American mainland, and then taking on cargoes of local provisions for other markets within the empire. Salem merchants, however, did not deal in English goods to this degree, rarely entered into commerce of this complexity, and followed more predictable routes instead.[19]

The vessels they employed were larger than had once been the case. Up until about 1720 Salem's overseas merchant fleet had been composed chiefly of sloops and ketches, averaging about 35 tons. By 1750 the vessels in the West Indian trade consisted mainly of schooners and brigantines averaging about 60 tons, and those employed on transatlantic runs tended to be larger still, up to 100 tons or more. Salem shipwrights had always been capable of building vessels of this size, but in earlier years, the markets that local shipping had serviced—mainly in the Chesapeake and the Caribbean—had been too small to justify the cost. Selling off a large cargo could be time-consuming in the plantation colonies of the seventeenth century, where seaports were few and people dispersed. Small vessels were appropriate to thin markets such as these, since they could dispose of everything on board in a limited number of stops, then turn around for home. By the middle of the eighteenth century, however, the plantation colonies possessed much larger populations and adequate small-vessel fleets of their own. New Englanders could sell more cargo in bigger parcels to traders and coasters familiar with the region, and the owners of these craft would take upon themselves the trouble and risk of distributing the goods locally.[20]

The tonnage and rig of Salem vessels was determined not only by markets but by the town's continuing connection with the cod fishery, and to the end of the colonial period, the local merchant fleet remained distinctive for its adherence to the two-masted fisherman's rig. Since any craft built for use in a North Shore community—even if originally intended for the merchant service—stood a strong chance of being converted to the fishery, shipowners understood the advantages of vessels suited to work on the banks. That was why Salem's seventeenth-century merchant fleet had been composed largely of ketches. With a fair-sized mainsail and a small steering sail aft, these craft had first achieved popularity in New England as fishing vessels mainly because on the fishing grounds they could easily lie hove to—that is, with their sails shortened and trimmed and their helm made fast so that they could remain fairly stationary on the same tack. Normally this technique was resorted to in bad weather, when normal sailing was impossible, but fishermen in past times made use of it so that they could tend their lines under circumstances where anchoring was inconvenient or impossible. Since heaving to was a balancing act that depended on wind strength and sea conditions, it was best suited to vessels with more numerous and smaller sails. For merchant purposes, however, ketches carried too little canvas to make good time, and by the early eighteenth century, they had largely been replaced by sloops and brigantines. Neither of these latter vessel types, however, was popular with fishermen. Brigantines were generally too large, and sloops, with their single, large mainsail, were unwieldy when hove to. Both were suited for trade and fast enough to perform well when pursued by privateers; so as long as the wars between 1689 and 1713 prevented the fisheries from staging a serious recovery, they seem to have been the dominant rigs. In the long run, however, to the degree that cod continued to dominate the economy of the North Shore, only a true, dual-purpose vessel— handy enough for fishing yet fast enough for trade—would answer the region's needs.

Massachusetts shipbuilders solved this problem effectively after peace returned in 1713 with their development of the two-masted schooner (Figure 3.2). With a fore-and-aft rig and a seaworthy hull, the schooner was well adapted to the changeable winds and bad weather with which sailors who fished and freighted on the North Atlantic were familiar. Having a mainsail of moderate size, these vessels could conveniently heave to while fishing; yet their two masts could carry a large enough spread of canvas to drive them along effectively in the trading lanes as well. More maneuverable than brigs or snows that depended heavily on square sails, they could better negotiate small harbors and keep a safe distance off dangerous shores while fishing. Spreading more canvas over more separate sails than

FIGURE 3.2 Schooner *Baltick*, 1765. This 70-ton Salem vessel was larger than most and carried a peculiar rig; it was essentially a topsail schooner with a briglike course (lower square sail) on its foremast. Notice that four of the six men are standing on the quarterdeck—obviously no officer's preserve. (Courtesy of the Peabody-Essex Museum)

a sloop, they combined power and flexibility in a way that allowed them to function simultaneously as small-scale bulk carriers and large-scale fishermen. Most schooners of the day ranged in size from 30 to 70 tons (on average about half-again the size of a ketch), and after 1715 they rapidly became the vessels of choice along the whole of Massachusetts's North Shore. By 1765 schooners accounted for almost 60 percent of all vessels clearing Salem's customshouse, and to the end of the colonial period they always accounted for most of the movement in and out of the harbor.[21]

Combining every element of Salem's shipping industry, the last hundred years of the colonial period constituted a period of undeniable growth. All told, between the 1680s and the 1770s, Salem's merchant fleet more than doubled in number of vessels—from 50 to 110—and multiplied fourfold in carrying capacity—from 1,500 to 6,000 tons. At the end of the colonial period, the business of manning and provisioning its shipping fleets continued to occupy the vast majority of the town's households; indeed, no visitor to colonial Salem ever recorded any other form of productive labor. Had all the vessels belonging to the town in 1771 been at sea simultaneously, they would have employed roughly nine hundred men —more than three-quarters of the males aged fifteen to forty-five living in town at the time. Never, of course, was the whole fleet abroad at once, nor were all the men who sailed them of local origin. Yet seafaring activity dominated local life in Salem every bit as thoroughly as these figures imply, and it was in this sense that a future president, John Adams, could in 1766 call Salem a "maritime Town."[22]

When Salem mariners of the eighteenth century first clambered on board ship, hauled their sea chests over the rail, gazed about the deck, and took stock of their situation, the great majority would already enjoy a fair idea of what to expect in the months ahead. The vessel they had spotted frequently at anchor in the harbor, the route they had probably sailed in the past, and the weather, if fickle, was at least a known commodity. What sailors shipping out of Salem knew best, however, was simply one another. Out of 617 mariners whose voyages on locally owned vessels were recorded in portledge bills or account books between 1690 and 1775, 80 percent lived in Salem or Beverly at the time, and 66 percent had been born there. In a community that numbered no more than a few thousand people, where life unfolded in a context of ceaseless interaction with one's neighbors over years and years, these eighteenth-century town dwellers had a sense of who was who that would stagger us today. That mariners in colonial Salem went to sea in familiar company was a central defining feature of their working lives.[23]

Occasionally crew members knew one another as family. When the sloop *Andrago* sailed to Bermuda in 1759, for instance, Capt. John Lovitt selected his mate and the rest of the crew from among his three sons, Thomas, John, Jr., and Peter. More important to recruitment, however, although difficult and enormously time consuming to measure quantitatively, were extended family connections. Thus Thomas Morong chose George Ashby, his brother-in-law, to be his mate on the *Hampton* in 1749. On board the *Rebecca*, which sailed to North Carolina in 1750, Benjamin Ellinwood was married to the sister of his crewmate Eben Corning, who in turn was married to the sister of another crewmate, Zachariah Batchelder. In the fall of 1759 Richard Derby employed his son, Richard,

Jr., to command a voyage to the Mediterranean in the brig *Neptune,* crewed by a mate, a cooper, eight seamen, and a "green hand." The mate was Richard's cousin, Henry Elkins, who had lived under the Derby roof with his mother since his own father's death several years before. One of the crew members, George Mugford, was another Derby cousin; the green hand, Samuel Sanders, was related to the Elkinses; and the remainder of the crew were residents of Salem, usually with family in town, although not closely linked to the Derbys. Nephews, cousins, and in-laws defined much of the pool from which sailors were recruited, and more distant family connections—though difficult to trace—probably drew in many more.[24]

It was not so much that owners and masters sought out their kin when trying to assemble crews; rather, the network of family relationships in and around Salem was so dense that they could scarcely avoid it. The ten individuals—owner, master, mate, and crew—concerned in the single voyage of the *Neptune* to Gibraltar were collectively related by blood or marriage, as immediate family, in-laws, cousins, uncles, or nephews, to at least 7.5 percent of the taxpaying population of the port. The seven men similarly connected to the voyage of the schooner *Beaver* to the Azores in 1753 could count more than 9.5 percent of the town's taxpayers among their near relatives. Whenever a cluster of local vessels weighed anchor for ports abroad, a large fraction of the town's inhabitants could have identified a close relative among the departing crews.[25]

Exactly how Salem shipowners sorted through this pool of neighbors and relations to choose masters for their vessels, and how masters did the same to select their hands, nobody ever described. One can only assume from the tangled integration of crew and town that the process must have been a domestic one, decided for the most part on street corners, across kitchen tables, and outside the meetinghouse door. In larger seaports, taverns and boardinghouses played an important role in facilitating the labor market, and shipping agents, popularly known as crimps, placed sailors with masters short of hands in return for a cut of their wages. In Salem, however, word of mouth probably sufficed, and masters chose their men on the basis of personal knowledge. The factors that weighed in these decisions are invisible today, but they must have included such issues as skill, strength, wit, and reliability, as well as family and neighborly obligation.[26]

The actual process of recruitment itself began a month or more before the vessel was due to leave, when the managing owner appointed a ship-master to oversee preparations for the voyage. Between merchant and master, there existed more often than not a close and long-standing relation-ship reflected clearly in the running accounts they kept with each other. Benjamin Bates, Jr., commanded a number of schooners owned by Richard Derby during the late 1750s and early 1760s, and on credit extended by Derby he purchased small amounts of salt meat, wine, flour, and cordwood for his household, as well as wholesale quantities of flour, rum, molasses, and fish that he plainly intended to trade on his own account while in the merchant's employ. Most important of all, Derby furnished him with suffi-cient cash before every voyage to advance a month's wages to every member of his crew and several times this sum when the vessel returned to pay the balance of what they had earned. Bates's account with Derby was ex-tremely active; the value of goods and sums of cash that changed hands between them every year often amounted to £100 or more, and dealings on this scale between shipowners and masters were entirely normal on Salem's waterfront. They were the financial expression of the tight per-sonal relationships that bound the two of them together, often for a sig-nificant portion of their lives.[27]

Over several weeks or even a couple of months, the shipowner and master, together with a succession of waterfront artisans and the gathering crew, readied the vessel for its voyage. Some of this work merely completed projects that had been ongoing for weeks or even months. Shipowners' accounts recorded steady purchases of boards, nails, pitch, tar, sailcloth, and oakum, together with the sums paid for labor performed by ship-wrights, sailmakers, riggers, carters, and blacksmiths, as well as regular treats of "rum & sugar" to keep the workmen on task as they repaired the damage from the last voyage and readied the vessel for the next. As the date of departure approached, however, the pace of work quickened. Crafts-men carried new sails, rigging, anchor stocks, and other equipment down to the shoreline to be freighted out to the waiting vessel; the owner delivered boatloads of beef, pork, bread, candles, rice, potatoes, beans, and other stores on board; and the shipmaster and his crew took responsibility for stowing the cargo both on deck and below. The preparations for every voy-age were expensive and involved dozens of skilled laborers drawn from across the town.[28]

Riggers, sailmakers, shipwrights, and coopers were as much a part of Salem's maritime community as were the mariners—indeed, many of them had spent time at sea as younger men themselves. The family connections among all these individuals, mariners and craftsmen together, was remarkably dense. Edmund Henfield, Timothy Orne's principal cooper, was the uncle of Gideon Henfield, who sailed twice to the Chesapeake in one of this merchant's vessels in 1771. Jonathan Neale, who carted ballast for Orne in the early 1760s, was father, brother, and uncle to three mariners who sailed for his employer during this period. Ebenezer Peele, a ship's carpenter who made masts for Orne, could count one shipwright and one coaster among his brothers, a shipmaster for a nephew, and two sailor sons of his own—all of whom worked for this same merchant during the 1750s and 1760s. Ebenezer's in-law, Robert Peele, was a tailor and, one would imagine, as shore-bound as any, but even he (or possibly his wife) contributed to these shipping ventures by fashioning ensigns for Orne's vessels. The crowd of men who swarmed over every schooner in the weeks and days leading down to its departure knew one another as neighbors and relations in a rooted and deeply integrated and maritime community.[29]

The core element in the income of all mariners was the wage, and the central characteristic of the mariner's wage—distinguishing it from most other remuneration in Salem—was the fact that it was paid almost entirely in cash. Most local people—indeed, most New Englanders generally—took a combination of goods, services, and notes of hand, as well as hard currency in payment for work they performed for others. To keep track of their obligations they maintained accounts of more or less formality that might be settled in a few months or stretch on for many years.[30] Mariners might open accounts with merchants and tradespeople around town, too, but not in order that they be paid for their work at sea. For that they received cash, advanced from the managing owner of the vessel to the shipmaster, who in turn paid them their wages for the voyage. For the investors who financed the voyage, this was an unwelcome expense, for they preferred to employ whatever specie they accumulated to settle debts in England. Thus cash was scarce in Salem, and undoubtedly these ship-owning merchants would have preferred that mariners took their pay— as craftsmen, farmers, and fishermen did—in shop goods, which they had in stock and on which they could turn a second profit. For a number of reasons, however, this would have proved unduly cumbersome. So many vessels were jointly owned by several merchants that resolving where the mariner would be expected to spend what portion of his income would have been complicated. Furthermore, although the great majority of sailors that shipped out of Salem may have been locally based and willing to receive part of their wages in goods and services, a measurable minority were not and needed their income in a portable form. This was even truer of larger ports, where a great many more hands were migrants, and over the centuries the cash wage had become a point of international maritime custom. Shipowners who gained the reputation of insisting on truck would have had to rely on local men alone to man their vessels, and while this strategy might work occasionally, it would in the long run have produced nothing but chronic shorthandedness.[31]

The wages that sailors were able to negotiate depended on many factors that we can only guess at today. Skill and experience must obviously have mattered; so did physical strength; and so, too, did the combination of personal characteristics—pliability, honesty, and responsibility—that made one a dependable hand. Most of these qualities were a function of age, and the wages that seamen commanded tended to rise rapidly through their youth to a peak reached generally in their late twenties and early thirties (see Graph 2, Appendix B)—much like professional athletes today. Beyond thirty-five, sailors might have a wealth of experience to offer any shipmaster trying to round out his crew, but in men who had spent fifteen or more years before the mast, the effects of age were beginning to tell, and the wages they commanded began to fall. So strenuous was the seafaring life that even the first hints of physical deterioration would lower one's competitiveness in the labor market.[32]

Another set of factors that bore on the wages that seamen could negotiate stemmed from the state of the maritime labor market in general. Help was scarce on the Salem waterfront—at least by comparison to the situation in London or Liverpool—and in peacetime, the wages an experienced, able-bodied seaman might expect were somewhat higher than could be obtained in England. Between 1750 and 1756, the standard seaman's wage in Salem was about 29s. per month; between 1764 and 1775, the wages were more variable but mainly a little higher, usually ranging between 30 and 40s. In England, by comparison, peacetime wages through the same period stayed remarkably stable at around 25s. per month. In wartime, however, the scene was dramatically reversed. During King George's War (1744–1748) seamen's wages negotiated in British ports ranged around 50–55s. monthly, and while the Seven Years' War raged they climbed to 60–65s. Plainly, the mobilization of the navy and the process of impressment strained to the limit the supply of labor in the mother country. In Salem, by contrast, the highest wage a seaman ever earned during this period was the 46s. 8d. per month paid to George Ashby on a voyage to the Leeward Islands in 1746, and the mean wartime rate was just over 31s. Since New England mariners worked in coastwise trades in which British vessels manned by British sailors seldom competed, the shortage of mariners in England would have had little impact on a market where British sailors rarely worked anyway. The full force of naval impressment, moreover, did not fall on the colonies as it did on the mother country and never drained seamen from Massachusetts seaports to the same degree that it did in Great Britain. Whether mariners were better paid in Salem than in London depended mainly on whether the North Atlantic was embroiled in war, which between 1689 and 1775 was true about 40 percent of the time.[33]

The wage scale on board Salem vessels was remarkably flat. On eighteenth-century English vessels engaged in foreign trade, masters normally earned about 120s. per month—a third again to twice the 60–90s. received by their mates, and anywhere from double to five times the 25–65s. paid to their able-bodied men. In Salem, by contrast, masters made no more on average than 38s., only 10–15 percent more than the mean of 34s. allowed to mates and only 25 percent more than the 30s. paid their men. Even on transatlantic voyages in large vessels, the pay differential was decidedly lower than that which prevailed in the English merchant service. In 1757 Richard Derby, Jr., took command of the *Neptune,* a 100-ton brigantine on a voyage to Gibraltar and the Mediterranean. Derby was as privileged a young man as could be found anywhere in Salem. His father, Richard, Sr., owned the *Neptune* outright in addition to all or part of eleven other vessels and was consistently rated among the richest men in town. Richard, Jr., would soon become a merchant himself, with several vessels of his own and attended in his elegant mansion house by a couple of black servants. Yet on this voyage, although Derby was paid 45s. per month, one of the highest wages ever earned by a Salem shipmaster during the eighteenth century, his mate Henry Elkins trailed him by only a shade at 42s., and all of the sailors save one made 37s. To the degree that wages mirror status, therefore, one can only conclude that the social distance separating even the privileged Derby from his men was not very great.[34]

Beyond the wage, however, Salem mariners also relied upon "portage," or what they earned by their own petty trading conducted in the course of the voyage. This reflected the general understanding, common to seafaring around the North Atlantic since the Middle Ages, that mariners were both servants and co-adventurers in the voyages they undertook. The precise balance between these two roles varied from country to country, industry to industry, and century to century. Fishermen and whalemen were usually co-adventurers recompensed in shares of the fish and oil they landed, whereas merchant seafarers were primarily wage earners paid sometimes by the voyage but mainly by the month. Wherever maritime labor was conducted on a small scale, as in lighterage, coasting, and the inshore fisheries, the laborers themselves frequently assumed the risks; in larger transatlantic ventures, however, the wage system usually prevailed. During the fifteenth and sixteenth centuries, portage and co-adventuring had been relatively more important, yet by the middle of the nineteenth century, wage systems had come to predominate. The merchant shipping industry of colonial Massachusetts stood close to the midpoint on most of these scores; hence portage still mattered to Salem mariners of the day.[35]

The practice was sometimes formally spelled out. A number of portledge bills allowed all hands the "privilege" of carrying so many bushels of wheat, quintals of fish, or barrels of rice freight-free in the hold. Mariners could either exercise their right, purchase the commodity as an adventure, and hawk it on their own when they reached their destination; or they could sell the right back to the owner of the vessel (or anyone else) and be credited for its value in currency. These rights were assigned to individuals by rank, with masters obtaining proportionately more than their mates, who in turn did better than the ordinary hands. Thus in 1757 David Felt, master of schooner Molly, negotiated a privilege of one hundred bushels of wheat on a Maryland voyage; his mate, John Flint, received one of fifty-five bushels; and the rest of the crew got forty-five bushels apiece. Captain Tobias Davis, Jr., of the schooner Esther, on a journey from South Carolina in the winter of 1759–1760, bargained for a privilege of six barrels of rice; his mate, Benjamin Henderson, obtained four; and the other members of the crew received two each. Plainly masters were favored here, though seldom did a master receive a privilege more than two or three times that of the rest of the crew.[36]

Most of the voyages in which privileges were extended to the crew as part of their shipping articles involved fishermen traveling south in the winter to employ themselves in the off-season. In November 1754 John Cloutman, with his crew, agreed to take the schooner *Fisher* south to Maryland on monthly wages with privilege attached and then "to go upon a Fishing Voyage . . . the next season upon common share." The wages they received were lower than those that prevailed in shipping agreements without privileges: Cloutman earned about three-quarters of the standard master's wage, and his sailors received two-thirds of what regular merchant seamen could expect to earn. We can only assume that the difference reflected the value of portage in the eyes of mariners and their employers —about one-third to one-half of their wage income. Fishermen were agreeable to these terms when sailing abroad as mariners because co-adventuring was part of fishing culture, where the men owned the fish until it was landed and sold and thus bore the risk of every voyage they undertook. Portage just extended this logic into their merchant shipping lives. Furthermore, because fishermen had to keep accounts with local merchant outfitters simply to obtain the gear and provisions necessary to their trade, their credit was established; although rarely wealthy, they could finance the purchase of trade goods with which to exploit their privilege.[37]

Even without a formally recognized privilege, most Salem mariners could, if they had the inclination and the means, purchase rolls of tobacco, boxes of raisins, bolts of cloth, or casks of wine and attempt to sell them abroad. If the item was bulky enough, the owners might insist on freight charges; but generally sailors simply slipped their investments into the hold or tucked them into their sea chests. The journals of early modern seafarers mention dozens of such adventures—some of them "in Small barralls of Tenn gallon Size, made to Stow between Small breakages in the hold," others simply carried in something as small as a pillowcase. That Salem mariners engaged in portage, beyond their formally contracted privileges, is known from the records of the shipowners for whom they worked. In one case, they formed part of the general accounting that occurred at the voyage's end. In the summer of 1772, when the Cabot family's schooner *Premium* picked up a cargo of flour in Philadelphia to carry to Bilbao, Captain Bartholomew Putnam purchased forty-six barrels of flour, which he stowed mainly "in the cabin" but also "between decks"; his mate, Andrew Gage, bought another six barrels; and the four "people" took seven between them. More generally, however, the practice of portage can be inferred from the acquisition of commodities in wholesale lots by mariners in between voyages. The accounts of mariners over the age of twenty-five are peppered with wholesale purchases—a quintal or two of cod, a few barrels of mackerel, or a hundred gallons of rum—that were too great for home consumption and can only have been intended to sell abroad.[38]

Exactly how widespread portage was in eighteenth-century Salem is hard to tell. Too much of this practice was carried on quietly in small amounts to have made much of a dent on the record-keeping process. The accounts of middle-aged mariners with local merchants contain many more adventures than those of their younger crewmates, but that may simply be so because the latter made these purchases on their fathers' tabs. The accounts of fishermen-sailors contain measurably more purchases than those of specialist mariners, but that may simply be a consequence of the fact that fishermen bought everything on credit, which was recorded in merchant ledgers, whereas specialist mariners more commonly made cash purchases, which were not. Christopher Prince of Kingston, Massachusetts, spoke of seaman's wages in Boston in 1766 as being "five dollars, and three barrels privilege," though he also noted that many seamen "were not able to put in one barrel" because they could not afford it. Prince was only fifteen, and as his father had not advanced him a single shilling, he assumed this would be his lot as well, until his merchant uncle stepped in, declaring, "You shall not go without an adventure," and advanced him enough money to purchase one to carry. Prince sailed to the West Indies, where he sold his adventure "at a great profit," and henceforth he purchased one on credit from his uncle on every voyage, apparently sending his wages home to his father but saving his trading profits "as my own property." In the British packet service of the 1780s, according to Samuel Kelly, adventures were mainly the business of "the officers, and those seamen that were married," and the same may have held true in Salem. There on the waterfront, as everywhere in New England, marriage signaled the beginning of an economic partnership, and a prudent wife who was able to manage affairs on her own could take upon herself the business of processing and marketing the goods that her seafaring husband brought home. Yet a mother could have done this as well; and if she were widowed, it might be her only means of support. In general, although access to a privilege seems to have been common in colonial Salem, the ability of a sailor to make use of it depended on the resources he had at his disposal.[39]

The one group of mariners who almost all engaged in portage on a large scale were shipmasters, who gained the most from this practice, mainly because of their access to credit. Almost all of them had long-standing relationships with at least one merchant in town, and alongside the cash advances they procured to pay their men, these masters also made regular purchases of commodities in wholesale amounts, chalked up to their tabs. Hogsheads of rum, fish, or molasses—the standard commodities of the trade—became the private adventures of shipmasters in this way. A few sea captains were almost merchants themselves. About one-third of the locally resident masters who cleared Salem harbor in 1761 owned trading stock, vessel tonnage, or money at interest sufficient to catch the town assessor's eye, and a couple of them ranked among the wealthiest men in town. By the same token, however, two-thirds of these masters did not possess any of these investments, and the majority were men of moderate estate, clustering in the middling deciles of Salem's taxpaying population. For them, the profits of portage were simply the means of maintaining a modestly furnished house in town, providing one's wife with the dry goods necessary to operate her domestic economy, and launching one's children into life—a vehicle to achieve and preserve what New Englanders termed a competency.[40]

To compare the incomes of officers and seamen in eighteenth-century Salem is no simple matter. Clearly the former lived better than the latter, and certainly shipmasters enjoyed opportunities for advancement into the merchant world that were only pipe dreams for most of their men. And yet the gap between the two—both in monthly earnings and in the prospects for commercial profit—was not nearly as wide in Salem as it seems to have been in the greater seaports that were home to larger vessels, richer cargoes, and grander speculation. If social distinctions that wages and portage reflected were real enough, they were a matter of degree, and they did not in this particular colonial seaport divide a class of managerial officers from one of laboring men.[41]

There have been almost as many characterizations of the sailor's life at sea as there have been authors who have attempted to describe it. Maritime historians cannot remember the age of sail personally, so they depend in the main on ship's journals, personal memoirs, private letters, and court records. Before the nineteenth century, however, sailors wrote very few letters (few that have survived, anyway), and ship's journals, though common enough, tend to be sparing in detail. Court records and personal memoirs survive in considerable number, provide buckets of the striking evidence a good tale requires, and plainly have a story to tell. It is a story of a particular type, however—one that emphasizes drama, danger, and difficulty. Court records deal disproportionately with problems that could not be solved informally by the parties at odds. They may reveal the character of conflicts on board ship, but they say little about the frequency with which such events happened. Memoirs cover a wider range of evidence—bad times and good—but they are just as selective in their own way. Mariners composed them relatively late in life as a summation of their experiences, and the events they recalled were generally those that dwelled on in their memories because they seemed to contribute in some distinctive way toward the story they were trying to tell. They tended to revolve around turning points and telling examples, and they usually passed over the humdrum events of each passing day, since most of these, at least in their specificity, had receded from the mind. Memoirs and court records both favor the extraordinary over the ordinary, and for that reason neither can be allowed to represent uncritically the seafaring experience as a whole. Rich as they are, they need to be complemented by an attention to what they do not say as well as to what one can reasonably infer from other more opaque source materials such as portledge bills, customshouse records, notarial records, ship's logs, and account books. It was the ordinary and expected, as much as the extraordinary and feared, that local mariners encountered when they shipped themselves on voyages overseas.

As adventures, most of the voyages out of Salem harbor during the eighteenth century were modest affairs that resembled the experience of the *General Wolfe* recounted earlier in this chapter. On vessels that were generally 80 tons or less in burden, accompanied by rarely more than a half-dozen familiar crewmates, and bound on itineraries that seldom lasted more than five or six months, most of these early American mariners would have found the experience of Captain Hodges and his men to lie well within the range of the expected. Life at sea involved an irregular sequence of steady sailing and shipboard maintenance, as well as sleep and recreation, all of which were punctuated by occasional emergencies and the consequent efforts to repair damages. This work environment, though administered through a structure of authority governed in the last analysis by a captain who was master of his trade, operated on a daily basis through a customary understanding of what had to be done.

Sailing itself involved a huge range of tasks adjusting the eighteenth century's most complex machine to the changing circumstances of wind and waves. Moderate breezes, light airs, calms, and squalls succeeded one another from different points of the compass, in fair or rainy weather, over long swells or choppy seas in an endless series of permutations—all of which demanded fine adjustment, a sense of which most seafarers acquired only over years of work. For the greatest portion of the time on any voyage, the main business of the crew was to set sails and shorten them, to trim them as the wind shifted, and to man the helm, all of which was generally accomplished in two groups or watches, one directed by the master and the other by the mate. Intermingled with the handling of the vessel, day in and day out, were the ordinary tasks of routine maintenance: scraping the decks, repairing the rigging, mending the sails, spinning and knotting yarn, fixing blocks, and putting on chafing gear. Yet much of this was complicated work. After two years of fishing on the banks, New Englander Christopher Prince felt that he had learned to "hand, reef, knot, splice, and steer," but not sufficiently that he could really claim to be able to "do my duty as a seaman"; two more years in the Caribbean trade were necessary to make him a "complete seaman . . . qualified to go . . . to any part of the world." In the nineteenth century seaman William McNally agreed that "a boy on board of a vessel for the first two years, would only earn his victuals and clothing; the third year he would earn wages; and the fourth year, be as good on most occasions as an able seaman." In the judgment of both mariners, therefore, four years' training constituted a practical apprenticeship for an able-bodied foremast hand.[42]

What Prince condensed into five words—hand, reef, knot, splice, and steer—amounted in reality to scores of different procedures, each of which required a distinct sequence of separate steps, defined in a vernacular language that every novice sailor had to learn. Listen to Richard Henry Dana, Jr., describe what would have been a common task on any sloop or schooner of the eighteenth century—the furling of a jib:

Go out upon the weather side of the boom. See your gasket clear for passing. The handiest way usually is, to make it up on its end, take a hitch over the whole with the standing part, and let it hang. Haul the sail well upon the boom, getting the clew, and having the sheet pennant hauled amidships. Cast the hitch off the gasket, take it in your hand, and pass two or three turns, beginning at the head; haul them taut; and so on to the clew. Pass the turns over and to windward. This will help bring the sail upon the boom and to windward. Make the end fast to the stay, to the withe, or the boom inside the cap, in any way that shall keep it from slipping back, which it might do if it were made fast to its own part around the boom. If there is but one hand on the boom, the first turns may be hauled taut enough to keep the sail up for the time; then, after the gasket is fast, go out to the head and haul each turn well taut, beating the sail down with the hand. Be careful to confine the clew well.

Multiply this set of instructions by many score, remembering that each might be undertaken in coordination with several other men under a wide variety of sailing conditions, and one can get a sense of what a seaman had to take in merely to do his job. There can be little doubt that sailing was skilled work.[43]

Some of the most sophisticated tasks, and those that set an able seaman apart from his less talented crewmates, involved maintaining and repairing the vessel. As Dana put it in 1840, an able seaman had to be "a good workman upon rigging," and there was nothing about the seafaring practices of earlier centuries that would have gainsaid this. Wherever yards or ropes wore, they had to be protected by "chafing gear." This could take several forms, called worming, parceling, serving, and so forth—each a different type of thread, yarn, and cord, manufactured on board from condemned sails and old junk and attached to the yard or rope in need of protection. Sometimes the rigging itself had to be replaced, and this required a host of different knots, splices, seizings, and coverings that might take years to commit properly to memory. Sails took a constant beating, and from time to time they needed patching as well. "A man's skill in this work," wrote Dana, "is the chief test of his seamanship."[44]

On larger vessels within the merchant and naval service, this work was delegated through a hierarchy of command that was by early modern standards both elaborate and formal. Masters handed down orders from the quarterdeck to their first mates, normally stationed forward, whose job it was to ensure that the tasks were promptly apportioned out to coopers, stewards, cooks, gunners, and the various grades of seamen. The complexity of three-masted ships required a level of coordination that could not emerge spontaneously from the crew, especially when they were new to the ship, to the voyage, and above all to one another. On the schooners, sloops, and smaller brigantines of New England, however, mariners plied well-known trade lanes in familiar company, and with smaller crews, the division of labor had to be more flexible. On either watch there might be only four, three, or even two men on duty, and this would require masters and mates to turn their hands to almost any task—even going aloft when the need arose. On ships manned by a dozen or more men both master and mate were generally spared from manual labor, but on schooners carrying crews of six or seven the officers worked alongside their men.

Even the most detailed mariner's diaries and memoirs from the seventeenth and eighteenth centuries, English or American, hardly ever describe the way in which routine work was performed at sea, and ship's journals are similarly mute on this matter. The purpose of the latter was to monitor and record the progress of the ship and its business, not to record who exactly performed which task. On occasion, however, they do hint at how certain elements of the work were divided. The most menial tasks, for instance, masters often described as explicitly seamen's work. "Sallors Employ'd in knotting yarns & Sondrey odd Small jobs," reported Capt. Francis Boardman on his trip to the West Indies in the spring of 1774. Certain specialized carpentry chores—trimming a tierce, hooping hogsheads, or carving bungs—journals plainly describe as the cooper's responsibility. Yet the regular work of shiphandling—setting, reefing, trimming and taking in sails, steering the vessel, as well as repairing rigging and canvas— masters almost always noted down in collective terms: "Rove New main Jib Sheets," "mended Several Rips in Sqr Sail & M.Sail," "unbent our Cables," and the like. Now it is possible that ship's officers preferred to stand aloof from this work, but it is difficult to imagine how they could have done so much of the time on vessels of this size. For the most part, masters and mates must have pitched in more or less constantly. Certainly those who were also skippers on fishing voyages were accustomed to taking part in every chore that fishing involved; such was the custom out on the banks. That a rigid hierarchy would have crept onto the same-sized vessels in their voyages to the Carolinas or the Caribbean and allowed officers to stand apart from physical work and transform themselves into pure commanders and managers stretches the imagination.[45]

When off duty, officers and crew alike were able to wash, mend clothing, swap stories, gamble, drink, sleep, and eat, and much of this recreational activity took place in the same physical space and informal spirit as regular work. On schooners and sloops, as on most other oceangoing vessels, the crew slept forward while the officers berthed in separate cabins aft, but the distinction between the two quarters was not the gulf one might imagine. The mate, after all, was allowed little more than room for a bunk, and even the captain's cabin, measuring on these vessels perhaps eight feet square, was relatively cramped, especially when stowed with the master's own portage. Both enjoyed a modicum of privacy, which the ordinary hands did not, but since each of them had to stand watch, the aftercabins were not the refuge they would have been on larger vessels. Indeed, it is only in that context of sleep and journal writing that masters ever made reference to them.[46]

Significantly, officers and men ate the same fare. Meals were plain, combining in a limited number of variations: beef, pork, lamb, and chicken, mixed with hard bread, beans, potatoes, or johnnycake and washed down with cider, beer, or rum. On short voyages, provisions did not deteriorate much, and colonial mariners were spared the worst sort of tainted meat, wormy biscuit, and stinking water that sailors in the long-distance trades had to stomach. Many Salem vessels carried livestock—chickens, pigs, and sheep—penned up on deck to be slaughtered and eaten fresh as the voyage progressed. The crew of the sloop *Adventure* on their way to the West Indies celebrated Election Day in 1774, for example, with "a large turkey for Dinner." Fishing added mackerel, cod, salmon, shark, barracuda, and dolphin to the menu. Dolphin was a special favorite—for its size and the ease with which it could be caught more than for its flavor: Ebeneezer Bowditch, Jr., recorded striking one four feet, two inches long on a voyage to Madeira in 1753, and Francis Boardman counted "16 Caught this passage" to the Caribbean in 1774. The pleasures of eating this fare and probably the work of preparing it were likely both shared informally among the crew as a whole. There is little explicit evidence about the social division of consumption on board these vessels, but without cooks or stewards or anything in the way of delicacies listed among the ship's provisions, we can only assume that officers and men ate together.[47]

Eating was the most commonly recorded form of shipboard recreation, but sailors relaxed in other ways as well. Cotton Mather of Boston had heard reports of how spare time was passed among the "Sea-faring tribe," and he was pretty certain that "Serious Piety" was not high on the list. Instead, he complained, sailors were much more interested in drinking, "Wicked Speeches," "Filthy Songs," gaming, superstition, sodomy, and masturbation. Drinking was indeed common. All vessels carried a modest communal supply of cider, rum, or sometimes beer, and a good portion of the mariners who shopped for their provisions at stores in port purchased enough rum to slip into their sea chest for forthcoming voyages. Only once, however, did any shipmaster-journalist from colonial Salem mention drunkenness in his journal. Returning from the West Indies in 1774, Francis Boardman of the *Adventure* complained: "I am much out in my Racking by a bad halm being kept and an log by a bad mat allious Drunk." His name was William Robinson, and according to Boardman, he had been "Drunk most of the Voige," though never incapacitated enough to merit any discipline, at least none that this shipmaster ever mentioned.[48] When the wind failed, some of the crew might take up fishing, and on one occasion, the captain reported "All hands over Board aswiming." Crossing the Tropic of Cancer always prompted a break from the regular routine as all green hands were "sworn in." By tradition, each one of these young men was required to pay a fine or be ducked into the ocean. Sometimes, the master seems to have taken charge here, though mostly the events were described as a collective rite involving the entire crew. In the course of one such affair, again on board the *Adventure,* a young man named John Lang fell overboard while fooling about on the deck stacked with timber and was in the water for an hour and a half before the crew could fetch him out again. Wrote Boardman: "I thout Saveril times never to have got him again Nobody Noes wat I felt for him."[49]

During emergencies, the chain of command certainly grew more taut. The normal, more casual routines of seafaring life could cease in an instant if an enemy vessel hove into sight or the weather took a turn for the worse. Then it was all hands on deck to deal with the predicament under the master's orders. In the case of pirates, privateers, or enemy frigates, the first object was to put on all sail possible and flee. New England trading vessels were not built for speed, and it took the combined seamanship of everyone on board—sometimes for several days at a time—to escape. On June 28, 1760, the sloop *Adventure*, laden with a cargo of fish and timber, was approaching the Leeward Islands from the north when it came upon three French privateers—two sloops and a schooner—which immediately gave chase. By late afternoon, "finding They came up very fast," the master, John Hathorne, ordered his men to loose the bundles of lumber stowed on deck and heave them overboard. This seemed to work, for "then We sayled as fast as either of them," and in the gathering twilight two of the privateers gave up the chase and disappeared. After dark the wind suddenly died, becalming the *Adventure* to the advantage of the remaining privateer sloop, which was able to put out its oars and row on through the night. Within a few hours, the privateers had caught up with Hathorne and his men, boarded the *Adventure*, and captured it. Episodes such as this were not uncommon during the colonial period—after all, between 1689 and 1763, the English were at war with the Spanish and/or the French almost half the time—and one can be certain that in every such emergency the skill of the master and the speed with which the crew could efficiently follow orders determined who escaped and who did not.[50]

The most dire and common emergencies, however, were the natural ones that were functions of the weather. Although tempests as serious as the one through which John Hodges and the *General Wolfe* passed were not common, most voyages had to confront at some time or another moderate gales, sudden squalls, thunderstorms, thick weather, and ugly seas— all of which demanded close cooperation, constant attention to duty, and a sharp ear for the master's commands. High seas and heavy winds could also damage the vessel itself, placing the crew under additional pressure and straining relationships with the officers. Few of the voyages that Francis Boardman commanded during the 1770s reached port without a few accidents of this kind. Different storms, for instance, carried away "the main after Shroud," "the Strap of the Sterboard Lift Block," "the paril Rop of the Top Sailyard," "thae Clue of the Main Sail," and so forth—all of which had to be dealt with in the short run and then later repaired. Heavy seas sometimes opened seams in the planking, forcing the crew to start pumping against the stream of water pouring into the bilge. Seldom was it possible to stop these leaks before the vessel made port, and so springing one added enormously to the burden of work over the remainder of the voyage, the general level of anxiety over the seaworthiness of the craft and the safety of the crew, and the tension among its members.[51]

The fact remains, however, that although almost every young sailor from Salem had been through scrapes such as these, most voyages out of this port unfolded at a more subdued tempo in an environment where for the greatest part of the time a customary understanding of work routine prevailed on board. True, shipmasters set the course and issued the commands that governed work on every watch, exercising general authority over their hands at sea in the same way as masters would over their men ashore. Yet they also shared in the physical labor they demanded of the crew, and most of the time that work, taxing as it may have been, would have amounted to what nearly all the sailors in this sloop and schooner fleet understood to be their duty.

Although no single vessel, voyage, trade, or port can stand for the social history of seafaring in its entirety throughout the eighteenth-century Atlantic, the journey of the *General Wolfe* and the story of the Salem fleet sat midway along a spectrum of experience in which the scale of operations was the most important variable. At one end lay the great seaports of Europe—London, Amsterdam, Seville, and a handful of others—where dwelled the wealthiest merchants, who dispatched the richest cargoes in great ships with large and heterogeneous crews on long voyages through distant waters to foreign parts. Such ventures were generally riskier, the tensions on board more severe, the discipline stricter, and the hierarchy of command more elaborate. At the other end sat a host of little outports —such as Lynn, Manchester, or Ipswich in Massachusetts—where commerce was conducted by mariners themselves, who freighted miscellaneous consignments in their own vessels for local people along familiar coasts with the help of a couple of neighbors at most. These operations ran few hazards and permitted a relatively cooperative work regime. By these measurements, Salem split the difference. On the one hand the town did possess an oceangoing fleet, owned by merchant shipowners and worked by wage-earning mariners, that transported major commodities over significant distances. On the other hand, it was home to a maritime community whose members sailed abroad on predictable routes in the company of people they knew under the command of masters who shared in the collectivity of work and leisure afloat. Across the range of maritime work experience within the North Atlantic, the seaport of Salem and the voyage of the *General Wolfe* both stood somewhere near the median.

More to the point, perhaps, Salem was the sort of town and the *General Wolfe* the type of vessel that most sailors encountered repeatedly throughout their careers. Even those who made their mark in the heroic episodes we love to recite—from dramatic naval battles to exotic long-distance trades —usually hailed originally from lesser ports and learned the ropes on smaller vessels. Likewise, mariners who labored most of their days in larger vessels out of greater seaports often returned to towns like Salem, where their families lived when it came time to wind down their careers and retire. Anglo-American seamen of the period were certainly men of the world, but that world must be defined to include not just its farther reaches but also those nearer and quieter waters where so much of their life was spent.

CHAPTER FOUR

The Eighteenth Century

SAILORS' CAREERS

THE ONLY COLONIAL AMERICAN sailor who left behind an account of his life in whole was Ashley Bowen, who grew up not in Salem but across the harbor in the "cragy and crasey" fishing port of Marblehead. Here was a different sort of town—tougher, less orderly, and more plainly stratified by wealth. The same travelers who complimented Salem on its "neat" and "pritty" appearance found in Marblehead only a "dirty, erregular, stincking place" with a few grand houses but many more cabins and crowded tenements jumbled in among the rocks.[1] Still, the two towns were less than half an hour apart by boat; they employed similar vessels in similar trades; and it is hard to believe that career patterns within the merchant seafaring population varied enormously from one community to the other. Ashley Bowen's life might have unfolded differently had he been born in Salem, but probably not by much, and since the course of this one mariner's career can be mapped—using diaries, memoirs, and ship's journals—with a remarkable degree of precision, his story furnishes a useful place to begin the analysis of seafaring careers in the region generally.[2]

The Bowen family hailed originally from Rehoboth in southern Massachusetts. About 1715 Ashley's father, Nathan Bowen, left there and moved to Boston, where as a young man in his late teens he seems to have obtained a position as a merchant's clerk. By 1719 he had married Sarah Ashley, a Boston girl with merchant connections, and the two of them settled in

Marblehead. Together they founded a large family—at least seven of whom grew to adulthood—and Bowen, who was a sharp man of affairs, supported them in growing style from his earnings as a trader, farmer, lawyer, notary public, teacher of navigation, and author of almanacs. By midcentury, at fifty years of age, he was a justice of the peace and gentleman farmer with two slaves, and he also possessed some mercantile interests on the side. On the eve of the Revolution—at the end of his public career—he was styled Esquire and stood comfortably within the affluent ranks of local society.[3]

Ashley Bowen, the youngest of Nathan's three sons, was born in 1728. Of his childhood we know nothing, for his autobiography begins only at the start of his seafaring career. In 1739, however, having just turned eleven, he made the acquaintance of some older youths from Salem and Marblehead who had come to learn navigation at the Bowen home. He was soon quite friendly with them, especially one Edmund Gale from Salem, and together they arranged for Ashley to join Gale and his father, master of the snow *Diligence,* as a ship's boy on a voyage that autumn to Spain. When the War of Jenkins's Ear broke out in October, Captain Gale chose to steer for North Carolina instead and took on a load of tar for Bristol. In England all of the crew was pressed—save Edmund and Ashley, who were probably too young. With new hands, however, the *Diligence* continued on to Swansea in Wales, where it obtained a lading of coal to carry back to Boston. Young Ashley arrived back in Marblehead in June 1740, six months past his twelfth birthday. At an age when most of his friends would have been punting around the harbor at home, he had gained a year of real seafaring experience.[4]

Two months after his return, the boy was turned on his ends when his mother, Sarah, died in childbirth. Nathan swiftly remarried—this time to a "fine rich widow" named Hannah Harris—and the new couple immediately decided that Ashley and his stepbrother, Nathaniel, "would lessen their family much if they were both bound out." Nathaniel was sent to live with a local house carpenter, and Ashley was bound out to Captain Peter Hall of Boston on a seven-year apprenticeship "at 13 years and three month old." To imply, as Ashley did, that the two parents wanted to rid themselves of their children may be a little unfair. Placing boys in other families to learn a trade was common strategy, and in Ashley's case the arrangement must have cost the elder Bowen a fair sum.[5]

For four years he sailed around the North Atlantic, from New England to the West Indies, to Britain, and into the Mediterranean, calling in at dozens of ports. The apprenticeship itself, however, turned into a disaster. Indeed, the chain of events that had begun with his mother's death he termed with some bitterness in later life "the greatest part of my ruining." Hall was not a kindly master, and Bowen's memories of these years were chiefly of the bullying, the beatings, and the string of petty injuries he endured at the captain's hand. On one occasion he was tied to the rail and stroked several dozen times for burning Hall's dinner and hiding away; on another he was whipped with the "cat" for dirtying his master's towel while scouring down the aftercabin. The pages of Bowen's memoir that cover his apprenticeship dwell chiefly on his shoddy treatment at the hands of this scoundrel.[6]

To compound his problems, Ashley learned next to nothing from Hall about navigation or anything else in the art of commanding a ship. In 1744 the captain quit the sea entirely to keep a store, with Ashley as shop assistant, at the British naval base in Minorca. The boy appealed to his father to terminate the apprenticeship, asked family friends to intercede for him, and even tried to join the navy—all to no avail. Then in 1745, just after Hall had resumed seafaring and their ship was lying to in the Dutch West Indian port of St. Eustatius, Ashley was taken sick and turned ashore. His master sailed away to St. Kitts to take on cargo, and in his absence Bowen saw an opportunity. With only his "duds" stuffed in a bag, he approached the commander of a Marblehead privateer moored in the road and persuaded his fellow townsman to take him on board. When the latter agreed they left that evening, passing Hall's ship in the moonlight, and in this way, after four years' harsh service, the young apprentice finally escaped.[7]

Leaving Hall in his wake, Bowen now embarked upon an eighteen-year career as a free mariner. It was a working life of extraordinary variety. In the merchant service, he visited most of the Caribbean Islands, every coastal town of consequence in North America, and many ports in England, Spain, and Portugal. Twice he interrupted his voyaging to work in other maritime industries—once fishing for cod off the south coast of Newfoundland and later hunting whales from the Outer Banks of North Carolina. In 1759 he enlisted as a midshipman in the British naval expedition on Quebec. That summer he spent on the St. Lawrence River, working (along with the future Pacific explorer James Cook) on H.M.S. *Pembroke*, assisting in the bombardment of the city and ferrying soldiers and arms around the siege. In a less heroic vein he spent many odd weeks throughout his career helping with the maintenance or construction of vessels or simply tending them in port. For Bowen, therefore, merchant seafaring was less a specialized trade than a single element within a broader pattern of maritime employment.[8]

Indeed, one of the persistent characteristics of his sailing career was the amount of time he spent on land. Most years, as Table 4.1 demonstrates, Bowen was based ashore in some port or other for five months or more. What he was doing there depended on circumstances. In St. Domingue he spent the spring of 1746 as a prisoner of war at Petit-Goâve, where he fell ill with smallpox and was "twice laid by as dead" before finally being exchanged. On another occasion he put ashore in Philadelphia for five months and worked first as an assistant in a rigging loft and then as a plasterer. In 1748 he interrupted his travels in Bristol to board with a Marblehead expatriate named James Perryman and study navigation. From 1753 to 1754, he dwelled in Greenwich, New Jersey, and worked as a boatman on the Delaware River. Finally, on several occasions, he "tarried" at home in Marblehead or Boston, probably unable to find any work at all. Bowen certainly considered himself a mariner; the sketches that illustrated his journal during these years were almost entirely miniature portraits of the vessels in which he sailed. But every one of these craft was pictured at anchor in some port or other, and rising prominently in the background was a profile of the waterfront. Keeping oneself fully employed in a business plagued by wars, storms, disease, and volatile markets was practically impossible, and Bowen as a sailor was as familiar with life in port as he was with work at sea. That he finished his sailing days with little property to his name may have resulted less from low wages or prodigality than from the general irregularity of maritime employment and the frequency with which the expenses of room and board ate up the pay he had earned afloat.[9]

Blessed with his father's money and connections, Ashley Bowen ought to have done well for himself. Plainly he intended to become a shipmaster, and his memoir is largely the history of that attempt. Yet the apprenticeship with Captain Hall failed so miserably that what should have been the first step on the path to promotion and the maritime equivalent of a competency actually lost him four precious years of training. By taking time out

Table 4.1

Ashley Bowen's Seafaring Career, 1749–1764

	JAN.	FEB.	MAR.	APR.	MAY	JUNE
1739	Marblehead					
1740	North Carolina to Great Britain to Boston					
1741	Marblehead & Boston				Boston to Philadelphia (return)	
1742	West Indies to Boston			Boston & Marblehead		
1743	Gibraltar		Gibraltar to Sardinia to Boston			
1744	Louisbourg to Gibraltar				Gibraltar	
1745	Port Mahon, Minorca					
1746	S.C. to W.I.	St. Domingue (in prison)			W.I. to Phila.	
1747	Marblehead to West Indies (return)					
1748	Gibraltar to Bristol			Bristol (learning navigation)		
1749	Charlestown			Marblehead to Barbados		
1750	Gloucester to Bilbao			Fishing Voyage from Bilbao		
1751	Boston to N.C.	North Carolina			North Carolina to London	

JULY	AUG.	SEPT.	OCT.	NOV.	DEC.
			Boston to North Carolina		
	Marblehead				
Boston to Gibraltar to West Indies					
Boston to Gibraltar		Gibraltar			
Boston			Boston to Philadelphia to Louisbourg		
Port Mahon, Minorca					
P.M. to W.I.	RUNS AWAY	West Indies to Philadelphia to Charleston, S.C.			
Philadelphia				Phila. to Mhd.	Mhd. to W.I.
	Marblehead		Boston to Bristol to Gibraltar		
Bristol to Boston		Charlestown			
& Louisbourg (return)				Gloucester to Bilbao	
to Newfoundland to Boston				Boston	
London				London to Jamaica	

(continued)

Table 4.1 (*continued*)

	JAN.	FEB.	MAR.	APR.	MAY	JUNE
1752	London to Jamaica & Philadelphia					
1753	Coasting between Rhode Island and North Carolina			Delaware River		
1754	Shore Whaling in North Carolina			Delaware River		
1755	Marblehead		Marblehead to Cádiz (return)			
1756	Marblehead			Salem to Lisbon (return)		
1757	West Indies			West Indies to Marblehead		
1758	Marblehead to West Indies (return)			Marblehead MARRIAGE		
1759	Marblehead					Naval
1760	Marblehead & Boston					
1761	Canada				To Mhd.	
1762	Marblehead					
1763	Marblehead				Coasting from Marblehead	
1764	Marblehead					

Note: Shaded areas represent periods when Bowen was based on shore. Philip C. F. Smith double-checked many of Bowen's dates.

JULY	AUG.	SEPT.	OCT.	NOV.	DEC.
Coasting between Rhode Island and North Carolina					
Coasting between Philadelphia and Rhode Island				Shore Whaling in North Carolina	
	Passenger to Marblehead			Marblehead	
Marblehead & Boston					
		Marblehead			Mhd. to W.I.
Marblehead					Mhd. to W.I.
Marblehead to Lisbon (return)				Mhd. to Maine	Mhd.
Expedition to Canada				Boston & Marblehead	
Boston to Canada					Canada
Marblehead					
Marblehead to Nova Scotia (return)					
Marblehead to West Indies		West Indies	West Indies to Marblehead		Mhd.
Marblehead					

Source: Philip Chadwick Foster Smith, ed., *The Journals of Ashley Bowen (1728–1813) of Marblehead*, 2 vols. (Colonial Society of Massachusetts, *Publications* [Boston, 1973]), 44:6–141.

from seafaring in 1748 to study navigation on his own account, he tried to remedy the situation, and he actually secured a berth as second mate on a voyage out of Bristol the following spring. This voyage, however, was canceled; and "all to leeward in my pl[ans]," he had to ship himself home to Boston once again as a foremast hand. "I had a promotion," he observed, "but short." Not until eighteen months later, at the age of twenty-two, did he finally get a post as second mate—on a snow, *Swift*, that crossed the Atlantic in the winter of 1750. Two years later he rose to first mate on a voyage to Louisbourg, and the year after that Thomas Mulford of New Jersey hired him as a "sailing master" to carry Mulford and his cargo on board the sloop *Susannah* to North Carolina. In his late twenties, therefore, Bowen could usually find employment as a mate or master on the smaller vessels that coasted the Atlantic shore between Rhode Island and the Delaware River, but the distinction of steady employment as a ship's officer on deep-sea voyages still escaped him.[10]

Approaching thirty, he now had cause to worry about whether he would ever rise to captain an oceangoing vessel. In the late summer of 1754, however, he heard of a vacancy for a mate in the employ of Robert Hooper, Jr., the wealthiest merchant in Marblehead. "I saw Mr. Hooper and offered my service . . . but the answer was 'I do not know you!' I said my name was A. Bowen. [He said] 'I know that, but as you have been master abroad I do not know your behavior.' I applied to Jerem[iah] Lee, and he gave me the same answer and said I must go a voyage before the mast before I should have any employ from here." Interestingly, Hooper's response spoke not to Bowen's class or family connections but to the fact that he lacked a local reputation. Bowen must have recognized this, for he took the advice and shipped himself out of Marblehead, first on a coasting voyage to Newbury that fall, and then across the Atlantic to Lisbon the following spring.[11]

Finally in 1757 he earned a berth as mate to Captain Philip Lewis on Hooper's schooner, *Swallow*, bound with a cargo of dried fish for the West Indies. It was on this voyage, at the age of twenty-nine, that an odd twist of fate finally provided him with his first chance at a real command. Ironically, the opportunity arose after he was captured again by a French privateer. Carried into Martinique, he managed to escape with Captain Lewis on board a schooner headed for St. Eustatius. There he met a merchant named James Freeman, who had just bought a sloop and intended to load it with a cargo of molasses for Marblehead. Freeman offered the command of the sloop, *Olive,* to Lewis, but the latter declined and recommended Bowen instead. Pleased with this turn of events, Bowen sailed around the island to collect a cargo, "got her full and down to Eustatius again, where I hoisted English colors and came home master." Unfortunately, the *Olive* was an "old bottom," and when it arrived home in Marblehead, the carpenters "opened her sides to shift her beams . . . [and] found every beam and knees rotten." It took Bowen five months to have the vessel repaired; then he sailed it back to St. Eustatius, "settled all my business with Mr. Freeman," and came home to Marblehead with his brother, Nathan. Twice more, in 1760 and 1762, he sailed as master, both times in command of small transport schooners carrying oxen, Indian corn, and other provisions to the British army at Quebec. But even this was little more than coasting. The plain truth of this mariner's career is that it never really took off, and on November 6, 1763, now married with a growing family in Marblehead, he went ashore for good to make his living in the rigging trade he had learned in Philadelphia fifteen years before.[12]

Although Ashley Bowen lived on for another half-century, he never went to sea again, save for a couple of short spells during the Revolutionary War, when the larder was bare and necessity forced him to take any work he could find.[13] We leave him here, however, in order to consider the typicality of his career afloat. Could the mariners of colonial Salem expect something of the same, or did other fates more commonly await them? At what age did these sailors first go to sea? How frequently were they promoted? How long did they continue voyaging, and why did they quit when they did? What sort of careers did they pursue after they retired from the deep? Above all, what sort of factors—class, geographic origins, merit, or the simple passage of years—governed sailors' fortunes most powerfully in this seaport town?[14]

When boys such as Ashley Bowen shipped themselves on board Salem vessels of the eighteenth century, they did so generally in the company of people they knew. Whether one employs the strict criterion of local birth or the looser one of local residence, either 66 or 80 percent of these crews were drawn from the Salem seaport community (defined in the eighteenth century as including Salem and neighboring Beverly). As children they had played together in the streets; their mothers had drawn water from the same wells; and their fathers had gabbed with one another on the waterfront. Indeed, on many vessels the links among the Salem-born were tighter still. Not only did a good portion of the crew share a common residency in the town as a whole; they often lived in the same neighborhood. Nearly half sailed with a master who dwelled in the same part of town as they did, and on some voyages the entire crew hailed from the same ward, a few minutes' walk apart. Every captain from time to time chose to round out his crew with newcomers and transients, and these always made up a sizable minority of the local seafaring labor force, but since theirs is a measurably different history, we will return to them after dealing first with those who had grown up within Salem itself.[15]

On occasion a locally born lad began his seafaring career, especially if his family was well-to-do, apprenticed to a shipmaster. For a fee, the captain would take him on, usually in his early teens, partly as a personal servant to fix meals, clean the cabin, and do laundry, but also on the understanding that the master would teach his apprentice the art of navigation, the skills of ship command, and the tools of business necessary to become a captain himself some day. Sometimes shipmasters took their own sons along with them in this capacity. The youngest ship's boy in the database was Thomas Lovitt of Beverly, who sailed with his father, John, to the Chesapeake in 1747 and later rose to become a master himself. Yet ship's boys were not common in the Salem fleet of the eighteenth century. Most vessels sailed without them, and one can only assume that the local maritime community believed the operation of vessels to be for the most part a practical matter that literate and competent sailors could best learn on the job under the supervision of officers and older seamen but without any formal apprenticeship. Servants would have seemed out of place, moreover, in the small, informal confines of a New England schooner. The handful of ship's boys identified in portledge bills seem to have been slightly advantaged in the scramble for officers' posts later in life. Indeed, of those who shipped on Salem vessels between 1745 and 1759, a full 62 percent went on to command vessels of their own before 1770, though whether this stemmed from their training or from the connections that their backgrounds afforded is difficult to tell.[16]

The great majority of Salem-born mariners (see Graph 3, Appendix B), went to sea initially as ordinary seamen sometime between fifteen and eighteen years of age. Single and still living at home, they divided their time for several years between sea and shore: sailing abroad, fishing on the banks, doing odd jobs around the waterfront, helping out their parents, and killing time when the work dried up. Their travels at sea took them to Spain and the Mediterranean, the Chesapeake and the Caribbean, Newfoundland, Nova Scotia, and the other mainland colonies of British North America. Over five years, they typically served on three or four different vessels under almost as many different masters and alongside a revolving mix of neighbors and acquaintances on every voyage. And yet seafaring proper usually took up only a portion of these young men's time. In 1747, the year he turned nineteen, Ashley Bowen worked a full ten months on the deep; yet in both the year previous and the year following he spent most of his months ashore. Another young mariner, George Glover, fished through the warmer months on the Nova Scotia Banks, sailed southward to Maryland and Virginia every winter, and worked by the day in between voyages both as a stevedore in Salem and as a hand on board Timothy Orne's sloop, coasting the New England shore. Samuel Gavet, who earned more than £11 on a voyage to the West Indies in 1752, added a further twenty shillings for work on board the same vessel after it had returned to Salem. Busy shipmasters such as George Williams and William Deadman usually spent between three and five months of the year at home in Salem, and they were normally in employ for about a month longer per voyage than the seamen they hired. Although every one of these men—masters and seamen alike—entered the records primarily as a mariner, most must have done many other things besides.[17]

Few New Englanders ever went to sea, however, with the intention of spending the rest of their working lives as ordinary hands afloat and common laborers ashore—even if that was sometimes how it worked out. Back in the early days of the colony, Lucy Downing had pointed out to her brother, John Winthrop, that without proper instruction in the art of navigation her sailor sons would never rise in rank: the lot of the "comman seaman," in her words, was "noe better than commane slauerye." What Mrs. Downing asserted with motherly bluntness, every mariner knew in his bones: that without at least a chance at promotion into an officer's post, seafaring could be a hard and unrewarding life. As Edward Barlow, the seventeenth-century English mariner put it, seafaring was "one of the hardest and dangerousest callings . . . all the men in the ship except the master being little better than slaves . . . which made me to take all the care

I could how I might become a master."[18] The question is, whether common seamen in colonial Salem could reasonably expect to rise to the quarterdeck, or whether theirs was an occupational dead end. One fact is plain: as age distributions for seamen under sail imply, most who had shipped themselves before the mast at age twenty had vanished from the forecastle by thirty. Something happened to them during this period of young adulthood that caused Salem-born seamen, aged thirty to thirty-four, to be only one-tenth as numerous in the forecastles of locally owned vessels as their twenty- to twenty-four-year-old compatriots. Indeed, their careers could take one of several different turns.[19]

Certainly, many of them disappeared. About 30 percent of all locally born seamen who were sailing out of Salem at the age of twenty had vanished from the records by the age of thirty.[20] What exactly happened to each of them is often difficult to trace, but demographic indicators suggest that most of those who disappeared had, in fact, died. A list of deaths kept by William Bentley for his waterfront East Parish between 1786 and 1805 allows one to calculate for this later period an age-specific mortality rate for men sixteen to twenty-nine years old of about 35–40 per thousand per annum, or slightly more than 30 percent per decade. That Bentley recorded 6.35 deaths per annum for males aged sixteen to twenty-nine years but only 2.3 per annum for women of the same age, and that so many of the male deaths Bentley reported actually happened abroad, suggest that the special risks associated with seafaring were the principal cause.[21] While similar evidence for the colonial period is lacking, other measurements suggest that the picture before 1775 had been much the same. Seafaring mortality has always tended to generate widows, and (if one can discount the effects of in- and out-migration) the proportion of widows within the population of a maritime community such as Salem is probably a rough index of the death rate among resident mariners. As it turns out, widows constituted a fairly steady proportion of the town throughout the late eighteenth century—falling slightly from 12 percent of all females in 1754 to 11.5 percent by 1785. Since 84 percent of those Salem widows who could be identified from account books and valuation lists from the period 1738–1775 had been married to Salem residents and were not in-migrants, it is probable that widowhood was a fairly stable function of *local* mortality and that the rates characteristic of Bentley's day can be read back into the period before the Revolution.[22] Similar rates have been reported for colonial

Boston, a seaport tied into the same commercial network, and they seem entirely plausible for Salem as well. Mortality would have been higher in Salem or Boston than in the New England countryside simply by virtue of their being commercial crossroads and centers for the transmission of disease. That young men were the primary victims, however, argues strongly for the deadly nature of what most young men in seaports shared in common—their broad involvement in maritime labor abroad.[23]

Seafaring itself was dangerous enough. Mortality records of the eighteenth century were usually sparing in detail, but whenever headstones, bible entries, newspaper notices, or parish registers in seaport towns made reference to the causes of death, then shipwrecks, drownings, and other accidental misfortunes figured prominently. Col. Robert Hale of Beverly was an unusually zealous reporter of tragedy, and his papers list a great many losses at sea during the later colonial period. Within the Thorndike family alone, for example: Paul, Jr., was "supposed to be lost in a hurricane, in the West Indies" in 1738; his cousin Benjamin "drowned at Philadelphia" six years later; Benjamin's brother, Andrew, "foundered coming from Philad[elphia]" in 1761; Paul's son, Ebenezer, and Andrew's nephew Daniel both died "coming from Gibralter" in 1760; and Paul's nephew John "foundered" in 1764. How exactly these Thorndikes perished we will never know. Possibly one of them lost his hold on the yardarm and fell from aloft; another may have been swept overboard by a wave breaking over the stern; yet another may have fallen out of the ship's boat while rowing ashore. And, as Hale's language plainly implies, some of the Thorndikes drowned along with all of their crewmates when their vessels sank.[24]

Fatal accidents at sea were sudden, horrible, and for that reason newsworthy events. Often hinging on momentary inattention or plain bad luck, they could carry off the most promising of young people without a trace. Even in cases where the dead were recovered, their bodies usually had to be committed to the deep and denied a normal burial on shore. To be "lost at sea" was to end one's life in an unnatural way, and there is no doubt that such accidents were recorded much more consistently than deaths of a more mundane stripe. They stare out at us from the historical records designed to keep track of mortality, yet they may not, in fact, have occurred quite as frequently as these records suggest. The journals of fifty-six merchant voyages in and out of Salem and other ports on Massachusetts's North Shore between 1753 and 1775 provide a more objective, shipboard view of maritime mortality, and they record not one accidental fatality among them. Not all of these journals are complete, and by their nature they recount the stories only of those vessels that avoided shipwreck and made it home safely. Still, the infrequency of serious accidents—fatal or not—on the voyages they document marks a real contrast to the picture afforded in records kept on shore, and they suggest that the dangers inherent in sailing on the deep may not have been the prime source of maritime mortality. Bentley's thorough mortality records of 1786–1817, which describe the cause of death in most cases and have the advantage of including shipwrecks, confirm that among young mariners from Salem in this later period, only 39 percent of deaths can be blamed on maritime accidents.[25]

Undoubtedly, the graver danger to officers and men alike, as Bentley's records and the ship's journals make clear, was the encounter with tropical disease. Fifty-four percent of the deaths of young men recorded by Bentley between 1786 and 1817 were attributable to illnesses, chiefly fevers of different sorts, including malaria and yellow fever, contracted more often than not in the West Indies. During his long career afloat, Ashley Bowen's only real scrape with death came in 1746 when he contracted the "fever and ague" in a French prison on St. Domingue. Twice "laid by as dead," he only just escaped being carted off by the guards who came to remove the corpses every morning. Five of the fifty-six accounts in ship's journals mention fatal illnesses—all of them in the Caribbean and most of them obviously fevers. In 1769, for example, the sloop *Elizabeth* picked up a young ship's carpenter in Dominica named Jonathan Siafoton "that hes ben hear this some time Sik" and offered to carry him home to New England. Three days later, however, while the vessel lay at anchor in St. Eustatia, he was "taken in fits and Died." The following morning, the crew of the *Elizabeth* constructed a coffin and "desently baread him in the Englis Church yard" before returning to their business. Plainly one cannot generalize from West Indian voyages to the entirety of Salem's shipping network. Voyages to other parts of the Atlantic carried with them the same risk of accident as those to the Caribbean, but tropical diseases were rarely a threat in Bilbao, Philadelphia, or Newfoundland. Throughout the colonial period, however, the Caribbean remained the principal destination for Salem vessels, and there were few local sailors who did not journey there on a regular basis. If the evidence from Bentley's death list can be applied in a rough way to the mid–eighteenth century, the stark and unavoidable truth remains that among locally born sailors three in ten never reached the age of thirty.[26]

If nearly all of those sailors who disappeared from Salem during their twenties can be shown to have died, then few could possibly have left. Local records, of course, seldom track the personal histories of those who moved away. The more industrious genealogists, however, of which New England has more than its share, have generally made an effort to follow individuals beyond town boundaries, and if one can assume that those possessed of no other record beyond that of their birth died young, then something on the order of 90–95 percent of those men born to families with strong seafaring traditions maintained Salem as their home through to the age of thirty. Seamen from Salem lived anything but sedentary lives; Ashley Bowen's peripatetic career on the deep was entirely normal. Yet like Bowen, they almost always returned home eventually, and their lives before the mast did not sever many of them from their family roots.[27]

Another 10 percent of these seamen quit merchant seafaring to take up other work. Some slid into side employments, the most popular of which were fishing and coasting. Even young and active mariners often spent part of each year on the banks of Newfoundland and Nova Scotia hand-lining for cod. Fishing involved frequent but shorter absences from home, and to those who had married and started families of their own it made for a more convenient if no more remunerative living. Benjamin Peters, for example, sailed as a young man to Virginia in 1751 but was outfitting himself, his son, and a hired man on a fishing voyage fifteen years later. Ferrying cargo up and down the New England coast and lightering ships in Massachusetts's harbors were further alternatives for married men who wanted to keep in closer touch with home. Other seamen quit the sea entirely and took up different trades. Benjamin Hawthorne, who sailed to Maryland as a teenager in 1747, was married, settled in Salem, and making hats by 1756, while Joseph Osborn, a young seaman who shipped himself to the West Indies under Richard Derby's command in 1759, was in the process of taking over his father's pottery business.[28]

This last case illustrates another important point—that the transition from ship to shore was rarely abrupt. Three years before his voyage with Derby, Osborn had begun selling earthenware on his own account; and for some period anyway he split his time between seafaring and pottery work. Ashley Bowen of Marblehead also wound down his seafaring career in stages. After his marriage in 1758, he decided to "not go any more to sea this winter, and . . . [stay] with my wife to see how it would suit to live on shore," yet this resolve lasted no more than a few months before he had left on the naval expedition to Quebec. Again in 1761–1762 he spent the better part of the winter at home rigging ships—a skill he had learned abroad during his earlier seafaring career. In the spring, however, he went coasting again, and that summer he sailed to the West Indies. Only in the fall of 1763 did he really leave the sea to open a full-time rigging loft in Marblehead. Trying to determine precisely who were still seamen and who had quit the sea masks a more gradual process by which individuals who failed to secure promotion circled steadily inward toward home.[29]

The salient truths about most foremast hands, however, not only from Salem but from everywhere else in the early modern world of the North Atlantic, was their youth and their seaside origins. Wherever they were bound in the longer course of their lives they took to the deep by virtue of having grown up within earshot of the surf, and their careers before the mast were defined primarily by their youth.

The most striking feature about Salem-born mariners revealed in this attempt to chart their life courses is the high proportion of seafaring men who rose into officer's posts. Of all native-born seamen who sailed out of the South River between 1745 and 1759 (including those who died in mid-career), 49 percent succeeded in becoming mates, and 27 percent went on to become shipmasters. If one counts only those who survived their years at sea, the rates of promotion were even higher—70 percent to mate and 39 percent to master. This is not to say that all of those promoted remained mates or masters for the rest of their working lives. Ship's officers could quit the sea as easily as anyone else; indeed, a clear mark of success in life was the speed with which a shipmaster could set himself up as a merchant in port or a shoreman with a fishyard. At sea, moreover, movement between ranks could occur in both directions. In a career that we can trace through eleven voyages between 1753 and 1761, James Cheever moved back and forth between master and mate several times over, and his story was not unique. Such a pattern could be rooted in a number of causes. Novice mates could prove incompetent shiphandlers, poor navigators, or insufficiently strict (or too strict) with their men. Young shipmasters might be gifted mariners but wretched businessmen. Both might be victims of intrigue at home in Salem, prone to row with the vessel owners, or simply jinxed. Sometimes mariners were willing to take a demotion in rank in return for the opportunity to ship themselves on a larger vessel. Although twenty-seven-year-old Benjamin Bray had obtained command of the schooner *Exeter* in 1747, he chose to sail as mate to Capt. Thomas Morong on board the brig *Betty & Molly* the following year. Thus the path of promotion in Salem was fluid, complicated, and quite reversible, but it was also relatively open, and masterships lay well within the reach of any ambitious young sailor.[30]

Even those who never became shipmasters on oceangoing vessels often turned to coasting—that is, commanding smaller vessels in the short-haul trades within New England waters. As coasters these men seldom cleared customs, and hence they rarely entered the records from which the promotion data were constructed. But if their proportion along the waterfront resembled their importance in the account books of Timothy Orne and Richard Derby (where they were one-third as common as masters), we can infer that almost 10 percent of foremast hands became coasters later in life. Many of these continued to combine coasting with deepwater sailing. After all, the line between the two was not very sharp. The same skills and the same vessels that could carry one to the mouth of the Kennebec could equally handle a voyage to Halifax. During the late 1750s, Israel Ober of Beverly was the skipper of another small sloop, the *Seaflower,* which he owned and operated in the local freighting business in partnership with the merchant Richard Derby. Early in his career, however, he began extending the scope of his travels, first to Nova Scotia, and then to the Carolinas and the West Indies. In 1762 he sold his share of the sloop to another coaster, Joseph Grafton, Jr., and embarked on a career as a full-fledged mariner, commanding large schooners and brigantines in voyages across the Atlantic and into the Mediterranean. Other coasters, however, stuck almost entirely to local freighting. For twenty years before the outbreak of the Revolutionary War, George Peele carried fish, timber, molasses, and "English goods" to and from Boston in his little sloop, the *Mary*—partly as freights for others and partly as ventures on his own account—and as with about half the coasters in Salem, his name never surfaced in the Naval Officer Shipping Lists as master of any voyage bound outside of Massachusetts. If we add skippers like Peele to the sum total of mates and shipmasters involved in foreign voyages, it seems safe to conclude that Salem mariners who survived their first decade at sea could reasonably aspire to an officer's berth and a decent chance at someday commanding a vessel of their own.[31]

Those who possessed the qualities needed to move upward through the ranks normally did so during their early twenties. The pattern of promotion can be viewed only indirectly through the age distributions by rank, but the data here imply that it was, indeed, during these years that mates and masters were generally recruited from the body of ordinary seamen. But what were these qualities? Promotion was common but by no means universal, and clearly there were certain characteristics that defined the mastery of seafaring and set some individuals above others in the scramble for command. Some of these are plainly beyond the historian's ken. Intelligence, toughness, self-control, business sense, and a great deal of technical knowledge all mattered vitally in the command of a ship, yet how individual mariners measured up to these criteria we can rarely even guess at.

There does survive, however, one fairly detailed account of a New Englander's *failure* to reach the quarterdeck—the autobiography of Ashley Bowen. Bowen undoubtedly felt he had been hard done by—that his talents had been overlooked. Yet a letter from his father, written in 1757 after discovering that Ashley had lucked into his one and only chance to command a deepwater vessel, reveals, if only by implication, some features of the young man's character that might have held him back. Wrote Nathan Bowen to his son in the West Indies: "I simpathize with you under your late Misfortune with Capt. Lewis, but hope you will retreive that loss by a due Improvement of the Oppertunities you now have, let me recommend you to a Steady Honest & Honourable pursuit of the Things of this World . . ." One can sense the intergenerational tension crackling across the waters here, but clearly Nathan felt that his son had hitherto not devoted sufficient attention to the "things of this world," and in some sense he was right. Ashley's career had so far taken him in many different directions over fifteen years, and although he was anything but idle during this period, he seems to have lacked the type of focused ambition and "steady . . . pursuit" that carried others to the mastery of their trade. Had he stayed in Marblehead, settled down earlier, and concentrated his energies on a "due improvement" of the "oppertunities" that the booming merchant shipping industry of that town afforded young mariners during the middle

decades of the eighteenth century, he might have become a more successful though probably duller man.[32]

That sort of locally focused persistence often paid off. Sailors who
shipped themselves out of Salem repeatedly, and so made themselves
known to local masters and shipowners, were far more likely to succeed
than those who did not. Of those who surfaced as seamen in surviving
crew lists three or more times, a full 48 percent became masters; of those
who appeared only once or twice, the rate of promotion was only 22 percent.
Ashley Bowen indeed understood the importance of a well-developed *local*
reputation. While trying to make a living as a coaster at the mouth of the
Delaware in 1754, he complained that he could not get the work he wanted,
in spite of his having "many friends here and relations," because, as an
outsider, he lacked proof of his maritime experience—"that I am as I assert to be." Yet when he returned to Marblehead in disgust several months
later, he discovered that he could not obtain an officer's berth there either,
since up until that point he had shipped himself principally out of other
ports. At this point Bowen attempted to mend his ways and base himself
in Marblehead, but at twenty-six years of age, he found that time and fortune had passed him by, and his career never did take off.[33]

Ashley's path to the quarterdeck might have been easier had his father
been a shipowner with a vested interest in placing his vessels under the
command of family members. Maritime historians have frequently drawn
attention to the advantages shipowners' sons and nephews enjoyed in the
scramble for promotion—mostly that merchants preferred to have men
they could trust conducting their business abroad. Yet while this logic may
have held in a great seaport such as London, it seldom operated in Salem.
Sometimes local shipowners placed their relations in command of their
vessels. Richard Derby, one of the wealthiest, appointed his son, Richard
Derby, Jr., to take the brigantine *Neptune* on several voyages to Europe
during the Seven Years' War. On the first of these, the young fellow was
only twenty-one, and yet his father placed him in charge of seven seamen,
a cook, and a mate who was twice his age. Most of the masters who commanded Derby's vessels during the colonial period, however, were not
members of his immediate family, nor were they related to him either by
blood or marriage. Timothy Orne employed even fewer family members.
Of thirty-one masters he hired for 117 voyages between 1737 and 1771, only
one was connected to him as brother, uncle, son, cousin, or nephew—by

either blood or marriage. Miles Ward, a smaller operator, who employed four different masters on 13 recorded voyages, depended entirely on men outside his family.[34]

Nathan Bowen's ability to help his son lay simply in his own personal status as a propertied member of his community. In Salem, evidence pertaining to twenty-nine locally born seamen who shipped themselves out between 1744 and 1759 and whose families of birth could be placed within the town's tax lists during this period in their careers suggests that the more property a father possessed, the stronger his son's chances for promotion. When we measure each father's taxable property at the time the seafaring son either turned twenty or married, it appears that among seamen from the wealthiest third of Salem's households, 40 percent rose eventually to master; of those from the middle third, only 27 percent did, and from the bottom third, only 15 percent. Poverty was not an absolute barrier to reaching the quarterdeck, but it made the process more difficult. How exactly parental wealth helped probably varied from case to case. With the Bowens, it provided the means for placing sons under apprenticeship. More commonly it simply placed the mark of confidence and credit upon the aspiring mariner—the brand that propertied men tended to see in others of their kind. Yet as the example of the Bowens amply illustrates, property and connection could not compensate for whatever young Ashley seemed to lack.[35]

Through the year he turned thirty, one of these failings was his inability to find a wife. In Salem the timing of promotion coincided closely to marriage, and this was no accident. Almost three-quarters of locally born sailors in the eighteenth century wed between the ages of twenty-one and twenty-six (and at a median age of twenty-four) regardless of rank—at about the time when they were beginning to sort themselves out into those likely to succeed afloat and those probably better suited to life ashore (see Graph 5, Appendix B). True, certain mariners made it to the quarterdeck and stayed single for a good many years before marrying. Thomas Cox of Beverly became a mate in his late teens, a master by twenty-three, yet he did not find a wife until the advanced age of thirty-seven. A few shipmasters remained bachelors all their lives. Richard Manning, who ran the schooner *Benjamin* aground while under chase by a French privateer on a voyage to Barbados in 1757, retired to Salem, where as a politician and man of affairs he "accumulated a great interest by Money letting."

"Reserved in his habits & temper" and perhaps a little too "attentive of his interest" to prove attractive to the opposite sex, he lived the rest of his days with his brothers and sisters in a large house on Bow Street. In general, however, most Salem mariners, like most New Englanders, married and usually did so in their early twenties.[36]

The logic connecting marriage with either promotion or retirement from the sea worked in several directions. The mariner's reasoning was fairly self-evident. Seafaring was never easy to reconcile with ordinary family life, and with the limited income that a common seaman could hope to earn, the task was much more difficult. Even with ten months of work in a year, the annual wages of a foremast hand would add up to only about £15—not much more than a farmhand—and although this could be a substantial contribution to a household with other sources of income, it was not much with which to launch a family of one's own. Furthermore, a seaman working under the command of a shipmaster was a species of servant, and servitude was not the status that heads of households in colonial New England aspired to hold. Some sailors did marry, of course, but they did so in the reasonable hope that in the not too distant future they would begin to climb the ladder of promotion or else move into some other less taxing work on land.[37]

Employers viewed promotion from the other side of the table, but they, too, probably thought that married men made better ship's officers —especially better masters. The issues here were responsibility, credit, and risk. A shipowner ran a considerable hazard every time he hired someone to command one of his vessels over the horizon and out of view. Not only had he delegated control over the vessel and its cargo to the master; he normally had also advanced the latter a considerable quantity of cash with which to finance the master's own trading activities, pay the sailor's advances, and cover other incidentals connected to the voyage. Shipmasters kept extremely active accounts with their employers, running up large debts every time they went to sea, and any shipowner could be excused for worrying whether or not his trust might be abused. One way of hedging his bets, however, was to select for the command of his vessels a married man. Not only did the latter have more to lose were he to trifle with his merchant employer's property; but he also possessed property of his own that his merchant creditor could easily seize if the mariner defaulted.

The same logic operated in a slightly attenuated fashion with mates.

These men conducted far less business than masters and rarely kept extensive accounts with merchants; in this way they resembled the seamen they supervised. Yet their responsibilities on board were considerable, including the obligation to take over command of the vessel should the master die or become incapacitated during a voyage. Shipowners and shipmasters alike were concerned about hiring dependable, trustworthy mates, and they chose at least three-quarters of them from among the ranks of married householders. For their part, sailors understood that promotion to mate augured well for the future. Not only did one's wages begin to climb, but having reached the rank of mate, a mariner knew that the chances of rising right to the quarterdeck were better than even—especially if he persisted in his quest. Among those with only one recorded voyage as mate, the rate of promotion was only 38 percent; but among those whose name surfaced on two or more, the rate was 77 percent. Knowing these odds, twenty-two-year-old George West, a fisherman and mariner, married Abigail Cook in 1751—the same year he first surfaced as mate on a winter voyage to the Chesapeake. For several more years he served in the same capacity, and then in 1756, predictably enough, he received command of the fishing schooner *Olive Branch*, which he took to the banks every spring and to the southward every winter for the next decade and more. Nothing automatic connected marriage and promotion. Rather, they were each expressions of the same impulse—a commitment to the local seaport community and its fleet—that tended to promote both.[38]

What difference did promotion make? Did it constitute such a fork in the road as to launch ship's officers on a radically different career path from their men? Certainly, the distinctions of rank mattered on board ship—though not for Salem vessels in anything like the autocratic terms that are often associated with the navy or the merchant service in larger ports. But did the relatively formal work relations that governed life afloat translate into a clear social hierarchy ashore? To answer this question, let us consider in turn the unfolding lives of those locally born sailors who ended up as career seamen, career mates, and career masters in Salem.

The aging foremast hand—gray, bent, and weathered by his service on the deep—was not unknown around the Atlantic basin of the eighteenth century, but in this particular maritime community he was, in fact, rather scarce. Death, promotion, retirement from the deep, or out-migration from the region removed sailors from Salem vessels at such a rate during the colonial period that no more than one-tenth of all foremast hands were older than thirty, and less than 2 percent were over forty. Spending time before the mast was an expected part of growing up for most young men in town, but to remain a sailor into middle age, after any realistic hope of promotion had vanished, was a mark of exceptional poverty and social dependence.

Timothy Mansfield was born in 1700 and as a young man followed his father into the maritime trades. At the age of twenty-four he married Abigail Foot—a young woman of identical background—and the two of them kept house together (or more precisely one-half of a house that they shared with another family) for at least forty years, while Timothy continued to follow the sea. A fisherman and merchant sailor, he was still shipping himself abroad at the age of fifty-six, making him the oldest common seaman in the database. In what sort of condition the Mansfields lived is hard to know, since no record of their personal estate or their dealings with shopkeepers has survived, but other career mariners who left probated inventories lived with their families in similar small, shared dwellings (sometimes rented but usually owned), furnished in plain fashion with pine tables and chairs, a bed or two, some chests to store their clothes in, and several items of basic kitchen equipment. Beyond this, creature comforts were few in number, low in quality, and worn in appearance. Abigail Mansfield's uncle, Thomas Foot, possessed eleven pewter plates, an old sword, and a set of brass compasses and dividers; while Benjamin Bush's wife, Mary, owned some table linen, a "small looking glass" to hang on the wall, and a set of "poor curtains" to cover the windows and maintain some privacy. The interiors of these homes were bare in the extreme. Moreover, career seamen owned very little in the way of productive property—no shipping, no merchandise, no animals, and few if any tools or equipment, such as a cart or a spinning wheel, that might support a by-employment for any member of their family. These households depended completely on wage labor to survive, and in the hierarchy of wealth holders inside Salem society (see Graph 6, Appendix B), they never escaped the lower rungs.[39]

Career mates, those who had left the forecastle and could be trusted to manage a vessel through an entire watch but who never received an independent command of their own, did little better in life materially speaking than the seamen they supervised. Their wages were only about 15 percent higher, and even at full employment—a near impossibility for any mariner —their earnings could not have topped £20 a year. Combined with fishing voyages and what their wives could earn on shore, such an income might support a family, but only on very plain fare. Jonathan Felt was one of these career mates—the son of a blacksmith and fisherman and eldest of five brothers who all followed seafaring trajectories in Salem. In 1744 Jonathan had married Sarah Reeves, daughter of a Marblehead fisherman, and in the late 1750s, while the two of them were raising a small family in a shared dwelling by the waterfront, he was fishing on the banks and shipping himself abroad as mate to make ends meet. He never commanded a vessel of his own, and throughout his life his wealth holdings, like those of most career mates, hovered close to those of career seamen and some-what below the Salem median. Christopher Bubier, a fisherman's son who was six years married and thirty years old when he died of a fever during a voyage on which he had shipped as mate to Surinam in 1705, owned a few small parcels of land that he may have rented out, and his wife carded and spun wool, probably to sell, but the house they lived in was rented, and their personal possessions were few and dilapidated.[40]

The true old salts of Salem's merchant fleet, and the only ones whose earnings allowed them to persist in their maritime careers in any number beyond the age of thirty-five, were shipmasters. These were, as we have seen, a numerically significant group. Indeed, most of those locally born mariners who truly wanted to become captains of their own vessels and were lucky enough to dodge the classic maritime fates of drowning and tropical disease eventually succeeded to a mastership and did reasonably well for themselves. Not only did their wages climb by about 10 percent over those of a mate, but as a master they also spent 20 percent more time in employ—mostly at the beginning but also at the end of every voyage —dealing with the cargo, hiring and paying the crew, and managing the vessel itself. An even greater advantage to the master was the improvement in credit he obtained. Whereas mates and foremast hands took their wages in cash and rarely if ever engaged in trading ventures, masters usually kept a number of running accounts with local merchants and did business constantly. Some acquired shares in vessels on credit obtained from local merchants. A few purchased sloops or schooners outright and freighted goods for a living. Many more, whether they owned shipping tonnage or not, supplemented their earnings through trading in timber, sugar, fish, and molasses—all the common commodities of the day. Taken together, 85 percent of mariners who called themselves masters or coasters in the accounts of Timothy Orne practiced one or another of the mercantile activities described here.[41]

Lewis Hunt, who sailed the trading lanes between Massachusetts and the Caribbean for thirty years in the late seventeenth and early eighteenth centuries, employed these strategies to climb into the highest decile among Salem's wealth holders before he was lost at sea with the rest of his crew returning from Barbados in 1713. His estate, totaling £369 sterling before an undisclosed number of debts were deducted, included a two-story house of his own close to the middle of town, comfortably if not opulently furnished with a collection of walnut and pine tables, leather upholstered chairs, looking glasses, and a good collection of pewter and plate. His second wife, Elizabeth, presided over a well-appointed kitchen equipped with a spinning wheel, which may have been plied by one of her daughters or perhaps the "indian girle" who was included in the estate. Hunt possessed no vessel tonnage when he died, but he owned a second house, which presumably he rented out, and the shop goods worth £7 and the bills of credit totaling £150 imply that he had over the years made good use of his trading privileges as master.[42]

The career of John Cloutman illustrates another course that an industrious seaman could chart toward the quarterdeck and the measure of comfortable independence it conferred. Born into a family that had been part of the maritime community in Salem for nearly a century, he rose through the ranks to become a skipper of fishing schooners in the early 1750s. In the summer he worked on the banks and in the winter he sailed southward with the same crew in the same vessel to sell his catch. On top of his wages and his share of the season's fish, he also carried ventures with him to trade. Thus in 1752, before taking the *Fisher* to Chesapeake Bay, he purchased fifty-three gallons of New England rum—obviously to sell there on his own account. Over the years, this brand of petty commerce must have paid off, for in taxable wealth he rose steadily through the ranks of Salem society, and on the eve of the Revolution he was a shoreman with a fishyard and a little schooner of his own.[43]

The professional mariners who were born in Salem and promoted to command—a majority of those who stuck to the sea and survived their years before the mast—combined their officer's wages with the fruits of their spouses' industry and the profits of trade won by both to acquire a competency by the time they had reached middle age. Virtually all of them owned their own homes—usually semidetached but comfortably furnished nonetheless. Many of Capt. John Cook's possessions may have been judged pretty "old," but he owned most of the basic householding necessities—from bedsteads to earthenware plates to a cupboardful of napkins, sheets, blankets, and pillowcases—and his oval table, brass candlestick, silver cup, and looking glass provided the house with a little distinction. James Foster's wife could stock her kitchen somewhat more handsomely, with brass, copper, and silverware, and her case of knives and forks even suggests a touch of gentility. Benjamin Stone's new pewter tankard, brass candle-sticks, pair of snuffers, and "belmettel scilet," ornamented the interior of his dwelling, while his gold ring and "the silver button on his breeches" lent his person a little elegance. William Cash's home was somewhat plainer, but he owned three servants (two boys and one girl), who assisted his wife while he was away at sea. The income of a sea captain could not support the standards of the new enlightened gentility developing around the Atlantic world during the eighteenth century, but these homes could compare in levels of comfort with those of competent farmers and artisans elsewhere in New England.[44]

In addition to their household goods, roughly half of these shipmasters possessed some modest quantity of shipping tonnage or stock in trade. Commonly, this amounted to no more than a one-eighth or one-quarter share in the vessel they commanded, purchased on credit from its manag-ing owner. Thus Samuel Carrel acquired part of a schooner he skippered, owned by Miles Ward, who graciously christened it after Carrel's wife, Hitty. Some probated estates of masters who died in midcareer also include a few hogsheads of rum, a bale or two of cotton, or what were lumped to-gether as "sundry shop goods" but might include a few yards of cloth, some chinaware, several cases of bottles, or a few boxes of buttons that a wife might sell out of her front door while her husband was away. Such households were modestly prosperous but hardly wealthy. Had their means allowed them, these shipmasters probably would have retired to a less strenuous gentleman's life on shore. That most of them continued to work at sea into their forties, about when they began to falter physically, and that only about a quarter were ever termed merchants, gentlemen, or esquires on any legal document they generated in later life, suggest that Salem shipmasters were precisely what their title implied: workingmen who had risen to become masters of their trade. Within the professional seafaring families that predominated on the Salem waterfront, such a career pattern—from youthful dependency to adult mastery and independence—would have been a reasonable expectation.[45]

Every seaport in the early modern world was a magnet for workingmen in search of employment, and Salem was no exception. Some of these hailed from parts overseas and deserted in Massachusetts, possibly because they had learned of the high wages that prevailed there or simply because they wanted to jump a disagreeable ship. Other prospective seamen drifted in from nearby villages along the North Shore, looking for adventure or at least the sort of steady employment that was increasingly difficult to find around home in the eighteenth century. Local shipmasters undoubtedly preferred to ship their crews from among local men—neighbors whose qualities they knew—but this was not always possible, and they often had to hire outsiders instead. Consequently, about 15 percent of all seamen who served on Salem vessels were newcomers who resided in town but hailed originally from other parts, while a further 20 percent were transients altogether.[46]

Unraveling the personal histories of the truly transient—those who came to Salem, shipped themselves on a voyage or two but never formed any permanent attachments there before they either died or departed—is very difficult. Labeling all of them strangers, however, would be inaccurate. At least one-quarter of the non–locally born can firmly be traced to other towns and villages in coastal New England, chiefly north of Boston; and judging from their New England surnames, many of the remaining three-quarters probably did as well. On the whole, like most migrants, they may have been slightly older than the locally born, but the difference was not significant, since they probably had not traveled far. Nor can we assume that because they were born outside Salem, they were always unknown to the masters who signed them on. Amos Stickney, a captain who took the *Beaver* to Barbados in 1750, came from Rowley, north of Salem, and hired all but one of his men from the Rowley area. We cannot be sure that they enjoyed the same prospects in life as their Salem crewmates; none of them remained long enough for this to be measured. Yet neither should we assume the opposite. Suggestive in this regard was the youth of those transients from elsewhere in Massachusetts whose age could be determined; these floaters, at least, were not old salts. Also suggestive was the large number of shipmasters who cleared the customshouse in Salem but had grown up and still resided in other towns along the North Shore (Table 4.2). Too few crew lists have survived from those ports to make sharply comparative statements on the rate of promotion there, but it is hard to imagine, given the number of masters who lived in these smaller ports and the smaller size of their merchant fleets, that promotion there would have been markedly more difficult than in Salem.[47]

Table 4.2

Town of Residence of 230 Shipmasters Clearing Port of Salem, 1751–1769

Town	Resident	Merchant Shipping Tonnage, 1771
Salem	90	7,963
Marblehead	40	4,793
Gloucester	32	1,858
Beverly	16	—
Elsewhere in Massachusetts	29	—
Outside Massachusetts	2	—
Unknown	21	—
Total	230	—

Sources: The 230 shipmasters clearing Salem Customs House, 1751, were randomly selected from Harriet Silvester Tapley, ed., *Early Coastwise and Foreign Shipping of Salem: A Record of the Entrances and Clearances of the Port of Salem, 1750–1769* (Salem, Mass., 1934). Their residences were determined from sources in Appendix 1. Tonnage for selected ports calculated from Bettye Hobbs Pruitt, ed., *The Massachusetts Tax Valuation List of 1771* (Boston, 1978), 48–67, 98–107, 130–155, 778; "Report on the American Fisheries by the Secretary of State," Feb. 1, 1791, in *The Papers of Thomas Jefferson,* ed. Julian P. Boyd et al. (Princeton, N.J., 1950–), XIX, 221, 223.

In the case of in-migrants—those among these outsiders who chose to settle permanently in Salem—we are on somewhat firmer ground. One of the more successful of them, at least in material terms, was William Wyatt. Born in Newbury, he sailed on Orne's *Beaver* under Amos Stickney in 1750. Moving to Salem shortly after, he met and wed Sarah Cheever, launching a long but turbulent marriage. A great consumer of rum, he was probably difficult to live with; in any event he clearly preferred the sea over his own hearth. Wyatt's career before the mast continued into his middle thirties, and even when he quit the deepwater trades he did not return to shore. Instead, he became a coaster, working first for local shipowners and later on a vessel of his own freighting goods between Salem and Boston. By the eve of the Revolution, he had acquired a house as well as a slave, and his property holdings placed him within the wealthiest third of Salem's taxpaying population. After the war he grew wholly estranged from his wife and took to living by himself on board his sloop —even while in Salem, when he moored it at the wharf on Winter Island and communicated with her when necessary through their daughter, Anna. Not until 1795, at the age of seventy, did he finally retire from coasting, and even then, rather than return home, he moved in with his son-in-law. The following year he and Sarah both died, just three weeks apart.[48]

John Ellison was another immigrant and one whose history was probably more typical. A British sailor of "uncommonly short" stature, he came from London about 1760, entered the local merchant service, married a New England girl, and decided to settle in Salem permanently. For fifty years he was a respectable fixture on the lower rungs of Salem society. Before the outbreak of the Revolution he acquired no assessable property, and the fact that he retired from the sea, apparently without promotion, to become a rigger implies that his seafaring career was not a successful one. That he served in the army during the War of Independence, even though he would have been in his thirties, speaks partly for his patriotism but also for the likely collapse of his rigging business in the face of the British blockade. As an older man, he was appointed to the town watch —possibly as a form of outdoor relief. When he died in 1812, William Bentley termed him with a touch of condescension "honest John . . . a man of great integrity & good reputation" but limited means.[49]

Those immigrants who settled in Salem did not fare as well in their careers as the locally born, almost certainly because they lacked the family and neighborly connections that generated trust and credit within the port. William Wyatt overcame this disability by marrying into the prosperous Cheever family; and Edward Gibaut trumped him by wedding a daughter of the well-to-do Crowninshields and later rising to become a minor merchant after the Revolution. But few in-migrant sailors were as fortunate. Only 15 percent of them became shipmasters, and although most of them managed to acquire some property in Salem, only a small fraction— between 5 and 13 percent, depending on one's standard of measurement —ever climbed into the higher ranks of taxpayers assessed for commercial property. Moses Townshend, a seaman–turned–house painter who died during the Revolution, left an estate in which the only productive equipment consisted of cooking utensils and a spinning wheel employed by his wife and "a chest with Paint Pots and Brushes," along with "half a Laith" and four turning tools with which to practice his own trade. Without access to the sort of credit that a host of local connections provided, these were the only capital goods Townshend ever managed to accumulate.[50]

What of those who left Salem to wander the oceans and settle down in other ports? Did they find it as hard to establish themselves abroad as did immigrants in Salem? Since nearly all of these individuals escape our research net entirely, we can only speculate as to what may have happened to them. Jack Cremer, an English sailor-journalist of the eighteenth century, certainly believed that his "roving mind" and "thoughtless . . . negligent" ways had been his undoing. Had he stayed put and concentrated on getting ahead, he wrote, "I might have made a fortin and lived happy in my old Age" instead of confirming the old saw that "a Rowling Stone never gathers Moss." If the experience of in-migrants to Salem mirrored in any way that of Salem out-migrants to other port communities, Cremer may well have been speaking for the lot of the wandering mariner in general. The number of these truly footloose mariners may have been relatively small, but their fate could be unusually hard.[51]

The labor system in which mariners made their living was extraordinarily complex. Even inside Salem itself, a great variety of forces combined in many different ways to chart dozens of different life courses along which sailors might journey. Remember that seafaring labor drew them into many other ports besides—witness the career of Ashley Bowen—and the range of possible futures that a young seaman might imagine was almost beyond measuring. Only in a very few cases did sailors ever reveal these speculations, but they knew how maritime employment operated, and they must have possessed some reasonable expectation of what was likely to happen to them.

Central to any understanding of this labor system was class. While at sea, Salem mariners were paid laborers in the employ of merchant capitalists, and while both parties shared an interest in the success of the voyage, they profited from it in different ways—one in wages, the other in profits —that frequently set them at odds. Shipowners wanted their cargoes delivered as quickly and as cheaply as possible, even if that meant requiring that the shipmasters they hired sometimes inflict physical danger, poor fare, and hard usage on their hands to economize on expenses and make the profits flow. Class also mattered in setting the broader rules governing the place of seafaring labor within the British Empire. Since the colonial and imperial governments were both committed to the advance of trade, they lent to merchants and shipmasters the force of law and the disciplinary arm of the state to exploit and control this maritime labor force in the pursuit of their commercial designs.[52]

Class is, however, a lived experience, and to be lived in the fullest sense, it must be lived for a lifetime. When one shifts one's focus from the shipboard experience of seafaring labor to the entire course of these mariners' lives, the influence of class begins to dim. People act not only in accordance with their present circumstances but also in light of what they anticipate from the future, and in eighteenth-century Salem, mariners understood that with the passage of time, their place within the power structure of maritime society would change. They knew as young men when they entered the merchant service that they would probably not remain foremast hands for more than ten or fifteen years at most. By the time they were thirty, most of them would either have risen to an officer's post or have quit the merchant service altogether and taken up another trade on land. Rarely, of course, did the seafarer thus transform himself from a laborer to a capitalist, but when he left the forecastle, his relationship to the merchant community of the town did change. If a ship's officer, he now acted as a manager of capital; he enjoyed some of the advantages that easy and abundant credit could afford; and in some limited fashion he could participate in commerce on his own account. If a farmer, shoreman, or shipwright, he began to deal with merchants as a skilled laborer with some productive property of his own. And if only a cooper, carter, or shoemaker, he was the practitioner of a trade with his own tools and possessed occupational skills that no merchant could claim. There were some career sailors who depended almost entirely on wage labor—at sea and ashore—to the end of their working days, but in Salem most seamen understood their status as hands to be transitory. This is not to negate the significance of class but only to suggest that inside this maritime society, where seafaring was part of normal experience, the distribution of capital, labor, and skill did not divide the town into mutually opposed camps.

It is important to remember that on balance, Salem merchants were not an overly genteel lot. Many of the richest shipowners in town had spent a few years before the mast and several more as active shipmasters before retiring to the countinghouse; and most of *their* fathers (moving a generation backward) had started out their lives in households where physical labor was an ordinary part of life. Two lists of Salem vessel owners, one constructed from Massachusetts Ship Registries, 1698–1702, and another compiled in 1765, list only one surname in common—that of Pickman. Not only had all the prominent merchant families of the late seventeenth century vanished from the field by the eve of the American Revolution, but none of the late colonial merchants, save Benjamin Pickman, could claim a family member who had mattered in the commercial hierarchy of the town sixty-five years before. For the most part, the grandfathers of this latter-day group had at the beginning of the eighteenth century been farmers, craftsmen, fishermen, mariners, or shopkeepers. Hard manual labor was a relatively recent memory. The shipowners of Salem were certainly a class, in that they controlled the shipping industry of the town at any given moment, but they were far from an impermeable club, for their membership was in constant transformation as newer families gradually replaced others who, by death, lack of interest, or bad fortune, dropped out.[53]

Class was further mitigated in Salem by the dense network of kinship that connected so many Salem families to one another. Although well born or upwardly mobile themselves, most members of the eighteenth-century merchant elite had rafts of cousins or in-laws, descended from or married into less successful branches of their families, who were still plainly laboring men. Richard Derby, for example, may have been the wealthiest shipowner in Salem in 1770, but he could number among his relatives not only merchants and shipowners but saddlers, shoemakers, coopers, farmers, and active mariners of all ranks. Kin relationships could be poisonous, but they were also tight, and in Salem they frequently cut across class lines and often served to complicate the operation of class power. When shipowners selected their masters, when masters chose their crews, and when master and crew slipped over the horizon on their voyages abroad, they carried with them an inheritance of obligations, resentments, family secrets, and fond memories that could well cut against the grain of economic exigency, and masters and men alike knew well that whatever they did to one another away would soon be known at home.

Even more important than kin in shaping the operation of this labor system was locality. In a town where a merchant like Miles Ward could count sixty-eight householders with thirty-three surnames to whom he was closely related, people must have believed they were at least distantly related to more or less everyone. Most voyages out of Salem were not socially cosmopolitan events, and given the preference accorded to local men on the ladder of promotion, one can understand why. Of course, this was not true in the fleets of all Atlantic seaports. Larger vessels sailing out of busier harbors tended to hire crews of greater regional, national, and ethnic diversity. Thus although 83 percent of mariners on ships that cleared London on transatlantic voyages described in depositions before the High Court of Admiralty, 1609–1733, termed London or one of its Thames-side suburbs as their place of residence, only 35 percent claimed to have been born there. Yet on shorter, more regular routes that resembled those pursued from Salem, including such massive ones as the Dutch grain trade into the Baltic Sea, local sailors predominated. It is fashionable now to speak of the Atlantic basin as a fundamentally international world, but the evidence from Salem suggests that the maritime labor market in much of that world remained deeply parochial.[54]

The principal defining feature of Salem's maritime labor market in the eighteenth century, however, was age. Local vessels were manned principally by young men who had gone to sea because in this waterfront society that is what young men did. Those who remained at sea beyond their youth into middle age, moreover, did so in the reasonable hope that they would someday acquire a ship's command—the principal marker of mastery and badge of adult competency in the seafaring world. Nowhere in colonial New England could employers depend on lifelong class dependency to generate the hands they needed, because too many men acquired elements of independence—if only as shipmasters, coasters, craftsmen, petty traders, or smallholding farmers—when they moved into middle age. Since the power of property ownership was insufficient to their demands, those in need of labor turned to other forms of compulsion (or habits of deference) to get things done. A few colonists employed indentured servants and slaves; more used a species of debt peonage; men depended upon gender; but everyone used age. The power of the old over the young could be condescending, exploitative, and even brutal, but in periods and places where a significant proportion of householders could expect to grow into some degree of economic autonomy, it got things done.

This is not to say that sailors lived in anything like a wholly open society. Within Salem proper they could see around them dozens of traders, shopkeepers, and shoremen and even a few true merchants who had once been working mariners like themselves; but nobody knew a local seaman who had ever taken a seat in Parliament, sat on the Board of Trade, or won acceptance into the Draper's Company of London. Clearly, there existed a world of wealth and privilege centered in England that they could not penetrate—the class of merchant capitalists, landed gentlemen, and government officials who benefited from property and connection and who profited most from oceanic trade. Nor is the claim here that all seaports resembled Salem in every respect. Larger cities—with greater ships, wealthier merchants, heavier labor demand, significant in-migration, higher anonymity, and more poverty—possessed class distinctions that divided mariners from their employers in a lifelong manner. In early modern London, for example, the foremast hands who offered testimony before the High Court of Admiralty were older than those who sailed out of Salem —almost certainly because it was harder there to climb out of the forecastle or set oneself up in a trade ashore.[55]

Yet most early modern sailors did not grow up in London, Bristol, or even Boston. They hailed from maritime regions that resembled Massachusetts's North Shore; they first learned the ropes in vessels that put out from towns like Salem; they spent several years crisscrossing the Atlantic; and then, like Ashley Bowen, many of them returned home when their sailing days were done. Seafaring enriched very few of them, but for most young men in the maritime societies of the age of sail, it was a customary apprenticeship for adult life.

CHAPTER FIVE

The Eighteenth Century

MARITIME SOCIETY ASHORE

MOST SAILORS WHO SHIPPED out of Salem in the colonial period spent a great deal of their time—not only at the beginning and end of their lives but even in the prime of their laboring years—not at sea but ashore. They may have earned their livings on the deep, but a host of other factors—family duties, the lure of landward employment, the pleasures of the harbor, physical infirmity and the inefficiencies of the maritime labor market—conspired to ground them in port throughout much of the year. Some of the time, these shoreside stints unfolded abroad—in the taverns, brothels, workshops, or prisons of foreign ports—but mostly they transpired at home in Salem. Mariners were undoubtedly seafaring men —possessed of a highly distinctive set of skills, a strong occupational culture, a technical language that was all but unintelligible to outsiders, and even a gait that betrayed their calling—and they were undeniably the most mobile of laborers. Their homes, however, lay ashore, and the great majority of sailors went to sea, time after time, to help support the households they left behind.

Ports differed one from another in their geographic settings, their population, the quality of their hinterlands, the trades they pursued, and the scale of the shipping they supported, and all of these factors bore on the character of the maritime society each one possessed. What set Salem apart from other Atlantic seaports during the colonial period was principally its limited size, its home-grown maritime population, and its small-vessel schooner fleet committed both to the cod fishery and the West India trade. This combination of circumstances created a labor system that was risky, even deadly, to its participants and yet full of opportunity for those lucky enough to survive, especially if they possessed local social connections. Maritime society in Salem rested, therefore, on the most earnest of lotteries.

Every large seaport in the age of sail—from London to Amsterdam to Bordeaux to Seville—possessed a waterfront neighborhood, where resident mariners made their homes and where visiting sailors could find lodging, refreshment, company, and eventually more work. Usually, these sailor-towns were warrens of narrow streets winding away from the harbor and lined with taverns, boardinghouses, tenements, little shops, and private homes—constructed of wood, frequently in disrepair, perpetually damp from their proximity to the sea, and rarely furnished with anything but the barest essentials. These were tough parts of town, where drink flowed freely and where young men cruised the streets looking for fun, trouble, or work, depending on their humor and how much coin remained in their pockets. Honest taverners, traders, and shopkeepers competed for their business, but so did a host of miscreant crimps and loan sharks, hoping to part them from their pay. The wives and mothers of mariners also mixed in with this crowd, tramping the lanes in their shopping rounds while their children swarmed under foot, dodging past the beggars, cripples, and prostitutes who also resided near the harbor. Sailortowns were long on character but short on community. Their populations were unusually transient, and even those who lived there the year-round were just as likely to have been born elsewhere. The human labyrinth of grandparents, cousins, in-laws, and other kin relations, through which most early modern people negotiated their way in life, was largely absent in this harborside world. As social settings, sailortowns were relatively pure constructions of merchant capitalism—defined less by the lineage of families who lived there than by the commodity and labor markets they sustained.[1]

Salem was an active and enthusiastic participant in the commercial expansion of the eighteenth century Atlantic basin, but it was nevertheless, in the opinion of Francis Goelet, little more than "a small sea port towne," with no glaring internal social differentials—by class or neighborhood— and it was certainly not a city large enough to support a sailortown. Alexander Hamilton in 1744 and Brissot de Warville in 1788 both described it as a "pritty place," and George Washington agreed that it was to all appearances a "neat Town." When Francisco de Miranda climbed Gallows Hill at the base of the peninsula after the Revolution, "the entire town and bay" struck him as "a beautiful view." While Salem did contain a few quite impressive houses, all of these visitors seemed more impressed by the number of "neat" and "attractive" dwellings "at a convenient distance from each other, with fine gardens back." Whereas Boston appeared to be built "Chiefly of Brick," the private and public buildings of Salem were of clapboard construction, and even the "genteel large houses" made only a pretense at permanence by having their outside wall "pland & Painted . . . in Imitation of Hewn Stone." Many local institutions catered to the shipping business and its maritime community: a number of public and private wharves, warehouses, and countinghouses, many different lofts and workshops where riggers, sailmakers, coopers, and smiths plied their trades, several active shipyards, a commercial newspaper called the *Essex Gazette,* a customshouse, a Marine Society for the mutual benefit of shipmasters, and a dozen or more taverns. For the most part, however, these were scattered throughout the town, not concentrated in any waterfront quarter. Taverns in particular are frequently associated with seafaring culture, but the licensed innholders of Salem were more likely to live around Town House Square or even in the agricultural "middle precinct," along the roads leading westward into the New England countryside, than to cluster around the North or South rivers.[2]

Salem had no sailortown principally because the entire community was a sailortown. Mariners liked to celebrate the conclusion of their voyages here as elsewhere by drinking to excess, feasting on fresh victuals, regaling their friends and families with stories from abroad, and renewing their acquaintanceships with women and girls. But for the most part, they engaged in all of these either at home or around the neighborhood. Although seafaring men tended to live in the town's eastern precincts, closer to Salem Neck and Winter Island where the fishery was based, a significant minority made their homes in the middle of town or even in its upper and western end (Map 5.1). Out of 141 taxpaying mariners found on the Salem Tax Valuation List of 1761, 28 percent lived in Ward One, 38 percent lived in Ward Two, 16 percent lived in Ward Three, and 18 percent lived in Ward Four. And even if the lower peninsula was marginally saltier in

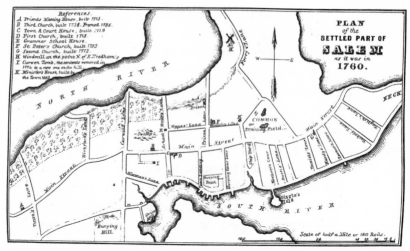

MAP 5.1 Map of Salem, 1760. Ward 1 lay mostly in the southeast corner of town, Ward 2 in the northeast, Ward 3 in the southwest, and Ward 4 in the northwest. Source: Joseph Felt, *Annals of Salem*, 2 vols. (Salem, Mass., 1845–1849), 1:282.

character than the rest of Salem, it was certainly no poorer. In fact, the mariners who dwelled in the easternmost wards tended to be among the more professionally successful, who paid higher taxes than those who dwelled uptown. Of those who lived in Wards One and Two, a full 54 percent rose to the quarterdeck at some point in their careers, whereas in Wards Three and Four only 38 percent did so; and of all mariners who lived in Ward One or Two, 55 percent ranked above the town median in taxable wealth, while of those who lived in Ward Three or Four, only 33 percent could say the same. Yet even here, the social differentiation from ward to ward was not profound. Salem was a sailortown from stem to stern.[3]

When travelers attempted to convey Salem's physical layout, they remarked, not on any pattern of neighborhood, but on the town's longitudinal character. As Dr. Hamilton bluntly put it, the seaport consisted "of one very long street running nearly east and west." Goelet concurred that "including the buildings back the towne," the town was about 2½ miles in length, with "a main street [that] runs directly t[h]rough." When Francisco de Miranda "took a walk through the town" as late as 1784, he still meant along the "principal street a mile and a half long." This main street (today's Essex Street) not only served as Salem's principal thoroughfare; it also provided the basic structural referent for the town's social geography. Indeed, when Benjamin Pickman decided in 1793 to write a history of Salem, he began by taking his readers on a stroll, house by house, down one side of the street and up the other, listing off all the "most ancient and respectable families" who lived there. When he had finished, he led them on a short detour up a single cross street where the courthouse was located, and then, seemingly exhausted, abandoned them back on Essex Street again near Town House Square.[4]

As far as Pickman was concerned—and as Hamilton, Goelet, and Miranda also sensed—Essex Street was the spine of Salem society. The physical work that sustained the town may have been conducted elsewhere— mostly along the waterfront, where goods were loaded, unloaded, and warehoused, where vessels were constructed and repaired, and where fish was dried—but it was on Essex Street that credit was obtained, justice dispensed, and the issues of local politics and administration decided. The homes that lined the street were more "elegant and grand" than others around town, and their occupants were commonly assessed during the eighteenth century for property worth ten, twenty, or thirty times the town's average. This was particularly true of the "mansion houses" constructed by the Ornes, Pickmans, Brownes, and Cabots along the part of Essex Street that stretched a couple of hundred yards either side of Town House Square, but even down closer to the Commons on the way to Salem Neck there lived a good number of prosperous shipmasters with sizable commercial interests.[5]

Yet if power was dispensed throughout Salem from a spine defined by this main street, access to that power by that very fact lay within easy walking distance of every other inhabitant. During the colonial period, the town's wealthiest families never hived themselves off geographically; indeed, they exercised much of their influence through social connections to those who lived nearby, on the lanes that ran from Essex Street down to the North and South rivers. Here the majority of Salem's working families lived. Their houses were seldom aligned in rows but rather set as close to or far from the public way as the original builder had seen fit and oriented in whatever direction he had wished. Each dwelling had a yard and garden; some had sheds, shops, or lean-tos attached, and a few even had barns. Many, probably most, of these houses were partitioned vertically and horizontally into halves, thirds, and even quarters, co-owned by several people. When the mariner Thomas Mascoll died in 1722, for example, the house he had built was divided into an easterly and westerly end among two of his sons—John, Jr., and Joseph. The easterly end later passed through several hands—from John to another mariner, Samuel Webb, to a third mariner, William Crispin, and finally to a ropemaker, David Hilliard. Meanwhile, Joseph sold his westerly end to a cordwainer named Zachariah Curtis, and upon his death, this half of the building was subdivided yet again between his son, Ebeneezer, and a ropemaker, Clifford Crowninshield. Portions of some houses were rented out to tenants, but for the most part, even along these byways, Salem remained a town of homeowners to the end of the eighteenth century.[6]

The social power that drove this maritime economy found its geographic expression in a residential pattern that emphasized chains of personal dependency far more than the sharp distinctions of class. Samuel Eliot Morison once wrote that "seaboard Massachusetts has never known such a thing as a social democracy," and Salem certainly fit this generalization. But power and inequality can assume different forms, and the degree of exclusivity and social distance that class implies simply did not exist inside this eighteenth-century town. And this matters to the social history of seafaring, for although Salem differed from London, Amsterdam, Seville, and the other large and more sharply stratified ports of the Atlantic basin whose vessels dominated the shipping lanes of that day, it resembled scores of maritime towns on both sides of the ocean, where the seafarers whose labors supported the commercial empire of the English Atlantic had grown up.[7]

How was it that in small seaports such as Salem seafaring formed so predictable a stage in the process of growing up? The manner in which young men first encountered the tug of seafaring life is now very difficult to recapture. The reality of childhood—not as observed or remembered by adults but as encountered by children themselves—is one of the history's shadowy corners. Boys and girls short of working age rarely if ever recorded their experiences; their activities seldom attracted the notice of business or the law; and few adults who tried to memorialize their upbringings spent more than a few pages at most upon their early years. Yet the character of childhood matters here, for in order to argue that seafaring came easily to young men who grew up in maritime societies, one must at least speculate about how their experiences in and around town during childhood might have predisposed them to regard work upon the ocean as something normal. In order to do this, we will have to cast our net widely around the North Atlantic for shreds of evidence that bear on the problem and employ a disciplined imagination to try to reconstruct a plausible picture of what a mariner's childhood in colonial Salem may have been like.

The sizable genre of nineteenth-century seafaring memoirs that has so thoroughly shaped our understanding of what seafaring meant in the American past describes experiences undertaken not by teenage lads but by young adults for whom the decision to go to sea was a matter of consciously considered choice. These memorialists believed that when they shipped themselves on merchant voyages or whaling cruises they were entering a different culture, and as writers they wanted to convey to the reading public an understanding of a maritime world that seemed to them decidedly exotic. They recognized their own decisions to follow the sea if only for a season as extraordinary, particularly in light of all the other employment alternatives that an expanding and industrializing America could offer them on land, and thus virtually all of them began with a justification —almost an apology—for why they went to sea at all. "I deem it but fair," wrote Ross Browne, a newspaperman's son bound whaling in 1842, "that the reader should know the circumstances under which I commenced my career of adventure." The voluminous genre of nineteenth-century sea narratives is rife with protestations of this kind. After all, those in poverty could have gone into the mills; those after adventure could have gone west; those in search of spiritual enrichment could have sought it within the various moral reform movements of the day. As individuals who chose the sea instead and discovered there things wonderful and terrible, these nautical narrators felt compelled to explain themselves and what it was they had found.[8]

Within the maritime societies of early modern times, however, going to sea was not a matter of individual choice as much as a local expectation. In ocean-fronting communities such as Salem, young men grew up in the company of older youths who regularly shipped themselves abroad, and it was only normal to follow in their wake. Ashley Bowen of Marblehead decided to seek out his first berth as an eleven-year-old when he made the acquaintance of a group of young sailors who had come to study navigation with his father. Jack Cremer was the son of a merchant shipmaster who grew up in Plymouth on the Devon coast and went to sea as a ship's boy about the age of eight at the urging of his uncle, a captain in the Royal Navy. Samuel Kelly of St. Ives, Cornwall, "was removed from school" to go to sea at the age of twelve by his seafaring father. Edward Coxere was raised in Dover on the English Channel, and although his parents tried to place him at the age of fourteen as an apprentice to a wine cooper, he quit after a week. "Not settling my mind to a trade," he wrote, "my lot fell to the sea." Gorham Low of Gloucester, Massachusetts, never once doubted as a child what lay in store for him. "As my father and all my brothers were sailors," he wrote, "I looked forward to the sea very naturally as my future home, always counting the years that must elapse before I would be old enough to commence a sea life." Likewise, Edward Beck found that "the kind of intimacy . . . with vessels" he had formed as a boy growing up beside the English Channel, simply on the basis of his "observations of the way others acted," enabled him to learn his duty swiftly. "In a boat," he wrote, "I was perfectly at home."[9]

Hector St. John de Crèvecoeur, though no seaman, spent some time in the whaling port of Nantucket, Massachusetts, where, he claimed, children grew accustomed to the sea from birth. "The roaring of its waves," they could make out as soon as they could listen, "and by early plunging" in the ocean, boys gained "that boldness, that presence of mind, and dexterity which make them ever after such expert seamen." As children, they heard their fathers "recount the adventures of their youth, their combats with the whales, and these recitals imprint[ed] on their opening minds an early curiosity and taste for the same life." Nantucket may have been a little unusual in that it was entirely surrounded by water, and there the ocean afforded almost the only living available, but even in Salem with the whole of eastern New England as its accessible hinterland, young men regarded seafaring as the employment of choice.[10]

Not every sailor of the day was bred to the sea in this manner. Edward Barlow was born a good distance from the ocean on a farm in Prestwich, England, and was so green when he first arrived on the Thames in London at the age of thirteen that he could not recognize the "things upon the water with long poles standing up in them" for ships, nor did he know that the sea was salt. Two years spent working in his uncle's tavern by the river in Southwark, however, gave him a rapid introduction to seafaring society and to the lure of distant parts. Sometimes while tramping the waterfront on his uncle's business, he later recalled, "I would stand where I could see the river for half an hour to see the ships and boats sail along, taking great pleasure therein." Barlow was the epitome of the adventure-loving youth. Although it was the poverty of his own family that originally forced him to seek employment outside the home, it was his deep-seated "mind to hear our neighbours and other people tell of their travels and of strange things in other countries" that drew him to spend his working life on the high seas. Repeatedly in his memoirs he questioned whether a sailor's life was worth it and wondered if he "had better to have taken any other employment upon me than have come to sea," and at such times he could only answer that his preoccupation with "strange countries and fashions . . . [had] made me bear these extremities with the more patience."[11]

Jacob Nagle of Pennsylvania came to the sea by an equally unconventional route. Born in the small agricultural market town of Reading, where his father had been a blacksmith, Jacob left home in 1777 as a teenager, not to venture overseas but to join Washington's army in the campaign against the British army under General William Howe. He returned home to avoid spending the winter at Valley Forge, but a year or so later his family moved to Philadelphia, where his father had opened a waterfront tavern, and perhaps as a consequence of the company he began to keep around that establishment, Nagle volunteered at the age of eighteen on a six-week cruise on board the U.S. Navy sloop *Saratoga*. As to his precise motive, Nagle said only: "I then inclined for the see."[12]

Barlow and Nagle were nevertheless exceptional. The great majority of sailors around the Anglo-American world—like Bowen, Cremer, Kelly, Coxere, and Low—grew up in seaside towns. Out of 112 mariners who gave depositions before the High Court of Admiralty in London between 1609 and 1733 and recorded their places of birth, only 13 percent were born in the countryside at any distance from salt water. A full 31 percent were from London itself—chiefly the Thames-side districts of Wapping and Stepney—and the remaining 56 percent hailed from dozens of coastal towns and villages elsewhere in Britain, on the European continent, or in the American colonies. These men were marginally older than their counterparts in Salem, but this was principally because the High Court of Admiralty sat in London—the port of call to which all Anglo-American sea lanes tended—and it heard sailors who had already left home and advanced far enough in their careers to find themselves there. Salem mariners were a few years younger principally because most of them were still living at home. Thus the pattern by which mariners such as Cremer, Coxere, and Kelly launched their careers on the deep from provincial seaports as teenage boys was probably the experience of most Anglo-American sailors of the seventeenth and eighteenth centuries. They went to sea in their early to middle teens to learn how to support themselves while relieving their family at home in what must have seemed a fairly conventional move—the maritime equivalent of service in husbandry.[13]

They could, of course, have chosen other lines of work. Samuel Kelly never mentioned any other possibilities, and Gorham Low clearly felt predestined to the sea, but had the fates unwound differently, the rest of them might well have ended up in another occupation. In the same year that Ashley Bowen became a ship's boy, his half-brother, Nathaniel, was bound out to a house carpenter. Edward Barlow at different times considered following his uncle into innkeeping, emigrating as an indentured servant to Virginia, or becoming a waterman on the Thames. Jack Cremer prefaced his seafaring career with two stabs at landward trades—cooperage and ship carpentry. Edward Coxere's parents would clearly have preferred that he stay on shore, badgering him with "What trade now?" even after he returned from his first voyage abroad. And yet none of these mariner-journalists, except Barlow the farmboy, who had truly cut his connections to home, ever felt that there was anything abnormal in choosing the sea, and they spilled no ink in justifying themselves. Having reached the age where it was customary to select a calling, they simply picked the one that in Marblehead, Gloucester, Plymouth, Dover, or St. Ives seemed the most obvious choice.[14]

The seafaring life, therefore, was something they first encountered as little more than children, and what they remembered of these early voyages in later life was the experience of being youths at sea. For one thing, like all young dependents in the charge of strangers, they were deeply worried about the issue of treatment. Decades later some of them still shuddered at the hard usage they had endured on board as children, and they remembered fondly those adults who had tried to protect them from it. Samuel Kelly recalled that as a twelve-year-old ship's boy entering the West Indian packet service, he had at his father's suggestion taken no wages at first, "in order to induce the captain to treat me well." In spite of this, however, he was abused by some of the officers on board. During several weeks of seasickness, he had to do without a hammock, and after a drunken boatswain pilfered his mattress, he "slept or rather lay about the deck, in holes and corners, being unable to eat or scarcely crawl, my chest of clothes was thrown down the main hatchway, having no one to look after it, and for want of exertion, by the sickness I became dirty and literally a neglected cast-away." At length, however, the sailing-master, Sampson Hall, took an interest in young Samuel, ordered a hammock to be slung for him, and made sure that he was washed and cleaned. Hall soon permitted the boy to hold the ship's quadrant while waiting for the sun to pass the meridian so that he might learn to take its altitude. All in all, though the sailing-master was a strict disciplinarian, Kelly was "happy to be taken some notice of." The chronically harsh treatment that he and other boys received in his early years at sea was a continual refrain in Kelly's memoirs.[15]

Gorham Low recalled plainly that on his first voyage across the Atlantic as a fifteen-year-old under the command of his brother, Capt. David Low, he had been ordered up to the main topgallant yard to furl a sail during a hard breeze. When the boy hesitated, his brother led the way up the rigging to show him how. "When we got up there it looked very wild to me," Gorham recalled, "for we were carrying a great press of canvas sail and the ship was well down on her side." When the foot of the sail hit him on the back, he grabbed onto the yard with both hands to keep from falling, but his brother urged him to the task and calmly hauled the sail in, advising, " 'One hand for yourself and the other for the owners.' " When they returned to the deck, the rest of the crew agreed that the captain had put his little brother to a test too severe for one his age, but Gorham Low was more impressed that a shipmaster had climbed up with him into the rigging at all. As he said, "It was not very common for a captain to go aloft at such a time to show a boy how to furl a sail, and we were watched from the deck very closely." As an issue of treatment, this was obviously a special case; few men served under their brothers. But Edward Coxere, Ashley Bowen, and Jack Cremer also commented frequently on the relative kindness and severity of the different masters under whom they served in their early years—a habit which faded as they grew older.[16]

As youngsters and the most powerless people on board, these novice sailors took particular delight in the mischief they played on their elders and the scrapes they got into. Many of Jack Cremer's memories of his first months on board ship were of all the "pranks we naturly took to on board those woodin worlds": stringing up hammocks so that they would fall when slept in; tying ropes across the hatchway to topple drunken sailors as they walked by in the dark; and hauling a dead body into the path of the ship's doctor to trip him up. Gorham Low's strongest memory of his first visit to St. Petersburg was of the day when the ship's cook, Jack Hogan, "believed by all the crew to have been a pirate," filched a pair of oars out of a Russian revenue boat they passed, provoking the police to take after them in another craft:

> Even now I can see the streak of white foam curling around the bows of the Russian boat, as the herculean rower bent to his oars in pursuit of us, and our degenerate cook pulling for dear life to escape. I was not a calm spectator of that scene, for I had heard of the prisons of Siberia and thought we should be sent there. I could do nothing but sit still and watch the progress of the race. At first I had a little hope, but I soon saw that the better boat of the Russians was gaining on us, and just as he was about to board us on the quarter, and I have no doubt sink us, for our boat was a mere cockle shell, Hogan brought his oar down on the head of the Russian with a force sufficient to have felled an ox. Before he had recovered his senses we were safe in the cook house.

Ruses to escape impressment—a deeply serious business but often conducted with true ingenuity—provided another common childhood memory. Edward Coxere once borrowed a suit of clothes from the owner of an alehouse in London and dressed up as a Billingsgate merchant in order to slip past the press and recover a venture he had left on board his ship. Jack Cremer similarly paid a boatman 7s. 6d for his passage from Gravesend to London "in a Watterman's boy's dres to proteckt me." Ashley Bowen recalled as a ship's boy stuffing his older crewmates into special cabinets called press-beds in the bulkhead of the captain's cabin. Although dodging the press was more than a game, there can be no doubt that all these youths relished their success in hoodwinking their elders.[17]

One of the foremost matters in any young sailor's mind, however, was the possibility of promotion. The life of a foremast hand was too hard and the rewards too meager for any young man willingly to envision it as his lot forever. Not everyone would be fortunate enough to succeed on the ladder of advancement—even as far as boatswain or gunner—but it was plain to see, as Edward Barlow put it, that a common seaman "past forty years of age . . . earns his living with more pain and sorrow than he that endures a hard imprisonment," and most youngsters did not plan to end up in that boat. Promotion itself rarely occurred in one's teens, but the eagerness with which young sailors attempted to pick up tools that might assist them on their way is plainly evident in the memoirs they penned in later years. "Whenever I had an opportunity," wrote Gorham Low, "I used to try to dig into the mysteries of navigation," though his progress was hindered by the enforced darkness of the forecastle. "The only place where we could see," he recalled, "was directly under the scuttle, and there, every now and then, would come a wave and wet the book and writing all over." Samuel Kelly took every occasion to obtain instruction in navigation and learn about the business of the different ports he visited. Jack Cremer studied arithmetic and Latin while a ship's boy in the navy and boasted that by his mid-teens, he had "lernt Estronomy and all parts of Sailing." Ashley Bowen's master, Peter Hall, never taught him any of these things; this, and the brutal treatment Hall dished out, were the principal reasons why Ashley decided to "try the title" of his apprenticeship and run away. Edward Coxere took pride in his languages—as a youth he learned French, Dutch, and Spanish—and he found that in foreign countries, his talents aided the business of the ship and attracted the favor of his master.[18]

Indeed, it is plain that the path of promotion—its barriers as well as the ways they might be overcome or the reasons they might not—was one of the main themes running through all of these early modern sea-faring narratives. It could well be argued that officers' posts were merely pipe dreams for most of these boys, except that every one of them—Barlow, Cremer, Coxere, Bowen, Low, Nagle, and Kelly—succeeded to the command of one vessel or another at least once in his career. Of course, these particular mariners were unusually literate and sufficiently proud of their accomplishments to make a record of them; the less educated and less fortunate may have been unable or unwilling to set their personal histories on paper. Certainly few mariners rose to become masters of East Indiamen or any of the larger traders that plied the transatlantic routes between London and the colonies. But as the case of Salem illustrates, there were plenty of smaller vessels out of lesser ports that needed experienced men to serve on the quarterdeck, and if these positions carried less prestige, they were masterships nonetheless—a legitimate aspiration for any young sailor.[19]

Even more universal, however, must have been the simple instinct for survival. All maritime journalists had by definition lived to tell their tales, and perhaps their memoirs simply presumed their survival, but one wonders how exactly sailors confronted futures in which, as they must have known, the odds of dying young were strong. Of course, they remembered any number of close shaves—shipwrecks, accidents aloft, bouts of disease, and so forth—but perhaps in the spirit of "overstrained manliness" remarked on by Richard Henry Dana, Jr., in the nineteenth century, they said little about how such near escapes affected their spirits. Edward Barlow presented his readers with a catalogue of dangers that sailors regularly faced—from leaky hulls to galley fires to gunpowder detonations—any of which might well be enough to prompt a young man to seek out another calling. He remembered storms "when the ship rolled and tumbled as though some great millstone were rolling up one hill and down another," and when summoned aloft, "half awake and half asleep with one shoe on and the other off," one could see "nothing but air above us and water beneath us, and that so raging as though every wave would make a grave for us." Still, the purpose of relating these perils was only to remind landsmen of how lucky they were, not to imply that in his mind they could not be borne. Ashley Bowen recalled lying as a teenager in a fever-ridden prison in St. Domingue where "one died of a day every day till we left the place," and where he was twice given up for dead himself. Even after his release, he was too sick for several months to get a voyage home, and yet once home it was only "but a little while" before he shipped himself back to the Caribbean again. It is hard to imagine that at some point or other in their youths, Barlow, Bowen, and others did not wonder whether these risks were really worth running, but if they ever felt this way, they seem never to have dwelled on it in public. One can only guess that in maritime society such doubts simply could not be expressed aloud. In a world where it was customary to go to sea, such fears were ultimately inadmissible.[19]

Custom is never constructed out of thin air, and if seafaring became a normal part of life in colonial Salem, it did so for basic, material reasons. It is a principle of maritime law that "freight is the mother of wages," and one could as easily claim that freight was the mother of the entire Salem economy.[20] Most people in this seaport town lived off either the profits of the shipping industry and foreign trade, their shares in the fishing industry that furnished Salem's principal commodity, the wages earned in voyaging overseas, or the business of constructing, outfitting, and maintaining the vessels that composed the local fleet. Salem was a commercial town, and the families that dwelled there supported themselves by dealing continuously within this commercial, urban economy. How exactly did they manage this? The rural economy of colonial New England is fairly transparent to the historian's eye because it depended so heavily on land, livestock, and farm equipment, all of which were regularly assessed and inventoried in a way that makes it possible to infer the types of work activity that men and women pursued. In urban settings, however, most working people of both sexes owned much less productive equipment, and as a consequence it is much harder to reconstruct with authority just how their household economies operated. Some of the work that men performed is described in court and business documents, but the tasks that fell to women, who were generally dependents and legally invisible, left only the faintest traces in the historical record of the day.

Mariners' households are particularly opaque. Paid in cash, sailors could spend their money wherever they pleased and they did not have to run up long tabs that local merchants or tradesmen recorded in account books. Consequently, we can only surmise how they, their wives, or their mothers and fathers employed this money to prosecute the domestic economy at home.[21] Shipmasters constitute a partial exception to this rule in that they did maintain large credit accounts with the managing owners of the vessels they commanded. Yet these accounts deal overwhelmingly with the business of voyages; they tell us little about shipmasters' own households. In the case of many urban trades—shoemaking, baking, weaving, and innkeeping, for example—one can imagine how entire households structured power and responsibility, setting husbands over wives and parents over children and servants to get things done inside what were essentially family businesses. Insofar as sailors were primarily wage laborers, however, they did not have a business—or at least not one in which women and children could regularly assist. Obviously, maritime families coordinated their efforts to sustain themselves as households, but exactly how did they manage to do so? More particularly, how did the absence of so many males for so much of the year in such risky endeavors affect the functioning of those households on shore?

Most obviously, it meant that the business of managing the domestic economy was much more thoroughly the responsibility of women. In addition to the normal female duties of cooking, sewing, washing, housecleaning, gardening, caring for the ill, supervising young children, and teaching one's daughters every one of these skills, a mariner's wife had to take on occasional business that a husband at home would normally have assumed. Jobs around the house that were customarily a man's responsibility would fall to her instead. If an autumn gale tore the shingles off the roof while her husband was off at sea, for example, she would have to put the house to rights herself or mobilize her own male relations to do so. From time to time, she might have to stand in for her husband to represent the family in dealings with neighbors around town. Thus in 1758, when her husband, Benjamin, was away in the Mediterranean, Mary Bates took it upon herself to pay off three debts ranging from 34s. to 46s. to Benjamin Cook, Edward Lester, and Richard Batton, all seafaring men. In addition, mariners' wives took some of the responsibility for marketing the ventures that their husbands carried home from overseas. Mary Coxere of Dover, England, sold the cloth her husband, Edward, brought home from abroad, and according to him, she, "having good friends, with her own industry kept me out of debt." This line of business involved peddling wares for cash in a manner that never needed recording, but it undoubtedly took place in Salem as well. Once in a long while, a mariner's wife might also intervene directly in her absent husband's maritime business, sometimes at his request. In 1698, for example, shipmaster John Beal sent a sight draft for £41 sterling, payable on presentation, home to his wife, Martha, with instructions to cash it immediately. When she attempted to do so, Joseph Tyler, who had signed the draft, refused to see her, even after a second attempt when she had taken two prominent male neighbors with her as witnesses. Finally, on behalf of her husband, she was forced to bring a suit against Tyler to cash the instrument.[22]

Seaport wives assumed, therefore, a degree of economic independence that struck contemporaries as unusual. Eleven years into his third marriage, Ashley Bowen copied down into his journal:

> If husbands e'er hope to live peaceable lives
> They must reckon themselves give
> The helm to their
> Wives
> For the evener we go Boys the better
> We sail
> And on ship-board the helm is
> Still ruled by the tail

Families acquire habits, and in a world where men's presence could not be counted upon, women grew accustomed to running a larger portion of household business.[23]

The role of the "deputy husband," however, should not be exaggerated. Few sailors spent more than half a year at a time overseas; instead, they often passed several months tarrying at home, repairing the property, chopping firewood for the winter, doing odd jobs for cash, and settling business matters around town before setting out again. Although merchant's accounts, mixing household purchases with wages and ventures, were active throughout the year, most by far of the purely commercial and legal business spanned the weeks or months that the mariner himself spent in port. Thus William Abbott, a shipmaster from Beverly who commanded vessels for Richard Derby between 1761 and 1764, transacted business in Derby's books during his time ashore amounting to about £180; his wife closed the account in 1768 by giving the merchant a note for a little more than £4. Scattered throughout almost every mariner's account, one can find mention of a "note from his wife" or cash "p^d his wife," but these are dwarfed in value by the commercial business that seafaring men insisted on conducting themselves.[24]

The business for which mariners' wives did take primary responsibility was the business of the household, which in good times was more than enough to keep them occupied. Much of it occurred entirely within the female economy, involving the exchange of personal services and provisions—child care for spare clothing for kitchen utensils for garden vegetables, and so forth—between women in a network of exchange where debts were surely monitored, if seldom recorded. Yet much of it also transpired with the public economy of Salem, where women negotiated directly with men. With a few pennies, a mother could send her daughter down to Town House Square to fetch a loaf of bread from a baker's stall; for sixpence she could purchase enough fresh mackerel from a peddler for dinner; and a couple of shillings would buy enough shalloon at a local shop to line a coat. Mariners spent some of their pay themselves while ashore, but the rest they left behind for their wives and mothers to disburse among the family as they saw fit.[25]

Since merchant seafarers and their families dealt mainly in cash, their spending habits left few traces in the historical record. Those who also fished, however, did keep running credit accounts with merchants, and the latter's books describe in some detail the way in which they and their wives spent these earnings—habits which can probably stand for those of mariners' families in general. Samuel Carrel commanded several schooners both on fishing expeditions to Nova Scotia and on trading voyages to the Chesapeake over a long career that lasted from about 1740 to 1770, and during this period, he took most of his pay in shop goods at the store belonging to the vessels' owner, Miles Ward. Like most mariners, he took responsibility for his own business affairs, purchasing fishing gear, buying barrels and hogsheads of cider and fish to sell in Virginia, and paying off the sizable debts that the Carrel family had run up around Salem. While Samuel was away, however, his wife, Abigail, shopped at Ward's store regularly for an even wider variety of goods: woolen cloth and pieces of silk; indigo to dye them with; tape and thread to tailor clothing; foodstuffs such as flour, salt meat, butter, sugar, cheese, chocolate, and ginger with which to cook; and cordwood to feed the hearth. None of these was a finished product; all required considerable labor on Abigail's part to render them useful. Indeed, it is quite possible that the value she added to the items she purchased in Ward's store amounted to more than their original cost. Women were responsible for much of the manufacture that took place in early America—in the towns as in the countryside—and Salem was no exception.[26]

Where seaport housewives such as Abigail Carrel differed from their rural counterparts was in their wholesale dependence on the commercial economy in which their husbands earned their wages and sold their ventures. Should a farmer fall ill or the price of corn drop, should a horse die or a servant run away, women in rural New England would certainly encounter rough sledding. But as long as some property remained in family hands, a farmwife could step into the breach—shift farm strategy about, work longer hours, go into the fields herself, or hire additional help. The garden, the chickens, the dairy, the barn, the orchard, the woodlot, and the fields remained, and with ingenuity and much hard work, the short-falls occasioned by these troubles could be accommodated. A sailor's wife had fewer options. When French privateers bottled the Salem fleet up in port, when the price of fish sank, or when seafaring husbands and sons sickened and could not work, the household was damaged twice over. Not only did the cash income for direct consumer purchases evaporate, but the household manufacture based on raw materials procured with that income became impossible as well. Maritime households could do well enough in flush times, but as wholly commercial operations, they were terribly vulnerable to misfortune.

The true measure of this vulnerability was revealed when a sailor-husband died at sea. Widowhood everywhere brought with it much suffering, but it was a particular problem in the maritime community, not the least be-cause the mortality of New England mariners was so high. The incidence of widowhood is hard to measure, because mortality records are incomplete, but available sources show that marriages of colonial Salem shipmasters terminated in the death of the mariner-husband 69 percent of the time and that first marriages were twice as likely to terminate in the death of the husband as in the death of a wife. The proportion of widows within the population of eighteenth-century Salem, moreover, was about double that of the agricultural towns surrounding it. A systematic sample drawn from the 1771 tax valuation lists shows that 7.5 percent of taxpayers in Salem but only 4.8 percent of taxpayers in the rural towns of Methuen, Wenham, Middleton, Ipswich, Lynn, Salisbury, and Rowley were women. A sample of households from the 1790 census reveals that in Salem a full 25 percent were headed by single women, whereas in the rural towns of Bradford, Haverhill, Ipswich, Wenham, Lynn, Methuen, Rowley, and Topsfield, only 12 percent of households fell into this category. While it is true that one-half of sailors' marriages lasted a quarter-century or more, suggesting that couples could reasonably hope their match to survive most of their child-raising years, the other half did not, and when it was the husband who died, which happened in 71 percent of examined cases from 1690 to 1775, a series of financial calamities commonly ensued.[27]

The first of these could be the probate process itself. It was customary in preindustrial times, across New England and probably throughout the Anglo-American world, for neighbors to allow book debts to stand for long periods of time without the creditor collecting interest or even insisting too vigorously on the debts being collected at all. There were exceptional periods, when an economic downturn or an interval of rapid inflation could prompt tighter lending policies and more frequent lawsuits, but by modern standards, the credit practices of colonial times were remarkably lenient. The one occasion in a man's life when it was considered appropriate to demand final reckonings was, ironically, when he died. The long, detailed accounts that accompany probate records are ample testimony to this. Creditors who had trusted the deceased with considerable obligations for years now arrived with statements in hand to demand payment, and in turn the administrators presented bills of their own to collect what was owed to the estate. In itself, this might not be a bad thing; if a dead mariner had been a net creditor, his widow would benefit from the collection. When Lewis Hunt was lost at sea in 1713, for example, about 40 percent of his estate lay in financial notes, which his wife, Elizabeth, proceeded to collect. If a mariner was seriously indebted or even insolvent, however, the deluge of creditors could doom his wife and children to indigence. A widow obtained some protection in this process, as she was guaranteed by law one-third of her husband's personal estate forever and one-third of his real estate during her lifetime, no matter how high the pile of debts against him might be, but against hungry creditors this type of protection was far less effective than that of a living husband. Elizabeth Elkins, the wife of an exceptionally promising young shipmaster in Richard Derby's employ, found herself widowed six years into their marriage in 1764. When the estate of her husband, Thomas, was inventoried, it included a comfortably furnished house as well as a bit of farmland and a few livestock worth altogether about £325 sterling—quite an achievement for a young man of twenty-six years. Even so, it proved insufficient to meet the demands of his creditors. Elizabeth received her widow's portion of something over £100, but it must have seemed cold comfort as she watched her home and most of its contents being auctioned off to pay her late husband's debts. Indeed, the protection she had enjoyed as Elizabeth Elkins —legally dependent on her husband but free in the enjoyment of her household possessions—must have seemed markedly preferable.[28]

A greater challenge than passing through probate, however, was that of survival in its aftermath. For a woman under thirty-five—youthful, attractive, strong, and capable of bearing children—the obvious solution was remarriage, and 56 percent of young widows are known to have succeeded in this, usually after several difficult years. Some of them chose mariners for their second husbands, but others did not—perhaps not as much out of preference as because the pool of men from whom they might have selected a spouse now included a good number of somewhat older men who had retired from the sea to pursue other trades on shore. Out of sixteen second husbands whose occupations could be identified, six were termed mariners, six were never termed mariners, and four combined seafaring with landward callings. Ashley Bowen's first wife, Dorothy Chadwick, married him when he was still a mariner, but his second and third wives, Mary Shaw and Hannah Graves—both young widows—wed him after he had put down roots in Marblehead and taken up ship-rigging. A study of colonial Woburn (a scant fifteen miles inland from Salem) shows that widows did not remarry easily, and at first glance, the seaport evidence would seem to suggest a happier conclusion. In reality, however, the Salem data reveal only the extraordinary mortality of young sailors—deaths that generated more young, relatively marriageable widows than would have been common in the New England countryside.[29]

Even in Salem, moreover, a significant number of young mariners' widows and the vast majority of middle-aged ones—a full 80 percent of those who lost their husbands between the ages of thirty-five and forty-nine—did not succeed in finding another mate. How they fared depended significantly on the resources they brought to widowhood. When Capt. Benjamin Pickman died in 1719 at the age of forty-eight, he left his wife, Abigail, ten years his junior, with several young children to raise but a sizable estate of £795 sterling, including two vessels, as well as a shop and warehouse, with which to manage. Abigail was the daughter of Timothy Lindall, one of Salem's more successful merchant shipowners, and following her husband's death she proved herself to be a capable businesswoman in her own right. After selling off one and probably both vessels, she concentrated her energies on running a large and well-stocked shop on Essex Street. Her shelves were filled with everything from dry goods such as stockings, coats, and fishhooks to grocery items like cheese, butter, sugar, and rum. Local fishermen ran up tabs at Abigail Pickman's store and then at the end of the season sold their fish to export merchants and asked

them to post a credit to her account on their behalf. Whether or not Widow
Pickman engaged in export ventures of her own is unclear, but she managed
the family estate well enough that Benjamin Pickman's estate never dropped
below the second decile of taxable properties in town throughout the period that it was entrusted to her care. In 1730, when her eldest son, also
Benjamin, reached his majority, she handed the business over to him and
retired from trade at the age of forty-nine. Benjamin proceeded to build
on the foundation his mother had laid, both in capital and in the business
training he had received by her side, to construct the largest family fortune
colonial Salem ever saw.[30]

Still, Abigail Pickman's story was highly unusual. The great majority
of seaport widows struggled mightily not to get ahead but simply to get
by. Out of all those living in Salem in 1771, only 4 percent possessed assessable merchandise, 3 percent owned livestock, 8 percent had money lent
out at interest, and 11 percent owned agricultural land. All told, only 17
percent were assessed for these types of productive wealth in any combination.[31] The widows of seafaring men may have been a little better situated
than other women in their position. Judging from the tax valuation list
of 1771, they were just as likely to own land or livestock, twice as likely to
possess money at interest, and five times as likely to own merchandise.
Thus Mary Ashton, Elizabeth Lee, and Elizabeth Sanders all kept shops,
Mary Eden had a fishyard, and Mary Grafton even owned some vessel tonnage. All of these propertied women had productive wealth to employ,
and one can assume that using their own wits, their children's assistance,
and the advice of family and friends, they managed well enough. One entry in a merchant's account of the 1760s, for example, catches fifty-year-
old Elizabeth Higginson in the act of purchasing two chests of Bohea tea
to stock the store she kept, while another records Anstiss Crowninshield,
now in her late sixties, arranging for the wharfage of her schooner and
the warehousing of the rice it had carried into port. But few of their widowed
neighbors practiced business on this scale. The plain truth remains that
the overwhelming majority of widows, seafarers' or otherwise, owned no
assessable property, and, indeed, were never listed on tax rolls at all.[32]

How then did these widows—those who did not inherit a schooner
or a warehouse full of codfish—support themselves and their families?
The immediate problem was that of finding a new source of cash income
to purchase the raw and semiprocessed goods that would enable the father-

less household to continue producing food, shelter, and the other amenities of life. A few women in this predicament went outside the home to earn this money. Sarah Mansfield became a "scooldame" and paid for the shalloon, garlix, camblet, and thread she purchased at Timothy Orne's store by instructing his little children. Ruth Tarrants worked by the day for Miles Ward (possibly in his fishyard) to help purchase cordwood, groceries, and her son David's fishing gear. It was a lot easier, however, for a mother to earn a living by working around home and building on the already functioning household economy she had to run anyway. Thus Mary Elkins, who had been married to Richard Derby's nephew Henry Elkins until he died in South Carolina in 1772, was able to pay for her firewood and rum as a widow by making and mending shirts. Mary Glover, widow of fisherman Joseph Glover, balanced her accounts with Timothy Orne in 1752 by boarding Benjamin Shaw, an eight-year-old lad who had just arrived from the country to ship himself as cabin boy on a voyage to Spain.[33]

Some colonial widows converted downstairs rooms into what were later termed huxter's shops or cent-shops, similar to the little store run by Hepzibah Pyncheon in Nathaniel Hawthorne's *House of Seven Gables*. Hawthorne, who had grown up in Salem in the early years of the nineteenth century, described Pyncheon's shop as a room with its own separate entrance "in the basement story of the gable fronting on the street," its floor "overstrewn with fresh blue sand." An old pair of scales sat on top of the counter; barrels of apples, flour, and Indian meal stood below; and the shelves behind were stocked with boxes of soap bars and tallow candles, a small supply of brown sugar, white beans, and split peas, as well as a few pieces of gingerbread and a tumbler of marbles. Benjamin Browne, another Salem resident who had grown up in the years after the Revolution, recalled:

> These shops were quite numerous about town at this period.
> They were generally kept by women, who thus eked out a
> support for the families dependent on them. They were in the
> houses where the proprietors lived. There would be a small
> room back of the shop, and in this, when no customer was in,
> she would be found knitting or entertaining her friends, and
> in this room she and her family would take their repasts. The
> door of the shop would be generally closed, and a bell attached

to it would give notice of the entrance of a customer, and from this we boys called them "ching-a-ling shops." In them might be found, in a small way, many articles needed for family use. They were eminently retail shops, and in some of them they would split a cracker, cut a candle, or halve a row of pins. Notwithstanding the variety of articles kept, the whole stock of some of them might be stowed into a bushel basket.

Although there is no documentary evidence of such establishments operating before the Revolution, eighteenth-century Salem homes often had lean-tos attached to the rear with a separate entrance, which may well have served as huxter's shops, and there is no reason why single women would not have operated them in colonial times.[34]

The most common and lucrative business in which the widows of Salem mariners engaged was the purveying of strong drink. That widows kept taverns in their own homes and retailed beer, wine, and liquor "out of doors" as well, under public license and often as a form of poor relief, was true throughout early America. Although the largest and most profitable public houses were usually owned and operated by men, widows obtained a sizable minority of licenses, especially as retailers. The best-known tavern in Salem—the Blue Anchor in Town House Square—was owned and operated for decades by the widow Margaret Pratt and later by her daughter Hannah. Sarah Adams, as the wife and then widow of shipmaster Jonas Adams, ran a licensed tavern where she sold rum that she had distilled for her on credit, hundreds of gallons at a time, by Richard Derby. Most widows who obtained liquor licenses, however, operated on a modest scale—often too small to be noticed by the town's assessors—either serving meals along with liquid refreshment in a "cakes and ale shop," or dealing out rum by the gallon over the counters of their cent-shops. With access to sufficient credit, they might have been able to compete with larger establishments, but women without property in colonial America found that credit in substantial amounts was nearly impossible to obtain.[35]

Tax lists imply that the great majority of Salem widows—something close to 80 percent—possessed no real estate or any productive assets, and without property or credit, they never entered the business world in any measurable way. For these women, widowhood meant moving into rented rooms or retreating into the homes of other family members—

parents or children—to become once again dependent on other men. Some were old enough to have essentially retired, but others had families to support and the talent and energy to do so, if they could gain access to some sort of a cash income to allow them to purchase the cloth, firewood, barreled foodstuffs, and other household inputs they needed to employ themselves productively. To this end, a great many widows poor in property sent their young sons to sea. Indeed, boys who had lost their fathers accounted for a full 63 percent of all teenage mariners, a proportion high enough to suggest that seafaring was the principal—almost the only— employment for the sons of single women in Salem.[36] The account books of the period are peppered throughout with the accounts of those whose chief source of income was the pay that their teenage sons received from fishing and merchant voyages. The widow Goutier survived the death of her husband, Lewis, by moving in to a neighbor's house as a boarder and dispatching her son Thomas to sea in the employ of Miles Ward to help pay the rent and provide her with credit at Ward's store. Mercy Beadle supported herself in part after her husband died by selling her house and retailing rum across the counter in the rooms she rented afterward; but the credit she needed to purchase spirits from merchant Richard Derby was underwritten by the wages her son earned on Derby vessels abroad. And account books only touch on the edge of this phenomenon, since any widow whose son received payment in cash, as most sailors did, would have spent the money around town as she saw necessary without leaving a paper trail that might document her business.[37]

The experience of Salem widows bears close examination in part because the sheer number of single mothers in need of cash and credit to power their own domestic affairs was a significant factor in Salem's maritime labor market, driving dozens of Salem youths into seafaring employment every year. Many of these young men must have quit the sea for landward trades when they reached the age of majority, but under their mothers' charge as teenage boys, they seem to have had no other choice than to go to sea. And this was not simply a problem for individual households. A great many extended families could count one or more widows within their ranks—and many of these single women did not possess sons of their own to finance them. The burden of supporting them, not in idleness but in order that they might employ themselves productively, fell collectively on the entire clan. A maritime society in which one-quarter of working-age women were widowed and potentially underemployed had to extend itself to solve this social problem, and it did so by driving teenage boys to sea.

On the deepest level, however, the case of widows simply illustrates in a particularly stark manner the way in which most households in this maritime economy depended to a significant degree on the cash and credit generated by seafaring wages and ventures to function. The management of these financial resources lay largely within the female province and involved less shopping for items of direct consumption than for the purchase of raw and semiprocessed materials that female family members would then work up into edible, wearable, and otherwise usable goods. But it was the income earned in profits and wages and rooted in freight that allowed them to do so in the first place.

If the abundance of widows placed real economic pressure on the households of colonial Salem, these difficulties were redoubled by the endemic underemployment of older men returned from the sea. There were no formal retirement parties in the eighteenth century. Sailors left off voyaging, just as landsmen shifted from one calling to another or withdrew from physical work altogether, one step at a time, by as many separate paths as there were people to walk them. Some sailors, as we have seen, discovered a lack of aptitude or distaste for seafaring and returned to live ashore, marry, and take up another trade sometime in their twenties. Yet others pursued maritime careers single-mindedly into their forties and early fifties before rheumatic joints and diminishing wanderlust moved them finally to cast their anchors at home. These men, who had spent their lives in physical labor on the deep, now faced the prospect of supporting families without a seafaring income.

A small but fortunate minority—shipmasters all—managed to climb after retirement into Salem's merchant class. Constituting about 10 percent of all those resident mariners who made it to their fortieth birthday, these men employed their accumulated capital, credit, and commercial expertise to construct some of Salem's largest personal fortunes.[38] Philip English, Benjamin Pickman, Richard Derby, and Timothy Orne all served before the mast, all rose to the quarterdeck, and all retired to conclude their careers in the countinghouse and become rich men. A few of these began their seafaring careers with no particular advantages save a good deal of ambition, a string of good fortune, a strong business sense, and a local family name. Take the case of Benjamin West. His father, John West, was a saddler of very modest means who died in 1751, leaving behind a widow, Mary, a daughter, Sarah, and two sons, George, aged twenty-one, and Benjamin, aged twelve. George, a fisherman, married later that year and probably assumed ownership of what seems to have been no more than a few rooms in a very small house; then shortly after, Benjamin went to sea as well to keep the household from collapsing. By 1754 young Benjamin was fishing through the summer with John Cloutman and accompanying him to Maryland as ship's boy for 10s. sterling per month plus the privilege of carrying twenty bushels of wheat home on the return voyage. In 1756 George was given command of a 40-ton schooner, the *Olive Branch*, and he began a long career both as a skipper on the banks and as a shipmaster in the short-haul provisioning trade to the southern colonies. Benjamin grew up in his brother's house, married as George had in his early twenties, and became a captain himself several years later. At this point, however, their careers diverged. George never left the fishery, never commanded a vessel larger than a schooner, never sailed farther abroad than Charleston, South Carolina, and never acquired any property beyond the one-half of a house he was assessed for in 1771. Benjamin, by comparison, became captain of a brigantine at age twenty-six and was soon sailing the entire coast between Newfoundland and the Caribbean, investing continually in small commercial ventures on his own account. By 1777 he had accumulated a stock in trade of £500, enough to catch the eyes of the town assessor, and after the Revolution, he erected a comfortable home on a fashionable stretch of Essex Street, where he joined the Gardners, Crowninshields, and Masons within the business elite of the town. At his death in 1809, Benjamin West was a merchant with an estate worth about $13,000. Most of these shipmasters-turned-merchants enjoyed a few more initial advantages than West could claim, but they all came from families where physical work was part of life.[39]

A somewhat larger number, about 35 percent of the whole, were also able to carve out places for themselves in Salem's waterfront economy, albeit on a more modest scale, as shopkeepers, taverners, shoremen, craftsmen, or coastal traders. These were also for the most part retired shipmasters, and by plying these businesses, they were able to maintain modestly comfortable homes for their families while accumulating the resources necessary to help launch their sons and daughters into more or less promising life courses of their own. George Peele had been master of his own coasting sloop until the outbreak of the Revolution, but when peace returned, this "honest, uniform, unsocial, not unkind" retired skipper kept a "little Shop" on the main street for twenty years, undoubtedly with his wife's assistance, until he died at the age of seventy-three. David Felt, who began his maritime career as a fisherman and became master of a schooner that he took to the banks every summer and sailed to the tobacco colonies each winter, purchased a fishyard sometime in the 1760s and became a shoreman. "He was a man of the greatest industry," wrote William Bentley in 1817, "& the last of those in Salem who supported himself by the Fishery, by actually maintaining fishing crafts & flakes." Thomas Ellis, who had been a prominent shipmaster earlier in the century, invested the profits earned during his years at sea in a variety of different directions so that when he died in 1743, he owned four different rental properties in Marblehead, Beverly, and Salem, a collection of woodcutting tools along with several thousand feet of pine boards, an old ferry boat, a cow and seven sheep, some bills of public credit, five young slave children, and possibly their mother, a "Negro Woman caled Rose." Dozens of men such as these invested in sawmills, imported firewood from down east, exported sale shoes, speculated in frontier lands, lent money, rented out small boats around the harbor, and imported molasses to be distilled into rum—trying their hands usually on a petty scale at an enormous range of different businesses.[40]

Most eighteenth-century Salem mariners, however—about 55 percent of those who survived their careers at sea—never acquired any productive property, at least none of the sort that the town bothered to assess. Once they had quit the sea for good, possessing little beyond their network of family connections ashore, a sparsely furnished home, and a set of accumulated maritime skills ranging from navigation to fishing to carpentry, they faced an uphill task just to maintain their families, let alone provide any real assistance for children heading out into the world. A few of them managed to turn some of what they had learned during their seafaring days to good account on shore. Ashley Bowen opened a rigging loft after he quit the sea; William Peele became a cooper; John Scollay, Jr., took up sailmaking; and Samuel Swasey, went into coasting and shoemaking. In none of these cases was the individual in question successful enough in his years on shore to prompt any real change in calling or identity. All of them, as well as most of their former shipmates, called themselves mariners when they died in spite of whatever other work they may have done during or after their seafaring careers, probably because they understood their work in port as an extension of what they had done at sea—the normal culmination of a maritime career.[41]

Most of those sailors poor in productive property, however, never managed to launch a second career at all. Some spent odd days laboring in one of the local shipyards or rigging lofts; others signed on to occasional wooding trips down east along the coast of Maine; and in a town constructed entirely of wood, there was always carpentry work to be had. On the whole, however, one is struck by the rarity of references, in account books or court records, to those who can be identified as retired mariners working by the day at anything. It would seem that most of them remained chronically underemployed for the rest of their lives. Much of the problem may have been plain physical breakdown. Even on land, New Englanders began to withdraw from strenuous toil outside the home once they had passed their fiftieth birthday, and the years of singular damage wrought on the bodies of mariners by injury, disease, and physical exposure at sea can only have accelerated the process. An assessment list of 1786, which rated Salem taxpayers not only by physical property but by earning potential (or "faculty") as well, reveals that 83 percent of retired colonial mariners owned some real estate, but only 28 percent were believed to have earned in the previous year any taxable income. The town authorities might have overlooked the odd times when forty-year-old Benjamin Abbott, once a sailor and now a laborer, hired himself out rafting boards, loading vessels, freighting fish around the harbor, or "helping up the sloop" that belonged to Timothy Orne, and they likely would have passed over the few days that John Muckford spent doing repair work on several schooners as a retired seaman in his mid-fifties. But it is hard to imagine Abbott or Muckford managing to cobble together much of a living from this brand of casual employment.[42]

How did they manage? Again, as did widows and, indeed, most families in Salem, they sent their sons to sea—at as early an age as possible. John Muckford may have worked a few weeks for Miles Ward in 1754 to pay off his store debt of £12 sterling, but the overwhelming balance of this obligation—90 percent of the total tab—was covered by his son's employment at sea. It is difficult to generalize about the relative importance of children's earnings within the family economy; after all, the elder Muckford and his wife may have been working for people other than Miles Ward. Contemporaries did recognize among seafaring households, however, a generational pattern of dependency. A petition to the Massachusetts General Court from Marblehead in 1770 asked for an abatement in taxes after a series of recent storms left "many Parents deprived of the earnings of their Sons which was their chief support."[43] Although these were primarily fishing families from Marblehead, the same pattern held true across the harbor in Salem. There, a full 42 percent of locally born merchant seamen had not yet reached the age of legal majority, and since almost all of these young men still lived at home, their earnings, as account books testify, normally passed over to their parents. That is certainly what Christopher Prince of Kingston, Massachusetts, remembered. "Let what would befall me," Prince remembered of a conversation he had with his father upon undertaking his first voyage at thirteen years of age, "he would be my friend, until I was 21 years old, and all my earning must go into his hands."[44]

Retired sailors short in property were, of course, not wholly inactive. They repaired their homes, hauled and cut firewood, went fishing in the bay, and conducted family business around town. Some of them filled local offices as constables, jurymen, fence viewers, or fish cullers. During his fifties and sixties, Ashley Bowen was able to keep at his rigging business a few days out of every month, but he also weighed fish for local shoremen, took charge of Marblehead's smokehouse during a smallpox epidemic, and dug in his garden. But his years of heavy labor were over, and he now depended heavily on the earnings of his two boys, Nathaniel and Edward. The responsibility for generating a cash income to power the domestic economy of his household, Ashley Bowen, like most aging mariners, delegated to his sons.[45]

Most young people in the early modern Western world, like the Bowen boys, found themselves under enormous pressure to begin making a productive contribution to their families at an early age. The combination of high fertility and high mortality characteristic of the period meant that households tended to be congested with children and short of adults capable of supporting them. The imbalance of hungry mouths over strong backs—what demographers refer to as a high dependency ratio—forced mothers and fathers to set their youngsters to work, usually inside the household at first, employing whatever discipline was needed. Some families that were prudent and lucky might produce a small number of healthy children and after perhaps ten or fifteen years of hardship could begin to enjoy the material benefits that their growing cohort of teenage offspring could generate. Others, like the "old woman who lived in a shoe" of nursery-rhyme fame—plainly an impoverished widow who "had so many children she did not know what to do"—lived constantly at their wits' end trying merely to survive. Across entire communities, however, these anomalies tended to average out. Sons and daughters, nieces and nephews, orphans and waifs: the sheer number of young people within any town constituted a social problem for everyone, and the variety of solutions designed to convert them into productive hands as quickly as possible framed the experience of childhood.

In rural New England the abundance of land and the general good health of the population mitigated the problem of excessive dependency. Though many were born, many also grew up, and in families that commonly possessed several dozen acres these children matured quickly into productive young adults. In Salem, however, the high mortality of young men—principally seafarers—meant that growing families were commonly robbed of a principal support precisely during the years when their numbers and needs were greatest. The physical punishment that work at sea inflicted on those who escaped death's axe, forcing many heads of families to withdraw from the maritime labor market into part-time employment on shore, only magnified this problem. Individual families might through good fortune escape the direct effect of such disasters, but entire family networks—including siblings, in-laws, cousins, and the like—could not. From time to time, almost all of them would feel the pinch of having to support different relatives—orphans, widows, or physically broken men—in varying degrees of hardship. Young men went to sea, therefore, in large part because there was no better way for a teenager to earn the hard cash that families facing these difficulties depended on.

The decision to go to sea, however, was not just an act of desperation. As we have seen, the prospects for a determined young seaman to climb the ladder of promotion were strong in colonial Salem, and it is not hard to imagine the lure that shipmastery held out. The title of "captain" carried a good deal of dignity in maritime New England, and the financial rewards that a successful shipmaster could obtain ran from basic competency to the possibility of considerable wealth. A number of factors bore on the prospects for promotion—including local parentage, talent, property, and persistence—but the most basic of all was simply the good fortune to survive. Any Salem youth who had reached the age of majority, who had shown some aptitude for seafaring, and who was determined to make it his career could reasonably expect to become a ship's officer with a solid chance at commanding a vessel of his own provided that he was not struck down by shipwreck, accident, or disease in the process.

In this sense, the local labor market resembled a self-propelled mechanism. The extraordinary mortality of mariners created openings for recruitment and promotion within the shipping industry at the same time that it forced families to send their sons to sea to make up for the shortfalls in household income that untimely deaths tended to create. The extraordinary mixture of risk and opportunity for men, and the unusual potential for autonomy and dependency for women were flip sides of the same coin —necessarily connected features of the human lottery that powered the shipping industry of colonial Salem.

CHAPTER SIX

The Nineteenth Century

ON THE FIRST OF June, 1774, Captain Francis Boardman of Salem was cruising through the West Indies when he spoke with a brig from New London and learned that a small fleet of transports carrying British regulars and accompanied by several men-of-war were bound for Boston to shut down the port in reaction to the Tea Party of the previous winter. "Trouble a nough gods Noes," he wrote. Back home, another mariner, Ashley Bowen, now retired and plying his trade as a ship rigger in Marblehead, witnessed the impact of the Coercive Acts firsthand. As the port of Boston was closed and the customshouse moved to Marblehead, Bowen saw the streets of his hometown fill with "tide waiters and other officers," all of them with "strange faces" that filled him with foreboding. "Sad times . . . Terrible times," he mused.[1]

Francis Boardman and Ashley Bowen were not alone in their apprehensions, and for good reason. To the maritime communities of eighteenth-century America, a rupture with Great Britain must have seemed as if it would change everything, as in truth it did. The American Revolution destroyed much of the familiar, largely coastwise, commercial system in which nearly all New England mariners had earned their daily bread. War and independence removed Massachusetts's merchant fleet from under the protection of the British navy and launched it on a tumultuous fifty years' passage through seas where it was now prey for attack by anyone strong and brazen enough to attempt it. The creation of the United States with its immense western hinterland radically redrew the social, economic, political, and spatial parameters of American life in a way that only compounded further the pace and complexity of change within seaports such as Salem. In a world where the profits of global commerce lured mariners into strange waters, far from any effective naval protection but bowsprit-to-bowsprit with the toughest commercial competition afloat, New England seamen began to run risks of all sorts that were fundamentally greater than those that had characterized colonial days.

The sailor's lot did change dramatically during the first decades of the republic, and the reasonable expectations that young foremast hands could entertain in Salem's larger, more capital-intensive, global fleet of the nineteenth century differed considerably from those of their colonial grandfathers. During their stints at sea, Cooper, Dana, and Melville encountered and then immortalized in literature a world characterized by risk and uncertainty that was obviously not for everyone. The portrait they offered has often been taken as a representation of seafaring in general, which it plainly was not, but their version of things was based on the actual experience of voyaging from American ports in the first half of the nineteenth century, and it did represent something real. As Salem's maritime history entered its final century, seafaring at last became a sort of exceptional activity and not just what one did when one grew up beside the sea.

The outbreak of war in 1775 brought New England's maritime economy to a shuddering halt. The port of Boston had already been shut down in 1774; the cod fishery petered out in the summer of 1775; regular overseas shipping disappeared later that year; and even Massachusetts's whaling industry based on Nantucket, although permitted by the British to survive in parts, shrank dramatically after 1776. Dependent as it was on the fish trade and connected to its historic markets through waters that were now patrolled by the enemy, Salem seaport saw its commerce collapse. Apart from some inshore fishing and sporadic coastal trade, dodging British frigates inside the sheltering hook of Cape Cod and eastward along the coast of Maine, regular waterborne business ceased and remained dormant until the early 1780s.

Faced with the prospect of massive unemployment and motivated by a resentment of British imperial arrogance, Salem shipowners and mariners began immediately to convert their sloops and schooners into privateers. The first of these, the schooner *Dolphin,* set out in the fall of 1775 and captured its initial prize, a sloop from Nova Scotia bound for the British encampment in Boston, at the end of November. Soon it was joined by a swarm of other vessels, each one crowding six or twelve guns and between thirty and sixty men onto one- and two-masted vessels that would normally have traveled unarmed and been manned by fewer than seven. Within two years, Salem and Beverly together could count at least thirty privateers crewed by something close to 1,300 men, and as the war progressed this fleet grew larger—in both tonnage and numbers. New Englanders proceeded to refit and dispatch every captured ship that was suitable for combat with a crew of its own to prey on the British merchant fleet, and since many of these were brigs, brigantines, and even full-rigged ships of 150–300 tons, they could be armed with as many as twenty-five guns and crewed by upward of a hundred men. Soon Salem merchants were commissioning similar vessels to be built in Massachusetts by local shipwrights. The greatest of these was the *Grand Turk,* a 300-ton ship constructed for Elias Haskett Derby in 1781 and remembered for taking the final prize of the war: an even larger Caribbean trader from London, which surrendered to the burly privateer off St. Kitts one month after the Treaty of Versailles but twelve days before the news of the peace arrived in Salem. At the end of the war, the combined fleet from Salem and Beverly—numbering 80–100 vessels, carrying 2,500 guns, and crewed by more than 3,000 men —could claim to have captured something close to 350 prizes.[2]

When the sailors of the *Grand Turk,* the *Julius Caesar,* the *Revolution,* the *Buccaneer,* and several dozen other privateers rounded Naugus Head and entered Salem Harbor in the spring of 1783, the physical prospect that greeted them would not have changed terribly from what they remembered from before the war. The town itself had never been occupied by the British and sat largely intact—the same church spires, warehouses, and waterfront buildings that had stood there in 1775. The population had grown a little since that time, but not enough to strike the eye. There were still only two principal wharves jutting out over the mudflats into the harbor, and most of the ropewalks, shipyards, smithies, and rigging shops stood where they had at the end of the colonial period. The seaport's tax collectors tallied five distilleries in 1784, just as they had in 1771. Salem's merchants (minus a few Tory emigrants) still made their homes on Essex

Street within a block or two of the waterfront, and the sailors and maritime artisans who had survived the war still lived in the lanes that ran from the main street down to the North and South rivers. Although many of the vessels at anchor a few hundred yards from the shore would have towered over those of colonial times, there were fewer of them, and the town's assessors counted roughly the same aggregate tonnage as before the war. In spite of having spent seven years operating as a corsair base—a Barbary seaport in America—Salem seemed much the same.[3]

Underneath, however, a great deal had altered—changes that would transform Salem as a seaport in the years to come. Most obviously, Massachusetts no longer belonged to the British Empire, and local vessels and the commerce they carried no longer sailed under either the protections or the restrictions that the imperial connection had provided. New Englanders now stood outside the trading system defined by the Navigation Acts, and the British Parliament reminded them of that fact immediately after the Treaty of Paris by barring all trade in American vessels with the British West Indies and forbidding the export of American fish to its Caribbean colonies in any vessel whatsoever. New England schooners no longer counted as British bottoms and ceased to enjoy their sheltered market inside the empire. Nor would the British navy now protect American vessels —against pirates, privateers, or anyone else. The largest merchant fleet in the world supported by the most powerful navy afloat was no longer a partner but a competitor.[4]

The new generation of Salem merchants who ran their eyes over the opportunities at hand thought long and hard about how exactly they might go about rebuilding their businesses. The town's own fishing fleet, like that of every other community on Massachusetts's North Shore, had effectively been destroyed. Fishing schooners made clumsy privateers, and during the war most of them had been dismantled for timber or hauled up on shore to rot. Yet the larger, faster vessels that had replaced them (Figure 6.1) possessed problems of their own. For one thing, it was difficult to imagine them profitably peddling mixed cargoes to Salem's traditional markets —those dozens of little islands and rivermouth seaports across the tropical New World. Nor, given their size and rig, were these ships and brigantines suited to fishing on the banks. And without quintals of cod—always Salem's prime export—collecting in local warehouses, what of value would these vessels carry anyway? None of these problems had easy answers.

FIGURE 6.1 Ship *Hercules*, 1809. This full-rigged ship of 290 tons, built in 1805, was typical of the type of vessel Salem merchants employed in global commerce during the first half of the nineteenth century. Here it is shown coming to anchor in Naples. (Courtesy of the Peabody-Essex Museum)

Yet New Englanders' exit from the empire also carried with it a corresponding array of opportunities. Most significantly, local merchants could now deal directly with any port in the world they pleased. They were no longer forbidden from importing cargoes directly from the continent of Europe—canvas from St. Petersburg, iron from Sweden, wines from Bordeaux, or books from Amsterdam—nor did they now have to ship those commodities enumerated under the English Acts of Trade directly to Great Britain. Now any Salem merchant could dispatch his vessel to pick up tobacco in Virginia, rice in South Carolina, or sugar in St. Domingue and freight it in his own vessel directly and legally to any market in the world he wished. Furthermore, independence placed Salem merchants outside of the monopoly held by the East India Company on British imperial trade beyond the Cape of Good Hope. New Englanders could now sail all the way to Canton or Calcutta to load teas, calicoes, nankeens, silks, chinaware, or sugar. Alternatively, they could purchase these same eastern commodities from middlemen in Cape Town on the southern tip of Africa or at the Isle de France (today's Mauritius) and carry them to market in Europe or America.

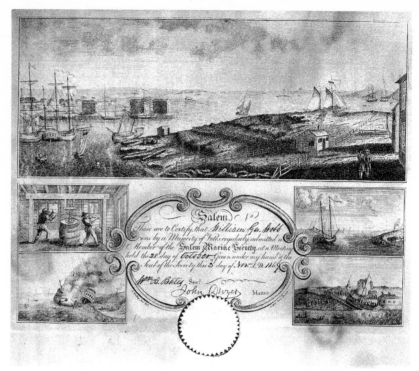

FIGURE 6.2 Salem Harbor, ca. 1797, from Salem Marine Society Certificate.
This engraving, based on a drawing by Abijah Northey, Jr., shows Salem's waterfront,
looking east toward the Atlantic. The old Union Wharf with three vessels moored
alongside is at the far left, and new Derby Wharf with three warehouses is immediately
behind it. Note the number of lighters and sloops at work in the harbor. (Courtesy
of the Peabody-Essex Museum)

But did Salem own any comparative advantages in these trades? Its
harbor, though snug, was as always difficult to approach, small in size,
and rather shallow (Figure 6.2). The mudflats that ringed the waterfront
did not make it easy to discharge a cargo. Eastern Massachusetts produced
no obvious commodities that were likely to interest foreign customers beyond codfish and whale oil, neither of which was in ample supply after
the Revolution. Salem itself constituted only the tiniest of markets, nor
was it, like New York and New Orleans, connected by any navigable river
to a larger cluster of consumers in the continent's interior. In the global
shipping game, Salem in 1783 held only one real ace—an extraordinarily
accomplished maritime and commercial community with no alternative

to earning its living upon the sea. Although not the only American seaport that prospered from the array of opportunities afforded the new nation after the Treaty of Versailles, Salem was the smallest of those that really competed across the seven seas, and its only true advantage lay in the knowledge about seafaring and markets that its residents had accumulated over the previous century and a half.

Independence did not propel Salem immediately into an economic boom. The local economy recovered fitfully from the Revolutionary War, and as late as 1788 the 179 foreign clearances noted by newspapers and customs officials had not even caught up with the 212 recorded in a twelve-month period in 1752–1753. Yet these vessels were larger now, and the courses they followed were often quite new. As early as 1784 Salem mariners were testing out the waters of the Baltic and the Mediterranean; those bound for the Caribbean islands began to call in at French, Dutch, and Spanish colonies; and in November of that year, Elias Hasket Derby dispatched the *Grand Turk* to trade for eastern merchandise at the Cape of Good Hope. Although the traditional markets of Spain and the West Indies still attracted most local shipping, voyages to new parts slowly multiplied, in both number and variety. The *Salem Mercury* of February 19, 1788, for example, noted in its shipping news twelve separate entries and clearances, including the arrivals of a bark from the Isle de France, two brigantines from France, one schooner from South Carolina, and two more from the Caribbean, as well as the departures of two brigantines to Cádiz and Senegal and four schooners to the West Indies, Madeira, and Virginia. The diversity of vessel types and trading routes recorded in the *Mercury* varied from issue to issue, but it outstripped anything common in colonial times.[5]

The outbreak of the French Revolutionary Wars in the winter of 1792–1793 presented Salem merchants and mariners with a new set of fresh opportunities as well as a whirlpool of potential problems. Certainly the conscription of European sailors by the tens of thousands into their respective navies eliminated much of the United States' foreign competition in the carrying trades, placing Americans in a position to profit handsomely as neutral shippers, and Salem merchants were not at all shy at seizing the chance. The number of vessels entering and clearing the port began to climb immediately, and the proportion that were ships and brigs of burdens ranging upward to 350 tons grew even faster. The registered tonnage of the Salem fleet rose from 8,652 in 1784 to 13,726 in 1790, to 19,636 in 1800, and to 36,272 in 1810, and most of this increase, especially during the 1790s and 1800s, was accounted for by brigs and ships, which soon replaced schooners as the principal workhorses of the local fleet. And these vessels now sailed the globe. Up until the early 1790s, the port's principal business remained the declining coastwise trade in timber, fish, and farm produce to the West Indies, but by 1805, Salem vessels might be bound anywhere on earth: to fetch gypsum from Nova Scotia or dry goods from New York, to load hemp in St. Petersburg or pepper in Sumatra, or to buy and sell hundreds of other commodities in scores of seaports in between. Since New England cargoes were unlikely to make these voyages pay, the same vessels were forced to tramp the oceans hauling freight for other nations, earning specie and gathering marketable goods that could be flogged on the Hooghly River in Calcutta or in the crowded seaports of the North Sea for goods that in turn might find a market at home.[6]

The complexity of these voyages is nicely illustrated by the log of the snow *Vigilant*, which left Salem under the command of John Murphy for the Indian Ocean in January of 1793. Stowed in her hold were barrels of flour, beef, pork, and rum, parcels of lumber and cordage, and a few saddles, most of which Murphy planned to trade at the Isle de France for a return cargo of sugar, coffee, and indigo. Although the first leg of the voyage unfolded predictably, Murphy decided not to return directly to Salem; after clearing the French colony in December, he headed instead for Ostend in Belgium, where he disposed of most of his eastern produce for cash. In ballast, the *Vigilant* then sailed eastward through the North and Baltic seas to Cronstadt outside St. Petersburg, where Murphy purchased a shipment of iron, hemp, sailcloth, rope, and a few miscellaneous dry goods, including a case of mirrors, for the New England market. Finally he put out for home, where he arrived in August 1794, after nineteen months abroad. Although the *Vigilant*'s voyage may have been longer than most, it represents clearly a degree of complexity in Salem commerce that was entirely new.[7]

The era of neutral shipping was a prosperous one for Salem. Between 1790 and 1810 the aggregate tonnage registered in the town had climbed by 160 percent, and the population rose from 7,921 to 12,613, making it the sixth-largest urban center in the United States. Yet much of this profit was attended by considerable economic risk and physical peril. Almost as soon as war had broken out between England and France, Salem ships began running into all manner of problems, both in foreign ports and on the high seas. French and British officials who believed that American visitors might be trading with the enemy thought nothing of placing their ships under embargo. Both privateers and naval frigates, off the European coast or more commonly in colonial waters, had seized so many vessels by the spring of 1794 that the merchants in Salem were prompted to complain to Congress that fully one-third of the West India fleet was now in British hands. It seemed to William Bentley that "neutral vessels have no advantages as one nation adopts the measures of its rivals, & makes the terms as severe." Even when not seized outright, Yankee vessels were frequently stopped at sea and inspected for cargoes bound to enemy ports and, in the British case, for sailors who could be removed and impressed.[8]

Nor did these problems diminish in distant seas. Bentley described in May 1794 the adventures of Edward Gibaut, who had just returned from a voyage to the Indian Ocean, "having been detained & embargoed in different ports 17 months." The *Astrea*, which he commanded on the outbound leg, was commandeered by a Burmese sultan to serve as a military transport and damaged so severely that after being returned it was judged unfit for the sea and condemned at Calcutta. Gibaut took passage to the Isle de France, where he met up with another Salem ship, the *Henry*. Somehow he was appointed master, and after purchasing a cargo he set sail for home, only to be waylaid yet again, this time "stopped at the Cape of Good Hope long enough to have a share of British Insolence." Finally he was released and returned to New England, after an absence of almost three years. Other trading relationships that New Englanders struck up after the Revolution—for pepper with the native peoples of Sumatra, for furs with those who lived on the northwest coast of North America, or for tropical products with the newly independent republics of South America—possessed different but serious political complexities that aggressive Yankee trading habits only exacerbated and often landed their ships in trouble. Long voyages were inherently risky, and although most Salem mariners made it home sooner than did Captain Gibaut, nobody could predict with any certainty how long or what route their adventures would take.[9]

Pirates were a further source of anxiety, especially those from the Barbary states of North Africa. Now that Americans stood outside the Empire, they could no longer depend upon the British navy to defend them or upon the protection money that Parliament had traditionally paid the corsairs to persuade the latter to leave British shipping alone. Through the 1790s the "Algerines," as Yankees termed them, were often as not "out again upon us in the Atlantic," and Salem mariners knew that if captured by the corsairs they could be imprisoned and "treated as Slaves, their heads shorn, chained together, dressed in frocks & trowsers, & employed upon the public works" until ransomed back. In waters that were more remote from the United States, piracy flourished even longer. Many peoples of the coast in the distant corners of the Indian Ocean regarded American vessels as either unwelcome intruders or easy pickings. In 1806 William Bentley learned of the "melancholy history" of a Salem ship, the *Essex*, sailing through the Red Sea under the command of Joseph Orne with $60,000 on board to purchase a cargo of coffee. In Mocha, some Arabs who had sought passage with them seized the vessel, plundered it, burnt it to the waterline, and murdered Orne along with all of his crew. The sole survivor was a Dutch cabin boy who was spared, then settled in the region, and told the whole story fifteen years later to the captain of a ship from New York. Similarly, in the waters off Sumatra, where Salem vessels cruised in search of pepper cargoes, Malaysian pirates often chased, attacked, and sometimes successfully captured Yankee vessels and their crews. Even on the coast of South America, piracy flourished in the early nineteenth century.[10]

This chronic vexation boiled over into formal conflict several times: once in the Quasi-War with France in 1798, again with the Tripolitan War with the Barbary States in 1801–1805, and yet again with the various diplomatic and military imbroglios with England that raged on and off from Jefferson's Embargo of 1807 to the Treaty of Ghent in 1814. The latter period in particular brought about two abrupt interruptions to Salem's foreign trade: one that lasted fourteen months between 1807 and 1809 and another that accompanied the War of 1812. Although the War of 1812 proved less of a hardship than the Revolutionary War, the British navy and British privateers did manage to chase most unarmed Yankee traders from the seas, and for several years privateering returned as the principal employment of Salem mariners and their vessels. Yet even in the absence of declared hostilities, the American merchant fleet walked a tightrope through this period, and one can fairly state that hardly a year transpired between 1792 and 1815 without Salem vessels running into trouble with one or another of many foreign powers.[11]

The Treaty of Ghent in 1814 marked an end to forty years of tumult and opportunity during which Salem's shipping fleet was transformed. By 1820, when the losses from the War of 1812 had been regained, the old colonial fish and timber commerce had shrunk into relative insignificance, and most merchants were sinking their shipping capital into larger vessels that tramped the lanes of transoceanic commerce carrying goods to and from markets outside Essex County, New England, or the United States entirely. Some schooners and smaller brigs continued to deal in the West Indian trade, principally now to Spanish and French islands, but the coastwise business inside the United States—principally to New York and Baltimore, with commodities from abroad to pay for flour and other foodstuffs that New England now had to import—accounted now for almost as much. An even greater portion of Salem's merchant shipping activity—both in bulk and in value—now rested strictly on foreign trade. Coffee, sugar, and pepper from the East Indies, as well as hemp, iron, wine, and manufactures from Europe and hides from South America, now filled the majority of larger vessels that had come to account for most of the registered tonnage that entered port. Quite commonly now, Salem vessels began their voyages by sailing to Boston or even New York, largely in ballast, with the intent of picking up a cargo and proceeding overseas. Likewise, the conclusion of a voyage might well involve the delivery of foreign produce directly to one of these larger markets before returning to Salem with a hold full of American provisions. William Bentley noticed the change as early as 1819, and Nathaniel Hawthorne, who worked for a short time in the local customshouse, wrote the same observation into *The Scarlet Letter*. Since the War of 1812, he noted, Salem had become less "a port by itself," mainly because "her own merchants['] and ship-owners['] . . . ventures go to swell, needlessly and imperceptibly, the mighty flood of commerce at New York or Boston."[12] The town on the North Shore was sometimes now an infrequent port of call, even for sailors who lived there.

Indeed, it is something of a puzzle how Salem remained in the nineteenth century a seaport of consequence at all. With a mediocre harbor, a hinterland poor in natural resources, and a host of powerful new competitors in cities such as New York and Baltimore much better situated for global commerce, why didn't the shipping industry in Salem simply collapse? Eventually it did, of course, but through the 1820s, 1830s, and 1840s, local merchants and mariners proved amazingly inventive in seeking out new destinations and new products, mainly in parts of the world where Americans had never ventured before. Vessels from Salem, for example, pioneered in the 1790s the Sumatran pepper trade and dominated it for several decades, serving as distributors to the world until eventually the trade was captured by shippers from larger ports. In the 1820s Salem imported from Brazil the first rubber boots Americans had ever seen. Brittle in winter and liable to melt in the hot summer sun, they retained a limited appeal until 1839, when Charles Goodyear discovered the vulcanization process and transformed an oddity into a national industry. Once again, however, a growing market attracted serious competition for the raw material, and Salem gave way to New York as the United States' principal rubber port. In the early 1830s Salem adventurers discovered that gum copal, a principal ingredient of varnish, could be purchased in great quantities at low prices in Zanzibar, and Yankees from the North Shore sailed there with "amerikani" cloth from Lowell to secure a near-monopoly through to about 1850 over the import of this commodity into the United States. Ships from Salem discovered and dominated for many years the import from West Africa of ivory and palm oil, the commerce from the East Indies in ginger and cloves, and even the sea cucumber trade between Fiji and Canton—all niche markets that Salem mariners were able to identify and exploit because over two centuries they had grown so skilled in waterborne capitalism. Back in the seventeenth century Edmund Randolph had been amazed at New Englanders' ability to "trye all ports to force a trade." To the end of Salem's history as a seaport, this skill remained the key to their success.[13]

The vastly larger fleet that Salem merchants assembled in the early nineteenth century—eventually six or seven times the tonnage of their colonial predecessors—required a great many more sailors than a town of this size could furnish. Larger vessels needed larger crews, and although the sloops and schooners that continued to ply the familiar routes of the North Atlantic may have carried on average only two officers and four or five hands—much as in the eighteenth century—the brigs and ships that sailed the globe and accounted for more and more of the seaport's business with each passing decade required at least three officers and anywhere from five to fifteen additional men. And as crews grew in size, so the proportion of sailors with roots of any kind in and around Salem declined. The fraction of seamen who were locally born as well as those who ever paid taxes in Salem both fell by roughly one-half over the early national period (Table 6.1). To assemble a crew in the nineteenth century, one had to cast one's net much farther afield.

Table 6.1

Birthplace and Residence of First Mates and Seamen Shipping out of Salem, 1690–1835

	SEAMEN		MATES
Date	Taxpayer in Salem	Born in Salem, Beverly, or Danvers	Born in Salem, Beverly, or Danvers
1690–1775	44% (n=490)	66% (n=617)	54% (n=164)
1783–1799	30% (n=125)	56% (n=113)	63% (n=30)
1805	31% (n=59)	37% (n=928)	62% (n=170)
1815	insufficient data	49% (n=450)	64% (n=98)
1825	26% (n=50)	39% (n=748)	70% (n=138)
1835	23% (n=26)	32% (n=451)	62% (n=93)

Sources: Crew Lists for Salem, 1805, 1815, 1825, and 1835, Massachusetts, Records of the U.S. Customs Service, National Archives Northeast Region, Waltham, Mass., mfm. edition owned by the Maritime History Archive, Memorial University of Newfoundland, St. John's, Nfld.; and the collection of portledge bills and biographical sources listed in Appendix A.

Ship's officers, especially masters, obtained their positions much as they had in the past, through reputation within a relatively small professional maritime community, connected by neighborhood and kinship to those who owned the ships. Typically, an officer might call upon some merchant who knew of his experience and ask whether the merchant had any ships readying to go abroad; alternatively, the vessel owner might write the mariner a letter, inviting him to apply. Gorham Low of Gloucester obtained several positions on Boston vessels through his older brother, who had sailed out of Boston, then settled as a trader there, and frequently recommended Gorham to his mariner and merchant friends. Charles Tyng from Newburyport began his career as a cabin boy on a ship owned by the Perkins brothers, who were brothers to his Uncle Samuel, and he proceeded to move upward through the ranks on Perkins family vessels, approaching them "to see if they had any vessel for me" whenever he was in need of work. Between 60 percent and 70 percent of all mates and possibly even a higher proportion of masters who shipped out of Salem in the first few decades of the nineteenth century came from Salem, Beverly, or Danvers, and grew up in a world where, much as in colonial times, promotion and preferment still went to the people you had known from childhood. Nathaniel Hawthorne, the son of a Salem sea captain, believed there was a type of spell that bound these men, generation after generation, to the town, the trade, and one another. Looking back from 1850, he wrote that "from father to son, for above a hundred years, they followed the sea; a gray-headed shipmaster, in each generation, retiring from the quarterdeck to the homestead, while a boy of fourteen took the hereditary place before the mast, confronting the salt spray and the gale, which had blustered against his sire and grandsire." Within this crowd, he insisted, there existed a "kindred between the human being and the locality," highly exclusive and based on "not love, but instinct," that caused local men to envision talent and reliability only among those whose ancestors had mingled their dust "with the natal earth." Hawthorne exaggerated the tightness of this network; it extended beyond family to friends, neighbors, and even acquaintances from adjoining towns. Yet the sense of preferment and entitlement that connected these men was as real as Hawthorne insisted, and it generated in a way that seemed to him almost inevitable the cohorts of officers that commanded Salem ships through his lifetime.[14]

The process Hawthorne alluded to and Low and Tyng experienced personally had once applied to all ranks within the Salem merchant service. During the colonial period, and indeed, up to the outbreak of the French Revolutionary Wars and the boom in neutral shipping, crews for local vessels had been composed of young men from Salem and the neighboring ocean-fronting communities along the North Shore, because that is what young men in maritime societies did. The recruitment process left little imprint on the historical record because it was simply the stuff of daily life—chance encounters on the road, plans concocted during meals, or promises made over drinks. This locally constituted labor market never disappeared, but as the Salem fleet grew in size and acquired its global range, shipmasters found these neighborly contacts insufficient to their needs. Even as the local population roughly doubled (from 5,000 on the eve of the Revolution to 11,000 by 1805) and the tonnage of the fleet multiplied fivefold (from about 5,500 in 1765 to about 28,000 in 1805), the absolute number of locally born mariners on Salem vessels climbed by only 70 percent (from 345 in 1765 to about 585 in 1805). As the nineteenth century proceeded, the number of native sons serving in the fleet may occasionally have topped the 1805 total, but the best evidence suggests that it was usually lower, and we know that by 1850 (when the population of the town had climbed to 20,264 and the tonnage of the fleet stood at 41,420), the census recorded only about 320 locally born mariners, of whom no more than 275 were of working age.[15]

At the same time, the number of strangers within this labor force began to rise. Across the period 1805–1835, only 30 percent of all foremast hands who signed articles on local vessels claimed Salem as their birthplace; the rest hailed from elsewhere in Massachusetts (35 percent), other seaboard states of the new republic (24 percent), or other (mainly European) countries around the Atlantic rim (11 percent). Roughly 10 percent of these crews were now African American—usually foremast hands, cooks, or stewards—sometimes local residents but much more commonly from other American cities and towns along the eastern seaboard mostly south of Boston. Salem vessels were probably a little more homogeneous in personnel than those from larger ports such as New York or Baltimore, but they were markedly more diverse in the early republic than they had been in colonial times.[16]

Indeed, it is quite possible that these crew lists underestimate the heterogeneity of these crews, for they reported only the birthplaces that captains and sailors chose to reveal. Since Yankee vessels could not clear customs without demonstrating that two-thirds of the crew were United States citizens, masters and men alike possessed a clear interest in making certain the crew looked (on paper at least) as American as possible. The crew lists from Salem, moreover, record outbound voyages only. Every vessel that lost men either to disease, discharge, or desertion while abroad would have been forced to ship replacements in the next port of call, and one can be certain that the number of Salem or even Massachusetts-born sailors hired in Copenhagen, Valparaiso, or Calcutta would have been low, indeed. On such voyages, the inbound leg would have been crewed by a measurably more heterogeneous lot.

Nathaniel Bowditch was told by his merchant friends in Salem that during the period of neutral shipping before the Embargo of 1807, at least one-quarter of the sailors employed in the merchant service in New England were foreign born, and that even in the shrunken fleet of 1815 between one-eighth and one-quarter of most crews hailed from overseas. Several decades later, in 1839, William McNally claimed that throughout the U.S. naval and merchant service, "not one-third" of the seamen were native born. The proportion was much higher—probably close to three-quarters, he admitted—in the fishing and coasting trades, and Salem as a smaller port probably continued to recruit more locally born sailors than New York City or Baltimore. Regardless of which estimates one prefers, however, there is no denying that Salem vessels of the nineteenth century shipped far more foreigners than they ever had before.[17]

To keep their vessels manned, Yankee shipmasters now had to resort to a variety of strategies unknown to their colonial ancestors. The simplest tool was cash. Through the period of neutral shipping and somewhat beyond—as long as the local fleet could profit from the disturbances of war and the advantages of having pioneered several highly lucrative markets —Salem captains managed to attract sailors into their service by offering them a generous return on their labor. As late as 1790 a foremast hand shipping out of Salem could expect to earn on average only between $7.50 and $8.00 a month: about $2.50 more than he might have earned as a laborer working by the month on a Massachusetts farm but not a lot to compensate him for the risks and hardships that extended voyaging entailed. After the outbreak of the French Revolutionary Wars, however, wages for seamen out of Salem shot upward, to heights that averaged out over the period 1793–1812 at close to $16.75 monthly (see Graph 7, Appendix B). True, most laboring men living around the Atlantic rim did relatively well during the age of the French Revolutionary and Napoleonic Wars. By comparison with the levels of 1790, the nominal wages of farm laborers in Massachusetts averaged about 25 percent higher; those of artisans and laborers in England reached a level 40 percent higher; and those of artisans and laborers in Philadelphia climbed by about 50 percent (see Graph 8, Appendix B). By contrast, over this same period, the wages of Salem seamen more than doubled. Widespread inflation ate away some of these gains, but even in relation to the cost of living, wages averaged around 50 percent higher between 1793 and 1812 than they had in 1790 (see Graph 9, Appendix B). Indeed, when Daniel Perkins, a twenty-year-old sailor from Dunbarton outside Glasgow, signed on in 1805 to the *Exeter,* bound from Salem to "one or more parts beyond the Cape of Good Hope," he earned a wage of $15 monthly—more than most ship's commanders had earned in 1790—and he was the worst-paid seaman on board! These elevated wages relapsed immediately after the War of 1812, once the British navy had discharged its many thousands of sailors upon the maritime labor market, and once American vessels lost their privileged and extraordinarily profitable status as neutral traders to the world. Yet by 1820 the monthly pay of Salem seamen in absolute terms had regained some of this lost ground, and because the cost of living had fallen decidedly since the period of the French Revolutionary and Napoleonic wars, the purchasing power of sailors wages during the 1820s probably stood at a level close to that which it had reached in the heyday of neutral shipping.[18]

In annual terms, moreover, sailors benefited from longer voyages because they spent longer periods in pay. In the colonial period, mariners had found it next to impossible to keep employed the year round, yet by the nineteenth century, a voyage to Europe or the Far East could obtain for a sailor anywhere from six months to a year or more in pay with relatively few unavoidable expenses. When the *St. Paul* returned from India in April 1840, for example, ordinary seaman Charles Trumbull disembarked with $95 in his pocket: the difference between the $114 he had earned at sea and the $19 he had been advanced in the course of his service. Some of his shipmates were less frugal. James Crabb earned the same as Trumbull but had purchased some cigars, several shirts, plus a few knives from the vessel's slop chest, and he had asked for cash advances at Manila and St.

Helena that reduced his take-home to $61. One suspects that while cruising the waterfront establishments of the Orient, the free-spending Crabb may have been better company than Trumbull, but whether one took one's pay in pleasures abroad or savings at home, these sums would well have exceeded whatever a colonial seaman would have earned in the course of a year.[19]

The other component of a sailor's earnings was what he could make from his private adventures, and although quantifying the importance of this income in any precise manner is not possible, the positive evidence for its importance is, in fact, stronger for the early republic than for the colonial period. Shipping agreements from the years after 1793 describe the privileges that hundreds of mariners—and not simply officers—were entitled to in addition to their wages. Nearly half of all deckhands were able to obtain the right to stow five hundred to a thousand pounds of goods in the hold—close in volume to the "three barrels" that Christopher Prince described as normal in Boston during the 1760s. Just as the rapid expansion of Salem's fleet after 1793 favored seamen in their negotiation of decent wages, so it permitted them to obtain a better chance of supplementing their income by trading on the side. What this meant in terms of actual opportunity, however, is difficult to measure. Many agreements made no mention of portage at all; does this mean that on such voyages private adventures were not allowed, or does it imply that they went without saying? And although most shipmasters had access to the sort of credit necessary to exploit their privileges, did the same apply in lesser degree for foremast hands?[20]

A variety of miscellaneous records do refer to private adventures. The Salem sloop *Nancy*, seized by a British privateer and carried into Jamaica to be declared a prize in 1794, possessed a cargo that included nine barrels of coffee and thirteen bags of cotton and coffee as the private adventures of the crew. Sailors sometimes purchased chickens or sheep that they penned up on deck and fed en route to nearby destinations. Shipping accounts kept by captains document regular advances in foreign ports to men of all ranks, some of which may have gone toward small speculations. A real sense of the overall importance of these adventures, however, is difficult to grasp. A shipping agreement from a voyage to the West Indies in 1808, stating plainly that "no officer shall have any privilege of carrying money or merchandise on board the ship nor shall any seaman, boy, or cook, have any, nor shall any officer or seaman have any adventure of money or goods home," may well imply that the practice would otherwise have been considered normal. Another agreement governing a voyage to the East Indies in 1795 declared that it was "agreed and understood between the master, mate and people that each one shall be entitled for his privilege to carry goods of the bulk which is affixed to each man's name and no more and that no mate or seaman shall sell or buy any goods—but that the master shall sell all their goods and lay out all their money." The need to make this explicit suggests that otherwise, all crew members would traffic freely on their own account. But how the profits from adventures compared to the remuneration from wages is ultimately anyone's guess.[21]

On the whole, however, it seems that before the 1830s, the combination of wages and privilege was sufficient to sustain a relatively informal labor market in Salem, and sailors could usually find berths through neighborly contacts and word of mouth. Salem fathers continued to place their sons with nephews, brothers-in-law, or fellow church members, just as they had in the eighteenth century. Yankee boys from along the coast traveled to Salem to find positions on the recommendation of family and friends. In 1822, at the age of sixteen, Gorham Low of Gloucester "yoked up the oxen for the last time" and signed on as a cabin boy to a brig bound for St. Petersburg commanded by his brother David. In this case, Gorham took the packet boat to Boston, and the Lows sailed from there, but a different train of events might just as easily have guided him to Salem. Other seafaring clans from up and down the North Shore—Obers from Beverly, Lees from Manchester, Boardmans from Ipswich, Toppans from Newburyport, and so forth—regularly traveled to Salem looking for work, and all of them had distant cousins living in the seaport with connections on the waterfront. Mariners from farther afield—from Cape Cod to Copenhagen to Calcutta—who found themselves ashore in Salem at the end of a long voyage probably put themselves up unobtrusively in a rented room for a week or so while they tramped the waterfront looking for an outbound berth, or possibly they took the stage down to Boston where it might be easier to find a vessel clearing for home.[22]

In the larger seaports of the early nineteenth century, sailortown institutions that facilitated the maritime labor market—shipping agencies, boardinghouses, brothels, and taverns—constituted a distinctive feature of the waterfront. While abroad, Salem skippers often had to deal with a variety of shipping agents, crimps, and runners whenever they ran short of hands and needed to replace them. The shipping accounts they kept to document expenses throughout their voyages sometimes contain the names of a dozen or more hands they had to hire along the way, and behind these accounts lay endlessly complicated negotiations. While in Le Havre on the English Channel, Richard Cleveland reported that "in the course of three weeks I shipped no less than four different men as mates, and as many different crews, and each, in turn, abandoned me." In Canton he found that "to procure a competent number of men was a task of such difficulty, that, when any one offered his services, I was not very particular in inquiring whence he came, or how well he was qualified." Charles Tyng of Boston hired men on one occasion through a merchant doubling as the American consul in Manila, who sent Tyng a note requesting him "to come up [to] the city, as some men had offered as sailors, and he wished me to see them and ship them." On another voyage, while in Havana, his entire crew deserted, probably "enticed away by one of the runners from the boarding houses," and Tyng "arranged with a sailors' landlord to ship me another crew, eight men, who were brought on board the night before we left . . . a big set of scoundrels." When most of Gorham Low's crew deserted him during a port stop in Savannah, he was forced "to pick up a crew from among the bartenders of the liquor shops who wanted to get away to avoid the sickly season." Negotiations of this sort became necessary to the completion of many voyages, once Salem embarked on global commerce, and dealing through the various institutions of the sailortown labor market often left masters at their wit's end.[23]

In Salem, by contrast, before the 1830s the workings of the maritime labor market were practically invisible—almost certainly because they still operated through informal channels. William Bentley moved to town just before the boom in neutral shipping and witnessed the transformation of Salem into a global seaport while ministering to the East Church two blocks from the waterfront, but never once in close to forty years of diary keeping did he ever make mention of any institutions catering to sailors interested in a berth. Indeed, Bentley scarcely mentioned visiting mariners as a presence in Salem at all. Benjamin Browne, who wrote a detailed memoir of life in Salem at the beginning of the nineteenth century, similarly failed to mention any shipping agencies, taverns, or boardinghouses with a maritime clientele. We know from crew lists that hundreds of

strange faces passed through Salem every year looking for seafaring employment, yet neither Bentley nor Browne nor anyone else felt them to
be a memorable feature of seaport life.[24] We can only conclude that during
the first real boom in Salem's shipping industry, personal connection operating in an attenuated manner up and down the New England coastline,
as well as plain high wages, drew in sailors without the assistance of commercial middlemen.

After the War of 1812 the terms of employment, in relative terms at
least, began to turn against the maritime community. During the decade
of the 1800s, seamen's wages had stood at a level nearly double that which
farm laborers in Massachusetts could obtain, but during the 1820s that
gap began to close, and by the 1840s farmhands in rural Massachusetts
were actually for the first time in history earning more than their seafaring
counterparts. After 1812, in comparison with other laboring men around
the Atlantic rim, Salem seamen did poorly. By 1825, moreover, local shipowners were growing noticeably stingier about granting any mariners the
privilege of carrying adventures freight free. Between 1793 and 1824, 47
percent of seamen had privileges explicitly guaranteed them in their articles of agreement; between 1825 and 1850 that proportion plummeted
to 4 percent. In real terms, the value of mariners' wages had probably not
fallen far—they may even have risen—but relative to other forms of available employment along the eastern seaboard, seafaring must not have
seemed the vehicle of opportunity in the 1830s that it had at the beginning
of the century. Sailing vessels were not on the leading edge of technologi-
cal and organizational innovation in the early nineteenth century, and shipowners found it hard to compete with landward enterprises in the labor
market, especially in a relatively advanced economy like that of New England. Finding men willing to work for wages that their neighbors on
shore could now earn with less hardship and fewer risks was not a simple
business.[25]

Given these conditions, Salem's maritime labor market could not be
expected to operate as easily as it had in the glory days of neutral shipping,
and during the 1830s a shopkeeper named Eben Griffin, originally from
Marblehead, opened an office on Lafayette Street by the shores of the
South River, where he began to operate Salem's first shipping agency. In
this capacity Griffin acted as a middleman between captains and prospective
hands. Seamen came to his door—often when their money ran out—to

find out who was looking for men and on what sort of terms. Over the counter, Griffin drew up shipping agreements, witnessed the advance pay that these men obtained, and then outfitted them on credit if necessary with clothing and other sundries for the voyage ahead. If a sailor ran into debt for his room and board, his outfit, or his bar tab, the agent sometimes agreed to cover his obligations in return for a lien on the wages he earned. If Griffin operated like other shipping agents, he probably maintained a clientele of boardinghouse keepers who housed sailors during their lay-overs in port and then recouped the room and board they were owed by forwarding them to the agent, who placed them on outbound vessels. Boardinghouses that may have operated in this manner could be found in 1837 scattered along Derby, Essex, and Water streets close to the wharves, usually run by widows, who would have relied on Griffin to guarantee that their boarders paid up.

How hard Griffin worked to draw mariners into any real dependence and whether or not he engaged in the heavy-handed tactics associated with crimping—advancing sailors money beyond their means of repay-ment, overcharging them for services, or colluding with shipmasters to keep wages down—the records do not reveal. His business must have been a profitable one, however, since during the 1840s he moved his prem-ises to the corner of Liberty and Vine Streets, closer to Salem's principal wharves, where he opened a boardinghouse of his own (Figure 6.3). It has long since vanished, but it must have been a fair-sized and busy establish-ment, for when the census enumerator stopped by there in the summer of 1850, he learned that 431 mariners, hailing from all around the Atlantic rim and ranging from seventeen to forty-eight years of age, had passed through recently enough and stayed long enough to call it their "usual lodging place." By 1850 Griffin had two professional competitors in the boardinghouse business, and dozens of Salem homeowners took in the odd sailor or two to make ends meet.[26]

Regardless of how they were recruited, the plainest feature about the seamen who shipped from this port in the nineteenth century was that they were no longer primarily neighbors. The motives that drove them to sea and the paths that brought them to Salem may have been as complex and variegated as the entire Atlantic world in which they worked. What they shared in common, however, was precisely this variety in origin, and nothing would have struck a Salem inhabitant strolling the wharves in

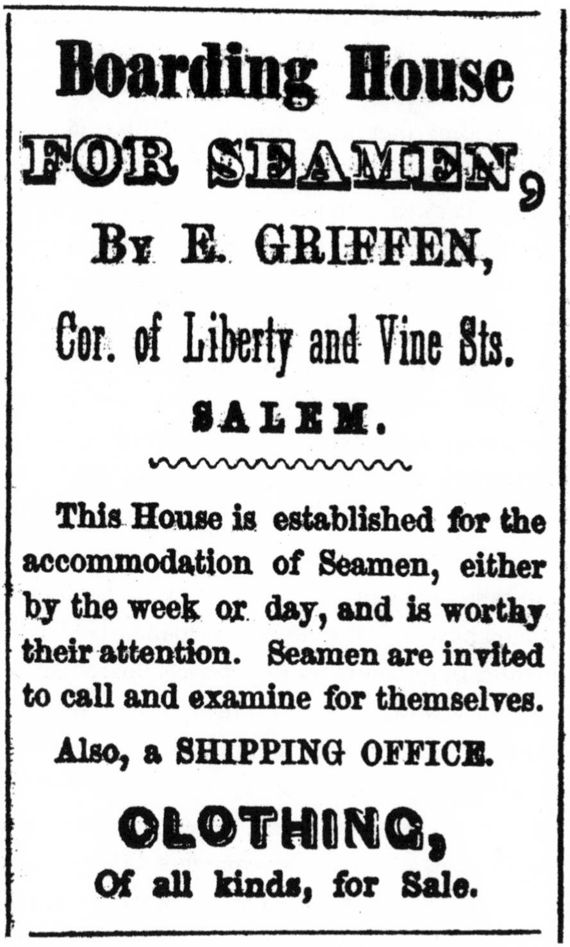

FIGURE 6.3 Seaman's Hotel Advertisement, *Salem City Directory*, 1850. This was Salem's first large, commercial boardinghouse. The advertisement documents the housing, outfitting, and recruitment functions of one nineteenth-century shipping master. (Courtesy of the Peabody-Essex Museum)

the antebellum period and watching a vessel discharge its crew more forcefully than the panoply of strange faces.

Early in the morning on September 29, 1825, a call from the chief officer summoned Thomas Boardman, seaman, on deck of the ship *Janus* to assist his crewmates in loosing the sails, bracing the yards, casting off

from Derby Wharf, and making way out of Salem Harbor bound on a voyage to the Far East. Boardman had grown up about fifteen miles north of
Salem, in Ipswich, where his father, Daniel, had been earning his living
on the ocean—as a mariner, fisherman, and lighterman—since before
the Revolutionary War. In 1823 Daniel died, insolvent, leaving young
Thomas as his mother's sole support, so the twenty-two-year-old decided
to join Captain Henry Bridges and ship himself abroad to help support
the family. That the younger Boardman, who had grown up along the
coast, would become a sailor like his father was entirely traditional. The
horizons that defined the respective working lives of father and son, however, could not have been more different: Daniel had spent most of his
seafaring career working in the waters along America's coast; Thomas
was bound around the world.[27]

Over the next twenty-one months, the *Janus* crossed the Atlantic,
Pacific, and Indian oceans, cruised the coasts of Asia, Africa, and the
Americas, and called in at an array of different ports and harbors, from
Baltimore to Valparaiso to Manila to Batavia to the island of St. Helena in
the South Atlantic. In the course of their travels Boardman and his crewmates battled their way through a good many violent storms but also experienced weeks of the steadiest sailing imaginable. They spotted what
they believed to be pirates in the South China Sea, witnessed waterspouts
off Cape Hatteras and the Bikini Atoll, talked with traders and whalers
they met along the way, and dealt with countless different peoples in their
ports of call en route. For five months on the outbound leg of its voyage,
the *Janus* sailed up and down the western coast of South America, hawking
produce and manufactures from around the Atlantic rim for silver, copper,
and other commodities Captain Bridges thought would find Asian buyers,
and then for even longer they tramped around the East Indies loading
sugar, coffee, and perhaps some pepper or indigo, all of which they transported home to markets in New England.[28]

Of the fifteen men who sailed out of Salem that September morning,
only ten returned—or at least returned on board the *Janus*. John Howell
of New Jersey and Samuel Averall from Kennebunkport, Maine, the two
oldest sailors on board, deserted on the South American coast—one in
Valparaiso, the other in Guayaquil, Ecuador. That both were older and
probably experienced suggests that something other than homesickness,
perhaps related to conditions on board, prompted them to it, but the ship's

log, which lay closed in port, tells us nothing more. Indeed, at no point in the voyage does the log even hint at issues of discontent. It is hard to imagine that sailors were not scolded, cuffed, or hazed routinely throughout the voyage, or that the daily practice of discipline did not generate problems that had plenty of time to grow and fester on a voyage of this length, yet it is significant that never during the cruise of the *Janus* did these troubles bubble over into a single disciplinary event—say a flogging or a dismissal—noteworthy enough to record.[29]

Three other members of the crew died abroad. The first, George Taylor of Newport, Rhode Island, breathed his last while the ship lay at anchor in the roads at Callao, Peru; the second, Jacob Ashton, Jr., of Salem caught a violent fever in Batavia and after fighting it at sea for fifty days finally succumbed, "without a struggle or a groan," off Ascension Island in the South Atlantic; and the third, a Dane named Christopher Lum, had been nursing a low-grade fever for months without seeming "in immediate danger" when he suddenly worsened and died a mere eight days short of reaching Salem again. Three such losses in twenty-one months may have exceeded normal rates of mortality by a little, but losing five men to the combination of death and desertion in a single voyage was by this period not highly unusual. When Thomas Boardman obtained his discharge in Salem and took passage in a coaster north to Ipswich to greet his mother with a couple of hundred dollars in his pocket, we can be certain that she was much relieved.[30]

The voyage of the *Janus* illustrates how remarkably the seafaring experience out of Salem had altered over fifty years. Although the basic elements of the seaman's duty—to hand, reef, knot, splice, and steer—remained familiar enough, the context in which they were performed had been transformed. Larger vessels, longer voyages, strange destinations, and cosmopolitan crews gave to life afloat in the nineteenth century a risky and uncertain flavor quite unlike that of colonial times. Mariners in eighteenth-century New England faced many challenges, but they knew for the most part what they were getting into; their nineteenth-century successors frequently did not.

This, of course, was part of the attraction. Longer voyages to distant parts provided a degree of adventure and novelty that Salem's colonial trades had lacked. The stories Yankee sailors told about their seafaring lives continued to dwell, as sailors' narratives traditionally had, upon the endurance and fortitude that their work entailed, the wit and ingenuity needed to triumph over their troubles, and of course the progress of their own careers. When this new generation of American mariners committed their narratives to paper, however, they dwelled now at much greater length on the lure of the strange and exotic. Sometimes they made the point explicitly. Richard Cleveland, who had first shipped out in 1792 at age nineteen, claimed later that he chose the sea partly for the same sort of motives that had inspired Salem boys for decades: "a predilection for nautical affairs" that he had "early in life, imbibed" by virtue of having grown up beside the sea, as well as his belief that a nautical career presented in a maritime society "the most sure and direct means of arriving at independence." To these traditional motives, however, he added the pursuit of adventure:

> that though the hardships and privations of a seaman's life
> be greater than those of any other, there is a compensation in
> the very excitement of its dangers, in the opportunity it affords
> of visiting different countries, and viewing mankind in the
> various gradations between the most barbarous and the most
> refined; and in the ever-changing scenes which this occupation
> presents.

The hunger for novelty was reflected even more obviously by the space that mariners devoted in their journals and memoirs to the peoples, the sights, and the customs of distant parts. Dana's description of his year and a half on the coast of California—gathering and curing hides, trading and visiting with Spanish colonists, and living on the beach with transplanted Hawaiian Islanders—is only the best known of hundreds of similar accounts recorded by every mariner-journalist of the day who set eyes on Calcutta, Manila, St. Petersburg, Zanzibar, Canton, Mocha, or the coast of Sumatra. And always, at least implicitly, the emphasis was on what distinguished these people and their ways from Yankees at home. In Salem shipmasters institutionalized this fascination by forming in 1799 the East India Marine Society, which charged its members among other duties with the task of bringing back from their travels artifacts of the Orient for display in the society's museum. Seafaring provided New Englanders with a window on a world that to them was utterly new.[31]

That these Americans should have memorialized this discovery in print and museum collections is hardly surprising. Travelers have always shown a disposition to regale the stay-at-homes with stories about what they are missing, and these were the first global wanderers that New England ever produced. They, along with their counterparts elsewhere in the United States, generated an entire genre of literature—the American seafaring narrative—designed to excite domestic readers with tales of true adventure. The flip side of adventure, however, was risk, and the vast majority of sailors experienced risk, not only as the mother of romance and opportunity but also as the accompaniment to trouble. The seas that Yankees began to frequent during the 1780s and 1790s may not have exposed them to much that was any more physically trying or dangerous to health than the waters they already knew. When Richard Cleveland reached into his memory for the quintessentially miserable voyage—the sort that might cause anyone to "pronounce the seaman's life to be the hardest, the most dangerous, the most irksome, the most wearing to body and mind, of any one of the pursuits of man"—he chose "a winter's passage from Europe to America." The North Atlantic kicks up as much dirty weather as any ocean on earth, and New Englanders had been battling it, sometimes to a briny grave, for a century and more. Nor was there anything novel about the threat of tropical disease. On the swampy coast of Sumatra or the seaports of west Africa, Yankee seamen did run the hazard of catching deadly fevers that, indeed, carried a good number of them off. Yet mortality rates in the colonial Caribbean were as high as any other region that New Englanders began to visit after the American Revolution, and generations of Salem widows could testify to the frequency with which husbands had sailed to the West Indies and never returned. Pirates, privateers, typhoons, and ship-rot: the trouble with global commerce from the sailor's perspective had less to do with hardships and dangers that had long been well within Yankee experience than it did with the difficulty of coping with these problems in contexts where they were so difficult to handle.[32]

Take a simple matter such as pumping. Sailors always hated it, both for the punishment to their bodies and for the strain on their minds. Masters often proved reluctant to put into port and repair the leak, and the tension that it wrought on board ship could be serious. Yet a short stint of pumping on a coastwise voyage of several weeks was nothing compared to the sort of drudgery this could inflict on a transoceanic voyage of several months. And the issue was not simply physical. Gorham Low lay in

Göteberg, Sweden, in the spring of 1831 preparing to weigh anchor for New England when his vessel suddenly began to take on water. Low decided to leave anyway, and even as they sailed through the North Sea into the Atlantic, the crew found themselves pumping around the clock at 800 to 1,300 strokes an hour, and "the worst of it," Low wrote, "was the constant anxiety we felt lest the gale should increase the leak beyond our power to keep the ship afloat." Although they arrived in Boston safely, Low termed it "one of the most anxious passages I ever made." Springing a leak on an India voyage could mean months of the same work without relief. Bound to the Far East and familiar with leaky vessels from past experience, Edward Beck trumpeted that this time "our ship is as tight as a bottle, which to us who for a whole India voyage were used to pump for ¾ hour out of 2 or 3, is a complete luxury." Although several shipmasters testified in a case before the federal courts in 1846 that on a voyage from Manila to New York a thousand strokes an hour around the clock was not an "extraordinary labor," it was still enough to prompt several sailors on board the *Moslem* to desert at the Cape of Good Hope, cause the remaining crew to demand, after leaving Cape Town, that the ship return for repairs, and drive several more sailors to mutiny as they labored northward through the Atlantic toward home.[33]

Another sensitive issue was food. Sailors put up with a plain and numbingly repetitive diet, but they did insist that food and water be plentiful and if not fresh then at least something short of spoiled. Even shipowners granted that a sailor was entitled to receive as a basic diet "tea or coffee night and morning, and flour, rice, or beans at dinner, in addition to meat," as well as about a pound of bread a day, and regular puddings sweetened with honey or molasses. At ports of call, many masters tried to procure extra fresh provisions and sometimes a few livestock to be penned up on deck and slaughtered later on for a midocean feast. Any fish caught in transit provided additional variety. Salt meat and hardtack were the staple in every trade, but on those that spanned shorter distances some variety was possible to sustain, and the consequences of running short were seldom severe.[34]

The longer voyages of the nineteenth century put provisioning to the test and were much more prey to any sort of accident, misjudgment, or stinginess. On October 20, 1849, the ship *Palmyra* made sail from Calcutta bound for New England with a crew of twenty-one and a single passenger on board. After a long and troubled voyage of 163 days, the *Palmyra* arrived in Boston, its stores exhausted and its crew hungry, thirsty, and sick. Two weeks later, the sailors submitted a libel to the First District Court of the United States, alleging that they had been living on short allowance for the better part of the voyage and demanding compensation for their suffering. For more than a month officers and crew battled with each other before the bench over the quantity of food and water necessary for such a voyage, whether the captain had purchased sufficient provisions in Calcutta, whether the food was edible, whether the crew had deliberately squandered their fare by tossing it to the hogs that were kept on deck, and whether the master had coerced his officers as well as the cook and steward into signing a paper claiming that the stores taken on in Calcutta were adequate and that the men were to blame for the shortfall. After listening to all sides, the magistrates found for the crew and awarded them more than 90 percent of their demands—a day's additional wages for every day on short allowance. If the libel was judged to be essentially true, we can assume that by the time they passed the Cape of Good Hope, the men had to make do with a quart or two of water per day (instead of the customary gallon) and eight to twelve ounces of salt meat (instead of fourteen ounces or more) and the same amount of ship's bread (instead of somewhat more than a pound). Much of the bread on the *Palmyra* was "wormy and unfit to be eaten," the meat was made "of ends of pieces," and by the time the basic stores began to give out, the other provisions laid in by the master —pumpkins, potatoes, yams, and onions—were either "wholy . . . [or] mostly gone." No wonder, as even the chief mate admitted, that the men were "kind of slow—always growling about their work" and "sick up and down" throughout the voyage. Lengthy voyages had this kind of reputation. "If . . . you have never suffered from thirst protracted, thirst tantalized or thirst disappointed and have any inclination to experience the sensations," wrote one retired sailor in 1830, "let me entreat you to make a voyage to Canton on a Boston Indiaman." Masters were not always niggardly to their men, but living on short allowance for weeks on end was a terrible hardship, and there are few topics that account for more legal actions than sailors' complaints about poor or insufficient grub.[35]

Another source of uncertainty whose importance multiplied over longer distances was the issue of changed voyages. By admiralty law, when a sailor signed shipping articles, he was obliging himself to complete the voyage described in the agreement, but not to continue in service if a master deviated substantially from the original destination. Yet masters in their search for markets did this all the time—shifting course for different ports, adding legs onto voyages, or even selling the ship in a foreign port outright and leaving the crew stranded. Sometimes the men did not care, provided the alteration was not too profound or the spot they were left to shift for themselves not too remote. But in certain circumstances, the changes masters insisted on were dramatic, even life changing, and sailors complained.

In the early 1840s the *Brookline* sailed from Boston with fourteen seamen on board, who had signed a set of articles drawn up by a shipping agent describing a voyage "from the port of Boston to a port or ports easterly of the Cape of Good Hope, or any port or ports to which the master should see fit to go, in order to procure a cargo." Instead, the ship proceeded to Ichaboe Island (off the coast of present-day Namibia), where the men were forced for thirteen weeks to dig out a cargo of guano for the American market. The work there was dangerous for a number of reasons. Anchored in an open roadstead, the *Brookline* lay "exposed to the winds and waves . . . [where] vessels were frequently dashed against each other and against the rocks," sometimes killing sailors on board. Even worse was the work on the guano, in pits as deep as forty feet and only ten across, where the odor was always "noxious and offensive," the "effluvia and dust . . . extremely annoying," and cave-ins burying men alive not at all unknown. Although the men were paid a tiny supplement of three pence a ton for their labors, they made it clear to the captain that they considered their contract violated, and when they returned to Boston, they brought suit in the Federal Court against the owners for extra compensation. The court agreed with them that "they had been cheated into the voyage, and engaged in services dangerous, nauseous, and unhealthy," and awarded the sailors $55 each, something close to a 150 percent bonus for the period they spent on Ichaboe. In this instance the master and owners did not get away with their nasty scheme, but plainly they imagined they could, seven thousand miles from home.[36]

When Richard Henry Dana was sailing the coast of California as a common seaman gathering hides in 1835, nothing bothered him more than the real possibility that he might end up trapped on those shores. Dana had been in San Diego seven weeks, loading the *Alert* with hides and waiting for the day of departure for home, when Captain Thompson summoned him aft and informed him that he could not leave until he found another sailor willing to take his old place on the brig, *Pilgrim,* which would remain behind on the Pacific Coast. This Dana knew to be impossible, "that it would be hopeless to attempt to prevail upon any of the ship's crew to take twelve months more upon California in the brig," and he nearly panicked. A year or so before the mast would not scar him permanently, he believed, but anything more "would . . . [make] me a sailor for the rest of my days," a fate he considered "worse than a Botany Bay exile." Desperate, he pulled rank and informed Thompson and his officers that he had "friends and interest enough at home to make them suffer for any injustice" they might do him. That apparently did the trick, and the captain sent Dana forward to be replaced in the *Pilgrim* by a poor English boy named Ben. When Ben discovered his fate, he returned to the forecastle, "looking as though he had received his sentence to be hung," and the crew descended on Dana. "Oh yes!" they said, "the captain has let you off, because you are a gentleman's son, and have got friends, and know the owners; and taken Ben, because he is poor, and has got nobody to say a word for him." Eventually Dana relented, and to save Ben (and his own reputation) he bought off another sailor named Harry Bluff with an order for six months of Dana's own wages, which Bluff then cashed as he gave up his berth in the *Alert*. Although this story says much about class and connection, it displays in particular the fear held by seamen far from home that they had lost control over their lives—that in the absence of courts and community sanctions, masters could ignore the terms of their shipping agreements and consign them to months or even years of labor to which they had not agreed.[37]

A key element of the new maritime regime operating out of Salem that compounded the uncertainties of working life in a global shipping industry was the heterogeneous social composition of nineteenth-century crews, for when a ship's complement was made up of people most of whom were strangers to one another, there simply was no telling where the interpersonal relationships within any crew might lead. Captains might be competent but also fools; chief mates could be easygoing or martinets; seamen could be endlessly long-suffering, chronic grumblers, or downright rebellious. Since few of the officers or men had grown up with one another, they did not know how exactly these unknown human elements would combine, nor would the truth often emerge until weeks or even months at sea. How, for example, could the sailors who signed on with Charles Tyng in 1831 have anticipated that as soon as the ship had left the wharf, Tyng would call each one of them separately down into the forecastle, demand that they open their sea chests, hack off the lids with an axe if they refused, haul out the jugs of rum they had purchased for the voyage, and heave the liquor overboard? How could Captain Horace Jenks of Salem have known that the second mate named William Farwell he shipped for a voyage to the East Indies in 1834 would prove incapable of supervising "much of the Ship's Work," ready to pick quarrels with some of the hands, and prone to fall asleep on his watch; that Farwell would eventually "lose all command over the Men by his improper Familiarity with them" to the point where disputes descended into shipboard brawls; and that in the end he would have to disrate this officer, send him forward to work as one of the crew, and eventually put him in chains when he refused? How could James Walker, cook of the ship *Nautilus* in 1823, have guessed that when he protested having to cook and serve the crew some fresh beef that had spoiled "on account of the warm wheather" to the point where it "smell'd like carrion," Captain Winslow would call for the chief mate, haul Walker aft, seize him up to the mizzen rigging, and deal him three dozen lashes with the bight of the mizzen topsail buntline? On a happier note, how could Richard Henry Dana have known when in 1835 he first boarded the *Alert* in San Diego that on this vessel he would make the acquaintance of the polymath English seaman Tom Harris, from whom he learned "more about foreign nations, the habits of different people, and especially the secrets of sailors' lives and hardships . . . than I could ever have learned elsewhere," making Harris "all in all, the most remarkable man I have ever seen." All of these eventualities were unanticipated. Of course, nobody ever guessed how exactly a journey by sea might turn out, even on a coastal passage in the company of friends. Nevertheless, an unplanned mix of strangers could be a recipe for pleasant amity or for real trouble, and Salem mariners of the nineteenth century had a dimmer notion than their colonial predecessors about whom to sail with and whom to avoid.[38]

Dana's account of his *Two Years Before the Mast* illustrates just how delicate the balance of human relations on board could actually be. Although the young New Englander sailed to California on one vessel and returned on another, his commander on both legs was the same Captain

Thompson. The outbound voyage on the *Pilgrim* was full of personal tension, climaxing in Thompson's flogging two of Dana's shipmates; the return voyage—though objectively much harder, including a terrible passage back around Cape Horn—transpired with relatively little human trouble. In Dana's view this was all owing to the different relationships that prevailed between Thompson and the two mates he hired for each voyage. The captain was "a vigorous, energetic fellow . . . always active and driving; severe in his discipline, and expected the same of his officers." With Andrew Amerzene, the mild-mannered mate of the *Pilgrim*, "a worthy man . . . honest, upright, and kind-hearted," Thompson could not help but grow "suspicious that discipline was getting relaxed." The captain "began to interfere in everything . . . and in his attempt to remedy the difficulty by severity, he made everything worse." In the end, wrote Dana, "we were in every respect unfortunately situated. Captain, officers, and crew, entirely unfitted for one another; and every circumstance and event was like a two-edged sword, and cut both ways." By contrast, the mate on the *Alert*, Richard Brown, "took everything into his own hands; and was more likely to encroach upon the authority of the master, than to need any spurring." Dana explicitly compared this mate, with his "hallooing and bawling, in all directions, making everything fly, and, at the same time, doing everything well," to Amerzene; Brown was "not so estimable a man, perhaps, but a far better mate of a vessel." Captain Thompson was a changed person on the voyage home to Boston, and the passage was, socially speaking, far smoother for the entire crew. Although Dana's particular psychology may be open to question, the broader point that the social experience of every voyage hinged on a set of interpersonal dynamics that was peculiar to every different crew and could not be anticipated among strangers is undeniable.[39]

Shipmasters responded to the problem of risk in all its dimensions by running a tighter ship: enforcing a greater division of labor by rank, making a clearer distinction between watches, and imposing a stricter form of discipline. The growing division of labor was reflected in the multiplication of ranks. By the nineteenth century, brigs always employed a cook and frequently a second mate, while ships carried both of these and often a steward and carpenter besides. The captain was still a master of his trade—usually the oldest man on board and possessed of the same personal, arbitrary, and physical authority as ever—but he no longer stood watch with the crew. In the larger vessels of the nineteenth century, he retreated to the quarterdeck or cabin and communicated with his men mainly through the chief mate. The mate in turn became more of a manager and less involved, except occasionally by example, in the physical work of the crew. Thomas Gregory, a mariner from Marblehead who engaged himself as mate on a voyage to Savannah in 1817 observed plainly that "the Trade is very Laborious but as I am a going Chief Officer my Duty is not very hard."[40] The division of hands into port and starboard watches grew more formalized on larger vessels. Edward Beck, an English sailor who sailed in both the coastwise and the East India trades, claimed that he appreciated this. When off duty, he wrote, he had "more time to myself," since the other half of the crew were numerous enough to handle the ship in all but the most severe weather without his being summoned to lend a hand. Still, the watch system, strictly observed, also served to augment the master's authority over the crew—not only by timing their labor but by spatially separating them in two separate groups.[41] Finally, as scores of cases before federal courts sitting in admiralty testify, shipmasters and their officers were much quicker to reinforce their commands with physical abuse. Whereas the New Englanders' coastwise fleet of the colonial period generated relatively little business for the vice admiralty courts of their day, the global fleet of the early republic presented the United States district courts with a regular stream of suits, and largely because the labor regime on board was more authoritarian.

Most voyages, of course, terminated without a visit to the magistrate. The *Lama*, to take a single example among thousands, sailed for Marseilles in June 1826 and returned six months later via Philadelphia with nothing more extraordinary in the mate's log than a brief patch of heavy weather three days out of Salem that parted the foretopmast studding sail, and few chance meetings with other vessels on the high seas—no chases, deaths, mutinies, or any disciplinarian incidents on board worth reporting. But a good index of how much more likely all of the tensions and stresses described in this chapter were to boil over into measurable discontent is the rising incidence of desertion. Since a deserter forfeited his right to any pay, one can measure its frequency by comparing outbound shipping agreements, listing those who obtained the customary month's advance pay against their voyages, with their inbound equivalents, detailing the total sums laid out on labor at the voyage's end. Men who received advances but no further pay we can usually presume to have deserted, although a small number may also have been discharged without pay for some other violation of maritime law. In the eighteenth century, the number of sailors who ran from Salem ships was small indeed. If we can take forfeiture of pay as an indicator of desertion, then only 3 percent of all Salem voyages between 1726 and 1800 lost hands in this way, whereas by 1801–1825 that proportion had jumped to 22 percent, and between 1826 and 1850 it had climbed to 33 percent. This is still not a majority; but even if most vessels returned to Salem with crews intact, men vote with their feet, and the rising proclivity to desert suggests something significant.[42]

Shipmasters believed deserters were simply scoundrels—the worst of a broadly unreliable pool of men from whom seamen were drawn—and sometimes they may have been right. Usually, however, sailors deserted for sound, practical reasons, one of which was pay. Those who signed on in a low-wage port (in Great Britain, for example) would often desert in a high-wage port (often in America), where labor was scarce and where they hoped to negotiate better terms. Since seamen who signed articles in Salem were comparatively well paid from the start, however, running away in most foreign ports would not have helped, and so the search for higher pay was probably not the issue there. The other principal motive for desertion, and the one that more probably pushed most of those who jumped from Salem vessels, was ordinary dissatisfaction. In extreme cases, when the sailor felt that he had been truly driven from the ship, either by the officers' brutality, the master's incompetence, the quality or quantity of the food, concerns over the seaworthiness of the vessel, or the fear that the voyage might be redirected in such a way as to prevent him from returning home in a timely manner, he sued the owners to win back the pay he lost when he left ship. Most deserters, however, never showed up in court, and we can probably assume that while their problems were real enough, they decided—for lack of evidence, the inconvenience and expense of standing trial, or the weakness of their case—that the chance of obtaining legal satisfaction was not worth the trouble involved. Still, it is hard to imagine that this rising incidence of desertion did not reflect something real that was changing in the quality of working life on board Salem vessels during the first half of the nineteenth century.[43]

At first glance, the difficulty in summarizing the experience of seafaring in an age of global shipping is rooted in the very variety of that experience. In a voyage to the far ends of the earth over six, twelve, or eighteen months a great deal could happen—much that was endlessly predictable, but much that was not. Yet it is the *range* of experience that is precisely the point. Going to sea had never been for the fainthearted, but when Salem's vessels followed coastwise trades, the spread of dangers and the array of opportunities could easily be summarized, for sailors had heard it all before. Once their descendants began to chase the sun across every line of longitude, the limit on experiences—good *and* bad—was effectively removed. Seafaring ceased to be something that every boy who grew up beside the sea could easily imagine doing.

What sort of a career, then, could Salem boys foresee in this era of global shipping? The changing age distribution of seamen suggests part of the answer. Although foremast hands of the early republic were still mostly young men commanded by their seniors, the numbers of older seamen had climbed significantly since colonial times, and we can only infer that the career expectations of mariners had changed (see Graph 10, Appendix B). To address this issue in a systematic, comparative way, one can pose the same question for the early nineteenth as for the mid-eighteenth century: what was likely to happen to young seamen between their early twenties and their early thirties (see Graph 11, Appendix B)? The answers presented here must be understood only as rough approximations, but even allowing for some margin of error, the only significant area of relative continuity with the world of their grandfathers was the chance that sailors would not survive their seafaring careers at all. Allowing for an age-specific mortality rate of about 40 per thousand per annum in the period 1786–1794, when the data are strongest, and extending that rate into subsequent decades on the strength of stable male life expectancy for the town as a whole, as well as a ratio of deaths at sea to general population that refused to drop, a sailor's prospect of dying within a decade at sea was still about 30 percent. There were some particularly deadly years during the early republic—as in 1800, when Bentley noted the deaths of fourteen young men, aged fifteen to twenty-nine, all to accidents at sea or fevers abroad usually contracted in the Caribbean. In other periods, as in the years following Jefferson's Embargo, when overseas trade dwindled, the mortality of mariners abroad dipped accordingly. Over the long term, however, as long as the majority of Salem vessels continued to steer courses principally toward fever-ridden tropical ports, the mortality of sailors was unlikely to fall.[44]

Those who survived their twenties faced a range of prospects that were quite changed from colonial times. For one thing, the chance of rising to a position of command was much thinner. Only about one-quarter of all locally born seamen ever became chief mates, and fewer than half of these mates eventually became masters. Promotion was nothing close to the customary expectation it once had been. In part, this was a simple matter of arithmetic: larger vessels with larger crews meant stiffer competition over the available mateships and masterships. Beyond probability, however, the advent of global shipping had altered the very nature of seaborne command, requiring knowledge and talents that well surpassed those necessary to the coastwise trades of colonial times. When John Crowninshield, commander of the ship *Belisarius,* called into Calcutta for sixty days in 1797–1798, he found himself responsible for renting premises on shore from which to conduct his business, hiring a local banyan (or commercial agent) through whom to buy and sell cargo; negotiating exchange rates for Indian currency and various precious metals, finding doctors for one sailor who had come down with venereal disease, trying to keep track of others who periodically disappeared (on sprees of their own or seized by British press gangs), hiring Indian workmen to help with lading the vessel, settling labor conflicts among his own crew, supervising weeks of difficult and extensive repairs to the ship, and surveying other vessels in port to determine whether or not they needed to be overhauled. Eighteenth-century Salem masters tended to sail repeatedly to the same ports and deal with the same merchants, the same currencies, and the same customs officials year after year. Difficulties cropped up, of course, but in relatively familiar settings. Colonial mariners did not have to learn how to negotiate in dozens of different countries, whose laws, business customs, and social relations in general differed so radically from those of New England.[45]

When hiring a master, a shipowner had always weighed candidates' purely nautical talents against other gifts for business and labor management, but on longer voyages with heterogeneous crews in larger ships to distant parts, the latter skills began to weigh more heavily in the balance. The complexity of commanding three-masted ships in unfamiliar waters should not be trivialized; it took longer to reach the quarterdeck after the Revolution than it had before, and part of the reason was undoubtedly that larger ships were more complex and harder to master. The new element in the owner's calculation, however, was the riskier business environment of global commerce, and for this reason they tended to select masters from within their own ranks—young men who had received their practical education not in boats along the waterfront or in years of service before the mast but in the shops and countinghouses of Essex and Derby streets. A few were sons of Crowninshields, Ornes, and the like—the offspring of Salem's true merchant elite. A much larger number belonged to the more successful shopkeeping, craft, or maritime families, where a combination of physical labor and business still occupied the day, and commerce was dinner-table talk. Capt. Nathaniel Hathorne (father of the famous author), for example, though unsuccessful in business himself, grew up in a comfortable three-story, hip-roofed house on Union Street—supported in part by his shipmaster father's investments in Salem's growing overseas trade. Although property and connection had never hurt in the search for promotion in this seaport town, they became more decisive during the early republic. Indeed, out of forty-nine cases in which fathers of Salem- or Beverly-born shipmasters, 1690–1775, could be traced on the Salem tax lists for the year closest to that on which the mariner turned twenty-one, only 37 percent ranked within the first or second wealth decile, but out of twenty-one similar cases, 1783–1850, fathers ranked within the first or second decile a full 62 percent of the time.[46]

Nowhere is this more clearly illustrated than in the case of Richard Cleveland. The son of a successful Salem shopkeeper, Richard spent his teenage years not punting around the harbor but dragging a quill across the pages of ledger books in the countinghouse of Elias Haskett Derby, the greatest merchant of his generation. As he admitted, Cleveland initially learned about ships not by sailing them but by watching them being built in Enos Briggs's shipyard on Stage Point across the South River. Writing his memoirs in later years, he heaped scorn upon the traditional saw that a shipmaster "should enter on board by the hawse-holes (or forecastle), and not by the cabin windows." As he put it:

> When I began, I was aware of the existence of this maxim, but doubted its truth; as I could not comprehend how the qualifications for command were to be acquired by living in the forecastle; or how nautical skill was to be advanced by practising the duties of tarring down the rigging, and slushing the masts.

I had therefore no ambition of attaining to a practical knowledge of these accomplishments. I came in at the cabin windows . . . in the capacity of captain's clerk; to live with him in
the cabin; to assist him in his business in port; and to do duty
as a foremast hand at sea. Nor have I, after my long course
of experience, been able to discover any way so desirable,
so eligible as this, for giving a young man a practical knowledge of seamanship, free from the vulgarity of the forecastle;
and of so familiarizing him with the manner of doing business in various countries, as to make him an accomplished
super-cargo.

And a shipmaster, he might have added, since that is where Cleveland's
particular career strategy landed him. Even in the nineteenth century,
most sea captains probably began their careers by doing a stint of several
years before the mast, but in their personal background as well as their
talents and inclinations, they were businessmen as much as navigators.[47]

Persistence before the mast helped a little in achieving promotion,
but not sufficiently, as in the eighteenth century, to make promotion to an
officer's berth a strong possibility. Out of all locally born mariners whose
last names started with A and whose careers at sea between 1803 and 1840
included at least five voyages, 14 percent made it to master, 14 percent to
chief mate, and 7 percent to second mate, while 64 percent were never
promoted. Of a comparable group whose careers included *fewer* than five
voyages, 8 percent made it to master, 8 percent to chief mate, and 4 percent
to second mate, whereas 80 percent were never promoted. Those who
served longer stood a slightly better chance of promotion, but doggedness
did not make the difference it once had.[48]

The compensation of senior officers reflected this fact. During the
era of neutral shipping, first mates saw their wages soar even more dramatically than those of foremast hands. In 1790 they had earned on average
about $9.00 per month, or about 20 percent more than the seamen under
their charge. Between 1793 and 1812, by contrast, that wage soared to
$22.75, or 39 percent more than a seaman could make. After the War of
1812, moreover, mates' wages did not return to earth as seamen's did, and,
in fact, there opened up between the two a gap that never closed (see
Graph 12, Appendix B). Whether this applied to shipmasters as well is

hard to know for certain, since ship's commanders received a great deal of their remuneration in the form of cargo space and the profits earned from trading on their own account. During the period 1825 through 1850 shipmasters who were allowed privileges earned a mean monthly wage of $25—slightly higher than that of a mate. Those denied privileges, however, garnered on average $22 more (a sum probably equivalent to the estimated value of a master's privilege)—earning a monthly wage of $47. Not only had the gap between mates and seamen widened, so too had that between masters and mates. And given the elevated responsibility of handling larger ships, managing more diverse crews, and doing more complicated business, nineteenth-century captains undoubtedly felt they deserved it.[49]

This sort of money, however, was little more than a pipe dream to most seamen of the nineteenth century, since so few of them ever succeeded to any senior officer's post. No marker of rising opportunity, it signified instead both the narrowing of the channel to promotion and the degree to which masters and mates were now more thoroughly the agents of capital. Facing a hurdle they could not surmount, some Salem youths, as in the past, quit the sea young and took up other trades in town, but even more remained mariners through their working lifetimes, even though they never succeeded in landing an officer's berth. Charles Atkinson was one of those who managed the transition to shore fairly successfully. Having survived at least a dozen years of voyaging around the world and reaching his late twenties, he married in 1811 the widowed daughter of an unsuccessful sea captain. How he managed through the War of 1812 is unclear, but after the return of peace he shipped himself as a seaman on one last voyage to India in 1815 and then in his mid-thirties quit the sea with almost nothing to his name. Some years later, however, he succeeded in launching a small grocery business on High Street in the west end of town, and he managed to get by fairly well until he and his wife both died of tuberculosis a few months apart in 1845.[50]

Yet Atkinson did better than most. The majority of Salem sailors in the nineteenth century never mounted second careers on shore, housed their families in rented quarters throughout their lives, and died in very plain circumstances, surrounded by a roomful or two of old furniture, a very modest wardrobe, the most basic of cooking and eating equipment, and only a few possessions of any decorative value—a picture on the wall, perhaps, or a couple of silver teaspoons. Out of seventy-three Salem sea-men who could be traced to nineteenth-century tax lists, 55 percent never acquired any assessable property, 64 percent were always assessed with property below the town median, and 78 percent were usually assessed below the median. The probated estates of nine nineteenth-century career seamen ranged in value from $20 to $247, but much of this was in the form of notes, probably wages due from a last voyage. Although men like Charles Atkinson did not leave the sort of paper trail one would need to plumb the motives guiding them through their lives, we know that their lot had become more common and that sailors could well anticipate spend-ing their entire seafaring careers before the mast.[51]

But what about those sailors who were not lifelong inhabitants of Salem—the ones who moved away from, moved into, or simply moved through the port? In the eighteenth century these may have been out-numbered by the locals, but in the nineteenth century men on the move constituted a decided majority in the forecastles of Salem vessels. In gen-eral, as the scarcity of officers from elsewhere indicates, men without es-tablished local ties fared poorly on the ladder of promotion. The proportion of mariners from the 1825 crew lists who were termed masters on the 1850 census was 33 percent among locally born mariners but only 11 per-cent among in-migrant mariners. If we can assume that those who left Salem fared no better in other ports than did migrants who settled in Salem, then officer's posts probably lay beyond their reach no matter where they sailed. The movers *through* are harder to evaluate. Those who returned home, where reputation and personal connection might aid them in their careers, may have managed passably, but the truly transient rarely made it to the quarterdeck wherever their travels took them.[52]

One of the latter was Jehiel Hard, who was born in Salisbury at the mouth of the Merrimack River in 1794 and came to Salem after the War of 1812 to ship out as an able seaman on voyages to Havana and then In-dia. In 1820 he married a Salem girl of plain origins named Abigail Gavett and decided to try to make a home in the seaport. For several years they lived together in one or two rented rooms furnished with several tables and fan-back chairs, a birch bedstead, a mahogany dresser, a mirror, a pair of brass andirons, and "a lot of crockery ware." Then in 1824 he shipped out one last time, as second mate on the brig *Indus*, and died abroad in Batavia that December at the age of thirty. Had Jehiel lived any longer, he could have come ashore to ply another trade in Salem or taken Abigail back to Salisbury, and the Hards might have moved into marginally easier circumstances, but they never got the opportunity, and after Jehiel's death, the family disappeared from town.[53]

In the age of global shipping, as seafaring from Salem became a more capital-intensive business and a personally riskier experience, the social gulf between masters and men began to widen, and the course of most mariners' lives turned measurably more proletarian. Although Yankee seamen had always been wage laborers, the status of a foremast hand in the colonial period was not one they had expected to put up with for their entire working lives. The majority experience was one of promotion into a position of authority, where the workplace, if not under a mariner's owner-ship, was at least under his effective control. Shipowners were at most a generation or two removed from active seafaring duty; shipmasters had almost all spent time in the forecastle and risen to command principally from their mastery of seafaring; and a ship's crew might include the sons of nearly any family in town. As Salem's maritime economy matured, however, many of these features weakened, sometimes to the point of dis-appearance. Promotion to mate or master could no longer be termed a reasonable aspiration for ordinary hands, the great majority of whom com-pleted their seafaring careers without ever having walked the quarterdeck. Most shipowners now inherited their wealth; most shipmasters acted prin-cipally as their agents; and most of the ship's crew were likely now to be strangers to them both.

In part, these developments stemmed from the transformation of Salem's shipping industry itself. With larger ships, broader labor markets, heavier discipline, and a wider gap between officers and men, Salem had simply advanced several rungs within the hierarchy of world ports. In the eighteenth century, Salem had been mainly a port of origin—the sort of place where sailors were born and trained, then either locally employed or launched for several years into an Atlantic marketplace of labor. In the nineteenth century it became as well a port of call and a magnet for sea-faring labor from elsewhere around the Atlantic rim. In part, the changes in seafaring as a lived experience were being driven by even deeper forces at work throughout American society that would transform maritime la-bor into a marginal activity, even within the seaports it supported, and it is to these that we now turn.

When Timothy Dwight passed through Salem in 1796, he described it as "a commercial town in the absolute sense"—much as it had been for the better part of two centuries. As had been other visitors before him, he was struck by Salem's lack of natural advantages: its relatively unproductive hinterland and a harbor that was still as shallow and "ill-fitted for commercial enterprise" as always. Yet the residents seemed "sober . . . [and] industrious"; the homes they inhabited were "generally decent"; and the town as a whole appeared among the most prosperous he had seen in his travels around New England. Although much in this account resembled the views of earlier visitors, there was also some suggestion of changes afoot. For one thing, Dwight was the first tourist ever to suggest that anyone in Salem earned a living apart from the sea. Although overseas commerce still supported most townspeople, Salem now also contained "its proportional share of mechanics and manufacturers." Furthermore, the town's internal geography was shifting. The "wide and handsome" Essex Street still constituted the major thoroughfare, as it had in colonial times, but Dwight also pointed out the new and fashionable neighborhoods around the "straighter and handsomer" Federal Street in the west end of town, where laboring people seldom lived. With every passing decade, Salem was becoming a town (Map 6.1) where class distinctions were easier to draw.[54]

Many of these developments were driven directly by Salem's maritime transformation. The waterfront was now under constant construction. Before the Revolution, only the Derby and Union Wharves provided ships with convenient mooring attached to the land. By 1800 workmen were constantly digging and filling along the shore, pushing new wharves out farther and farther into the harbor. Wrote Bentley one day in the summer of 1802: "Mr. Barker is putting a Cobb wharf near to Dodge's, between the remains of Nurse's wharf & Collin's tan yard & wharf . . . [while] another man is filling in that part of English's lot to the eastward . . . which is below Becket's building yard . . . [and this] will give another landing below English's former wharf, & higher to the Neck than any wharf has yet been." The modern reader can be forgiven for not following Bentley in topographical detail, but his entry resounds with the financial capital and human energy that Salemites were pouring into waterfront development. Five years later, the minister observed that a dilapidated wharf in the middle of town had just sold for $9,000, which he guessed to be ninety times what the property would have fetched when he arrived in Salem in 1784.[55]

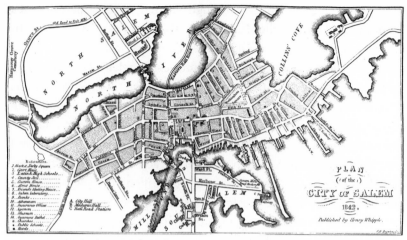

MAP 6.1 Map of Salem, 1842. Source: Joseph Felt, *Annals of Salem*, 2 vols. (Salem, Mass., 1845–1849), 1:310.

There was little suitable room on either side of the Salem peninsula to construct any new shipyards during the neutral shipping boom, but the existing yards kept busier through this period than ever before. Except in the dead of winter, the framing of sloops, schooners, brigs, and ships went on throughout the year at the Becket yard close to Salem Neck, the Briggs yard on Stage Point, and the Mann-Turner yard on the North River. All of them operated on a much larger scale than in the eighteenth century —requiring far more timber and many more men—and every couple of months one of their products would slide down the ways to the cheers of a large, appreciative audience. A host of other craftsmen, including black-smiths, blocksmiths, sailmakers, pump makers, riggers, finish carpenters, and boatbuilders descended first on the shipyards and then onto the vessels themselves, once launched, to ready them for the sea. Although none of these trades was new to Salem, the volume of business and employment they enjoyed was unprecedented.[56]

In colonial times most of the material used in the construction and outfitting of vessels had been imported, but with the boom in neutral shipping, enterprising craftsmen in Salem began to manufacture many of these goods themselves. Although ships consumed vast quantities of rope, there were very few ropemakers in colonial Salem, and when Bentley arrived in 1784, there was, he claimed "but one proper Rope walk in Town." By 1800, however, several large businesses were in operation, and dozens of men were spinning miles of line the year round. The buildings themselves had to be as lengthy as the longest cable required, and Salem's two wealthiest ropemakers, Joseph Vincent and Thomas Briggs, constructed walks of several hundred yards on piles built out over the mudflats of Collins Cove. Benjamin Browne, who grew up in the neighborhood, recollected that since "all the work being then done by hand, and not by machinery, a great number of men were employed in the walks." In particular, he remembered the day in 1799 when the ropemakers from Briggs's walk, "arranged two and two," carried the anchor cable of the frigate *Essex* through the town, bearing it on "woolering stick[s]" resting on their shoulders, to the yard where the vessel was being finished, while drummers and fifers played "Yankee Doodle." Browne also remembered how the ropemakers operated something in the collective manner of a guild, sharing difficult work between the walks and celebrating the feast of St. Catherine every November 25 with "a procession in the early part of the evening, a salute at intervals from cannon placed on the common, and an entertainment by the owners in their dwellings to a circle of their friends and patrons, and a liberal table spread for the workmen in the walks," where the ropemakers caroused until early the next morning. Although Pastor Bentley disapproved of this "folly," he could not deny the revelry of the day, with its "uncommon shew & noise, guns firing, flags displayed, etc."[57]

Less directly connected to seafaring was a cluster of other industries that made their appearance early in the nineteenth century. Shoemaking was one of these. Salem sat just to the north of the rapidly growing shoe city of Lynn, and some of this manufacture was put out to shoemakers and their families in Salem. By the 1830s there were more than five hundred men and women cutting leather and stitching shoes in dozens of homes and workshops around town. A few hundred more workmen toiled in the tanneries around Salem Commons, transforming the hides brought into port from South America into leather sides and uppers for the shoemakers in Salem and Lynn. In 1796 Bentley claimed that since the Revolution the number of local tanyards had multiplied from one within the town as a whole to eight within its eastern wards alone. A stroll through the western suburbs in 1815 revealed three more "doing business upon a large scale" on the banks of the North River under the brow of Gallows Hill. In other parts of town, tobacconists set up small "manufactories," where yet another few hundred people, chiefly women and girls, rolled tobacco carried from Virginia into cigars.[58]

Like other towns across America, Salem was alive with entrepreneurial experimentation in the early nineteenth century, and if many of these businesses failed to last more than a few seasons, taken together they employed all sorts of people in jobs their grandparents could not even have imagined. In 1790 the town donated land on Broad Street for the construction of a little factory to weave sailcloth that could compete with the Russia duck that local merchants had traditionally imported to suit their vessels. The factory was still in business a decade later and kept a dozen or more weavers and spinners busy as long as it lasted. During the War of 1812 a couple of chemists started manufacturing alum and vitriol for local physicians and did well enough that in 1819 they constructed larger premises across the North River; by 1832, as the Salem Laboratory Company, they were employing twenty-five men refining a variety of chemical products for sale around the United States. William Bentley made a hobby of touring such establishments, and during his pastorate, he visited dozens of them—ironworks, cotton factories, bark mills, weaving shops, breweries, chocolate mills, mustard mills, and others—pointing out repeatedly how these businesses had "greatly multiplied" in recent years. By 1837, when Salem's first city directory was published, it is clear from the lists of names and occupations that the town had diversified enormously and that maritime employment no longer commanded the labor market.[59]

For the first time in Salem's history, people began to speak of seafaring as being confined to a certain community within the town—a small but identifiable sailortown, where mariners tended to congregate and maritime social institutions flourished. Sailors had always tended to live in the eastern end of the peninsula, generally in the lanes off Essex Street that were handy to the fishyards and the harbor, but then so had many of the shipowners who employed them. During the era of neutral shipping, this pattern began to change. For a while, many of those who prospered from the European and East India trade, being practical men with personal ties within the maritime community, built comfortable homes for themselves around Salem Common or on the lower reaches of Essex Street, close to their business and the sailors they depended on. By 1805, however, Salem's merchant elite had begun to lay out for themselves far statelier homes in the west end of town, most famously along the new and fashionable Chestnut Street. In mansions constructed no longer of wood but now of brick, many designed by Samuel McIntire in the classically elegant federalist style and furnished with luxuries carried to Salem from the four corners of the earth, these families began to hive themselves off from the waterfront where they and their forebearers had once made what could now legitimately be called their fortunes.[60]

As rich and established families moved out, poor and transient single men replaced them. The history of this process is difficult to chart, but by tracing the taxable wealth of Salem's four wards across time some rough sense of the chronology does emerge. In 1800 Salem's first ward, which ran from Essex Street down to the harbor, accounted for 36 percent of the taxable wealth and 26 percent of the propertied taxpayers in town. Until the late 1820s and early 1830s, the taxable wealth of the first ward held up reasonably well, owing mainly to a small number of wealthy merchants who continued to make their homes along Essex and Derby streets. Yet even by that date the gradual removal of propertied families with middling estates to the western precincts of town had begun. By 1840 the first ward ranked last in both of these measures, and by 1850 it accounted for only 14 percent of the taxable wealth and 16 percent of the propertied taxpayers. The manuscript census of 1850 reveals in more precision exactly how much had changed. At midcentury, master mariners could still be found scattered throughout Salem, either renters or homeowners, but in no sense clustered in any neighborhood. The majority of ordinary seamen or mariners, by contrast—63 percent of all those named in the census— now dwelled in the first ward, and the great majority of these were boarders. As early as 1837, when Salem's first city directory was published, more than half of all the boardinghouse keepers in Salem lived in the block or two between Essex Street and the harbor, and in 1850 the two establishments that specialized in housing mariners—one owned by Eben Griffin and the other by John Collins—were both located within the first ward.[61]

Beyond the counting of heads, moreover, this part of Salem now felt like a sailortown. Benjamin Browne of Salem remembered that in his childhood days in the opening decade of the century, he and his schoolmates used to feud constantly with their rivals from the East School in the heart of Bentley's Parish. According to Browne, his opponents, "being of rougher stamina," were frequently the victors, and he termed them "Wapping boys" after the Thames-side neighborhood in London, where many mariners lived and many more boarded, victualed, and entertained themselves in between voyages. Similarly, Nathaniel Hawthorne recalled the view eastward from the customshouse where he worked in the 1840s, giving "glimpses of the shops of grocers, block-makers, slop-sellers, and ship chandlers; around the doors of which are generally to be seen, laughing and gossiping, clusters of old salts, and such other wharf-rats as haunt the Wapping of a seaport." By 1850, the year Hawthorne published these lines, this was a quiet sort of a Wapping, for although the seaport's registered tonnage employed in deepwater commerce was still considerable, local vessels spent most of the year far from home lugging freight between distant seaports and only periodically discharging crews on Salem's shores. So although "a Lascar or East Indian might sometimes be met in the street" or a few masters of rusty schooners carrying firewood from down east—"a rough-looking set of tarpaulins," as Hawthorne described them—the jostling, rowdy press of humanity that crowded the real Wapping, or the Bowery, or even the North End of Boston, Salem never really replicated.[62] Nevertheless, what had once been the business of the entire town had now been reduced to that of its maritime quarter, and while this was still an active seaport, seafaring itself had become the exceptional livelihood of a minority.

From the period of settlement, Stage Point in South Salem, directly across from Derby Wharf, had been a center of maritime business. It was the site of the town's earliest fishing stages, where men unloaded cod to be split, salted, dried, and barreled for shipment to market. In the eighteenth century, mariners used to haul their schooners up on the gravelly beach there for careening and graving, and a few shipwrights pressed for space on the other side of the harbor began to lay down their ways on its sloping shores and constructing entire vessels there. During the era of neutral shipping, some of Salem's largest vessels were framed at Stage Point. Behind the beach as late as 1780 lay open farmland, the so-called South Fields, where a few of the more prosperous retired mariners and their families grazed animals and mowed hay for winter fodder.[63]

During the 1820s, however, a number of local entrepreneurs purchased lots in this fairly inexpensive part of town and founded a rather different group of businesses. Near the end of Harbor Street opposite Derby Wharf, Caleb Smith built a sperm oil and candle factory that lasted about ten years. On ground nearby, a group of investors built a lead manufactory in 1826 that employed more than 150 men at its peak, though it too failed in time.[64] Then, in 1839, another consortium, led by Nathaniel Griffin, formed the Naumkeag Steam Cotton Company and purchased the land beside the defunct lead mill with the intention of building Salem's first real textile factory. The greatest construction event in Salem's history began several years later in 1845. Frank Moreland, who grew up on the point during these years, remembered an army of workmen leveling the site and shoveling fill into Salem Harbor, teams of oxen hauling great stones for the underpinning and huge timbers for the floors and roof, and the coming and going of ships at the seawall unloading bricks, mortar, and hardware. When the building was complete, it stood four stories tall and four hundred feet long, with two square towers on the southern side and a wide door opening on each story. Moreland recalled the workmen, "most of whom had been sailors at some time or other," hoisting the machinery to these doors hand over hand to the accompaniment of sea chanties, while their foreman, "brawny, thickset, his . . . ears adorned with little gold rings, and above all endowed by nature with a voice of tremendous power," cried out the time from the top of the tower. The skills and habits of maritime Salem had been turned to this industrial project.[65]

The mill began carding cotton fiber in January 1847, spinning it into thread shortly after, and weaving the thread into cloth within just more than a year. In 1848 with the company fully operational, six hundred operatives were tending 29,696 spindles and 642 looms in what was briefly one of the largest and most modern mill buildings in the United States. On the other side of Harbor Street, the company constructed a range of boardinghouses on the Lowell model, where young women—mainly from rural New England and Ireland—lived while they worked in the mills. A few years later, the old Union Wharf—Salem's first—was extended and converted into a bridge to allow millworkers living in the other wards to commute easily to the factory; some time after that developers began to carve up the South Fields into house and tenement lots for families of operatives; and in short order the mill became the geographic center of town. By the 1850s Salem (Figure 6.4) had effectively become a mill town.[66]

Although the shipping industry in Salem did not die immediately, the arrival of factories in Salem did mark the beginning of the end. By 1850 the customs officers recorded more entries from Nova Scotia—

FIGURE 6.4 View of Salem from the South, 1854. The foreground shows the intersection of Harbor and Lafayette streets, in what had a few decades earlier been the South Fields. The new cotton mill can be seen at the far right, and although the harbor is still visible, opening to the eastward and stretching past the extended Derby Wharf toward the ocean, it is not central to this image at all. Lithograph by J. W. Hill, del. J. H. Colon Lith. Printed by Endicott and Co., published by Smith Brothers and Co., New York. (Courtesy of the Peabody-Essex Museum)

mainly carrying gypsum to plaster the walls of urban and industrializing America—than all other foreign ports combined. By 1860 that ratio had climbed to 3:1, and by 1870 to 13:1. The last voyage to Manila set sail in 1858, and the last for Sumatra was launched in 1860. The arrival of the bark *Glide* from the Indian Ocean in 1870 marked the last entry from beyond the Cape of Good Hope; and when the schooner *Mattie F.* made port in 1877, it represented the last foreign entry from any port beyond the maritime provinces of Canada. The Salem firm of Silsbee, Pickman, and Allen did construct a small fleet of fast ships for the hemp trade after the Civil War, but they operated only out of Boston. And in 1896 the last of these, the *Midoro,* was towed to Derby Wharf and cut down to a coal barge.[67]

It was the clattering of cotton machinery and not the moaning of the wind that sounded loudest in the ears of Salemites after midcentury. Black smoke belched over the harbor where white canvas had once billowed; the Naumkeag mill itself yearly spilled farther out into the shallows where schooners had once taken on their hogsheads of fish and brigs had discharged their bales of calico. Salem at last produced something of its own —miles and miles of power-loomed cotton cloth—but most of it left town by rail and not by water. The old merchant families of Pickmans, Ornes, and Gardners finally concluded that banks, mills, and railroads made better investments than ships and cargoes, and as an older generation of merchants slipped into retirement, a new cohort of industrialists and businessmen took their place in the office buildings that now lined Essex Street. When Joseph Peabody, the richest merchant by sea that Salem ever produced, died in 1844, his widow and two sons reinvested much of their inheritance in real estate, securities, and industrial enterprises. George became a banker, Francis a mill owner, and the fortune that had once constructed eighty-three vessels and shipped more than seven thousand seamen was rechanneled inland. At the same time, as the manuscript censuses of midcentury reveal, the young men from the families who had worked those ships for generations—the Webbs, Brays, Cloutmans, Bowditches, and others—decided that their prospects as machinists, bookkeepers, curriers, or teachers were perhaps a little less thrilling but a great deal easier to reconcile with the ordinary duties and aspirations of working-class Americans. A new generation of immigrants, mainly from Maine, Nova Scotia, French Canada, England, Scotland, and Ireland, moved into town, not to board along the wharves and take their place before the mast but to rent rooms in the tenements of South Salem and find work in the town's new industrial economy. Regardless of their origins, the people of Salem had turned their back on the ocean and embraced the United States as a continental home.[68]

CHAPTER SEVEN

Mastery and the Maritime Law

NOTHING ARGUES MORE STRONGLY for the distinctiveness of the seafaring life than the persistence of the maritime law. From ancient times through the end of the age of sail, jurists recognized that the civil and criminal codes operating on land simply did not work in the fluid context of seaborne activity. Accordingly, in seafaring cases they dispensed a particular brand of customary, international justice called maritime or admiralty law. At the hub of the maritime law stood the captain. Agent of the owner and master of the crew, he possessed a range of powers and responsibilities unusual and extensive enough to dominate the text of all the maritime legal customaries descendent from the Middle Ages. This extraordinary status Richard Henry Dana, Jr.—a sailor turned lawyer—summarized in plain language:

> I have no fancies about equality on board ship. It is a thing out of the question, and certainly, in the present state of mankind, not to be desired. I never knew a sailor who found fault with the orders and ranks of the service; and if I expected to pass the rest of my life before the mast, I would not wish to have the power of the captain diminished an iota. . . . He has great cares and responsibilities; is answerable for everything; and is subject to emergencies which perhaps no other man exercising

authority among civilized people is subject to. Let him, then, have powers commensurate with his utmost possible need; only let him be held strictly responsible for the exercise of them. Any other course would be injustice, as well as bad policy.

In Dana's view—echoed ever since by novelists, poets, and historians— the experience of working in a confined space on the open sea under the extraordinary authority of a shipmaster constituted an activity without parallel on earth. Seafaring made uncommon demands on human beings; it placed them in an environment where their freedom was severely curtailed; and few men would choose this way of life unless they had to.[1]

Yet the story of Salem and its merchant shipping fleet suggests a rather different picture. Indeed, for most of this seaport's history, the experience of going to sea was not exceptional at all. True, Dana's account may have characterized accurately enough some of the trades plied by Yankee mariners in the 1830s, but seafaring in earlier times from this and scores of similar ports constituted a far more commonplace line of work—occupationally different from labor ashore but hardly a world apart. One should not carry this argument too far. Claiming that captains ran their vessels in the same way that shoemakers ran their shops stretches beyond what common sense will bear. Dana's voyage round Cape Horn to California involved physical risks and social tensions that were more intense than anything he would have encountered in the workshops of coastal New England. Yet mastery at sea clearly constituted a special case of mastery in general, and to the end of the age of sail, a form of labor discipline in which personal authority was guaranteed by the right to inflict corporal punishment would have seemed entirely normal. The personal power of the shipmaster could be exercised along a broad spectrum—from the sort of community-mediated patriarchy that governed Salem's fleet in colonial times to the harsher class-based regime that prevailed on board its global fleet in the early republic. Yet the model of the captain's authority that prevailed in all periods covered by this book involved a mixture of control and responsibility over the seaman's person as well as his labor that was rooted less in ownership than in the traditional notion of mastery.

Still, this leaves us with a problem. On the one hand, the very existence of a separate body of maritime law—uniformly applicable across the seas for hundreds of years—suggests the exceptional character of maritime life. On the other hand, the real experience of working on the ocean was something so widely shared, in Salem's experience at least, that it is hard to imagine that for those brought up within the sound of the surf, maritime life was exceptional at all. Redrawing the romantic portrait of seafaring life demands that we reexamine the maritime law in the light of actual experience and, in doing so, try to determine the actual nature of mastery at sea.

In 1650 the Massachusetts General Court appointed a committee to look over the *Lex Mercatoria* of Gerard Malynes, a recent compendium of commercial and admiralty law, and draw up some ideas for the construction of a legal code to regulate New England's burgeoning maritime economy. Whether the committee reported back on this matter, the records do not say, but in the fall of 1667, the legislature, responding to the "many occasions dayly grouing among us respecting maritime affairs & admiraltie cases," appointed another committee to develop a code of laws that would enable local justices to deal consistently with the raft of maritime disputes that were now clogging the colonial courts. Since there were as yet no admiralty courts in America, and few magistrates had much direct experience with cases of this kind—save through occasional contact with maritime affairs in the local courts of the old country—the representatives clearly recognized the need to regularize proceedings. A year later, in 1668, the General Court enacted a Maritime Code of twenty-seven articles, "that there may be knowne lawes & rules for all sorts of persons imployed therein . . . & that there may be one rule for the guidance of all Courts in their proceedings." Although this was neither the first nor the last occasion when the assembly attempted to construct or amend admiralty law, it constituted a signal legislative initiative—one of the most comprehensive that Massachusetts attempted during the seventeenth century. In 1674 the colony's Court of Assistants was empowered to begin hearing cases in admiralty, and it began almost immediately to constitute itself in that fashion several times in every sitting, dealing with exactly the sort of issues that the Code addressed.[2]

Clearly inspired by the *Lex Mercatoria,* the Massachusetts Code of 1668 descended from the numerous maritime customaries of Europe, most famously the Rolls of Oléron, and one cannot suppose that it necessarily reflected the customary experiences of shipboard life on New England vessels. By its nature the maritime law was constituted to deal with trouble, and trouble normally arose on the longest and most strenuous voyages, on which social tensions ran highest. The General Court knew that local magistrates sitting in admiralty would have to deal with all manner of shipping, much of which originated in England and arrived in Boston and Salem only after two months of beating across the North Atlantic against the prevailing westerlies, often in seasons of the year when sailing the deep could be a nasty experience. Although the code was plainly designed to address the flashpoints of shipboard life—matters that frequently arose before local magistrates and were sources of real practical concern—and the maritime law was something within which New England seafarers were expected to operate, one cannot assume that *all* vessels, local and foreign, tested the outer limits of the law equally.[3]

At root, the code was enacted to govern trade in and out of Massachusetts ports in the interests of cargo—those who furnished it, purchased it, and dealt in it, which meant most householders in the colony, though merchants and traders foremost. This regulation it accomplished for the most part, in typical nascent capitalist fashion, by locating the focus of authority in the person of the master and working primarily through him. In the words of a contemporary English legal commentator, "a Master of a Ship is no more than one who for his knowledg of Navigation, fidelity & discretion, hathe the Government of the Ship committed to his care and management," and he must bear the responsibility "if misfortune happens, if they be either through negligence, wilfulness, or ignorance of himself or his Marriners." Following this logic, almost every section of the Massachusetts Code placed the responsibility for the success of the voyage in the hands of the shipmaster and aimed at governing the industry as a whole by empowering or restraining him in the exercise of his authority in relation to the owners and shippers on the one hand and his own crew on the other.[4]

In relation to the owners of the vessel he commanded, the ship's captain was at once an employee, a labor manager, a business agent, a coadventurer, and the master of a highly technical trade. Accordingly, the social connections between owner and master could often be quite complex. In a legal sense, however, these relationships were essentially contractual, and could be considered an extension of ordinary commercial law. Some were expressed explicitly in plain language on the sheaf of legally binding papers—letters of instruction, bills of lading, charter parties, cargo manifests, and portledge bills—that every shipmaster signed before clearing port. Others were unspoken privileges and obligations defined only by the maritime law. Any captain who had run out of cash in a foreign port, for example, did not require formal permission to sell off the merchant's cargo or borrow against the "bottom" of the vessel to pay for necessary expenses. Facing a storm that threatened the survival of his ship, he possessed the right to pitch overboard sufficient cargo to save the vessel. The master's obligations to direct the salvage of cargo from a shipwreck, to defend the ship from pirates, to care for his sick mariners, and so forth were never mentioned in the formal documents that defined every voyage, but they were entirely understood within the custom of the sea.[5]

Written or not, explicit or implicit, all of these promises were essentially contractual in nature, and the principles that lay behind them would not have perplexed anyone versed in commercial law. What brought these rules into being as a separate body of law was not a distinct maritime logic but rather the need to adapt commercial law to the peculiar circumstances of seafaring. This was necessary, first and most obviously, because mariners confronted physical perils far more frequently than did landsmen. On shore there may have been bandits on the roads, enemies in the woods, and blizzards in the winter—all of which might on occasion have disrupted one's business sufficiently to generate a lawsuit—but they were not the continual problem they were at sea. Large sections of the Massachusetts Code of 1668 as well as all the older maritime customaries were prompted by the real likelihood of breaking up on a lee shore, damaging cargo in a gale, losing a vessel to pirates or privateers, or finding goods spoiled in the hold after a long voyage through tropical latitudes. An important purpose of maritime law was simply to spell out how in each of these different emergencies the pattern of responsibility was structured.[6]

Second, maritime law was peculiar in that it dealt with parties who by the very nature of their mobile business often found themselves at great distance from one another and beyond the effective reach of local justice. Farms, smithies, and ropewalks did not move. They remained subject to one law, their proprietors could normally be served with writs, and their premises could always be attached. Whole areas of maritime law came into being as a consequence of the communication problems that were endemic to seafaring. The rights of a shipmaster to borrow against the bottom of a vessel in foreign ports, to sell the ship's provisions to other vessels in distress, or to deviate under certain limited circumstances from a voyage's original planned course were just three of many rules that arose from the difficulty in making decisions in a workplace under sail and far from home. Similarly, the rule that a master must follow the terms of his letter of instruction and not deviate from the voyage they described also arose from the difficulty of communications over water. No rational shipowner would wish his master hamstrung under a welter of restrictive laws and regulations that would hamper the latter's freedom to carry out each voyage to a profitable conclusion. Yet the potential for fraud was enormous, for if the master who conducted nearly all of his significant business over the horizon were not reined in somehow by rules more explicit than those laid out in the common law, he might succumb to temptation and fleece his employers at will.[7]

Every one of the maritime codes was shot through with anxiety over this problem, and much of their verbiage was poured into a somewhat contradictory agenda of empowering and disempowering the men on whom the profitability of the industry depended. A few articles in the Massachusetts Code of 1668 focused squarely on the problem of fraud and presumed no certain identity of interest between a master and his employer's business. Article 4, for instance, made it very plain that a master might be far from "sufficient to discharge his place," that he might choose to "imbezel the ouners stockes or time, or . . . suffer his men to neglect their due attendance on board, and that he or his mate might not stay "on board euery night, to see good orders kept." Article 8 admitted that masters could well feel tempted to steer a course for ports other than those named in their charter parties or bills of lading in order to do business on their own account, and it established plain rules to prevent this. Yet other sections of the same code presumed exactly the opposite—that the master identified entirely with the property under his command. Thus Articles 26 and 27 required that seamen "doe their vtmost endeauour to asist the master in saving ship & goods and not desert him," and in the case of shipwreck to "without dispute, vpon their getting on shoare . . . to save the ship or vessell, tackle, & apparell, as also the merchants goods," yet neither article saw any need to place any explicit obligation on the master. That he would do his best to protect the property under his charge was here simply taken for granted. Masters who read through the entire code might well be excused for thinking they were being delivered a mixed message. Given the fundamental ambiguity of their position, however, this was the best that this or any other body of maritime law in the age of sail could ever manage.[8]

The perils of the sea, the mobility of the ship, and the ambiguity of the shipmaster's position notwithstanding, it would be wrong to overemphasize the exceptional character of the law that covered maritime business. The vice admiralty court that sat in Boston from 1696 onward handled many cases involving shipmasters' commercial dealings, but so too did all the other county and provincial courts that administered justice at different times during the colonial period. The magistrates who presided over these courts lived in a maritime society where the ways of the sea were broadly understood, and they judged maritime cases and common-law cases in rapid succession at every sitting. The contracts that organized every voyage were more complicated than most, and the oceanic circumstances in which they were carried out added a good many twists to their various terms, but in the broadest sense they resembled similar agreements hammered out on shore as well. Fundamentally, they delegated the responsibility for an enterprise from a merchant with capital but no practical understanding of the labor involved to a master who brought to the task a lifetime of skill learned on the job and who assumed the responsibility for carrying the project to completion. This was the logic that connected merchant capital to the practical businesses of production and transport throughout the early modern world, and the shipping industry shared in its general characteristics. That maritime law should have fit comfortably within commercial law in general stands to reason.

Can the same be said of the labor law that governed relationships between shipmasters and their men? Was it simply a species of early modern labor law in general? Conventional wisdom has generally argued no: that labor relations at sea during the age of sail were framed by a distinctively authoritarian body of law quite distinct from that which held sway on shore. Yet labor law everywhere in early modern times was authoritarian —on land and sea. Nowhere was the legal assumption that servants obey their masters seriously in question. If the codes of law governing maritime labor in the seventeenth and eighteenth centuries in the Anglo-American world strike us as somewhat more oppressive than those that operated on shore, they resembled landward rules in their fundamental character, and the differences that did exist constituted, as in commercial law, a peculiar expression of such rules inside the maritime world.[9]

Under Anglo-American law of the seventeenth and eighteenth centuries, most men who worked for others fell under one of four categories: they were laborers, artificers, apprentices, or servants. A laborer or artificer was an adult householder who was responsible for his own maintenance and entered employment under strictly limited conditions. He remained subject to his employer's command only during the working day and returned to his home at night; and he was free to quit employment once the day, week, or particular task for which he had contracted was complete. In short, these workers "had made the master responsible not for their persons but only for their hire." Apprentices and servants, by contrast, were generally young people with little or no property of their own, who stood to their masters, much as children to their parents, in a state of personal dependence. Throughout the entire term of service, which could be months or years in length, an apprentice or servant fell under his master's legal control and was expected to carry out the latter's orders or to suffer correction for his negligence. In return, masters were required to recompense their charges, either in the form of vocational training (in the case of an apprentice) or with a monthly wage (in the case of an ordinary servant), and they had to furnish all of their dependents with adequate housing, food, clothes, and medical care. At no time during this period could a servant or apprentice absent himself from his master, and under the law, neither party was free to terminate the employment agreement unilaterally unless the other had violated the terms. There was some regional variation in servants' rights as the law was altered to suit local conditions, but the central principle that a master possessed a form of authority over his servant that was more personal than contractual was general to their relationship.[10]

Although maritime labor law followed neither of these forms in strict detail, it is plain from the medieval customaries to the admiralty commentaries of the nineteenth century that in most respects shipmasters were masters, and seamen were servants. Even Charles Abbott, composing in 1802 his authoritative *Treatise of the Law Relative to Merchant Ships & Seamen* as a London barrister in the heart of the most advanced capitalist society on earth, stated plainly that the shipmaster's powers over his men were analogous to those "of a parent over his child, or of a Master over his apprentice or scholar." Like a master and servant on land, the captain and his crew were bound together on board ship for a period of employment that was measured in months. A sailor could not quit midvoyage—that would be desertion—nor could he absent himself from the vessel at any time without the master's permission. If he took to his heels with a month's advance in his pocket before the voyage had begun, he could be pursued, in the words of the Massachusetts Code, "as a disobedient runaway servant." The shipmaster, for his part, could not dismiss any of his seamen before the voyage's end, unless he could prove that the latter was so negligent, disobedient, dishonest, or drunk as to render him unfit for duty. Like a master on shore, moreover, a captain had a broad range of powers over the seaman's person. He could set the latter to work at any time of the day or night at any task that he felt necessary to the completion of the voyage, and he could physically punish a sailor who refused his duty. For the length of the voyage, the captain commanded the leisure time of his men as well—granting access to the ship's stores, regulating the forms of recreation permitted on board, and determining when sailors were to be allowed the liberty to go on shore. Furthermore, the shipmaster owed most of the same obligations to his men as masters on land did to their servants: housing them in the forecastle, provisioning them with food, and caring for them when sick or injured or placing them ashore if they could not continue at sea in the hands of people who could nurse them back to health.[11]

Shipmasters, in short, maintained broadly speaking the same sort of personal and arbitrary authority throughout the early modern era that all masters possessed—an authority derived not fundamentally from their ownership of capital but from seniority and mastery of their craft. At the core of that mastery was the right to command obedience. Thus Gerard Malynes, the author of *Lex Mercatoria*, urged sailors in a general sense not only to pay "all due obedience to the Master" but also to suffer his wrath when they did not. The medieval Rolls of Oléron ruled that a master or his mate was always to be allowed "the fyrste buffet, be it with fyst or with the flat of the hand," to which seamen had to submit. A sailor who struck back at the first blow or launched a preemptive attack was subject to heavy fines and could even have his hand severed. Down into the nineteenth century, the maritime law always condoned the master's right to "moderately correct and chastise" a recalcitrant sailor. Yet in terms of legal privilege this was nothing more than was allowed on land. Throughout the Anglo-American world, masters were allowed to chastise "for negligence or other misbehavior" any disobedient servant. The courts made a distinction between chastising and beating; the former was legal, while the latter, which possessed the connotation of repeated action—that is, beyond the "fyrste buffet"—was not. Vaguely expressed as it usually was, however, the right of corporal punishment was as much a master's prerogative inside the household as it was on board ship.[12]

Shipmasters also derived considerable authority over their hands from the maritime laws regulating desertion. Since the Middle Ages, sailors had bound themselves whenever they joined ship to complete the voyages on which they had signed or else forfeit their wages and risk additional fines and imprisonment. Under exceptional circumstances, a mariner could obtain release from his obligations—for example, if the destination of a voyage was altered, if the vessel was judged unsafe, or if the master had abused his authority in matters relating to discipline, victuals, or medical care. But to leave one ship in midvoyage simply to obtain a better situation elsewhere, or to entice a sailor to attempt the same was both a civil and a criminal offense. This principle formed part of all the ancient maritime codes and was repeated in English and American statute law several times during the early modern period.[13] Yet servants of farmers and craftsmen were not at liberty to desert their masters, either. Signing a formal indenture always bound one to complete the term specified, and in the early modern period one who ran away from servitude was liable to recapture, imprisonment, and restoration to one's master with criminal penalties attached. Oral contracts could be just as restrictive in the case of individuals hired by the year. New England farmers and craftsmen tended not to keep servants and relied instead on family labor supplemented by hired hands in busy seasons, but those they called servants—principally youths employed for longer terms on apprenticeships or indentures—were no freer than servants elsewhere to quit of their own accord. During the eighteenth century, the criminal penalties for deserting one's master may have diminished—at least for those who had not signed indentures—but even servants under oral agreement knew that if they left employment in midterm and were caught, they would be returned. Desertion was more of a headache for sea captains than for most other employers, since sailors tended to run away in foreign ports where they were difficult to replace.

Hence the penalties for desertion persisted longer at sea than on land. But the principle behind desertion laws—that a servant was not free to come and go as he chose—was entirely traditional within early modern labor law.[14]

The crime of piracy—a capital offense since the Middle Ages—was plainly unique to the seas, but in essence it was merely a particular species of the sort of serious felony that was often punishable by death on shore as well. In most corners of the Anglo-American world, bandits who seized property worth hundreds of pounds were certain, if caught, to end their lives on the gallows. The opportunity to commit a crime of this nature and get away with it was obviously better on the high seas than the highways, and at different times piracy became a serious enough problem to generate a considerable quantity of particular legislation. In the final analysis, however, seizing vessels on the deep was only an extreme form of larceny.[15]

Mutiny, like piracy, was also more common afloat than ashore, and for the same reason, since the prospect of punishment was distant. And like piracy, the penalties involved could be severe—anywhere from whippings and heavy fines, if the issue involved nothing more than insubordination, to imprisonment afloat and even execution ashore if the master was physically attacked or killed. Yet once again, it should be remembered that mutiny was only a special form of collective disobedience that was a criminal offense everywhere, and combinations among servants on land were treated seriously in the early modern period and often punished without mercy. Where and when it occurred, collective resistance on shore commonly resulted in lashings, imprisonment, deportation, and execution, just as it did afloat.[16]

Where the maritime law did invest the master at sea with more authority than a master on land lay not in the character of offenses for which seamen might be punished but in the fact that sea captains combined in one person the practical authority of a master with at least some of the power of a magistrate. They could not actually administer the law themselves. As Abbott put it, they possessed "no judicial authority to punish the criminal," but could only "secure his person, and cause him to be brought before a proper tribunal."[17] But the law plainly recognized that shipmasters faced an unusual problem in their responsibility to keep order in the absence of formal justice. Accordingly, a wide range of punishments —fines, whippings, confinement, and different sorts of public humiliations

—that magistrates alone had the right to administer to free men ashore, captains themselves could dispense at sea.

In some degree, shipmasters had to be invested with quasi-magisterial powers simply because formal justice was out of reach, and it was felt that the perils of the sea demanded summary justice. Decisions on the deep often had to be made swiftly, and the pressures of command in emergency, especially during long voyages, forced masters into a harsher mode of discipline than was common on land. As one U.S. District Court judge stated in 1824, a ship's command often required that authority "be exercised with promptitude, often under circumstances of extreme excitement, with but little time for reflection, and little opportunity of weighing in critical scales the just amount of punishment against the magnitude of the offence." The same view was echoed by another judge, who ruled that masters could apply "personal chastisement to the crew whilst at sea, to compel the execution of lawful orders . . . upon the principle that the emergency of the service demands of seamen implicit obedience."[18]

Yet in and of itself, this cannot be considered a complete explanation, for there were many arms of the sea service—especially coasting and fishing conducted out of smaller ports in smaller boats—where masters possessed few or none of these extraordinary powers. What weighed pre-eminently in the logic of the maritime law was the issue of scale. Common as shorter trips in slighter vessels with fewer sailors from smaller communities may have been, the law had to account for the types of disagreement that would arise in the most stressful voyages it could imagine—the longest and most dangerous, usually carried out in the largest vessels from the greatest ports, where a community of origin among the crew could not be presumed. The maritime law was designed to handle trouble, even if it was only on the most ambitious voyages that trouble usually brewed.[19]

Capitalism was, of course, the engine that drove maritime commerce into a progressively more ambitious scale of operations, and with the passage of time, the role of the shipmaster gradually lost some of its original ambiguity. Much of the trouble that brewed on the larger vessels that plied the longer transoceanic routes between the greater ports was rooted in class conflict, and on voyages such as these the gap between master and crew undoubtedly widened. Certain ancient rules that limited the authority of shipmasters—requiring them to consult with their crew when deciding whether or not to leave port, jettison cargo, or cut away the masts in a storm—had by the eighteenth century been dropped. Medieval law had also placed certain explicit restrictions on their disciplinary powers— allowing sailors sanctuaries on board ship or specifying the number of blows that a seaman had to suffer before striking back in self-defense— that later codes never mentioned. By the early nineteenth century in America, Judge Joseph Story could observe that:

> the very necessities of the sea service require this stubborn
> support of authority. On the ocean the officers can have but
> little physical power compared with that of the crew. They
> may, at any time, become the victims of a general conspiracy
> to revolt; and unless they can subdue obstinacy and indolence
> by the moral influence of command, and enforce a prompt
> and uncomplaining obedience by punishment, the ship and
> cargo must soon be at the mercy of the winds and waves.

Story was not alone in his presumption that, at least by the 1820s, masters and seamen in the American merchant service were staking out ground on the opposite sides of a class divide, and this logic surely applied in earlier centuries in other merchant services that operated on the same scale of advanced capitalist enterprise.[20]

And still, for all of the special authority that shipmasters possessed as quasi-magistrates or, increasingly, as agents of capital, the fact remains that legally speaking the essential nature of the relationship between shipmaster and seaman retained most of its master-servant quality through the end of the age of sail. In the arbitrary power that masters retained over the persons of seamen, in the personal obligations they owed to their hands, and in the length of the contracts that bound the two parties together, mastery best expressed the spirit of the maritime law. Nor should this in the last analysis surprise us, since the great majority of foremast hands were until well into the nineteenth century still young men taking orders from those who were many years their elders and distinguished from them principally not by their ownership of capital but by technical knowledge, physical maturity, and the habits of authority that came with age.

When the colonial courts first began to hear maritime labor cases in the second half of the seventeenth century, they dealt with them much as English and American judges of the period dealt with master-servant cases in general. At sea as on shore, the state set out to enforce a standard of authority in the workplace that was at the same time strict, hierarchical, physical, and legitimate. Lawsuits might formally be concerned with a wide variety of pleas, but more often than not cases were really grounded in the twin issues of authority and obedience. When a master brought suit—principally for absence or negligence—he was complaining about the servant's refusal to show up for work as requested or to follow orders satisfactorily. When a servant sued—almost always for wages—he was normally disputing his master's claim that he had been negligent and did not deserve his pay. In either case, the issue under investigation before the courts usually returned to a string of incidents in the workplace revolving around the personal relationship between the two parties.

How did justices deal with these matters when sitting in admiralty? In 1729 two mariners, one named Sellman, the other Spencer, complained separately before the Vice-Admiralty Court of Rhode Island that their master, Benoni Gardner, had assaulted them in the guise of regular discipline on a voyage to Surinam. In Sellman's case the two parties had already been feuding for some time when one day an argument broke out on the afterdeck, and in a fit of passion Captain Gardner heaved the companionway door in Sellman's direction. Sellman left the helm, ran forward, and would not return despite Gardner's orders, whereupon the master "took hold of him and hauld him along the Deck to get him aft and as he was hauling he gave him some blows," although these seem to have drawn no blood. A second quarrel ensued later when Gardner ordered Sellman to mend a sail. This time, when Sellman refused, claiming he had no marlinspike, the captain first threatened him with a "Billet of Wood," then beat him with a rack of some sort, bloodying the sailor's cheek. The court considered Sellman's complaint for assault but dismissed it. A few days later, Sellman's crewmate Henry Spencer brought a similar complaint against Gardner before the same court. Apparently, while in Surinam, Gardner refused Spencer permission one day to go ashore. Whether Spencer actually left the ship is uncertain from the evidence, but the next time the two met, Gardner accused him of being absent without authorization and struck Spencer "with the End of the Fore Brace." He then ordered the mariner carried ashore and confined for several hours in the Dutch fort, and while he was there the master in a fit of fury emptied out a barrel of shallots belonging to Spencer onto the steerage floor, where they were trod upon and spoiled. When the court considered Spencer's suit, they sustained it.[21]

What sort of evidence did the court consider relevant? On the simplest level, it tried to reconstruct the actual disciplinary events complained of to determine whether they were excessive. The implements masters used and the manner in which they wielded them were almost always a subject of inquiry. Captain Gardner was more inventive than many in seizing on the companionway door, but brutal masters might reach for almost anything at hand to punish their men. If the master could demonstrate that he had used an open hand or a relatively small weapon, such as a thin rope or a rattan cane, that he had struck just once or twice, and that the sailor bore no permanent marks from the attack, he could argue that such punishments stood within limits that the law allowed. Cases describing milder discipline of this sort rarely came before the courts, not because sailors did not resent it but because they knew they would not win. When crew members did complain of treatment, they spoke, as Sellman and Spencer did, of main braces and wooden billets, and the courts often took evidence to establish down to the inch just how long and thick these implements were. Witnesses were asked how many blows they counted, how much blood was shed, and how permanent were the injuries sustained; and here in spite of Gardner's temper, the absence of any serious damage to life or limb probably favored the captain. Part of the court's assignment, therefore, was to decide whether the master had moved beyond moderate chastisement.[22]

More than anything, however, disciplinary cases hung on the circumstances surrounding the case. The court was interested in the characters of the different parties: laziness, insolence, or incompetence on the part of the sailor; vindictiveness, passion, or cruelty from the master. Witnesses were queried at length about the general background to the fray. Had the sailors been placed on short rations, for example, or were their tempers frayed from weeks of pumping? The courts inquired into the precise sequence of events that had led up to the incident. Had the officers or men been drinking? Did the sailor actually disobey an order? Did the officer explain to the sailor why he was being punished and was he given a chance to mend his ways? Who spoke exactly what words to whom, and in what tone of voice? Ultimately, it was not the question of whether or not a particular disciplinary convention had been violated that concerned these magistrates. As one nineteenth-century judge put it, "We do not look for the manners of a drawing-room on board of a ship." Admiralty courts cared mainly that good order and subordination be preserved in a strict but relatively general sense, and this required weighing all the elements of the story.[23]

That is why Sellman lost and Spencer won. Although the magistrates left no written justification for their decision, several differences between the two cases stand out. Most important is the question of provocation. Sellman twice refused his duty—for understandable reasons perhaps, but in the eyes of the law he was a disobedient servant. Spencer, by contrast, certainly talked back to Gardner, but there was no conclusive proof that he actually disobeyed him. Indeed, two of his crewmates claimed that he never went ashore at all. Certainly, the type of punishment Captain Gardner had chosen to inflict carried some weight in the case—his treatment of Sellman in particular amounted to more than gentle correction—but in the final analysis the decisive issue was that of the shipmaster's authority. Our modern sensibilities may respond more dramatically to Sellman's corporal punishment, but to an eighteenth-century admiralty judge, it would have seemed legal if not commendable.[24]

The reason for this, of course, is that early modern master-servant law pursued very much the same logic on land. Compare for a minute the sort of brutality exercised by Gardner over his New England crew during this voyage to the Caribbean with that which was, in fact, quite tolerated inside New England households at home. Cases pitting servants against masters over matters of alleged assault pepper court records in colonial Massachusetts, and the courts worked in very similar ways to uphold the master's right to compel obedience through what was held to be legitimate corporal punishment. In 1681, for example, a farmer from Bradford named John Simmons presented his servant, Thomas Bettis, and demanded that he be punished for running away. Bettis did not deny the allegation, but he accused his master of stepping so far over the limit of legitimate punishment that flight was the only possible response. On one occasion, Bettis charged, Simmons had beaten him with a stick so large that in order to wield it effectively in the house, he had to break it in two over his knee. At other times his master had tied him to pieces of household furniture for further abuse, driven him into the fields while he was still nursing his injuries, and deprived him of proper clothing. "I haue bin so abused," pleaded Bettis, "that I am afraid to liue with him ani more or ani longer and if your honars please to order me to liue with ani other master I am willing, but not to liue with him." The court called in various witnesses, including other servants from the same household, and they confirmed many of Bettis's complaints, including that his master had failed to clothe him properly against the weather and had beaten him so hard that he fainted. As a fellow servant revealed, Simmons on one occasion tied Bettis to a cradle, "having pulled off all his clothes to his shirt, and whipped him with three cords tied to a stick so that he brought blood, while he asked the boy if he loved him."[25]

And yet Simmons won his case. The Essex County court ordered Bettis to return home with his master and serve him an additional six months in recompense for the damage wrought by his running away, and the only reproof Simmons received was the magistrates' advice that he use greater "moderation" in the future and that "if he could agree with some other suitable person, to dispose of said servant." As in the case of Captain Gard-ner, the court was interested in the details of Bettis's punishment—the implements, the bloodshed, and the injuries—and it also received testi-mony on the manner of his clothing and diet, as well as the history of re-lations between master and servant, in trying to contextualize the beating and the flight. But again, as in the Rhode Island admiralty case, it was the issue of authority that proved decisive. Witnesses agreed that Bettis had been "a very naughty boy" and "rude in the family whenever his master was away," so in the eyes of the law his refusal to acknowledge authority justified discipline, and Simmons's discipline did not justify flight. Lacking the wisdom to control himself, it was held, he occasionally needed quite literally to have some sense knocked into him.[26]

Master-servant actions such as that between Bettis and Simmons were a common feature of court sittings everywhere in England and the colonies, and in both procedure and spirit of inquiry there was little to distinguish between cases before the regular courts and those that were heard in admi-ralty. The same search for the details of punishment and the same interest in the overall context of authority characterized each.[27] There even seems to have been considerable similarity in the social structure of litigation and in the pattern of outcome. In late-eighteenth- and early-nineteenth-century England, where the results of master-servant trials have been mea-sured, servants were more frequent plaintiffs than masters; servants usually sued for wages while masters tended to sue for absence; and in either instance, whether master or servant, the plaintiff usually won. Equivalent cases before the Massachusetts Vice-Admiralty Court earlier in the eighteenth century displayed the same pattern: sailors launched suits more often than masters; they mainly sued for wages while masters sued for desertion; and in either case, the plaintiffs were successful most of the time. That so many seamen (and other servants) were able to use the courts and win testifies, of course, to the customary imbalance of power under which they labored. Since sea captains, like all masters, held most of the cards—above all, the right to initiate discipline and the power to withhold wages—they rarely felt the need to come into court and demand justice. Seamen had to use the courts because, like all other servants, they were required to submit to their master's authority in the workplace and seek redress from a magistrate later. And again, like other servants, they won so frequently when they chose to sue because sea captains, as governors of their ship, could trample roughshod (at least in the short run) over the limits of customary discipline and generate cases that were relatively easy to prosecute.[28]

Master-servant logic continued to dominate maritime labor law down to the abolition of flogging in the middle of the nineteenth century, led, in fact, by the United States, which outlawed the practice in 1850. Up to that date, however, admiralty courts persisted in using traditional language and procedures to protect and monitor the strict, hierarchical, personal, and physical regime of authority that they felt was vital to the successful operation of sailing ships and the interests of commerce. Magistrates continued to seek out detailed and measurable information about the character of the discipline that sailors thought excessive. In 1831, for example, a Capt. Thomas Saunders tried to protect himself from a charge of assault by denying he had clubbed the ship's cook with a ship-carpenter's hammer of two or three pounds but admitting having hit him with a "light and small" hammer that a little boy on board had used for cracking nuts. Five years later, one Capt. Charles Christianson told the court he had not knocked a green hand to the deck with the end of the main-tack, "a very hard rope, about two inches in diameter," but he acknowledged hitting him with the royal mizzen-brace, "one of the smallest and loosest ropes on board the ship," about half an inch thick, presumably because he knew the law would not object. In Saunders's loss and Christianson's victory,

particular facts—measured down to the inch and the ounce and taken seriously by the courts—decided the case.[29]

In the tradition of master-servant law, the courts continued into the
nineteenth century to try to establish for each case the broader context of
the event under investigation to see whether or not the personal authority of the master had really been violated. In 1837, for example, one Henry
Dean, a seaman belonging to a New England brig, the *Dove*, libeled his
captain, John Huffington, for assaulting him during a port stop for repairs
in Cartagena, Spain. The altercation occurred one night when the captain
returned from shore and discovered that all hands had turned in without
a watch being set. He went forward, called the crew up from the forecastle,
berated them for their negligence, and threatened to flog those responsible
the next time it happened. Dean then spoke up and told the captain something close to "you don't seize nobody up here." Enraged, Huffington struck
him with his hand once or twice; Dean replied in kind; the captain reached
for a weapon (some said a broomstick, others a broken handspike); and
Dean fled the ship.[30]

By admiralty standards, the fracas itself was pretty minor—the mate
termed it a scuffle—and the two parties did not differ significantly over
the sequence or severity of the blows exchanged. The case hung only on
the question of whether or not the blow was deserved. Accordingly, Judge
John Davis questioned several of Dean's fellow mariners and one passenger
at length principally about the plaintiff's character, the history of his relationship with Huffington, and, indeed, the entire atmosphere on board
the *Dove*. Apart from details regarding the ship's routine and how watches
were normally set, the judge wanted to know about Dean's "general character," his "conduct . . . as a mariner," and whether he "was frequently disobedient to the captain's orders." He also questioned witnesses about Huffington, his treatment of the men, and whether they were fed properly.
The exact words that the two of them exchanged, the tone of voice that
Dean employed, and whether the altercation had bred a general "appearance
of mutiny" among the crew were all central to Davis's determination of
the case. After two weeks of argument, Davis sided with Huffington and
decided that Dean had, indeed, launched an unacceptable challenge to
the captain's authority and that the latter had acted quite within proper
limits by striking him in return. What made the discipline appropriate
could not be reduced to some clear and definable rule that Dean had bro-

ken. Rather it lay in the character of the whole and entirely unequal personal relationship that had bound master and servant together under maritime law for a very long time.[31]

By the nineteenth century, however, this traditional vision of labor relations that persisted at sea was rapidly disappearing on land. In the context of commercial and industrial development surging across New England and America in the early republic, there arose instead an understanding of the workplace that was just as unequal but somewhat more contractual. Under the law, an employer now purchased nothing but the employee's labor, no longer controlled the person of the employee outside of working hours, and no longer bore any responsibility for his or her general welfare. Although workers were still held to be servants in the sense that they had fewer rights to abandon their contracts free of penalty, to combine with one another, and so forth than their bosses, that subordination was no longer "established in the form of the individual will of the master" and his power to control, physically if necessary, their persons. Henceforth, jurists argued, it should be contracts and rules that governed labor—in a workplace of laws, not of men.[32]

Accordingly, when these same nineteenth-century judges sat in admiralty and defended both the powers of the shipmaster and the now rather antiquated degree of personal authority with which he still was invested, they felt obliged to spill a great deal of ink justifying themselves. Part of this argument they advanced in terms of the emergency character of sea service; masters needed special authority because they so often had to make rapid life-and-death decisions that could brook neither opposition nor delay.[33] But another part hinged on an argument that mariners were a different sort of people: "a strange race of men." In character, "simple and somewhat rude," "fearless, intrepid, and daring," "thoughtless, hasty, and choleric," "heedless and improvident," they were said to possess a degree of "hardihood, sometimes approaching almost from necessity to ferocity." Men of this breed, "partaking in a measure of the violent and tempestuous nature of the element on which they spend their lives" generally needed "prompt and energetic government," but also a "peculiar indulgence" to their "defects of temper and manners." The personal rule of traditional master-servant law might seem increasingly irrelevant to the regulated world of the factory floor, but it still seemed appropriate to the task of running a ship under sail.[34]

In previous centuries, admiralty jurists had always stressed the author-ity of shipmasters plainly enough. For Charles Molloy, he was the one who "hath the supream Rule a Shipboard"; for Gerard Malynes, he had "the whole power and charge of the Ship." Before the nineteenth century, however, they rarely felt the need to justify the personal character of the shipmaster's authority because early modern people encountered the per-sonal authority inherent in mastership everywhere. In an age of industriali-zation, by contrast, when entire nations began to focus their energies on transforming the way things were made on land, seafaring began to seem different and marginal. This was doubly true in the United States, where people were simultaneously consumed by the project of conquering the continental West, and where even in port towns like Salem so many men and women were now turning their backs on the sea. The condescension of traditional master-servant law survived in admiralty, partly because it had worked on sailing ships for so many centuries, but also because sailors —now poorly paid and frequently foreign—were becoming a culturally constructed other that needed the sort of close supervision that this legal tradition allowed.[35]

If the right to inflict corporal punishment was a central defining feature of the master-servant relationship in the early modern period, it does not follow that this right had to be in constant exercise. The assertion of per-sonal authority and subjection that a beating signified, however, did distin-guish this from other freer labor forms. That shipboard discipline was physical scarcely bears repeating. But just how brutal it actually was is difficult to recover from the surviving evidence.[36] On the one hand, it could be that the mass of cases we can recover from the admiralty court records of the early modern period represent only the tip of the iceberg. Sailors might have had any number of valid reasons for not wanting to sue their shipmasters—the cost, the inconvenience, or the fear of being blacklisted being only the most obvious—and so for every abuse that came before the courts a dozen or more may have passed unrecorded. On the other hand, since the vast majority of voyages returned home without generating any business for the courts whatsoever, it may also be that the records of admiralty courts are simply a register of crimes and give no more represen-tative a view of seafaring life than family courts do of normal parenting. There is no way to evaluate the relative truth of these two positions in any absolute measurable sense, and even if we could, the exercise of calculating the frequency of beatings would tell us next to nothing about the real character of labor discipline at sea. Its function to terrify the assertive sailor, potential mutineer, or idle sluggard into a "proper frame of mind" did not depend on its universal application. Most mariners may well have escaped any serious punishment in the course of their careers, yet they had only to witness one man seized up and flogged or pass by one pirate's corpse hanging in chains from a gibbet to be reminded for life of where the costs of disobedience might run.[37]

One can turn, of course, to other sources—ship's logs or seamen's memoirs—to find evidence on disciplinary issues, but those sources have problems of their own. Logbooks are terribly spare and offer us only the view from the bridge, while autobiographies are richer but highly selective. Neither can help us measure the customary exercise of discipline, which would have largely passed beneath their notice. Still, the problem may be surmounted in some measure by approaching it from the side. What sort of punishments did shipmasters when hauled before the bench confess having inflicted? These admissions may help us to establish a minimal definition of what level of discipline was considered unexceptional at sea. Similarly, what sort of punishment did mariners describe in passing— inadvertently in the context of telling an unrelated story—that might tip their hand as to what they considered normal? Finally, when in the course of a trial, a logbook entry, or a memory committed to paper mariners tried to draw attention to some particularly dramatic episode, what were the circumstances that most commonly seemed to kindle the brand of discontent, disobedience, and discipline likely to rage up into confrontations of a memorable stripe? Comparatively speaking, these circumstances varied over time and space in patterns that can be recovered.

To begin at the bottom, the most basic discipline was imposed simply to hurry the pace of work, and the ship's officers who administered it spoke of it as routine. The seventeenth-century mariner Edward Barlow, after spending fifteen years before the mast and the rest of his career as first mate, observed that many seamen were of a "lazy, idle temper," and "when they do anything it is with a grumbling unwilling mind, so that they must be forced and drove to it." This was "a great trouble and vexation" to a ship's officer such as himself since he was "forced to strike them against their will when fair means will not do it." These words followed an incident in which Barlow had dealt one of his men "several blows with a cane" for not stowing cargo properly and was then denounced for doing so by a second sailor—"an idle fellow who I had struck sometimes in the term of our voyage." Although Barlow thought he was reckoned "rather too mild than too harsh to bear command over a parcel of seamen," the tone of his language suggests that he felt no compunction about using a couple of clouts to hasten his men to their tasks. Indeed, he had been doing the same for many years and had never before been called to account.[38]

In a similar vein, Jack Cremer recalled how as mate on one voyage he got into trouble with his master simply because "one evening being dark, and calling out all hands in a hurry, the Captain being the Last, I, by mistake Struck him, taking him to be a common fellow." This was no mean blow, for the master ended up with two black eyes. But the mate's language clearly implies that the last one on deck, regardless of who he was (and Cremer could not see for the dark), might expect to receive a fairly powerful cuff to speed him on his way. Although the captain was furious with him, Cremer was unrepentant, for in his view (and he had been at sea since the age of eight), this sort of casual violence seemed exactly what a "common fellow" who was slow off the mark might expect. Almost all of this lighter discipline passed beneath the notice of the courts. What one maritime legal treatise called "the punishment of the moment . . . necessary to quicken the caviller and the lazy" was something that sailors undoubtedly resented but rarely complained of openly, since maritime law explicitly allowed it and master-servant practice generally admitted it as well.[39]

Ship's officers did not blanch, however, at delivering uglier forms of punishment if they felt their authority threatened. Some evidence of these can be found in the official responses they offered to the courts when facing assault charges. Though no plain reflection of events as they actually transpired, these probably do represent what masters and mates considered a minimal standard of punishment—what they felt anyone in their shoes would do. On one occasion, for instance, when a sailor refused to turn to when called, the chief mate acknowledged striking him three or four times with "small ends of rattling not larger than a common goose quill," then a few minutes later kicking him twice in the rear with feet clad in "thin & much worn canvas shoes." On another voyage, for a cook's insolence in spilling water repeatedly over the deck, the second mate admitted to striking him "two or three times with a bucket strap . . . it being a rope about two feet long and an inch and a half in circumference." For physically threatening the chief mate, another sailor was struck "two or three times with a rope," which the captain asserted the mate "had right to do." For embezzling several bottles of wine belonging to a passenger, a steward was said by his captain to deserve "two dozen blows with a cowskin on his back and shoulders" with his shirt on, as "a reasonable and moderate correction for the offense." For shamming injury, one seaman received "a gentle Blow with the Catt." For spreading rumors that might have sparked a revolt on a slaving voyage, another sailor twice received about two dozen lashes—"not Severe or violent" enough to cause bloodshed, but a flogging nonetheless. These are simply answers to assault libels, of course. They represent not what actually happened but rather a version of reality concocted by shipmasters or their mates to convince the courts that no criminal act had occurred at all—merely what they felt would be considered customary.[40]

Heavier discipline of the sort that pushed into the realm of the criminal seems to have been much rarer. In ship's logbooks, captains and mates were advised to record their version of any serious disciplinary episode for which they might later be sued, and in Massachusetts logbooks of the eighteenth and nineteenth centuries, only 3 percent of voyages contain any disciplinary references at all. If their keepers followed recommended practice, then the scarcity of references probably reflects the rarity of truly criminal acts.[41] Similarly, the majority of voyages described in sailors' memoirs did not generate floggings or beatings worthy of mention. On only three of the eight merchant voyages Jack Cremer recounted in his memoirs of the period after Queen Anne's War did he record any actual discipline—several beatings and one flogging with a set of cross-jack braces. In twenty-three years of merchant seafaring that took him all over the world during the early republic, Jacob Nagle mentioned only one incident of punishment—being put in irons for three days after attempting desertion on a voyage to India. The pugnacious Charles Tyng recorded five disciplinary episodes during fifteen years at sea; the more mild-mannered Gorham Low over a similar career mentioned only one.[42]

If most voyages passed without major problems, it is equally true that almost all of these sailors experienced several incidents over their careers when they or their crewmates were victims of something more than casual discipline, and a good number of them describe episodes that were really

terrifying. As a young man in the packet service, Samuel Kelly once witnessed from a distance two naval seamen being flogged, "fixed to a kind
of gallows in a boat, and exposed to the tropical sun whilst going through
their punishment." One of them, he later found out, died from the beating.
William McNally claimed "never to have had a weapon of any kind raised
to me," but the fists, boots, sticks, and cat-o'-nine-tails that rained down
on some of his fellow seamen during two different merchant voyages,
combined with stories he had heard from other sailors, prompted him to
write a book on the subject. Thus if the physical experience of more than
casual discipline seems to have been relatively uncommon in the age of
sail, the personal knowledge of it was not.[43]

The sporadic character of heavy discipline raises the question of when
and where sailors were most likely to encounter it. Much of the answer
to this lies in the realm of social chemistry; some voyages had hard masters;
others had brutal mates; still others had troublemakers in the forecastle;
and a great many were blessed with none of these. Any sailor's autobiography can be read as a commentary on the variety of crews with whom he
shipped, and clearly the most powerful variable to account for this variety
was chance—who was in town and looking either for men or for work
during the week when the vessel sailed. Beyond the luck of the draw, however, there was a logic that focused harsh treatment on particular circumstances that made certain sorts of individuals prone to abuse and certain
types of voyages likely to engender trouble.

One lightning rod for punishment was youth. In almost every trade
and every period, young sailors seem to have borne more than their share
of harsh treatment. Some of this was a form of vigorous hazing. In his
early teens Edward Coxere served under one master who enjoyed trying
to "harden me to the sea" by running after him with a rope's end. "Though
they did it in jest," he remembered, "I took it in earnest . . . for I did not
like such kind of sea-tricks"; it prompted him to think of quitting the sea
altogether. Jack Cremer remembered about the age of ten all the boys on
the ship being forced during calm weather "to run the hoop to raise a gale
of wind," that is with "theair left hand tyed to a hoop, and in their right
hand a cat-of-Nine-Tailes to flog the boy before them." Decades later Cremer
had not forgotten this "barborous" practice, in large part because it fell
into a broader pattern of physical abuse that he and other mariners often
experienced as children. Samuel Kelly knew all about this from his expe-

rience as a youth in the packet service of the late eighteenth century, and he knew he was not alone. On one vessel, he recalled "about twenty boys had deserted . . . by the turbulent and cruel disposition of the master," who thought nothing of striking them "with a large iron bolt about two feet long." As a shipmaster, Kelly claimed to "have allowed no one to chastise the boys but myself"—plainly, one can infer, because he knew how novices might fare at the hands of others. In a sense, one could say that most corporal punishment on board ship was administered along the axis of age—as were most orders—but the degree of bullying that fell upon the shoulders of teenage sailors seems to have been unusually pronounced.[44]

To some degree, masters and mates may have picked on the young because they were nervous about tackling the grown men on board who could match them in size and strength. A few days after leaving Grinnock, Scotland, for the Caribbean about 1810, Jacob Nagle, a highly experienced seaman in his mid-forties, was standing watch in the middle of the night when the chief mate, "a verry stout man" named Cameron, warned him that if he allowed the apprentices to fall asleep on their watch, Cameron would "swet" him for it. The two of them had exchanged harsh words the day before, and the mate had made it clear: "I shall mark you on the voige." When later that night Cameron actually caught one of the boys dozing, he asked Nagle if he remembered his threat. Nagle replied: "I do, Sir, and I [k]now the old grudge, but I now swear to you if ever you lift a hand to me, we will both go overboard together. That is one word for all. Are you that man? You may try as soon as you pleas." After a moment's silence, wrote Nagle, Cameron "walked aft and said no more, and I walked forward. From that time we never had words." It took an unusually self-possessed, adult mariner, however, to face his superiors to a standoff. Had a younger sailor spoken back to the mate in the same language, he probably would have received a drubbing.[45]

A second factor that shaped the distribution of punishment on board ships was race. Maritime labor had always been attractive to people of color within the Atlantic world, for as confining as shipboard life might be, it afforded them better treatment, higher wages, and more liberty than they were normally allowed ashore. This was undeniably true for slaves in the Americas, who were sometimes sent to sea by their owners and doubtless found work at sea vastly more attractive than the principal alternative of plantation labor. But even free black men knew that in the face of a hurricane, the color of one's skin mattered less than one's strength, skill, and willingness to risk one's life for others, and it is no wonder that so many of them left menial service jobs or common labor on land and turned to seafaring instead when the opportunity presented itself. Yet if racism afloat did not match what African Americans experienced ashore, it hardly vanished. Africans had been serving at sea within the Atlantic economy from the time that economy came into existence, and it is hard to imagine that the sort of racism that undergirded slavery on land evaporated entirely at sea. Measuring treatment is always difficult, especially in earlier periods, when records are scarce, but the degree of abuse that fell on black sailors on New England vessels in the early nineteenth century on voyages that are relatively well documented was really quite remarkable. Although cooks and stewards (virtually all of whom were black) made up only about 14 percent of the nonofficers on board Salem vessels, they accounted for 35 percent of the incidents of physical punishment recorded in ship's logs and district court records of the period.[46]

The very language advanced in these cases reinforces the importance of race in the disciplinary logic of the day. Masters and mates justified their treatment of African Americans, not simply in the regular terms of the disobedience, laziness, and incompetence that they attributed to everyone they punished, but also for the brazen speech, dirty work habits, and filthy personal hygiene that they seem to have associated especially with black skin. When William Dobbins, cook on board the ship *Esther,* complained of having been assaulted, flogged several times, and put in irons during a voyage to China, the captain, along with several members of the crew, described the punishment as entirely justifiable in light of not only Dobbins's disobedience and lack of culinary skills but also his manner. Different crewmates described him as "saucy," "very sulky," "unmannerly," or "a negro and pretty obstinate." When one of the more sympathetic hands asked Dobbins why it was they flogged him so often, he replied he did not know "unless it was because he was a black fellow." After Charles Parker, cook on board the ship *Louisa,* bound for Cuba and St. Petersburg in 1829, claimed to have been beaten and flogged repeatedly during the voyage, the master defended himself by arguing that not only had Parker failed in his duties and embezzled the ship's stores, but he was given to impudence and had once even dared to use the master's hairbrush, leaving it "dirtied and filled with negroes hair." Yankee ship's officers always tried to cast their actions as reasonable responses to attacks on their authority, but the frequency with which they used the word "insolent" to describe the punishable behavior of their black crew suggests what the latter had actually done to get under their skin.[47]

By far the most important factor in shaping the disciplinary atmosphere on board oceangoing vessels in the age of sail, however, was the scale of the enterprise concerned. Shorter voyages departing lesser ports in smaller vessels were seldom the scenes of serious social strain or the settings for heavy discipline. Vessels departing New England for the Carolinas or the Bay of Fundy, for example, generated very few admiralty cases at any period covered by this book. The huge coastal trading networks around the North Sea—for coal, grain, and timber—seem also to have plied their business year in and year out during the early modern period without much shipboard trouble. Those few sailors who recounted their experiences in these trades—Benjamin Bangs on the American coast and Edward Beck in the Irish Sea, for example—never mentioned floggings, beatings, or confinement of any sort. Shorter voyages could not have transpired without trouble all of the time. The great majority of them were capitalist operations facing many of the same bottom-line pressures that divided masters from their men on longer and more ambitious voyages. Still, they unfolded within familiar waters where the risks that capital and labor ran were inherently smaller and where problems—from incompetence to leaky hulls to low prices—had less chance to fester and were more easily repaired. When trouble did arise, moreover, captains and their crews alike were almost certainly more reluctant to test the limits of the law, since the institutions of home were closer to hand, and they feared they might get caught.[48]

Those sorts of inhibitions did not operate in anything like the same way on longer voyages. By far the lion's share of evidence for social violence at sea comes from voyages of three or more months in length, crossing significant bodies of water, and ranging long distances from sailors' native turf. The farther the destination, the harsher the discipline, the quicker the rebellion, and the more likely these conflicts could spiral out of control. Mutiny, piracy, and brutal punishment might sometimes occur a few days out of one's home port, but the bulk of serious shipboard struggle occurred not hundreds but thousands of miles from home. Thus in the case of New England, voyages to Europe, Africa, South America, and the Caribbean were far more troubled than those bound along the coast, and those that extended into the Indian and Pacific oceans were the most prone to conflict of all. Yankee voyages to Canton, Calcutta, Manila, and Sumatra—like those conducted by the East India Companies of Great Britain and the Netherlands in earlier centuries—were the settings for the harshest treatment sailors were likely to encounter anywhere outside the navy.[49]

The equation between distance and discipline was something of which mariners around the Atlantic world were quite aware. According to Nathaniel Ames, a nineteenth-century Yankee sailor with fifteen years at sea behind him: "Whoever has been off soundings in a merchantman cannot help having observed that the commander, although naturally a good-tempered man, has some poor devil of a butt upon whom to vent his spleen." Yankee skippers, he noted, "when beyond the reach of a New York jury," could be "overbearing, tyrannical, and inhuman" in their conduct toward their men. Richard Henry Dana, who also spoke from experience, agreed that "it is on long voyages, to distant coasts, where there are none to see and hear but the crew themselves, that seamen need most the preventive protection of the law." Echoing Ames, he pointed out that while a captain might "preserve a respectable appearance" at home, he could at sea, "far from all the restraints of friends and superiors and public opinion, possessed of despotic power, and with none to see or hear him but those who stand to him in the relation of slaves . . . show himself a very fiend." It was not distance of itself, but distance from the enforceable law and the sanctions of community that allowed mistreatment to flourish. Longer voyages in larger vessels created an atmosphere conducive to conflict not just because such voyages were difficult to conduct, but because they were no longer socially rooted in the seaports that launched them.[50]

In a case tried in Massachusetts in 1823, Judge John Davis, though in sympathy with the master, made substantially the same point. The ship *Hamilton* had just returned from a forty-three-month voyage around the world from Boston to Canton and home again. During the two "long and monotonous" years the crew had spent in the Pacific Northwest trading for otter skins to sell in Canton, a pair of contentious incidents had occurred in rapid succession: first, a mutiny followed by the confinement of thirteen crew, then a skirmish with local Indians during which one of the mutineers, John Healey, was severely wounded. When he returned to Boston, Healey launched a suit against Capt. William Martin for personal injury, which he lost. In his summation of the case, Judge Davis made a number of predictable points regarding the importance of "wholesome discipline," but he also tried to explain why voyages of this sort required a particular type of authoritarian command by drawing a comparison that is worth quoting at length:

> The best concerted plans for the prosecution of these remote
> and circuitous expeditions will be defeated if strict discipline
> be not preserved. The cod fishery has its peculiar character, and
> may be conducted . . . with all the familiarity and simplicity
> of domestic economy or of rural occupations. The various oper-
> ations at sea and on the fishing-ground, are subjects of mutual
> consultation, and the skipper is little more than primus inter
> pares. It is far otherwise on voyages to the northwest coast. . . .
> They require, in a great degree, the subordination, strict obe-
> dience, and deference to command, which are practised in
> military regimen. . . . Without the utmost vigilance, strict sub-
> ordination, and perfect command of the whole strength of
> the ship, assaults from the savages and fatal destruction must
> be expected to ensue.

Davis plainly chose his examples from the opposite ends of what he believed to be a spectrum of danger. The cod fishery operated close to home in a customary routine and could afford a cooperative regime afloat. The *Hamilton,* by comparison, was engaged in an adventure so perilous—given the distance from New England, the length of the voyage, and the tensions surrounding the fur trade—as to demand a quasi-naval brand of discipline.[51]

And yet, born and brought up in Plymouth, William Davis must have known that handlining for cod from little schooners in the frigid waters of the North Atlantic during the gales of November was at least as hazardous an enterprise as anything Healey and Martin were prosecuting in the Pacific Coast. Although he may not have stated this clearly, the real defini-tion of the spectrum he identified depended not simply on the character of the voyage but also on the social construction of the crew and the culture of authority within the community that mounted the voyage in the first place. Habits of mutual consultation could handle the emergencies that arose out on the banks precisely because fishermen from the outports knew one another and could transfer the domestic habits of authority from land to sea without heavy coercion. Maritime history is sometimes written as if the voyage of the *Hamilton* and the troubles it encountered can stand for the generality of seafaring experience in the heyday of merchant capital. They cannot. As Davis implied, the voyage stood at the extreme end of a continuum defined by risk and scale of operations, and the authoritarian practices of Captain Martin come much closer to expressing the limits of the disciplinary regime under sail than its norms.

Even though he might be "under twenty years of age," wrote Nathaniel Ames in 1835, "the commander of a merchantman . . . is invariably called the 'old man.'" If Ames exaggerated the youth of these "old men" (95 percent of whom were, in Salem anyway, twenty-five years of age or older), he was quite right about the ubiquity of the term. Melville described Ahab that way, as Dana did Captain Thompson. It was a kinder epithet than many that circulated in the forecastles of the day, but it referred nonetheless to the style of patriarchal authority that shipmasters had wielded for centuries, and it stuck because it described that authority so well. Operating in the patriarchal mode, a captain had the power to control not only his men's labor but their persons as well; he need answer to no authority on board; he could guarantee the observance of his orders by the right to physically punish in the sight of the crew anyone who contested his authority; and his mastery over the ship derived not from ownership or birth but primarily from talent, experience, and age.[52]

Mariners took this, the most common form of authority known in the preindustrial West, with them when they went to sea. Patriarchy could be adapted to many different purposes, however, and as our study of Salem has shown, it worked differently in the coastwise trades of colonial times than in the subsequent period of global shipping. In the seventeenth and eighteenth centuries, seafaring was simply what male New Englanders who grew up in Salem did in their youth. Born for the most part within a few minutes of the beach, they learned about boats, tides, and the weather from an early age, and to none of them would the notion of going to sea have seemed unusual. Furthermore, in a town where households were frequently short of productive, wage-earning, adult men, youths often had little choice but to join their older brothers and neighborhood companions in voyages abroad to finance the operations of their families at home. In a succession of short and relatively straightforward voyages to the Chesapeake, the Caribbean, the Wine Islands, or the Mediterranean, they served under the direction of masters whom they knew from around town in a disciplinary regime that may have been strict but was tempered both by the predictability of the work and by the force of community sanction. They knew, moreover, that if they were persistent enough and could avoid being struck down by tropical fevers or lost overboard, they could expect as adults to receive promotion and a strong chance at command. Although mastery of a vessel gave no assurance of riches, and it seldom worked to transform maritime laborers into capitalists, it was a badge of middling respectability to which most young men in colonial Salem could reasonably aspire. Patriarchal power generally drove the ketches and schooners of that period at a profitable pace that brooked no laziness, yet it was a power enforced through example, accompanied by curses and cuffs, not by the wholesale terror of irons and whips.

With the transformation of Salem's shipping industry into a global operation during the period of the French Revolutionary Wars, the style of authority afloat shifted. The rapid expansion of commerce, increasingly carried in ships and brigantines needing two or three times the men that could handle a schooner, soon outstripped Salem's ability to generate enough young men to crew the local fleet. Accordingly, masters in search of hands now began to recruit within a labor market that extended all along the Massachusetts coastline, down the Atlantic seaboard of the United States, and throughout the maritime regions of western Europe. When signing articles these sailors could no longer claim to know their masters or many of their crewmates personally, nor could the majority of them reasonably expect that someday they would climb to the quarterdeck and become masters themselves. In the era of neutral shipping these problems were compensated for by higher wages and more abundant privileges, but after 1815 seamen saw the return on their labor diminish, at least in comparison with landward employment, and the future that the seafaring life afforded ordinary workingmen in Salem grew steadily less attractive. Bound abroad with a crowd of strangers on transoceanic, even global, voyages of many months into unknown waters and distant seaports, they saw the risks inherent in their work and the strains of enforced cooperation afloat begin to mount. Under these circumstances, the patriarchal power of Salem shipmasters took a different, harsher form. Sailing farther from the institutions of home, and driving men they did not know, often beyond reasonable limits, captains from time to time supplemented traditional tools of persuasion and light discipline with a rounded measure of terror, documented by the rising incidence in assault cases before local courts and reflected in the climbing rates of desertion abroad. The personal, arbitrary, and physical tone of mastery survived, administered as in the past over lines of age, but now in a measurably more authoritarian key.

Capitalism in its nascent stages commonly delegated the management of labor through patriarchal modes of authority that varied in character just as widely throughout the entire Atlantic economy as it did in the different branches of merchant seafaring. Commercial agriculture in early modern Europe used servants in husbandry and family members to perform much of the routine daily work. Manufacture, though increasingly financed by merchant capital through various outwork systems, depended on patriarchal authority over wives and daughters to produce the finished goods. Many extractive industries, such as fishing, mining, and lumbering, used the truck system, whereby credit was extended to householders in exchange for their promise to organize family and friends to gather and deliver the commodity and receive pay in goods in return at the company store. Indentured servitude placed young men from Europe in the settlements of the New World, where masters who had bought their service on credit could drive them into the fields and produce staples to pay back the debt and earn a profit besides. Slavery, too, adopted a twisted form of patriarchal power to win fortunes for the sugar, tobacco, rice, and indigo planters who constructed these, the most profitable capitalist enterprises of the early modern age, on the backs of imported African labor. These labor systems exhibited huge diversity from farm to farm, shop to shop, and village to village, and they differed enormously among one another in the scale of brutality and exploitation they employed. But along with seafaring they shared in common a style of authority and discipline that was personal, arbitrary, and physical, and in the early modern period, they did capitalism's work.

Toward the end of the eighteenth century, a growing fraction of the ruling classes throughout most of the Western world began to doubt the legitimacy of patriarchal authority as a mode of organizing labor outside the family. In part they may have been moved by the libertarian arguments of the Enlightenment; in part they may have been frightened by the popular revolutionary upheavals of the period; in part they may have felt that patriarchy was simply not very efficient; and in part they may have believed that as a system it sustained other, more traditional portions of the ruling classes with whom they were struggling for power. The modernists were not opposed to authority. Indeed, the industrial labor systems of the nineteenth century demanded more of it, not less. But they hoped that in a more enlightened age they could create through a variety of institutional means a new sense of internalized self-discipline that would be more humane, more rational, and ultimately more powerful in governing labor relationships outside the home than patriarchy had ever been.

When reformers imbued with these thoughts looked at slavery, servitude, the truck system, and the brand of shipboard discipline enshrined in the maritime law and practiced on ships from Salem and dozens of other ports around the Atlantic in the early nineteenth century, they saw a style of authority that appeared to be an anachronism. In purely economic terms they were frequently wrong. Storekeepers in Newfoundland, shoemakers in Massachusetts, planters in the cotton South, and shipowners in Salem all knew that for a number of different reasons peculiar to their respective businesses, the personal, arbitrary, and physical powers of patriarchy still worked. But in a liberal society, these powers now seemed, when exercised outside of the family, to be at best exotic, and at worst repulsive. So when Dana, Melville, and other maritime writers of the nineteenth century returned from the sea, they felt as if they had explored another world and lived for a time among a separate tribe of men, whose social relations were structured by the traditional master-servant relationships that were now disappearing on land. The very phrase "the old man" was invented in the nineteenth century; Nathaniel Ames's usage of 1835 is one of the oldest on record. It made its appearance not because shipmasters were really any older but because authority stemming from age seemed increasingly anomalous.[53]

Seafarers in colonial Salem would not have needed a term like "the old man," because to them, the style of command it embodied would have seemed entirely natural. Shipmasters as patriarchs could lead by example or reach for a cane, but the control they exercised over the persons of those under them in the early modern period was but another adaptation of the most customary mode of authority on land. In a maritime society as Salem had been, where labor at sea was a stage in the lives of most men, it was a matter of habit to carry aboard ship the patriarchal assumptions of social relationships on shore. This, more than any witchery of the deep, was what shaped the relationship between young men and the sea.

Conclusion

ON A PRESENT-DAY MAP of the United States, Salem sits at the far northeastern corner—truly on the geographic periphery of the nation. This is no coincidence. Modern American atlases are designed to portray the land, and on any regional map—say, of New England or the Pacific Northwest—seaports are always sited on the edge, surrounded only by their hinterlands. How these coastlines related to other shores within the United States or overseas such maps do not reveal. Yet they suit the present day, for Americans possess a national identity that for the better part of two centuries has been deeply continental. There is no state in the union that anyone calls "maritime," because the vast majority of our citizens have grown accustomed to training their vision toward the interior and away from the sea. "Middle America" sits somewhere in Ohio or Kansas, not in Massachusetts. In cultural terms, seafaring also sits now on the periphery of the American consciousness. As fewer and fewer people employ the ocean as a normal medium of travel or transport or participate directly in plumbing its natural resources, maritime activity has acquired an exotic character that seems at odds with what normal people do. The practice of mapping the maritime world geographically and conceptually out of the American mainstream has been growing since the period of the early republic, and it now seems rather conventional.

Today it is difficult to reimagine an early American past when the frontier extended in all directions and when the Atlantic, rather than the continental West, stood at the center of our country's geographic consciousness. In that world, Salem was not peripheral but fully enmeshed in the central historical developments of the age. Though never a commercial metropolis on the scale of London or New York, Salem participated at one time or another in as many branches of maritime activity as any port in the Atlantic. At different periods local vessels fished for cod off the northeastern coast of the continent, chased whales in more distant seas, engaged in the staple trades of the colonial New World, launched privateering voyages against the French, Spanish, and British, and traded all over the world —fetching pepper from Sumatra, palm oil from Africa, hemp from Russia, and rubber from Brazil. Salem was at various times a place where sailors were born, a place where sailors came looking for work, a port of origin, and a port of call. Remembered now principally as the site of America's only major witchcraft episode, it was best known in its early history for its connection to the sea.

Through most of the seventeenth and eighteenth centuries, the men who worked Salem's vessels were nothing more or less than the generality of young men who had grown up on Massachusetts's North Shore and resided in the town. Sons of craftsmen, farmers, shopkeepers, merchants, and other mariners, they represented a cross-section of local society distinguished only by their sex and their age. Like other New Englanders, they had homes and families. Some were devout, and others were not. Most of them worked afloat for part of their lives and ashore for the rest. All of them performed their duties at sea within a context of master-servant relationships that were normal to early modern life, and most could reasonably expect to someday acquire sufficient mastery of their trade to rise into a position of command—as either chief mate or master of a local vessel. They did possess a distinctive occupational culture, composed of skills, habits, traditions, and language that identified them as mariners, but this culture did not mark them as a breed apart whose mode of life distinguished them fundamentally from their neighbors on land.

Only during the nineteenth century did seafaring from Salem begin to seem like something more exceptional. Partly this happened because the rest of the world was changing. As the United States pushed westward across the continent, much of the human energy that had been spent on maritime labor, as well as the financial capital that had been earned in oceanic shipping, was redirected toward the land. Fields of corn and cotton, railways, and factories absorbed a rapidly growing and finally dominant portion of American economic life. Even those men who had grown up in Salem recognized that as seamen's wages and shipping profits declined in relation to the returns that laborers and investors could obtain on land, the maritime economy was descending into a second-rate field of endeavor. The new industrial world brought with it, moreover, regularized habits of life in comparison with which the more erratic rhythms of seafaring began to seem increasingly anomalous. As large numbers of people grew habituated to the internal disciplines inculcated by schools and workplaces—structured by rules and driven by the clock—the arbitrary and corporal discipline of the ship began to strike many as old-fashioned and even barbaric.

Seafaring also began to seem exceptional in Salem during the nineteenth century because it was itself changing. Voyages grew longer and riskier, promotion became tougher, seamen were more likely strangers to town and spent more of their lives before the mast. Class divisions became more pronounced at sea, and a spirit of noticeably harder usage began to infect the discipline that officers imposed upon their men. At the same time as Americans were growing more sensitive to patriarchal styles of labor management, therefore, the actual character of maritime discipline on these Yankee vessels was hardening as well. It is no wonder that as the century wore on, seafaring ceased to be something in Salem that ordinary people did.

When the great American sea-authors of the nineteenth century—Cooper, Dana, and Melville—shipped themselves before the mast, seafaring from American ports like Salem was changing into something increasingly foreign to the ways of work and life that prevailed on land. Indeed, it was the very strangeness of the deep, the unusual ways of the ship, and the seemingly outlandish manners of the men who now chose this manner of life that drew these authors to it. The stories they told gripped the imagination of their readers largely because their subject matter constituted such an extraordinary foil to modern life—so different from anything one encountered on the main streets of eastern cities, let alone in the cornfields of the Midwest. Yet in cleaving too closely to the particular picture they drew of the "maritime" as exceptional—a definition that disengages mariners too radically from their homes on shore—we risk forgetting that in much of the world and through most of America's age of sail, maritime labor was not all that exceptional. In Salem it was simply what young men did when they grew up beside the sea.

Primary Sources

THE RESEARCH THAT UNDERLIES *Young Men and the Sea* is mainly embodied in a series of related data files constructed within a Paradox 8 database program. Since the task of describing the contents of this database inside individual notes would expand the referencing apparatus many times over, we have chosen instead to describe the database in a comprehensive manner here in this appendix. Certain other sources examined are described in the relevant notes.

The database is based around a series of core voyage files that included 10,451 man-voyages between 1641 and 1850. Mariners qualified for inclusion in these files if they could be identified by name and rank on a voyage of known date, and unless otherwise specified, each mariner was counted for each voyage on which he sailed. The sources for these voyages included:

1. *Legal Records.* George Francis Dow and Mary G. Thresher, eds., *Records and Files of the Quarterly Courts of Essex County, Massachusetts, 1636– 1686,* 9 vols. (Salem, Mass., 1911–1975); "A Volume Relating to the Early History of Boston Containing the Aspinwall Notarial Records from 1644–1651," in Registry Department of the City of Boston, *Records Relating to the Early History of Boston* (Boston, 1903), vol. 32; Archie N. Frost, comp., *Verbatim Transcriptions of the Records of the Quarterly Courts*

of Essex County, Massachusetts, 1636–1694, 57 vols. (Salem, 1939); Files of the Essex County Inferior Court of Common Pleas, property of the Supreme Judicial Court, Division of Archives and Records Preservation, on deposit at the James Duncan Phillips Library, Peabody-Essex Museum, Salem, Mass.; Essex County Notarial Records, 1697–1768, *Essex Institute Historical Collections,* 41 (1905), 182–192, 381–398; 42 (1906), 152–168, 245–256, 346–354; 43 (1907), 49–64, 223–232; 44 (1908), 89–92, 147–152, 325–331; 45 (1909), 90–96, 130–136, 212–220; 46 (1910), 81–96, 114–128, 273–288, 325–332; 47 (1911), 124–132, 253–260, 333–340; 48 (1912), 72–78, hereafter cited as *E.I.H.C.;* Records of the Court of Admiralty of the Province of Massachusetts Bay, 1718–1747, 3 vols., Massachusetts Supreme Judicial Court Archives, Suffolk County Court House, Boston.

2. *Town Histories.* Sidney Perley, *The History of Salem, Massachusetts,* 3 vols. (Salem, 1924–1928); James Duncan Phillips, *Salem in the Eighteenth Century* (Boston, 1937); James Duncan Phillips, *Salem in the Seventeenth Century* (Cambridge, Mass., 1933).

3. *Account Books.* George Corwin, Account Books, 1663–1672, 1671–1684, Curwen Family Papers, 1641–1902; Philip English Account Books, 1664–1718, 1697–1710, English/Touzell/Hathorne Papers, 1661–1851; William Pickering, Account Book, 1695–1718; Joseph Orne, Account Book, 1719–1744, Timothy Orne, Account Books, 1738–1758, 1762–1767, Orne Family Papers, 1719–1899; Richard Derby, Account Book, 1756–1790, Derby Family Papers, 1716–1921, all in James Duncan Phillips Library, Peabody-Essex Museum, Salem, Mass.

4. *Customs Records.* Naval Officer Shipping Lists for: Massachusetts, 1686–1765, C.O. 5/848–851; Barbados, 1678–1737, C.O. 33/13–16; Leeward Islands, 1683–1720, C.O. 157/1; Nevis, 1704–1729, C.O. 187/1, 2; Bermuda, 1716, C.O. 41/6, and Jamaica, 1683–1702, C.O. 142/13, 1709–1722, C.O. 142/14; Maryland, 1689–1754, C.O. 5/749; Harriet Silvester Tapley, ed., *Early Coastwise and Foreign Shipping of Salem: A Record of the Entrances and Clearances of the Port of Salem, 1750–1769* (Salem, Mass., 1934); Crew Lists for Salem, 1805, 1815, 1825, 1835, 1850, Salem Crew Lists, 1803–1850, Massachusetts, Records of the U.S. Customs Service, National Archives Northeast Region, Waltham, Mass.

5. *Shipping Papers.* Curwen Family Papers, 1641–1902; English/Touzell/ Hathorne Papers, 1661–1851; Orne Family Papers, 1719–1899; Ward

Family Papers, 1718–1945; Derby Family Papers, 1716–1921; Felt Family Papers, 1717–1915; Goodhue Family Papers, 1684–1858; Cabot Family Papers, 1712–1862; Townshend Family Papers, 1787–1887; Benjamin Pickman Family Papers, 1763–1843, all in James Duncan Phillips Library, Peabody-Essex Museum, Salem, Mass.

6. *Vital Records. Vital Records of Salem, Massachusetts, to the End of the Year, 1849,* 6 vols. (Salem, 1916–1925); *Vital Records of Beverly, Massachusetts, to the End of the Year, 1849,* 2 vols. (Topsfield, Mass., 1906–1907); *Vital Records of Gloucester, Massachusetts, to the End of the Year, 1849,* 3 vols. (Topsfield and Salem, Mass., 1917–1924); *Vital Records of Newburyport, Massachusetts, to the End of the Year, 1849,* 2 vols. (Salem, Mass., 1911).

7. *Ship Registries.* Massachusetts Vessel Registrations, 1697–1714, Massachusetts Archives, 7:19–515.

8. *Provincial Records. The Acts and Resolves, Public and Private, of the Province of the Massachusetts Bay,* 21 vols. (Boston, 1869–1922); Nathaniel B. Shurtleff, ed., *Records of the Governor and Company of the Massachusetts Bay in New England,* 6 vols. in 5 (Boston, 1853–1854).

9. *Tax Records.* Salem Tax Valuation List, 1758, 1762, Salem Tax and Valuation Lists, 1689–, microfilm copy in possession of James Duncan Phillips Library, Peabody-Essex Museum, Salem, Mass.

From this group of mariners, a sample of 2,620 (including all of those identified from the period 1641–1800 [n=1,716] and a random sampling of those identified from the period 1800–1850 [n=904]) was selected for more detailed biographical analysis. In addition to the foregoing sources, the following were searched to flesh out the life courses of these mariners and selected members of their families: William P. Upham, ed., "Town Records of Salem, 1634–1659," *E.I.H.C.*, vol. 9 (1868); "Salem Town Records, 1659–1680," *E.I.H.C.*, vols. 48–49 (1912–1913), vols. 62–67 (1926–1931); "Salem Town Records, 1683–1690," *E.I.H.C.*, vols. 68–69 (1932–1933), 83 (1947), 85 (1949); *Vital Records of Marblehead, Massachusetts, to the End of the Year, 1849,* 3 vols. (Salem, Mass., 1903–1908); *Vital Records of Manchester, Massachusetts, to the End of the Year, 1849,* 3 vols. (Salem, Mass., 1903); George Francis Dow, ed., *The Probate Records of Essex County, Massachusetts, 1635–1681,* 3 vols. (Salem, 1916–1920); Probate Records of Essex County, Massachusetts, Massachusetts Archives, Boston; Miles Ward, Account Books, 1745–1753, 1753–1764, 1765–1777, Ward Family Papers; Salem

Tax and Tax Valuation Lists, 1683–1850 (up to 1776, these can be found in Ruth Crandall, comp., *Tax and Tax Valuation Lists of Massachusetts Towns Before 1776*, 25 reels (Cambridge, Mass.), reels 8, 9; after 1776, they are held in microfilm form by the James Duncan Phillips Library, Peabody-Essex Museum, Salem, Mass.); Bettye Hobbs Pruitt, ed., *The Massachusetts Tax Valuation List of 1771* (Boston, 1978); William Bentley, *The Diary of William Bentley, D.D.: Pastor of the East Church, Salem, Massachusetts*, 4 vols. (Salem, 1905–14; rpt. Gloucester, Mass., 1962); "Parish List of Deaths Begun 1785, Recorded by William Bentley, D.D., of the East Church, Salem, Mass.," *E.I.H.C.* 14 (1877), 129–148, 224–232, 286–298; 15 (1878), 86–100; 16 (1879), 18–36, 191–203; 18 (1881), 73–80, 129–144, 206–223; 19 (1882), 18–39, 91–104, 176–182; Essex County Deeds, Bound Transcriptions, Registry of Deeds and Probate Record Office Building, Salem, Mass.; 1850 Manuscript Census for Massachusetts, using Family Tree Maker, *Massachusetts, 1850 from the National Archives of the United States* (Novato, Calif., 1998); the extensive genealogical collection of the James Duncan Phillips Library of the Peabody-Essex Museum; and the FamilySearch website of the Church of Jesus Christ of Latter-day Saints (http://www.familysearch.org/).

These sources were combed to provide the information of various sorts about the lives of mariners and their families. Given the nature of the evidence, there are gaps in our knowledge of even the best-documented cases. Hence, although the size of the database remained constant throughout, the number of cases that actually provided evidence for each given question varied considerably. One needs a date of birth, for example, to calculate a sailor's age. The single most difficult technical problem in the entire project was that of record linkage, trying to decide, for example, whether the John Manning on a portledge bill was the same John Manning whose marriage was recorded the following year. Our principle was to admit the linkage and include the evidence if there seemed no plausible alternative to the linkage under consideration, but to reject it if there was more than one possible linkage. This led to a great many blanks on our data entry forms, and a huge number of judgment calls over what data were admissible and what had to be rejected. In every case, we erred on the side of caution and dropped uncertain cases, even though that seriously reduced the quantity of data we eventually had to work with. The evidence was gathered under the following major headings:

Biographical. For each mariner, we collected basic demographic data, including place and date of birth, marriage and death, spouse's and parents' names, and father's occupation.

Wife. A parallel set of records was assembled for all mariners' wives, including, in addition to the above, evidence on all known previous and subsequent marriages.

Business. For each seventeenth- and eighteenth-century mariner, all of the Salem account books referred to earlier were searched for information regarding work performed on shore, along the coast, or in the fisheries, as well as consumption patterns and commercial investments.

Probate. The estates of mariners whose estates passed through probate were examined to determine the value of physical estate, the evidence of having adopted a subsequent nonmaritime career, the extent of maritime investments, and the quantity of livestock, land, and household equipment that their family may have employed.

Taxes. To help chart the patterns of mariners' careers and measure their residence in (or departure from) Salem, we constructed a database including the taxable property holdings of all the 51,398 Salem taxpayers listed for roughly every fifth year between 1683 and 1850. Through the end of the colonial period, all that survives are the records of taxes paid; from 1777 onward, the surviving records are assessment lists counting (and often describing in some detail) the value of taxable property and "faculty" or earning potential not generated by property (a type of primitive income tax). In each year selected, the taxpayers were sorted from richest to poorest and (to facilitate measurement of their relative wealth) divided into deciles, from 1 (representing the wealthiest 10 percent) to 10 (representing the poorest 10 percent). Taxpayers were also assessed for polls, the number of adult males in each household sixteen years of age and older. Those households with greater or fewer than a single poll were adjusted in our ranking so that their assigned decile reflects only their property and faculty. Producing these files was an ambitious project, and copies have been deposited with the James Duncan Phillips Library of the Peabody-Essex Institute for use by other researchers. These lists were searched for evidence on all mariners from the period up to 1800, a random sampling of mariners from 1800 through 1850, and all mariners' fathers in the year the mariner turned twenty-one, as well as the year the mariner married. By "year" is meant the five-year interval closest to the actual date in question (e.g., for 1719, we searched the 1720 list).

Crew Lists. All mariners found in the 1825 Salem Crew Lists were traced through the Family Tree Maker's indexed CD-ROM version of the Massachusetts Manuscript Census of 1850 in an attempt to trace the course of their subsequent careers.

Nineteenth-Century Mariners with Surnames Starting with the Letter A. Research in depth was performed on all 196 mariners whose surname began with the letter A and who sailed on Salem vessels between 1803 and 1812. Each of these men was traced through all subsequent Salem crew lists (almost 5,000 in total) to the end of his career. The last of these men retired in 1840. Then all of them were traced through vital records, tax lists, probate records, and census records to try to flesh out the rest of their lives. This group is referred to hereafter as the A-mariners.

Currency Conversions. During the colonial period, Massachusetts currency was subject to serious inflation and dramatic revaluations. In the interests of easy comparison over time, all currency amounts for the period before 1776 were reported in the relatively stable British sterling. Conversions were made using the tables in John J. McCusker, ed., *Money and Exchange in Europe and America, 1600–1775: A Handbook* (Chapel Hill, N.C., 1978), 138–142.

Graphs

A NOTE ON LIFE COURSE GRAPHS 4 AND 11

The method by which the data were prepared for most of the tables and graphs that follow is fairly self-evident. The two pie charts that attempt to describe the life courses of seamen in Salem between their early twenties and their early thirties are more complex constructions, and since they are fundamental to the argument of the book, they require separate treatment. Each chart measures the same categories of outcome (died, promoted to mate, etc.), and here we will describe, outcome-by-outcome, how the percentages reported were reached. It is critical to remember that the sizes of each slice are approximations rounded to the nearest 5 percent. This was done in part because exact percentages would give the charts a spurious sense of hyper-accuracy and in part because it is quite possible that a seaman could fall into more than one category. A seaman who was promoted by twenty-five but then died before reaching thirty would be categorized as "died"; one who was promoted at thirty but drowned at thirty-five would be categorized as "promoted." Although as graphics the slices of the pie would be presented more truthfully if they blended into each other—that is, if the borders between them were not so firm—such a chart would be very difficult to read and so we stayed with the rigid, if slightly misleading form that the pie chart allows. Readers should understand that the purpose of these graphs is to present rough tendencies and not precise measurements.

Still Seamen. This percentage reflects the ratio of the total number of those seamen aged 30–34 to those aged 20–24. Knowing that the most common reported ages for seamen ranged from 18 to 23 (1745–1775) and from 18 to 25 (1800–1850), it seemed reasonable to assume that 20–24 was the age range at which almost all of those who ever went to sea had gone to sea. In a stable population, the ratio of those aged 30–34 to those aged 20–24 should reflect the proportion of seamen still serving before the mast in their early thirties. For the period 1744–1769 this ratio was 0.11 (n=93); in 1805–1850 the ratio was 0.20 (n=367). We concluded that about 10 percent of seamen were serving before the mast in their early thirties between 1745 and 1769. This logic hangs on the annual recruitment of new seamen remaining relatively stable over time, which it did not. Since both periods are long enough to include upswings and downturns in the shipping economy of Salem, however, we felt that age distributions of seamen reflect in an approximate manner sailors' persistence before the mast. Data on ages were drawn from the sources listed in Appendix A.

Promoted to Master. Of those 154 seamen born in Salem or Beverly who sailed before the mast between 1745 and 1759, 41 (27 percent) later cleared Salem's customshouse as master on a voyage bound for foreign parts between 1751 and 1769. A slightly different test was performed on 55 Salem-born seamen of known age, employing every available source listed in Appendix A to answer the question: What were they doing in the year they turned thirty? Of these seamen: (i) 16 percent were active masters, (ii) 9 percent had been masters but had retired from the sea, (iii) 4 percent had been masters but were now fishermen, and (iv) 2 percent were dead. Those from category (i) clearly belong in the promoted to master category, but those in categories (ii), (iii), and (iv) could equally fit in others (e.g., died). Assigning all of (i) and half of (ii), (iii), or (iv) to the "promoted" category results in a promotion rate of 23.5 percent. Splitting the difference between our two tests and rounding to the nearest 5 percent results in an estimated promoted to master rate for the period 1745–1769 of 25 percent. The names of seamen were drawn from the portledge bills listed in Appendix A.

A similar calculation could be performed for the period 1800–1850, but the lack of a set of customshouse records indexed by masters' names would make this too complex and prone to error. In order to construct a measure of promotion that could be compared with the 25 percent rate from the eighteenth century, we posed the question as follows: How many seamen were serving as master on voyages from Salem to destinations outside the thirteen colonies or continental United States *exactly* ten years after we identified them as seamen? This test was performed on every member of two groups of locally born seamen, each time he sailed: (1) all those who sailed during the years 1745–1759 (*n*=201); and (2) all those who sailed in the years 1805, 1815, and 1825 (*n*=866). The promotion rates under this stricter definition fell from 4.2 percent (1745–1759) to 2.2 percent (1805–1825). We concluded from this that the likelihood of promotion to master was only about 52 percent as strong between 1805 and 1835 as it had been between 1745 and 1769. If the promotion rate was 26.6 percent in the earlier period, then the promotion rate in the latter period must have been 13.8 percent. We would be inclined to round this upward to 15 percent, except that promotion rates among the locally born A-mariners (*n*=45) by age thirty-four was only 9 percent. The sample size among the latter group was smaller, but the measurement of promotion was more direct. Accordingly, we rounded the two results down to 10 percent. The seamen in this test were drawn from the Salem Crew Lists as described in Appendix A.

Promotion to Mate. All mates during the period 1745–1759, born in Salem or Beverly, were tested for promotion to mate using the same sources as in the previous section. Out of 45, 26 (57.8 percent) were promoted. That means the ratio of unpromoted to promoted was 0.73. Thus if 26.6 percent of all seamen or boys were promoted (through mate) to master, then 26.6 × 0.73, or 19 percent, of these were promoted to mate but no farther. We rounded this up to 20 percent. To produce a comparative figure for promotion in the nineteenth century, we performed the strict ten-year test on the same 866 locally born seamen, 1805–1825, as were tested for promotion to master. Whereas 2.2 percent had become masters, a full 3.8 percent had become mates. This suggests a considerably higher promotion rate for mates than masters. Among the 45 locally born A-mariners, however, promotion to mate was achieved by only 9 percent, which inclines us to round the promotion rate higher than that for masters, but only slightly, at 15 percent.

The attentive reader will notice that the promotion rates described in the life course pie chart imply that mariners who survived their twenties had almost entirely graduated into officers' posts, whereas the stacked bar for ages 30–34 in Graph 3 describes a ratio of masters to mates to seamen of approximately 1:1:1. This discrepancy results from the fact that many seamen served officers' berths only once or twice in their careers and then either returned to the forecastle, retired from the sea, became fishermen, or turned to coasting. Hence the fact that they were promoted at all places them into the "Promoted" slices, even though they may have been doing other things in their early thirties.

Died. Annual rates of age-specific male mortality and population at risk were estimated from the following sources: "Parish List of Deaths Begun 1785, Recorded by William Bentley, D.D., of the East Church, Salem, Mass.," *E.I.H.C.* 14 (1877), 129–148, 224–232, 286–298; 15 (1878), 86–100; 16 (1879), 18–36, 191–203; 18 (1881), 73–80, 129–144, 206–223; 19 (1882), 18–39, 91–104, 176–182; U.S. Department of State, *Return of the Whole Number of Persons Within the Several Districts of the United States . . . 1800* (Washington, D.C., 1801), 8; William Bentley, *The Diary of William Bentley, D.D.: Pastor of the East Church, Salem, Massachusetts,* 4 vols. (Salem, 1905–14; rpt. Gloucester, Mass., 1962), 1:7, 222; U.S. Bureau of the Census, *Heads of Families at the First Census of the United States Taken in the Year, 1790: Massachusetts* (Washington, D.C., 1908), 9. The calculated rates of deaths per thousand per annum were: 40 for males aged 16–29 (1786–1794); 35 for males aged 16–25 (1795–1805); and 37 for males aged 26–44 (1795–1805). If we assume an annual rate of 37 per thousand, the resulting rate over a ten-year period would be 31.4 percent per decade, which we rounded down to 30 percent. Reading these rates forward into the nineteenth century is much more difficult, since with every passing decade the assumption that most young adult males were seafarers grows steadily weaker. We reduced the mortality rate slightly from 30 percent to 25 percent on the grounds: (i) that the ratio of deaths at sea to total population did fall from 0.0031 (East Parish, 1786–1794) to 0.0021 (Salem, 1821–1830), though this was partially accounted for by the growing number of youthful Salem residents not at sea and not at risk to die; (ii) that Maris Vinovskis believes that mortality in Salem "remained the same or decreased only slightly" between 1818 and 1861; and (iii) that the main cause of death abroad was disease, and Salem vessels were still sailing

mainly to tropical ports where these diseases were common. See Maris
Vinovskis, "Mortality Rates and Trends in Massachusetts Before 1860,"
Journal of Economic History 32 (1972), 207.

Left Salem. To measure this for the eighteenth century, we employed the
research of genealogists who have traced the history of out-migrants
from Salem. Out of 155 males who were born to prominent Salem maritime families (Archer, Beckford, Bowditch, Bray, Cook, Foot, Gardner,
Glover, and Punchard) between 1690 and 1745 and appear to have survived childhood, only 7 percent had left town by age thirty. On the one
hand, this figure may overstate the out-migration relevant to Graph 4,
since some of these young men may have left Salem before they reached
seafaring age. On the other hand, it may understate it since a small
number of men did disappear from the records for reasons unrecorded;
some of these may have been out-migrants, though given the high mortality rates and the underregistration of deaths in the colonial period,
it is almost certain that most of this latter group had, in fact, died. See
Sidney Perley, *The History of Salem, Massachusetts,* 3 vols. (Salem, 1924–
1928), 1:69–71, 214–215, 368–369; 2:43–45, 136–137; 3:19–20, 38, 48–
49, 353–355, and the genealogical collection of the James Duncan
Phillips Library, Peabody-Essex Museum.

Small pieces of circumstantial evidence also suggest the rarity of seaman
out-migration in this period. Five mariners in our database who sailed
out of Salem in the period before the Revolutionary War—John Henfield,
Benjamin Lang, Jesse Smith, Moses Townshend, and Benjamin Webber—filed pension applications with the federal government of the
United States in the nineteenth century. These pension applicants could
be positively linked to the mariners in the database via matching names,
birth dates, birthplaces, and/or wives' names. All of these retired mariners applied for pensions between 1820 and 1843, and not one of them
had moved away from the town he was living in when first identified
as a merchant mariner. See Pension Files S19700, W15011, S19469,
S30167, W14101, Revolutionary War Pension and Bounty-Land-Warrant
Application Files, Record Group 15, Records of the Veterans Administration, National Archives, United States of America, Washington, D.C.

For the nineteenth century, we performed two tests. First, we traced the
histories of 41 seamen who were born in Salem, Beverly, or Danvers
whose surnames started with A and whose careers began during the

period 1803–1813 through all available records (including every outbound crew list between 1803 and 1840); of those, 46 percent had either died or left town by the time they reached thirty years of age. If 25 percent had died, as we calculated above, then 21 percent left town. Another sample group of seamen born in Salem, Beverly, or Danvers found in nineteenth-century crew lists were traced to the 1850 manuscript census for Massachusetts, and here it was found that 23 percent (n=99) were living elsewhere within the state. Although this last figure must be considered a minimum, since other seamen may have moved out of Massachusetts entirely, it cannot be much greater if we are to account for those whom we know remained in the region or died. Since this latter measurement dates from the end of the period, however, when other opportunities on shore connected to industrialization and west-ward expansion were presumably drawing young men away from Salem, we rounded the result downward to 20 percent for the period 1805–1850. See the Salem Crew Lists, 1803–1840, the Manuscript Census for Massa-chusetts, 1850, and other sources listed in Appendix A.

Retired to Shore. Of all seamen of known age born in Salem 1690–1745 (n=55), 9 percent had retired to land to practice a nonseafaring trade by age thirty. We rounded this figure up to 10 percent. Performing the same test on the seamen whose names began with A and whose careers began between 1803 and 1810 (n=41), 12 percent had returned to land to practice another trade. We rounded this result down to 10 percent.

Graph 1

Population of Salem, 1683–1776

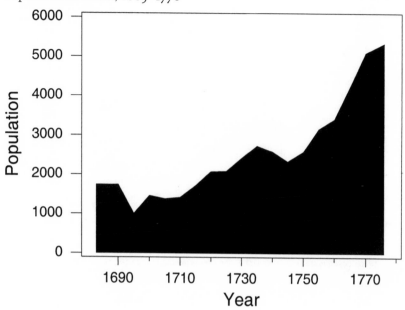

Graph 2

Wages of Salem seamen by age cohort, 1746–1771

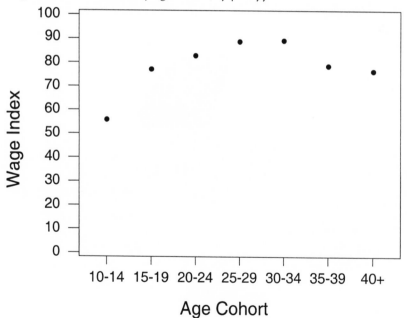

Graph 3

Age distribution by rank on Salem vessels, 1690–1775

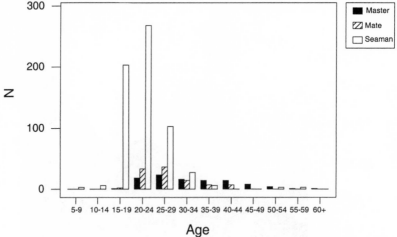

Note: Graph represents total number of mariners needed to man 100 typical vessels of the period.

Graph 4

Fate of Salem seamen between early twenties and early thirties, 1745–1775

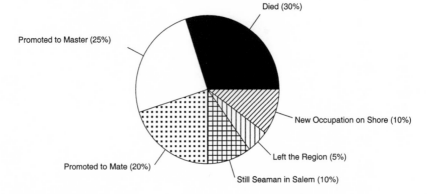

Graph 5

Age distribution of seamen and officers, aged 18–27, on Salem vessels,
1745–1775

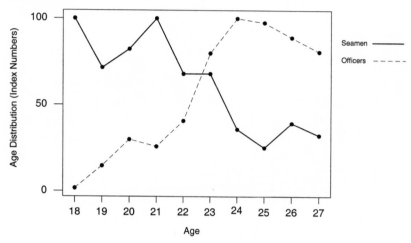

Graph 6

Mean wealth deciles of Salem mariners by age relative to year of
marriage, 1690–1775

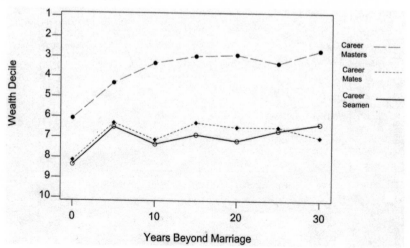

Graph 7
Monthly wages of Salem seamen by destination, 1750–1850

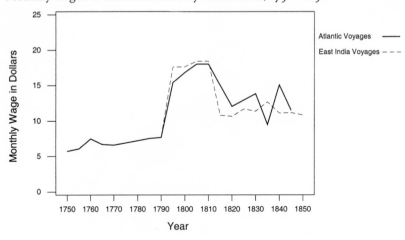

Graph 8
Wage index for selected occupations, 1785–1845

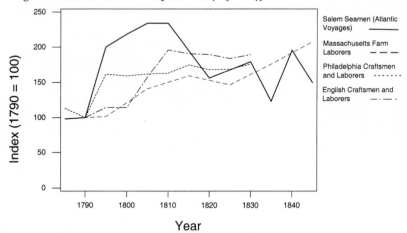

Graph 9

Index of real wages for Salem seamen, 1750–1850

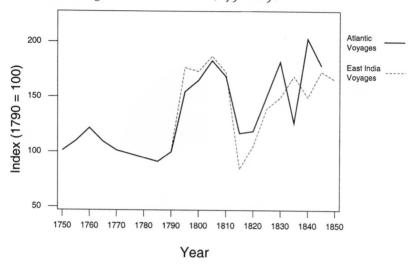

Graph 10

Age distribution of mariners born in Salem, Beverly, or Danvers on Salem vessels, 1805–1850

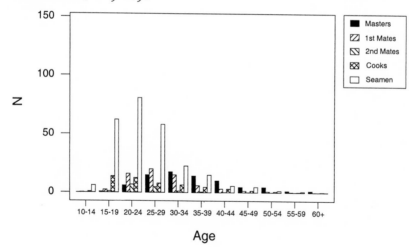

Graph 11

Fate of Salem seamen between early twenties and early thirties,
1800–1850

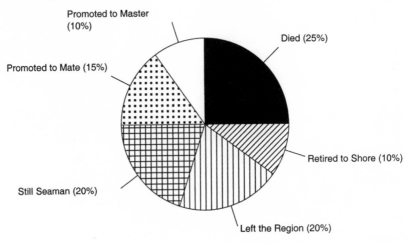

Graph 12

Monthly wages of seamen and mates on Salem voyages with Atlantic
destinations, 1750–1845

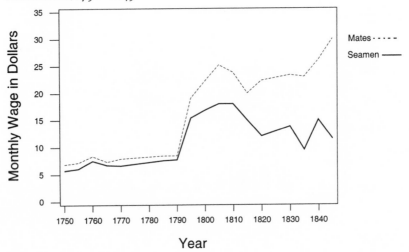

Graph 13

Age distribution of mariners born outside Salem, Beverly, or Danvers
on Salem vessels, 1805–1850

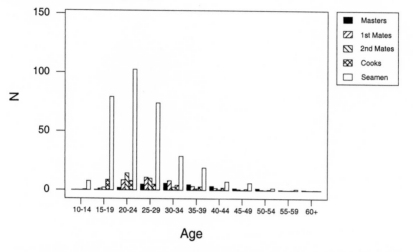

Ship's Logs

ONE SOURCE FOR THE quality of life on board Salem ships of the eighteenth and nineteenth centuries is the voluminous Marine Logbook collection of the James Duncan Phillips Library, Peabody-Essex Museum, Salem, Massachusetts. We analyzed all logbooks dating from before 1782 and a sampling of those from 1783–1850, searching specifically for evidence on provisioning, work routines, encounters with other vessels, experiences in foreign ports, discipline, desertion, and mortality, and more broadly the general character of seafaring life. These logbooks included those kept on board, in alphabetical order, sloop *Adventure* (1773–1779); brig *Alfred* (1826); ship *Arab* (1806–1807); schooner *Brittan* (1771–1772); schooner *Defiance* (1768); bark *Derby* (1825–1827); schooner *Dollar* (1825–1826); schooner *Dolphin* (1764); vessel *Dolphin* (1764); schooner *Dolphin* (1772); schooner *Eagle* (1753–1755); brigantine *Eliza* (1787); sloop *Elizabeth* (1768–1769); bark *Emily Wilder* (1850–1851); schooner/brigantine *Essex* (1765–1766); schooner *General Wolfe* (1768–1769); brigantine *Hind* (1784–1786); schooner *Hopwell* (1770); ship *Janus* (1825–1827); brig *Lama* (1826); schooner *Lively* (1772); schooner *Nabey* (1768–1769); brig *Ocean* (1784); schooner *Olive Branch* (1766–1771); schooner *Polly* (1772); schooner *Polly Virginia* (1763); schooner *Pompey* (1769); ship *Prudent* (1804–1806); schooner *Rockingham* (1772–1773); brigantine *Romulus* (1781); ship *Salem* (1765); schooner *Salem* (1772–1783); schooner *Sally* (1769–1770); bark

Sea Men (1849–1850); ship *St. Paul* (1749–1751); schooner *Swan* (1760); bark *Tom Corwin* (1849–1850); ship *Vaughan* (1767); brig *Washington* (1804–1805); brig *William* (1805–1806); schooner [name unknown] (1758–59). These forty-one vessels conducted ninety fully or partially chronicled voyages.

NOTES

INTRODUCTION

1. Herman Melville, *Moby-Dick; or, The Whale* (Harmondsworth, 1972), 93; John Masefield, "Sea-Fever," in *The Oxford Book of Travel Verse*, ed. Kevin Crossley-Holland (Oxford, 1986), 21; Rudyard Kipling, "The Long Trail," in *Moods of the Sea: Masterworks of Sea Poetry*, ed. George C. Solley and Eric Steinbaugh (Annapolis, Md., 1981), 55.

2. Samuel Eliot Morison, *The Maritime History of Massachusetts, 1783–1860* (Boston, 1921; rpt. Boston, 1979), 106; Marcus Rediker, *Between the Devil and the Deep Blue Sea: Merchant Seamen, Pirates, and the Anglo-American Maritime World, 1700–1750* (Cambridge, 1987), 80; Margaret Creighton, *Rites and Passages: The Experience of American Whaling, 1830–1870* (Cambridge, 1995), 57; Jesse Lemisch, "Jack Tar in the Streets: Merchant Seamen in the Politics of Revolutionary America," *William and Mary Quarterly*, 3d ser., 25 (1968), 375.

3. *OED Online* (2d ed., 1989); Rediker, *Between the Devil and the Deep Blue Sea*; Creighton, *Rites and Passages*; W. Jeffrey Bolster, *Black Jacks: African American Seamen in the Age of Sail* (Cambridge, Mass., 1997); Lisa Norling, *Captain Ahab Had a Wife: New England Women and the Whalefishery, 1720–1870* (Chapel Hill, N.C., 2000); Paul A. Gilje, *Liberty on the Waterfront: American Maritime Culture in the Age of Revolution* (Philadelphia, 2004). One volume that differs markedly from the above in the similarities it draws between life at sea and life on land is Eric W. Sager, *Seafaring Labour: The Merchant Marine of Atlantic Canada, 1820–1914* (Kingston, Ont., 1989).

4. *OED Online*. There are exceptions to this generalization. Histories of fisheries often follow the second definition more closely than the first. See Rosemary E. Ommer, *From Outpost to Outport: A Structural Analysis of the*

Jersey-Gaspé Cod Fishery, 1767–1886 (Montreal, 1991); Daniel Vickers, *Farmers and Fishermen: Two Centuries of Work in Essex County, Massachusetts, 1630–1850* (Chapel Hill, N.C., 1994); Sean T. Cadigan, *Hope and Deception in Conception Bay: Merchant-Settler Relations in Newfoundland, 1785–1855* (Toronto, 1995); Jerry Bannister, *The Rule of the Admirals: Law, Custom, and Naval Government in Newfoundland, 1699–1832* (Toronto, 2003). Likewise, historians of seaport women employ the second definition to handle the subject, although the exceptional character of sailors' lives remains an assumption in their work. See Norling, *Captain Ahab Had a Wife*; Elaine Forman Crane, *Ebb Tide in New England: Women, Seaports, and Social Change, 1630–1800* (Boston, 1998). Michael Jarvis successfully employs both definitions in "'In the Eye of All Trade': Maritime Revolution and the Transformation of Bermudian Society, 1612–1800," Ph.D. diss., College of William and Mary, 1998.

5. For several decades, historians have been trying to explain that social phenomena are not timeless categories but historical creations—the product of struggle. The realization that class, gender, and race all "happen" (see Edward Thompson, *The Making of the English Working Class* [Harmondsworth, 1968], 9) has allowed a generation of scholars to construct around the principle of human agency a rich social history of ordinary people unimaginable fifty years ago. We recognize what has been gained from the strategy of foregrounding the collective activity of ordinary people, but we depart from it in the attention we pay to individuals once they have exited the particular social stage that drew our attention to them in the first place. The focus on struggle and agency tends to highlight the deeds of individuals in particular historical roles, usually articulating some vision of gender, race, or class. These visions mattered at critical points in the past, for they gave social movements their shape, and that is why this approach has been so fruitful. Yet in its insistence on history as process, this type of scholarship has sometimes downplayed the way people as individuals are in process too.

1. LANDSMEN ON THE WATER

1. Philip L. Barbour, *The Three Worlds of Captain John Smith* (Boston, 1964), 200.

2. William Bradford, *Of Plymouth Plantation,* ed. Samuel Eliot Morison (New York, 1952), 59, 61–62.

3. Ibid., 64–72, 89–90; Alexander Young, ed., *Chronicles of the Pilgrim Fathers of the Colony of Plymouth* (Boston, 1841; rpt. New York, 1971), 171, 172, 199, 214–218; George F. Willison, *Saints and Strangers* (New York, 1964), 156–180; Joseph F. Cullon, "Colonial Shipwrights and Their World: Men, Women, and Markets in Early New England," Ph.D. diss., University of Wisconsin, Madison, 2003, 52–55.

4. George D. Langdon, *Pilgrim Colony: A History of New Plymouth, 1620–1691* (New Haven, 1966), 16–18, 36; Cullon, "Colonial Shipwrights," 55–64; Young, *Chronicles of the Pilgrim Fathers,* 224–229, 293, 299–305, 308–309;

Bradford, *Of Plymouth Plantation*, 94, 110–111, 113–115, 121–123, 132, 178, 181, 182, 219–234. Commercial fishing proved less successful. See Bradford, *Of Plymouth Plantation*, 145–146.

5. Christopher Levett, *My Discovery of diverse Rivers and Harbours, with their names, and which are fit for Plantations, and which are not*, in *Sailors Narratives of Voyages Along the New England Coast, 1524–1624*, ed. George Parker Winship (Boston, 1905; rpt. New York, n.d.), 261–262; Bradford, *Of Plymouth Plantation*, 103–115, 133–138, 145–147.

6. James Kendall Hosmer, ed., *Winthrop's Journal: "History of New England," 1630–1649*, 2 vols., *Original Narratives of Early American History* (New York, 1908), 1:67, 68, 82, 141, 166, 334; Daniel Vickers, *Farmers and Fishermen: Two Centuries of Work in Essex County, Massachusetts, 1630–1850* (Chapel Hill, N.C., 1994), 91–92; Darrett B. Rutman, *Winthrop's Boston: Portrait of a Puritan Town* (Chapel Hill, N.C., 1965), 167–169, 180–181; Langdon, *Pilgrim Colony*, 37. Quotation on vessel types is from Thomas Lechford, *Plain Dealing; or, News from New England* (1641), ed. Darrett B. Rutman (New York, 1969), 110; Stephen Innes, *Creating the Commonwealth: The Economic Culture of Puritan New England* (New York, 1995), 279–287, 300–306.

7. James Phinney Baxter, ed., *The Trelawney Papers*, Maine Historical Society, *Collections*, 2d ser. (Portland, 1884), 3:18, 19, 20, 23, 28, 29, 114, 145, 155–156, 192–195, 212, 218; Hosmer, *Winthrop's Journal*, 1:107, 109, 126, 128, 131, 160, 176, 183, 185, 187, 194, 238, 260, 291, 2:17, 18, 70, 73–74, 157, 176, 248; Edward E. Hale, ed., *Note-Book Kept by Thomas Lechford, Esq., Lawyer, in Boston, Massachusetts Bay, from June 27, 1638, to July 29, 1641* (Cambridge, Mass., 1885), 47–48, 214–215, 224–226, 362–363. The last entries in Winthrop's journal that identify voyages to the West Indies and to southern Europe as newsworthy commercial achievements can be found in Hosmer, *Winthrop's Journal*, 2:92–93, 227.

8. William Wood, *New England's Prospect*, ed. Alden T. Vaughan (Amherst, Mass., 1977), 64; Samuel de Champlain, *The Voyages of the Sieur de Champlain*, ed. and trans. W. F. Ganong, in H. P. Biggar, ed., *The Works of Samuel de Champlain*, 6 vols. (Toronto, 1922–1936), 1:334–339.

9. See George Francis Dow, ed., *The Probate Records of Essex County, Massachusetts, 1635–1681*, 3 vols. (Salem, 1916–1920), 1:5, 20, 22, 30, 36, 39, 42, hereafter cited as *Essex Co. Prob. Recs.*; George Francis Dow and Mary G. Thresher, eds., *Records and Files of the Quarterly Courts of Essex County, Massachusetts, 1636–1686*, 9 vols. (Salem, 1911–1975), 1:3, 5, 20, 22, 25, 27, 28, 38, 43, 64, 2:23, hereafter cited as *Essex Co. Court Recs.*

10. *Essex Co. Prob. Recs.*, vols. 1–3; *Essex Co. Court Recs.*, 1:27–28, 2:23–26; Sidney Perley, *The History of Salem, Massachusetts*, 3 vols. (Salem, 1924–1928), 1:254; William A. Baker, *Colonial Vessels: Some Seventeenth-Century Sailing Craft* (Barre, Mass., 1962), 151.

11. David Hackett Fischer, *Albion's Seed: Four British Folkways in America* (New York, 1989), 31–36; Virginia DeJohn Anderson, *New England's Generation: The Great Migration and the Formation of Society and Culture in the Seventeenth*

Century (Cambridge, 1991), 224; James Duncan Phillips, *Salem in the Seventeenth Century* (Cambridge, Mass., 1933), 65–66; Hosmer, *Winthop's Journal*, 1:55–56; Wood, *New England's Prospect*, 29; Robert Charles Anderson, *The Great Migration Begins: Immigrants to New England, 1620–1633*, 3 vols. (Boston, 1995), 2:737–739.

12. Hosmer, *Winthrop's Journal*, 1:141, 166. On Sewall's character see James Savage, *A Genealogical Dictionary of the First Settlers of New England*, 4 vols. (1860–1862), 4:53.

13. *Essex Co. Court Recs.*, 1:3, 4:98; Hosmer, *Winthrop's Journal*, 1:83, 137; Wood, *New England's Prospect*, 64; Nathaniel B. Shurtleff, ed., *Records of the Governor and Company of the Massachusetts Bay in New England*, 6 vols. in 5 (Boston, 1853–1854), 1:246; Perley, *History of Salem*, 1:404–408.

14. Bradford, *Of Plymouth Plantation*, 148–157, 165–166; Hosmer, *Winthrop's Journal*, 1:83, 183–189, 228; Francis Jennings, *The Invasion of America: Indians, Colonialism, and the Cant of Conquest* (Chapel Hill, 1975), 206–209; Thomas Morton, *The New English Canaan*, ed. Charles Francis Adams, *Publications of the Prince Society* (Boston, 1883) 14:263.

15. Hosmer, *Winthrop's Journal*, 1:183–185; *Winthrop Papers*, 5 vols. (Boston, 1929–1947), 3:87, 141, 156, 170, 275, 433, 457, 4:184, 190; Savage, *Genealogical Dictionary*, 2:222–223.

16. Perley, *History of Salem*, 1:319, 361, 375, 456, 461, 2:9, 403; Savage, *Genealogical Dictionary*, 2:529; *Winthrop Papers*, 3:434, 435; Hosmer, *Winthrop's Journal*, 2:17.

17. Hosmer, *Winthrop's Journal*, 1:231, 307, 2:18, 35–36, 62.

18. Hosmer, *Winthrop's Journal*, 1:183.

19. Bradford, *Of Plymouth Plantation*, 126–127, 139, 150, 155, 165, 167, 226, 237, 252, 256, quotation on 255; *Winthrop Papers*, 2:262n; Hosmer, *Winthrop's Journal*, 1:49, 71, 92, 94, 221, 228, 260, 278, 293, 2:34; Anderson, *The Great Migration Begins*, 3:1472–1478; Karen Ordahl Kupperman, *Providence Island, 1640–1641: The Other Puritan Colony* (Cambridge, 1993), 172, 310, 325, 335, 339–341.

20. Hosmer, *Winthrop's Journal*, 1:24, 65, 80, 102, 103, 104, 152, 153, 2:157; *Winthrop Papers*, 3:150, 151, 155; 5:2, 244; Thomas Bellows Wyman, *The Genealogies and Estates of Charlestown, Massachusetts, 1629–1818* (Boston, 1879; rpt. Somersworth, N.H.: New England History Press, 1982), 432.

21. *Winthrop Papers*, 3:155–156; Hosmer, *Winthrop's Journal*, 2:70, 92–93, 248–249; Wyman, *Charlestown*, 227–228.

22. Anderson, *The Great Migration Begins*, 1:145–146; Hosmer, *Winthrop's Journal*, 1:24; Wyman, *Charlestown*, 72, 952; *Winthrop Papers*, 3:161, 199; 5:280, 368. The only other master mariners who took up residence in New England before 1645 were John Cutting, William Goose, Edward Payne, William Quick, and Edward Wetheridge. See sources in Appendix A.

23. Quotation from John Winthrop in Hosmer, *Winthrop's Journal*, 2:70; quotation from Lucy Downing to John Winthrop, ca. January 1641, in *Winthrop Papers*, 4:304. See also *Winthrop Papers* 2:58n, 105n; 5:89, 290–291, 296–297.

2. SALEM'S FIRST MARINERS

1. Francis Higginson to His Friends in England, July 24, 1629, in Everett Emerson, ed., *Letters from New England: The Massachusetts Bay Colony, 1629–1638* (Amherst, Mass., 1976), 22.

2. William Wood, *New England's Prospect*, ed. Alden T. Vaughan (Amherst, Mass., 1977), 64; Francis Higginson to His Friends at Leicester, September 1629, in Emerson, *Letters from New England*, 30, 31; Sidney Perley, *The History of Salem, Massachusetts*, 3 vols. (Salem, 1924–1928) 1:14–15.

3. The three best accounts of the settling of Salem remain James Duncan Phillips, *Salem in the Seventeenth Century* (Cambridge, Mass., 1933); Perley, *History of Salem*, vol. 1; and Richard P. Gildrie, *Salem, Massachusetts, 1626–1683: A Covenant Community* (Charlottesville, Va., 1975).

4. Phillips, *Salem in the Seventeenth Century*, 90–101, 171–187. See George Francis Dow and Mary G. Thresher, eds., *Records and Files of the Quarterly Courts of Essex County, Massachusetts, 1636–1686*, 9 vols. (Salem, 1911–1975), 1:3, 255, hereafter cited as *Essex Co. Court Recs.*

5. Quotation from Edward Randolph, "Report to the Committee for Trade and Plantations," Oct. 12, 1676, in *Edward Randolph Papers*, ed. Robert Noxon Toppan, *Publications of the Prince Society* (Boston, 1898; rpt. New York, 1967), 25:249; Bernard Bailyn, *The New England Merchants in the Seventeenth Century* (Cambridge, Mass., 1955; rpt. New York, 1964), 45–111.

6. See the references to canoes, skiffs, boats, and lighters in *Essex Co. Court Recs*, vols. 1–9; George Francis Dow, ed., *The Probate Records of Essex County, Massachusetts, 1635–1681*, 3 vols. (Salem, 1916–1920), hereafter cited as *Essex Co. Prob. Recs.*

7. *Essex Co. Court Recs.*, 1:134, 292, 2:29, 95, 96, 3:284–285, 7:257, 8:215.

8. *Essex Co. Court Recs.*, 4:97–98; *Essex Co. Prob. Recs.*, 2:214. For other examples, see *Essex Co. Court Recs.*, 4:212, 6:51, 8:331, 9:164–165. The estimate of business for Salem lighters is based on the conservative assumptions that Salem possessed a fleet of sixty ketches during the 1680s, that their mean tonnage was 30, that they made at least three voyages (either fishing or trading), half-laden, every year, and that they were loaded or unloaded in boats that could carry up to 750 pounds of cargo. This piece of informed guesswork produces almost fifteen thousand boatloads of cargo, or about fifty for every working day of the year. Naturally there were many idle days during the winter months, a great many trips that carried people and no cargo, and a great deal of business involving foreign-owned vessels and local coasters— none of which are included here. See Perley, *History of Salem*, 3:296 (size of fleet); Naval Officer Shipping Lists for Barbados, C.O. 33/13; 14, Nevis, C.O. 187/1, 2; St. Kitts, C.O. 243/1; and Jamaica C.O. 142/13 (mean tonnage); Philip English Account Books, 1664–1708, 1678–1690, English/Touzell/ Hathorne Papers, 1661–1851, James Duncan Phillips Library, Peabody-Essex Museum, Salem, Mass. (voyages per year).

9. Perley, *History of Salem*, 2:100, 201; *Essex Co. Court Recs.*, 1:16, 298; *Essex Co. Prob. Recs.*, 1:133, 2:73–74; John J. Babson, *History of the Town of Gloucester,*

Cape Ann, Including the Town of Rockport (Gloucester, Mass., 1860; rpt. Gloucester, 1972), 173.

10. *Essex Co. Court Recs.,* 4:15, 47; Daniel Vickers, *Farmers and Fishermen: Two Centuries of Work in Essex County, Massachusetts, 1630–1850* (Chapel Hill, N.C., 1994), 65–67.

11. *Essex Co. Court Recs.,* 4:47, 7:257. On the age structure of men's working careers in Essex County, Massachusetts, see Vickers, *Farmers and Fishermen,* 64–77.

12. *Essex Co. Court Recs.,* 1:5, 4:98; Laurel Thatcher Ulrich, *A Midwife's Tale: The Life of Martha Ballard, Based on Her Diary, 1785–1812* (New York, 1990), 5, 7, 39, 103, 167, 182. Boats, canoes, lighters, ferries, and hoys are mentioned in connection with 216 individuals, only two of them women, between 1636 and 1683 in the *Essex Co. Court Recs.,* vols. 1–8. The best study of women's daily activities in Massachusetts during this period is Laurel Thatcher Ulrich, *Good Wives: Image and Reality in the Lives of Women in Northern New England, 1650–1750* (New York, 1980), a book that uses the *Essex Co. Court Recs.* to document a wide range of women's activities. That boating was not among them seems significant.

13. See *Essex Co. Prob Recs.,* vols. 1–3.

14. George Corwin, Account Book, 1652–1655, Curwen Family Papers, 1641–1902, James Duncan Phillips Library, Peabody-Essex Museum, Salem, Mass.

15. David Thomas Konig, *Law and Society in Puritan Massachusetts: Essex County, 1629–1692* (Chapel Hill, N.C., 1979), 76–78; *Essex Co. Prob. Recs.,* 1:34–35, 2:13; *Essex Co. Court Recs.,* 9:497; Naval Officer Shipping Lists for Barbados, C.O. 33/13; 14, Nevis, C.O. 187/1, 2; St. Kitts, C.O. 243/1; and Jamaica C.O. 142/13, P.R.O.

16. Charles F. Carroll, *The Timber Economy of Puritan New England* (Providence, R.I., 1973); *Essex Co. Court Recs.,* 1:263, 296–300; David Van Deventer, *The Emergence of Provincial New Hampshire* (Baltimore, 1976), 33–39, 93–95; *Essex Co. Court Recs.,* 6:366, 8:11–12, 164, 328.

17. Vickers, *Farmers and Fishermen,* 85–141.

18. Ibid., 116–129; *Essex Co. Court Recs.,* 3:14–15, 210–211, 261.

19. *Essex Co. Court Recs.,* 3:261; 7:167–168.

20. Carroll, *Timber Economy,* 140. These figures are for Boston only; the customs records for Salem have been lost, but they certainly carried the total of clearances from Massachusetts ports to more than 10,000 tons.

21. These generalizations are based on a file composed of sixty-one mariners involved in eighty-nine commercial coasting voyages before 1690 identified from sources in Appendix A. On the Cross brothers and their coasting business, see Savage, *Genealogical Dictionary,* 1:478; Thomas Franklin Waters, *Ipswich in Massachusetts Bay Colony, 1633–1917,* 2 vols. (Ipswich, Mass., 1905–1917), 1:465–466; *Essex Co. Court Recs.,* 3:87–88, 396, 4:50, 247, 5:186, 6:17, 248, 286, 366, 430, 7:261–262, 9:261–262.

22. *Essex Co. Court Recs.,* 3:398, 399, 400, 4:76–82, 235, 242, 5:78, 139; Waters, *Ipswich,* 2:73–74.

23. On John Lee see *Essex Co. Court Recs.*, 4:82–83, 5:143–147, 186–188, 227–230, 6:368–369, 8:11–12, 164, 327–328, 9:329; Savage, *Genealogical Dictionary*, 3:71; Ulrich, *Good Wives*, 120–121. On the Dutch family and the warehouse fire, see *Essex Co. Court Recs.*, 3:349, 6:12, 7:167–168, 366–374; Savage, *Genealogical Dictionary*, 2:84. On Mordicai and Edith Cravett see Perley, *History of Salem*, 2:221, 228; *Essex Co. Court Recs.*, 1:256, 258, 2:100, 3:43–44, 104–105, 210–211, 260–263, 330–333, 344, 352–353, 420–421.

24. On Thomas and John Chubb see Perley, *History of Salem*, 1:365; *Essex Co. Court Recs.*, 3:463, 4:124–125, 5:23–25, 221, 6:27, 7:187, 325, 8:21–22, 291, 299, 315, 9:206–208, 336. On Thomas Chick see *Essex Co. Court Recs.*, 7:81–82, 149, 271, 308–310.

25. On Robert Nash see *Essex County Court Recs.*, 1:263; Savage, *Genealogical Dictionary*, 3:262; Jay Mack Holbrook, *Boston Beginnings, 1630–1699* (Oxford, Mass., 1980), 182.

26. Nathaniel B. Shurtleff, ed., *Records of the Governor and Company of the Massachusetts Bay in New England*, 6 vols. in 5 (Boston, 1853–1854), 1:109, hereafter cited as *Recs. of Mass. Bay*. On coasters and churches see sources in Appendix A.

27. Michael Pawson and David Busseret, *Port Royal, Jamaica* (Oxford, 1975), 71, 76; Arthur Pierce Middleton, *Tobacco Coast: A Maritime History of Chesapeake Bay in the Colonial Era* (Newport News, Va., 1953), 60–90.

28. Bailyn, *New England Merchants*, 76–86; Darrett B. Rutman, "Governor Winthrop's Garden Crop: The Significance of Agriculture in the Early Commerce of Massachusetts Bay," *William and Mary Quarterly*, 3d ser., 20 (1963), 401–407; James G. Lydon, "North Shore Trade in the Early Eighteenth Century," *American Neptune* 28 (1968), 265–268.

29. James Kendall Hosmer, ed., *Winthrop's Journal: "History of New England,"* *1630–1649*, 2 vols., *Original Narratives of Early American History* (New York, 1908), 2:23–24, 31, 60, 152, 157, 177, 289, 345; Joseph A. Goldenberg, *Shipbuilding in Colonial America* (Charlottesville, Va., 1976), 10–23; Stephen Innes, *Creating the Commonwealth: The Economic Culture of Puritan New England* (New York, 1995), 271–275, 287–295; *Recs. of Mass. Bay* 4, no. 2, 203, 211; Randolph, "Report," Oct. 12, 1676, *Randolph Papers*, 25:250.

30. John Hull quotation cited in Carroll, *Timber Economy*, 135. See also ibid., 131, 139; "The names of such ships & masters that have Come in and gone out of our Harbours and Given bond for his Majesty's Customes," Aug. 16, 1661, to Feb. 25, 1662, Massachusetts Archives, 60:33; Naval Officer Shipping Lists for Barbados, 1686–1688, C.O. 132/13, 14, Public Record Office.

31. Randolph, "Report," Oct. 12, 1676, *Randolph Papers*, 25:250; Carroll, *Timber Economy*, 131; Bernard Bailyn and Lotte Bailyn, *Massachusetts Shipping: A Statistical Study* (Cambridge, Mass., 1959), table 1.

32. Todd Gray, ed., *Early Stuart Mariners and Shipping: The Maritime Surveys of Devon and Cornwall, 1619–1635*, in *Devon and Cornwall Record Society*, new series (Exeter, England, 1990), 33:96–98, 117–122; Bailyn and Bailyn, *Massachusetts Shipping*, 20–21.

33. Vickers, *Farmers and Fishermen*, 145–167.

34. Richard Davenport to Hugh Peter, 1637, in *Winthrop Papers*, 5 vols. (Boston, 1929–1947), 3:342; "A Volume Relating to the Early History of Boston Containing the Aspinwall Notarial records from 1644–1651," in Registry Department of the City of Boston, *Records Relating to the Early History of Boston*, 32 (Boston, 1903), 177–178; *Essex Co. Court Recs.*, 4:299, 7:310–312, 9:397–398; Perley, *History of Salem*, 1:430, 2:347, 364, 371; George Corwin, Account Books, 1663–1672, 1671–1684.

35. On Salem's trade with the West Indies see *Essex Co. Court Recs.*, 5:47–49; 301; George Corwin, Account Books, 1663–1672, 1671–1684; Naval Officer Shipping Lists for Barbados, C.O. 33/13; 14, Nevis, C.O. 187/1, 2; St. Kitts, C.O. 243/1; and Jamaica C.O. 142/13.

36. *Essex Co. Court Recs.*, 6:392, 7:221, 326, 328.; Philip English, Account Book, 1664–1718, English/Touzell/Hathorne Family Papers, 1661–1851, James Duncan Phillips Library, Peabody-Essex Museum, Salem, Mass.; Phillips, *Salem in the Seventeenth Century*, 289.

37. Paul J. Lindholdt, *John Josselyn, Colonial Traveler: A Critical Edition of Two Voyages to New-England* (Hanover, N.H., 1988), 117; Perley, *History of Salem*, 1:366–367, 2:37–39; 298–299; Phillips, *Salem in the Seventeenth Century*, 140–141, 190–191. On Brown, Corwin, and Lindall as shipowners see *Essex Co. Court Recs.*, 5:169, 7:196, 8:25; George Corwin, Account Books, 1663–1672, 1671–1684. On "traders by sea" see Jacob Price, "Economic Function and the Growth of American Port Towns in the Eighteenth Century," *Perspectives in American History*, 8 (1974), 138–139. On English and Hardy see Perley, *History of Salem*, 1:286, 3:37, 70; *Essex Co. Court Recs.*, 5:348, 6:356; *Essex Co. Prob. Recs.*, 1:147; Philip English, Account Book, 1664–1718, English/Touzell/Hathorne Family Papers, 1661–1851, James Duncan Phillips Library, Peabody-Essex Museum, Salem, Mass.

38. *Essex Co. Court Recs.*, 7:61–66; Perley, *History of Salem*, 1:286–287, 2:186. On the same pattern in Philadelphia see Thomas M. Doerflinger, *A Vigorous Spirit of Enterprise: Merchants and Economic Development in Revolutionary Philadelphia* (New York, 1987), 41–45.

39. *Essex Co. Court Recs.*, 2:164, 4:394–395, 5:339; Perley, *History of Salem*, 1:391.

40. Phillips, *Salem in the Seventeenth Century*, 203, 209, 217, 218, 219, 235–236, 250, 270. Catherine Alice Young, *From "Good Order" to Glorious Revolution* (Ann Arbor, Mich., 1980), 50–52; Gildrie, *Salem*, 61, 103, 137–138, 158–160; Inventory of George Corwin (1685), in *Essex Co. Court Recs.*, 9:492–503.

41. Perley, *History of Salem*, 3:296; Naval Officer Shipping Lists for Barbados, C.O. 33/13, 14. Working from Edward Randolph's estimates for all of Massachusetts cited earlier, James Duncan Phillips guessed that the fleet included five ships of 100 tons or more and seventy or eighty brigs and ketches of 30 tons or more. Since Randolph's figures seriously exaggerated the dimensions of the shipping industry as a whole, however, Phillips's figures are probably too high. See Phillips, *Salem in the Seventeenth Century*, 282.

42. With 366 militia recorded for Salem and Salem Village in 1690, and assum-

ing a population-to-militia ratio of 5 to 1, the population of Salem would have been 1,830. With 590 polls in 1689 and a ratio of polls to population of 4 to 1, the population of Salem would have been 2,360. The estimate of 2,000 is intended as a rough compromise. See Evarts B. Breene and Virginia D. Harrington, *American Population Before the Federal Census of 1790* (New York, 1932), xxiii, 20.

43. On John Marston see *Essex Co. Court Recs.*, 2:126, 3:324, 4:144; Perley, *History of Salem*, 2:78; Savage, *Genealogical Dictionary*, 3:160. On Henry True see Perley, *History of Salem*, 1:314, 316, 2:194, 165; Savage, *Genealogical Dictionary*, 4:334; *Essex Co. Court Recs.*, 5:174; *Essex Co. Prob. Recs.*, 1:311–312.

44. On Richard More see Robert Charles Anderson, *The Great Migration Begins: Immigrants to New England, 1620–1633*, 3 vols. (Boston, 1995), 2:1283–1287; *Essex Co. Court Recs.*, 5:400, 7:310–312, 9:368; Perley, *History of Salem*, 3:80.

45. Vickers, *Farmers and Fishermen*, 131.

46. On Robert Starr see Perley, *History of Salem*, 2:193, 405; *Essex Co. Court Recs.*, 7:239–240; Philip English, Account Book, 1664–1718; Sidney Perley, "Salem in 1700, No. 21," *Essex Antiquarian*, 9 (1905), 168. Of all mariners who settled in Salem, Marblehead, and Beverly between 1660 and 1689 ($n = 135$), 36 percent were active fishermen at some time in their careers. See sources in Appendix A.

47. Length of voyages were estimated from Harriet Sylvester Tapley, ed., *Early Coastwise and Foreign Shipping of Salem: A Record of Entrances and Clearances of the Port of Salem, 1750–1769* (Salem, 1934).

48. Vickers, *Farmers and Fishermen*, 100.

49. Ibid., 133–134.

50. Winter to Trelawney, July 7, 1634, July 10, 1639, *The Trelawney Papers*, ed. James Phinney Baxter, Maine. Historical Society, *Collections*, 2d ser. (Portland, 1884), 3:44, 164; Capt. Staffd. Fairborne, "Account of the Fishery at Newfoundland," Sept. 11, 1700, in *Calendar of State Papers*, ed. W. Noel Sainsbury et al., Colonial Series, *America and the West Indies*, 40 vols. (London, 1860–1939), 18:522, hereafter cited as *CSPC*; Marcus Rediker, *Between the Devil and the Deep Blue Sea: Merchant Seamen, Pirates, and the Anglo-American Maritime World, 1700–1750* (Cambridge, 1987), 136–137. On Job Tookey see *Essex Co. Court Recs.*, 8:330–332, 337–338; Paul Boyer and Stephen Nissenbaum, *Salem Possessed: The Social Origins of Witchcraft* (Cambridge, Mass., 1974), 206–208. On Stephen Griggs see *Essex Co. Court Recs.*, 3:155, 5:49, 114, 7:306–307, 8:330–338, 9:468–469; George Corwin, Account Book, 1663–1672.

51. *Essex Co. Court Recs.*, 4:146–148. On Edward Woodman see *Essex Co. Court Recs.*, 7:402, 9:193–199; Archie N. Frost, comp., *Verbatim Transcriptions of the Records of the Quarterly Courts of Essex County, Massachusetts, 1636–1694*, 57 vols. (Salem, 1939), 51:118. See also *Essex Co. Court Recs.*, 2:52, 9:59; Naval Officer Shipping Lists for Barbados, C.O. 33/13; Philip English, Account Book, 1678–1690.

52. Jack Cremer, *Ramblin' Jack: The Journal of Captain John Cremer, 1700–1774*,

ed. R. Reynall Bellamy (London, 1936), 113. This reference dates from the early eighteenth century, but the English pamphleteer Ned Ward may well have been referring to the same point when he noted that New England women were "not at all inferiour in Beauty to the Ladies of London." See Ward, *A Trip to New-England with a Character of the Country and People, both English and Indians* (London, 1699). Out of forty nonofficers who moved into Salem during the period 1660–1689, twenty-one married identifiable New England women. Of the remaining nineteen, some may also have married women from elsewhere in New England and escaped our dragnet. See sources in Appendix A.

53. On John Tawley see Perley, *History of Salem*, 2:357, 361, 3:116, 125, 128, 145, 421; Estate of John Tawley (1690), Probate No. 27290, Essex Prob. Recs. (unpubl.); Naval Officer Shipping Lists for Barbados, C.O. 33/13; Naval Officer Shipping Lists for St. Christophers, C.O. 157/1; Frost, *Essex Co. Court Records: Verbatim Transcriptions*, 46:59. On Nicholas Durrell see *Essex Co. Court Recs.*, 6:241, 282, 7:155, 161, 323, 343; Perley, *History of Salem*, 3:99; Savage, *Genealogical Dictionary*, 2:83; *Records of the Suffolk County Court, 1671–1680*, ed. Samuel Eliot Morison, *Publications of the Colonial Society of Massachusetts*, vols. 29–30 (Boston, 1933), 29:249–50. Percentages of settling mariners are based on the histories of ninety-two masters and seamen who shipped out of Salem on locally owned vessels for ports outside New England, 1660–1689. See sources in Appendix A.

54. On John Archer see *Essex Co. Court Recs.*, 3:324, 463, 9:470–471, 522; Perley, *History of Salem*, 1:214; *Vital Records of Salem, Massachusetts, to the End of the Year, 1849*, 6 vols. (Salem, 1916–1925), 1:44. Out of 154 Salem or Beverly mariners who sailed between 1680 and 1689, 57 were locally born. See sources in Appendix A.

55. On Robert Bray see Naval Officer Shipping Lists for Barbados, C.O. 33/13, 14; *Essex Co. Court Recs.*, 7:30, 9:145; Perley, *History of Salem*, 3:48, 419; George Corwin, Account Book, 1663–1672. On John Ruck see *Essex Co. Court Recs.*, 7:221, 326, 328; Perley, *History of Salem*, 1:316, 2:5, 9, 10, 97, 159, 160, 189, 401–403, 3:421.

56. *Essex Co. Court Recs.*, 4:389.

57. Shurtleff, *Records of Massachusetts Bay*, 4, no. 2, 203, 211; Randolph, "Report," Oct. 12, 1676, *Randolph Papers*, 25:250; "Order in Council," May 5, 1676, *CSPC*, 9:226.

58. Greene and Harrington, *American Population Before 1690*, xxiii, 13, 19–21; Randolph, "Report," Oct. 12, 1676, *Randolph Papers*, 25:250.

59. Alain Cabantous, *Le ciel dans la mer: Christianisme et civilisation maritime, XVIᵉ–XIXᵉ siècle* (Paris, 1990), 53.

3. THE EIGHTEENTH CENTURY: SAILORS AT SEA

1. Ship's Journal, schooner *General Wolfe*, May 25–31, 1767, Marine Logs and Journals Collection, James Duncan Phillips Library, Peabody-Essex Museum, Salem, Massachusetts.

2. Ibid., June 1–18, Nov. 4, 1767. The entire crew was listed together at their discharge. See the collection of portledge bills listed in Appendix A.

3. Ship's Journal, schooner *General Wolfe*, June 24–July 27, 1767.

4. Ibid., May 25–June 18, July 27–Aug. 13, 1767. On Dominica in the late colonial period, see Patrick L. Baker, *Centering the Periphery: Chaos, Order, and the Ethnohistory of Dominica* (Montreal, 1994), 57–67; Lennox Honychurch, *The Dominica Story: A History of the Island* (London, 1975), 58–82.

5. Ship's Journal, schooner *General Wolfe*, Aug. 24–Oct. 14, 1767. The robbery occurred on Oct. 13.

6. Ibid., Oct. 14–Nov. 4, 1767.

7. Vince Walsh, "'Up Through the Hawse Hole': The Social Origins and Lives of Salem Shipmasters, 1640 to 1720," M.A. thesis, Memorial University of Newfoundland, 1995, 88n; Ian K. Steele, *The English Atlantic, 1675–1740: An Exploration of Communication and Community* (Oxford, 1986), 285, 287; Naval Officer Shipping Lists for Barbados, C.O. 33/13, 14.

8. Naval Officer Shipping Lists for Barbados, C.O. 33/13; Perley, *History of Salem*, 3:296–297, 298, 306, 308, 312, 317, 321; Philip S. Haffenden, *New England in the English Nation, 1689–1713* (Oxford, 1974), 94–99.

9. Carol F. Karlsen, *The Devil in the Shape of a Woman: Witchcraft in Colonial New England* (New York, 1987), 51; Mary Beth Norton, *In the Devil's Snare: The Witchcraft Crisis of 1692* (New York, 2002), 82–111; Walsh, "'Up Through the Hawse Hole,'" 89–90; Salem Tax Lists, 1689–1695, in Salem Tax and Valuation Lists, 1689–, microfilm copy in possession of James Duncan Phillips Library, Peabody-Essex Museum, Salem, Mass., hereafter cited as Salem Tax Lists, 1689–.

10. Haffenden, *New England in the English Nation*, 205–271; quotation from Francis Nicholson and Samuel Vetch to the Earl of Sunderland (1709), cited ibid., 228–229; Naval Officer Shipping Lists for Salem, Massachusetts, 1716, C.O. 5/848.

11. James G. Lydon, "North Shore Trade in the Early Eighteenth Century," *American Neptune*, 28 (1968), 261–274; Daniel Vickers, "'A Knowen and Staple Commoditie': Codfish Prices in Essex County, Massachusetts, 1640–1775," Essex Institute, *Historical Collections*, 124 (1988), 192, 194.

12. James G. Lydon, "Fish for Gold: The Massachusetts Fish Trade with Iberia, 1700–1773," *New England Quarterly*, 54 (1981), 544–545; Lydon, "North Shore Trade," 264, 265; Naval Officer Shipping Lists, Salem and Marblehead, Massachusetts, 1716, 1752–1753, 1765, C.O. 5/848, 849, 850; Daniel Vickers, "The Price of Fish: A Price Index for Cod, 1505–1892," *Acadiensis*, 25 (1996), 96.

13. John Barnard, "Autobiography of the Reverend John Barnard, Nov. 14, 1766," Massachusetts Historical Society, *Collections*, 3d ser., 5 (1836), 240; Christine Leigh Heyrman, *Commerce and Culture: The Maritime Communities of Colonial Massachusetts, 1690–1750* (New York, 1984), 330–365.

14. George Francis Dow and Mary G. Thresher, eds., *Records and Files of the Quarterly Courts of Essex County, Massachusetts, 1636–1686*, 9 vols. (Salem, Mass., 1911–1975), 2:52, 6:302–305, 331–332, 392, 9:323–325, 393–396.

As late as 1716, twenty-nine vessels from the British Isles entered inward at the port of Salem, whereas by 1753, only one British vessel did the same. See Naval Officer Shipping Lists for Salem and Marblehead, Massachusetts, 1716, 1753, C.O. 5/848, 849; Lydon, "North Shore Trade," 272.

15. Account of George Peele, Jonathan Archer, Timothy Orne, Account Books, 1738–1758, 1762–1767, Orne Family Papers, 1719–1899; Richard Derby, Account Book, 1756–1790, Miles Ward, Account Book, 1753–1764, 1765–1777, all in James Duncan Phillips Library, Peabody-Essex Museum, Salem, Mass. See also Naval Officer Shipping Lists, Salem and Marblehead, Massachusetts, 1765, C.O. 5/850. Harriet Silvester Tapley, ed., *Early Coastwise and Foreign Shipping of Salem: A Record of the Entrances and Clearances of the Port of Salem, 1750–1769* (Salem, Mass., 1934).

16. Duty of Tonnage on Fishing and Coasting Vessels, 1756–1762, in Salem Tax Lists, 1689–; Timothy Orne, Account Books, 1738–1758, 1762–1767; Richard Derby, Account Book, 1756–1790; Naval Officer Shipping Lists, Salem and Marblehead, Massachusetts, 1765, C.O. 5/850.

17. Naval Officer Shipping Lists, Salem, Massachusetts, 1714–1717, C.O. 5/848; Accounts of Eleazar Moses, William Pickering Account Book, 1695–1718, James Duncan Phillips Library, Peabody-Essex Museum, Salem, Mass.; Lydon, "North Shore Trade," 264–271; James Duncan Phillips, *Salem in the Eighteenth Century* (Boston, 1937), 72–92; Daniel Vickers, *Farmers and Fishermen: Two Centuries of Work in Essex County, Massachusetts, 1630–1850* (Chapel Hill, N.C., 1994), 145–153.

18. Naval Officer Shipping Lists, Salem, Massachusetts, 1715–1717, C.O. 5/848; Naval Officer Shipping Lists for Barbados, 1715–1716, C.O. 33/15; Portledge Bills, Sloop *Mary*, July 1711, Nov. 1711, Nov. 3, 1712, Philip English to William English, Nov. 11, 1711, Letter of Instructions to William English, Dec. 14, 1713, box 2, folder 4, English/Touzell/Hathorne Papers, 1661–1851, James Duncan Phillips Library, Peabody-Essex Museum, Salem, Mass. Quotation from Edward Randolph, "Report to the Committee for Trade and Plantations," Oct. 12, 1676, in *Edward Randolph Papers*, ed. Robert Noxon Toppan, *Publications of the Prince Society* (Boston, 1898; rpt. New York, 1967), 25:249.

19. Tapley, *Early Coastwise and Foreign Shipping of Salem*; Jacob Price, "Economic Function and the Growth of American Port Towns in the Eighteenth Century," *Perspectives in American History*, 8 (1974), 142–143.

20. Naval Officer Shipping Lists for Barbados, 1686–1688, C.O. 33/13, 14; Salem and Marblehead, Massachusetts, 1716, 1753, 1765, C.O. 5/848, 849, 850. See the references to local coasting operations in Anne Pérotin-Dumon, "Cabotage, Contraband, and Corsairs," in *Atlantic Port Cities: Economy, Culture, and Society in the Atlantic World, 1650–1850*, ed. Franklin W. Knight and Peggy K. Liss (Knoxville, Tenn., 1991), 64–66; David Geggus, "The Major Port Towns of Saint Domingue in the Later Eighteenth Century," ibid., 93, 99; Arthur Pierce Middleton, *Tobacco Coast: A Maritime History of Chesapeake Bay in the Colonial Era* (Newport News, Va., 1953), 60–90.

21. See Naval Officer Shipping Lists, Salem and Marblehead, Massachusetts,

1716, 1765, C.O. 5/848, 850. On the sailing qualities of a schooner, see Basil Greenhill, *The Merchant Schooners*, 2 vols. (1951; rev. ed., New York, 1968), 1:24–27, 34–37, 40–41, 51; Howard I. Chapelle, *The History of American Sailing Ships* (New York, 1935), 220. During the nineteenth century, the schooner became a popular vessel in many different specialized trades, but the fact that it reached its first popularity in New England and that it so swiftly came to dominate fleets on Massachusetts's North Shore argues for our emphasis on the fishery.

22. See Alexander Hamilton, *Gentleman's Progress: The Itinerarium of Dr. Alexander Hamilton, 1744*, ed. Carl Bridenbaugh (Chapel Hill, N.C., 1948), 119, 121–122; Francis Goelet, *The Voyages and Travels of Francis Goelet, 1746–1758*, ed. Kenneth Scott (Flushing, N.Y., 1970), entry for Oct. 21, 1750; James Birket, *Some Cursory Remarks Made by James Birket in His Voyage to North America, 1750–1751* (1916; rpt. Freeport, N.Y., 1970), 15–16; John Adams, *Diary and Autobiography of John Adams*, 4 vols., ed. L. H. Butterfield (Cambridge, Mass., 1961), 1:318–319. For fleet size in 1689 see "Letter from Rev. John Higginson to his son, Nathaniel Higginson, Aug. 31, 1698," Essex Institute, *Historical Collections*, 43 (1907), 183, hereafter cited as *EIHC*. For fleet size in 1771 see Bettye Hobbs Pruitt, ed., *The Massachusetts Tax Valuation List of 1771* (Boston, 1978), 130–155; "Report on the American Fisheries by the Secretary of State," Feb. 1, 1791, in *The Papers of Thomas Jefferson* ed. Julian P. Boyd et al. (Princeton, N.J., 1950–), 19:221, 223; Bailyn and Bailyn, *Massachusetts Shipping*, 124. The 1771 estimates were revised downward from the 9,463 tons actually recorded in the Valuation List by (i) 20 percent to account for vessels actually based in Boston and (ii) an additional 1,500 tons devoted primarily to the fishery. The number of hands on Salem vessels in 1771 was estimated on the basis of 8 men per fishing schooner, 6.5 men per merchant vessel, and 3 men per coasting sloop. The population of men aged fifteen to forty-five was estimated on the assumptions that (*a*) the ratio of taxable males to the entire population was 1:4, and (*b*) the age distribution of Salem males in 1771 resembled that of the same group in 1801. See Evarts B. Green and Virginia D. Harrington, *American Population Before the Federal Census of 1790* (New York, 1932), xxiii; U.S. Department of State, *Return of the Whole Number of Persons Within the Several Districts of the United States . . . 1800* (Washington, D.C., 1801), 8.

23. See sources in Appendix A. Although Danvers split off from Salem in 1752, it was considered part of Salem for the purpose of this calculation.

24. Tapley, *Early Coastwise and Foreign Shipping of Salem*, 121; Portledge Bills, brigantine, *Neptune* (1757, 1759), box 5, folder 9, Derby Family Papers; Portledge Bills, brigantine, *Neptune* (1759, 1760, 1761), box 5, folder 13, Felt Family Papers, 1717–1915, James Duncan Phillips Library, Peabody-Essex Museum, Salem, Mass.; Portledge Bills, sloop *Andrago* (1759), box 1, folder 3, schooner *Hampton* (1749), box 6, folder 5, sloop *Rebecca* (1750), box 8, folder 8, Orne Family Papers.

25. Portledge Bill, schooner, Beaver (1753), box 2, folder 3, Orne Family Papers;

Portledge Bill, brigantine, *Neptune,* Felt Family Papers, box 3, folder 13. The family genealogies were reconstructed using the sources in Appendix A.

26. Marcus Rediker, *Between the Devil and the Deep Blue Sea: Merchant Seamen, Pirates, and the Anglo-American Maritime World, 1700–1750* (Cambridge, 1987), 81; Judith Fingard, *Jack in Port: Sailortowns of Eastern Canada* (Toronto, 1982), 194–241.

27. Accounts of Benjamin Bates, Jr., Richard Derby, Account Book, 1756–1790.

28. These preparations are recorded in considerable detail for numerous voyages in Timothy Orne, Ship's Ledger, 1758–1768, Orne Family Papers.

29. These family connections are of individuals who conducted business with Timothy Orne and were related to those who took part in the preparations for the voyage of the brigantine *Essex* to Bilbao in the winter of 1763–1764. This voyage is described in Accounts of brigantine *Essex,* Timothy Orne, Ship's Ledger, 1758–1768; Tapley, *Early Coastwise and Foreign Shipping of Salem,* 59; Portledge Bill, brigantine *Essex* (1763), box 5, folder 1, Orne Family Papers. The dealings that Timothy Orne pursued with these men and their relations can be traced in Accounts of Edmund Henfield, Gideon Henfield, Jonathan Neale, Ebenezer Peele, George Peele, Robert Peele, Jonathan Peele, Jonathan Peele, Jr., Timothy Orne, Account Books, 1738–1758, 1762–1767; Portledge Bills, schooner *Endeavor* (1745), box 4, folder 10, schooner *Molly* (1771), box 7, folder 13, schooner *Betsey* (1760), box 1, folder 6, sloop *Charming Sally* (1763), box 3, folder 3, schooner *Eunice* (1764), box 5, folder 4, schooner *Hampton* (1755), box 6, folder 7, Orne Family Papers.

30. Vickers, *Farmers and Fishermen,* 162–164, 240–244. That credit payments dwarfed cash payments in early modern England is argued in Craig Muldrew, *The Economy of Obligation: The Culture of Credit and Social Relations in Early Modern England* (New York, 1998), 98–103.

31. Of thirty-three Salem "vessels engaged in foreign trade" enumerated in 1765, only sixteen were owned by a single merchant; the rest were owned in shares. See "A List of Salem Vessels in 1765," *EIHC,* 62 (1926), 8–11.

32. This curve is almost identical to that reported for eighteenth-century New England fishermen in Vickers, *Farmers and Fishermen,* 180.

33. Wage estimates are based on the portledge bills cited in Appendix A. For a similar picture of wages in Boston, see Gary B. Nash, *The Urban Crucible: Social Change, Political Consciousness, and the Origins of the American Revolution* (Cambridge, Mass., 1979), 414. On seamen's wages in England, see Ralph Davis, *The Rise of the English Shipping Industry in the Seventeenth and Eighteenth Centuries* (London, 1962), 137. On impressment in the colonies, see John Lax and William Pencak, "The Knowles Riot and the Crisis of the 1740s in Massachusetts," *Perspectives in American History,* 10 (1976), 163–214; Jesse Lemisch, *Jack Tar vs. John Bull: The Role of New York's Seamen in Precipitating the Revolution* (New York, 1997), 13–49; Richard B. Morris, *Government and Labor in Early America* (Boston, 1981), 272–278.

34. Average wages of Salem mariners are calculated from 902 cases drawn from portledge bills, 1746–1771, listed in Appendix A. English equivalents

are taken from Davis, *Rise of the English Shipping Industry,* 137–140. On
Richard Derby, Jr., see Portledge Bill, brigantine *Neptune* (1757), box 5, folder
9, Derby Family Papers; Perley, *History of Salem,* 3:146; Salem Tax Valuation,
1758, in Salem Tax Lists, 1689–; Pruitt, *Massachusetts Tax Valuation List of
1771,* 132–133.

35. The best treatment of this subject is Peter Pope, "The Practice of Portage in
the Early Modern North Atlantic: Introduction to an Issue in Maritime Historical Anthropology," *Journal of the Canadian Historical Association,* 6 (1995),
19–41. Allan A. Arnold, "Merchants in the Forecastle: The Private Ventures
of New England Mariners," *American Neptune,* 41 (1981), 165–187, is also
interesting, though most of the evidence here comes from masters, not
foremast hands as the title implies.

36. Portledge Bills, schooner *Molly* (1757), box 7, folder 11; schooner *Esther* (1752),
box 5, folder 2, Orne Family Papers. For other examples, see Portledge Bills,
schooner *Beaver* (1749, 1750), box 2, folder 1; brig *Cicero* (1762), box 3, folder
7; schooner *Esther* (1762), box 5, folder 3; schooner *Eunice* (1762), box 5,
folder 4; schooner *Fisher* (1752, 1754, 1756, 1757), box 6, folders 1, 2; schooner
Louisa (1760), box 7, folder 6; schooner *Molly* (1755), box 7, folders 10, 11;
schooner *Rowley* (1756), box 9, folder 4; sloop *Rebecca* (1751), box 8, folder 8,
all Orne Family Papers.

37. Portledge Bill, schooner *Fisher* (1754), box 6, folder 1, Orne Family Papers;
Vickers, *Farmers and Fishermen,* 110–112, 161.

38. Edward Coxere, *Adventures by Sea of Edward Coxere,* ed. E. H. W. Meyerstein
(New York, 1946), 76, 78, 79, 109, 120–121, 126, 127, 139, 148; John Cremer,
Ramblin' Jack: The Journal of Captain John Cremer, 1700–1774, ed. R. Reynell
Bellamy (London, 1936), 175–176, 189; Edward Barlow, *Barlow's Journal of
His Life at Sea in King's Ships, East and West Indiamen, and Other Merchant-
men, 1659–1703,* ed. Basil Lubbock, 2 vols. (London, 1934), 1:204, 248, 252,
271, 277, 284, 2:406–407, 425; Samuel Kelly, *Samuel Kelly: An Eighteenth
Century Seaman,* ed. Crosbie Garstin (New York, 1925), 28, 34, 44–45;
Account of Adventure on Board schooner *Premium* from Philadelphia to
Bilbao (1772), box 1, folder 1, Cabot Family Papers, 1712–1852, James Duncan
Phillips Library, Peabody-Essex Museum, Salem, Mass. Fifteen of twenty-
seven deep-sea mariners in Timothy Orne, Account Books, 1738–1758, 1762–
1767; Richard Derby, Account Book, 1756–1790; Miles Ward, Account Book,
1745–53, 1753–1764, 1765–1777, were aged twenty-five to thirty-four years
when they began their portage practices; the remainder were older.

39. Christopher Prince, *The Autobiography of a Yankee Mariner: Christopher Prince
and the American Revolution,* ed. Michael J. Crawford (Washington, D.C.,
2002), 19–20; Kelly, *Samuel Kelly,* 70; Coxere, *Adventures by Sea,* 51, 76, 78,
79, 119–120.

40. Examples of private adventures can be found in Accounts of John Cloutman,
Timothy Orne, Account Book, 1738–1758; Accounts of Samuel Carleton,
Timothy Orne, Account Book, 1738–1758, Richard Derby, Account Book,
1760–1790, and Miles Ward, Account Books, 1745–1753, 1753–1764. For

shipmasters' assessments see sources in Appendix A, and Tax Valuation List, 1761, in Salem Tax Lists, 1689–.

41. Ralph Davis has made this point in regard to England in Davis, *English Shipping Industry*, 138–139.

42. Prince, *Autobiography*, 19–20; William McNally, *Evils and Abuses in the Naval and Merchant Services; With Proposals for Their Remedy and Redress* (Boston, 1839), 47; Richard Henry Dana, Jr., *The Seaman's Friend: A Treatise on Practical Seamanship* (Boston, 1879; rpt., Mineola, N.Y., 1997); W. Jeffrey Bolster, *Black Jacks: African American Seamen in the Age of Sail* (Cambridge, Mass., 1997), 68–101.

43. Dana, *Seaman's Friend*, 60–61.

44. Ibid., 159–160.

45. Ship's Journal, sloop *Adventure*, July 28, 30, 1774, Jan. 28, 1775; Vickers, *Farmers and Fishermen*, 151.

46. Howard I. Chapelle, *The History of American Sailing Ships* (New York, 1935), 21, 34–35, 38–39; Ship's Journal, sloop *Adventure*, June 22, 1775.

47. Ship's Journal, sloop *Adventure*, May 26, Oct. 24, 1774; Ship's Journals, schooner *Eagle*, Aug. 17, 1753. The Derby, Orne, and Ward Account Books cited above all contain dozens of lists of ships' provisions, but they are unusually well recorded in Timothy Orne, Ship's Ledger, 1758–1768.

48. Cotton Mather, *Sailour's Companion and Counsellor* (Boston, 1709), ii, 13, 37–42; Ship's Journal, sloop *Adventure*, Apr. 3, 6, 1774. Of seamen who kept accounts with Richard Derby, Miles Ward, or Timothy Orne during the middle decades of the eighteenth century (*n*=17), 59 percent were credited for substantial rum purchases. Timothy Orne Account Book, 1738–1758, 1762–1767; Richard Derby, Account Book, 1760–1790; and Miles Ward, Account Books, 1745–1753, 1753–1764, 1765–1777. Of course, these mariners may well have bought additional rum elsewhere.

49. Ship's Journal, sloop *Adventure*, May 26, Oct. 22, 27, 1774, July 9, 1775; sloop *Elizabeth*, Aug. 25, 1769.

50. John Hathorne, Protest, Aug. 23, 1760, "Essex County Notarial Records, 1697–1768," *EIHC*, 46 (1910), 330. For other examples of chases by pirates and privateers, see Essex Notarial Recs., *EIHC*, 41 (1905), 186–187, 390; 42 (1906), 156, 160; 44 (1908), 152; 46 (1910), 86–88, 328–329.

51. Ship's Journals, schooner *Salem*, June 16, 1773, sloop *Adventure*, May 23, July 25, 1774, Sept. 4, 1775.

4. THE EIGHTEENTH CENTURY: SAILORS' CAREERS

1. Quotations from Alexander Hamilton, *Gentleman's Progress: The Itinerarium of Dr. Alexander Hamilton, 1744*, ed. Carl Bridenbaugh (Chapel Hill., N.C., 1948), 122; J. P. Brissot de Warville, *New Travels in the United States of America, 1788*, ed. Durand Echeverria (Cambridge, Mass., 1964), 362; Francis Goelet, *The Voyages and Travels of Francis Goelet, 1746–1758*, ed. Kenneth Scott (Flushing, N.Y., 1970), entry for Oct. 20, 1750.

2. Philip Chadwick Foster Smith, ed., *The Journals of Ashley Bowen (1728–1813)*

of Marblehead, 2 vols. (Colonial Society of Massachusetts, *Publications,* 44–45 [Boston, 1973]), hereafter cited as Bowen, *Journal.*

3. Bowen, *Journal,* 44:vii–viii, 4, 6, 7; Bettye Hobbs Pruitt, ed., *The Massachusetts Tax Valuation List of 1771* (Boston, 1978), 100–101.

4. Bowen, *Journal,* 44:6–7.

5. Ibid., 44:7–9; 45: appendix 2.

6. Ibid., 44:8, 9–24.

7. Ibid., 44:11, 13, 22–23, 23–24.

8. Ibid., 44:24–137.

9. Ibid., 44:25–27, 29, 33, 41, plates 2–20.

10. Ibid., 44:28–44.

11. Ibid., 44:42–43.

12. Ibid., 44:44, 45, 107–137, 225.

13. The remainder of Ashley Bowen's life is recounted in Daniel Vickers, "An Honest Tar: Ashley Bowen of Marblehead," *New England Quarterly,* 69 (1996), 544–553; Daniel Vickers, "Ashley Bowen of Marblehead: Revolutionary Neutral," in *The Human Tradition in U.S. History: The Revolutionary Era,* ed. Nancy Rhoden and Ian Steele (Wilmington, Del., 2000), 99–115.

14. The answer to these questions rests on a biographical database describing the lives of 1,165 mariners who shipped out of Salem between 1690 and 1775. Systematically tracing these sailors through a wide variety of public and private records allows one to reconstruct their seafaring careers and to situate those careers within the context of their entire lives. To the twenty-first-century statistical mind, the results of such an exercise have a seductive feel of objectivity that must continually be resisted. The sources on which these biographies are based, described fully in Appendix A, all have their own biases, and almost every query aimed at the database had to be framed in the knowledge that the answer was certain to be selective in one way or another. What follows employs the methods of social science but in a manner tempered with a spirit of skepticism.

15. Geographic origins were measured from sources in Appendix A; Vince Walsh, "Recruitment and Promotion: The Merchant Fleet of Salem, Massachusetts, 1670–1765," *Research in Maritime History,* 7 (1994), 35–36. During the period 1715–1717, Dutch shipmasters from the town of Hindeloopen in the province of Friesland recruited two-thirds of their crew from among residents of that town and a full 86 percent of their men from among residents of that province. See Jaap R. Bruijn and Elisabeth S. van Eyck van Heslinga, "Demand and Supply of Seamen in Dutch Shipping During the 17th and 18th Centuries," in Colloque international d'histoire maritime, *Seamen in society / Gens de mer en société,* ed. Paul Adam (Bucharest, 1980), 2:59.

16. On Thomas Lovitt, see Portledge Bill, schooner, *Beaver* (1747), Orne Family Papers, 1719–1899, James Duncan Phillips Library, Peabody-Essex Museum, Salem, Mass.; *Vital Records of Beverly, Massachusetts to the End of the Year, 1849,* 2 vols. (Topsfield, Mass., 1906–1907), 1:218; Harriet Silvester Tapley, ed., *Early Coastwise and Foreign Shipping of Salem: A Record of the Entrances and*

Clearances of the Port of Salem, 1750–1769 (Salem, Mass., 1934), 88. Out of thirteen ship's boys who shipped on Salem vessels between 1745 and 1759, eight went on to command vessels of their own before 1770. See sources in Appendix A.

17. Portledge Bills, schooner *Fisher* (1754, 1757), box 6, folders 1, 2; schooner *Molly* (1753, 1754), box 7, folder 10; schooner *Rowley* (1752), box 9, folder 2; Accounts of Mary Glover and Samuel Gavet, Timothy Orne, Account Book, 1738–1753, all in Orne Family Papers. The ratio between time at sea and time ashore was 2.06:1, measured for eighteen voyages by William Deadman (May 22, 1758–Aug. 7, 1760), Joseph Grafton (Apr. 19, 1751–June 8, 1753), George Williams (Feb. 16, 1752–Oct. 3, 1758), and Thomas Kimball (Feb. 16, 1751–June 10, 1752, Feb. 4, 1755–Aug. 7, 1756). See Tapley, *Early Coastwise Shipping*, 78, 136, 192. On average, the length in pay for mariners who departed Salem between 1740 and 1775 was 5.7 months in the case of masters (n=97) and 4.6 months in the case of both mates and seamen (n=422). See the portledge bill collections listed in Appendix A.

18. Lucy Downing to John Winthrop, ca. Jan. 1649, *Winthrop Papers*, 5 vols. (Boston, 1929–1947), 5:296; Edward Barlow, *Barlow's Journal of His Life at Sea in King's Ships, East and West Indiamen, and Other Merchantmen, 1659–1703*, ed. Basil Lubbock, 2 vols. (London, 1934), 2:339.

19. See, for example, Ira Dye, "Early American Merchant Seafarers," *Proceedings of the American Philosophical Society* 120 (1976), 335; Marcus Rediker, *Between the Devil and the Deep Blue Sea: Merchant Seamen, Pirates, and the Anglo-American Maritime World, 1700–1750* (Cambridge, 1987), 299; Judith Fingard, *Jack in Port: Sailortowns of Eastern Canada* (Toronto, 1982), 67; Eric Sager, *Seafaring Labour: The Merchant Marine of Atlantic Canada, 1820–1914* (Kingston, 1989), 154; Helge W. Nordvik and Jan Oldervoll, "Seafarer and Community in Norway: An Analysis Based on the 1801 Census," in Adam, *Seamen in society / Gens de mer en société*, 3:85. The Norwegian data report that only 66 percent of deckhands were under the age of thirty (the lowest figure obtained in any of these studies), but this is characteristic of census data, in that people often retain occupational titles for some years after they have ceased to actually practice the trade.

20. See sources in Appendix A.

21. "Parish List of Deaths Begun 1785, Recorded by William Bentley, D.D., of the East Church, Salem, Mass.," Essex Institute, *Historical Collections* 14 (1877), 129–148, 224–232, 286–298; 15 (1878), 86–100; 16 (1879), 18–36, 191–203; 18 (1881), 73–80, 129–144, 206–223; 19 (1882), 18–39, 91–104, 176–182, hereafter cited as Bentley, "Parish List of Deaths."

22. Elaine Forman Crane, *Ebb Tide in New England: Women, Seaports, and Social Change, 1630–1800* (Boston, 1998), 15. Salem widows, 1738–1775 (n=134), were identified from Pruitt, *Massachusetts Tax Valuation List of 1771*, 130–155; Timothy Orne, Account Book, 1738–1758, 1762–1767; Richard Derby, Account Book, 1756–1790, Derby Family Papers, 1716–1921; Miles Ward, Account Book, 1745–1753, 1753–1764, 1765–1777, Ward Family Papers 1718–

1945, James Duncan Phillips Library, Peabody-Essex Museum, Salem, Mass.; and their origins were traced through the sources in Appendix A. On the issue of migrancy among widows, see Douglas Lamar Jones, "The Strolling Poor: Transiency in Eighteenth-Century Massachusetts," *Journal of Social History*, 8 (1975), 29, 34–36, 38; Jones, *Village and Seaport: Migration and Society in Eighteenth-Century Massachusetts* (Hanover, N.H., 1981), 29–33, 104–113.

23. The average mortality rate per thousand for the period, 1701–1774, in Boston was 37.2. See John B. Blake, *Public Health in the Town of Boston, 1630–1822* (Cambridge, Mass., 1959), 247–249. These rates are slightly lower than those for late-eighteenth-century Philadelphia reported in Smith, *The "Lower Sort*," 42, 205–209. Note that during the period 1807–1815, when for diplomatic reasons Salem's shipping business was very slow, Bentley, "Parish List of Deaths," counted for the same cohort 2.8 male deaths per year and 2.0 female deaths per year. On the greater incidence of female householding (meaning for the most part widowhood) in urban as opposed to rural New England in the late colonial and early national periods, see Daniel Scott Smith, "Female Householding in Late Eighteenth-Century America and the Problem of Poverty," *Journal of Social History*, 28 (1994), 89, 92, 97.

24. *Vital Records of Beverly*, 1:326–329; 2:302–305, 574–576.

25. Accidents at sea were traced through the colonial logbooks listed in Appendix A. Rates of maritime accident, 1786–1817, are based on references to sixty-one deaths of mariners under the age of thirty in Bentley, "Parish List of Deaths."

26. Bentley, "Parish List of Deaths"; Bowen, *Journal*, 44:26; Ship's Journals, sloop *Elizabeth*, Sept. 16, 30–Oct. 2, 1769; schooner *Nabby*, Nov. 15–Dec. 12, 1769; schooner *Salem*, Nov. 16, 1772, Jan. 4, 1763; sloop *Adventure*, July 15, 1775; schooner *Sally*, Dec. 5, 1769, Marine Logs and Journals Collection, James Duncan Phillips Library, Peabody-Essex Museum, Salem, Mass.

27. See Appendix A.

28. See Appendix A. On Benjamin Peters see Portledge Bill, schooner *Sea Flower* (1751), box 10, folder 3, Orne Family Papers; Accounts of Benjamin Peters in Timothy Orne, Account Book, 1738–1758, and Miles Ward, Account Book, 1764–1772. On Hawthorne see Portledge Bill, schooner *Swallow* (1747), box 1, folder 3, Ward Family Papers; Perley, *History of Salem*, 1:285. On Osborn see Perley, *History of Salem*, 3:60; Account of Joseph Osborn, Miles Ward, Account Book, 1753–1764, Ward Family Papers.

29. Bowen, *Journal*, 44:45, 51.

30. For rates of promotion, see Appendix A. On James Cheever see Portledge Bills, schooner *Rowley* (1753, 1754), box 9, folder 3; sloop *Dolphin* (1758, 1759, 1760), box 4, folders 3, 4; schooner *Rebecca* (1758), box 8, folder 11; sloop *Polly* (1761), box 8, folder 6, Orne Family Papers. On Benjamin Bray, Jr., see Portledge Bills, schooner *Exeter* (1746), box 5, folder 6; brig *Betty & Molly* (1747), box 1, folder 9, Orne Family Papers. On the issue of promotion in the early American merchant service, see the disagreement between Samuel

Eliot Morison, *The Maritime History of Massachusetts, 1783–1860* (Boston, 1921; rpt. Boston, 1979), 106–107, and Jesse Lemisch, "Jack Tar in the Streets: Merchant Seamen in the Politics of Revolutionary America," *William and Mary Quarterly*, 3d ser., 25 (1968), 371–380. On the complexity of one individual mariner's life see Vickers, "An Honest Tar," 531–553.

31. See the accounts of twelve coasters and forty-one masters in Timothy Orne Account Book, 1738–1753, and those of eight coasters and twenty-two masters in Richard Derby, Account Book, 1756–1790. On Israel Ober see *Vital Records of Salem, Massachusetts, to the End of the Year, 1849*, 6 vols. (Salem, Mass., 1916–1925), 4:135; 6:98, hereafter cited as *Salem Vital Records*; Accounts of Israel Ober, Timothy Orne Account Books, 1762–67, Orne Family Papers; Richard Derby Account Book, 1756–1790; Miles Ward, Account Book, 1753–1764, Ward Family Papers; Tapley, *Coastwise Shipping of Salem*, 6, 14, 64, 129, 151, 183; Salem Tax and Valuation Lists, 1689–, microfilm copy in possession of James Duncan Phillips Library, Peabody-Essex Museum, Salem, Mass., hereafter cited as Salem Tax Lists, 1689–. On George Peele see Accounts of George Peele, Timothy Orne Account Books, 1762–1767, Orne Family Papers; Richard Derby Account Book, 1756–1790; Miles Ward, Account Book, 1753–1764, Ward Family Papers; Bentley, *Journal*, 2:366. Out of sixteen coasters who took out licenses to conduct their business during the Seven Years' War, only seven also cleared customs for foreign parts at some point during the period 1750–1769. See Tapley, *Coastwise Shipping of Salem*; Lists of Licensed Coasters, 1757–1762, in Salem Tax Lists, 1689–.

32. Nathan Bowen to Ashley Bowen, May 24, 1757, cited in Bowen *Journal*, 44:44n.

33. For sources of promotion data, see Appendix A. Quotation from Bowen, *Journal*, 44:41–42.

34. Portledge Bills, Derby Family Papers, Felt Family Papers, Orne Family Papers, Ward Family Papers. See especially Portledge Bills, brigantine *Neptune* (1757, 1759), box 5, folder 9, Derby Family Papers; brigantine *Neptune* (1759, 1760, 1761), box 3, folder 13, Felt Family Papers. On the Derby family see Perley, *History of Salem*, 3:146. Derby's mate in 1757 was Henry Elkins; see *Salem Vital Records*, 3:329, 330; 5:227. Davis, *Rise of the English Shipping Industry*, 128, 159. Evan Cotton in *East Indiamen: The East India Company's Maritime Service* (London, 1949), 25–26, makes a similar argument for the importance of family connection and political cronyism in the path to promotion on company ships.

35. See sources in Appendix A.

36. On Thomas Cox see Essex County Notarial Records, 1697–1768, hereafter cited as Essex Notarial Recs., Essex Institute, *Historical Collections*, hereafter cited as *EIHC*, 42 (1906), 159; 44 (1908), 150; Registry of Massachusetts Shipping, Massachusetts Archives, 7:459; Naval Officer Shipping Lists for Salem and Marblehead, 1715, C.O. 5/848; Naval Officer Shipping Lists for Barbados, 1715 C.O. 33/15; Accounts of Thomas Cox, William Pickering Account Book, 1718–1729, James Duncan Phillips Library, Peabody-Essex

Museum, Salem, Mass.; Perley, *History of Salem*, 1:402; 3:315; *Vital Records of Beverly*, 1:91; 2:75. On Richard Manning see Essex Notarial Recs., *EIHC*, 46 (1910), 274–275; Perley, *History of Salem*, 2:389; Bentley, *Diary*, 1:84, 225, 336; 4:1; Bentley, "Parish List of Deaths," *EIHC*, 19 (1882), 93. That 81 percent of Salem seamen eventually married (*n*=222) is calculated from Perley, *History of Salem*, vols. 1–3, and sources in Appendix A.

37. Daniel Vickers, "Competency and Competition: Economic Culture in Early America," *William and Mary Quarterly*, 3d ser., 47 (1990), 3–29. For wage rates, see portledge bill collections cited in Appendix A.

38. Between 75 percent and 85 percent of all mates who were residents of Salem, 1690–1775 (*n*=58), married during or before the year they sailed. See Perley, *History of Salem*, vols. 1–3, and sources in Appendix A. On George West see Accounts of George West, Timothy Orne Account Book, 1738–1753, Orne Family Papers; Accounts of George West, Miles Ward, Account Book, 1753–1764; Portledge Bills, schooner *Fisher* (1752, 1754), box 6, folder 1; schooner *Sea Flower* (1751), box 10, folder 3, Orne Family Papers; Tapley, *Coastwise Shipping of Salem*, 100, 125, 126; Perley, *History of Salem*, 2:305; *Salem Vital Records*, 2:411; 4:453; 6:322.

39. The personal wealth of several career seamen is detailed in Estate of Benjamin Bush (1726), Probate No. 4291; Estate of Thomas Foot (1714), Probate No. 9749; Estate of David Hilliard (1702), Probate No. 13313, in Probate Records of Essex County, Massachusetts, Massachusetts Archives, Boston, hereafter cited as Essex Probates (unpubl.). On Timothy Mansfield see Portledge Bill, schooner *Rebecca* (1756), box 8, folder 9, Orne Family Papers; Perley, *History of Salem*, 1:368–369; 3:14; Pruitt, *Massachusetts Tax Valuation List of 1771*, 134–135.

40. On Jonathan Felt see Perley, *History of Salem*, 3:226–227; Pruitt, *Massachusetts Tax Valuation List of 1771*, 144–145. On Christopher Bubier see Essex Notarial Recs., *EIHC*, 42 (1906), 164; Perley, *History of Salem*, 3:303; Estate of Christopher Bubier (1707), Probate No. 3910, Essex Probates (unpubl.).

41. On wages see portledge bill collection described in Appendix A. See also the accounts of fifty-eight masters and coasters in Timothy Orne, Account Book, 1738–1753; and supplementary evidence in Derby, Account Book, 1756–1790; Ward, Account Books, 1745–1753, 1753–1764, 1765–1772, Ward Family Papers.

42. Lewis Hunt's voyages are recorded in Naval Officer Shipping Lists for Barbados, C.O. 33/13; 14, Jamaica, C.O. 142/14; Perley, *History of Salem*, 2:365; 3:303; Essex Notarial Recs., *EIHC*, 42 (1906): 247, 348; Registry of Massachusetts Shipping, Massachusetts Archives (Boston) 7:83, 281, 329, 416. On Hunt's life in Salem, see Perley, *History of Salem*, 3:182; Estate of Lewis Hunt (1717), Probate No. 14257, Essex Probates (unpubl.).

43. Account of Joseph Cloutman, Timothy Orne, Account Book, 1738–1758; *Salem Vital Records*, 1:187; 5:161.

44. Richard L. Bushman, *The Refinement of America: Persons, Houses, Cities* (New York, 1992), 110–127. The estimate of home ownership is based on the tax valuations in Pruitt, *Massachusetts Tax Valuation List of 1771*, 130–155.

For home furnishings of masters who died in midcareer, see Estate of John Cook (1721), Probate No. 6240; Estate of James Foster (1724), Probate No. 9880; Estate of Benjamin Stone (1703), Probate No. 26656; Estate of William Cash (1729), Probate No. 4817, Essex Probates (unpubl.).

45. Out of thirty-five active shipmasters on the Salem Valuation list of 1761, thirteen owned trading stock, warehouses, or vessel tonnage. Out of twenty-eight shipmasters aged forty years or less in 1771, sixteen owned such investments. See Salem Tax Valuation of 1761, in Salem Tax Lists, 1689–; Pruitt, *Massachusetts Tax Valuation List of 1771*, 130–155; Estate of Thomas Beadle (1734), Probate No. 2182; Estate of William Cash, Probate No. 4817; Estate of Eleazar Lindsay (1717), Probate No. 16813, Essex Probates (unpubl.). For Samuel Carrel see Account of Samuel Carrel, Miles Ward Account Books, 1745–1753, 1753–1764; *Salem Vital Records*, 3:193; 5:140. For a nineteenth-century parallel in England's outports, see Basil Greenhill, *The Merchant Schooners*, 2 vols. (1951; rev. ed., New York, 1968), 1:192–193.

46. See sources in Appendix A.

47. Portledge Bill, schooner *Beaver* (1750), box 2, folder 1, Orne Family Papers. On the crew, see Appendix A. Thirty percent of all mariners who did not reside in Beverly or Salem but shipped out of the latter port between 1690 and 1775 came from other coastal towns around New England, principally in Essex County. The median age of 21 seamen or boys, 1690–1775, born outside the Salem-Beverly area was twenty-three; that for 202 born in Salem or Beverly was twenty-one. See sources in Appendix A.

48. On William Wyatt see Portledge Bills, schooner *Beaver* (1750, 1751), box 2, folders 1, 2, Orne Family Papers; brigantine *Neptune* (1760), box 3, folder 13, Felt Family Papers; *Salem Vital Records*, 3:209; 6:347; Account of William Wyatt, Richard Derby, Account Book, 1756–1790; Bentley, *Diary*, 1:15, 227, 338, 410; 2:116, 206, 208, 294–295.

49. On John Ellison see Portledge Bill, brig *Essex* (1764), box 5, folder 1, Orne Family Papers; *Salem Vital Records*, 3:331; 5:228; Pruitt, *Massachusetts Tax Valuation List of 1771*, 144–145; Bentley, *Diary*, 3:105; 4:86–87.

50. Promotion rates are calculated for thirty-nine in-migrant seamen, 1745–1759. The property holdings of thirty-one of them were traced through the tax lists, and of these, only seven ever rose into the top three deciles, where virtually all the holders of commercial property were found. See sources in Appendix A. Out of twenty-one non–locally born seamen who could be found in the 1771 tax valuation list for Salem, only one, John Handy, owned any commercial property (£75 worth of trading stock). See Pruitt, *Massachusetts Tax Valuation List of 1771*, 130–155. On Edward Gibaut see *Salem Vital Records*, 3:412; 5:278; Estate of Edward Gibaut (1804), Probate No. 10803, Essex Probates (unpubl.); Bentley, *Diary*, 1:18, 224; 2:429. On Moses Townshend see Portledge Bill, schooner *Beaver* (1757), *Salem Vital Records*, 4:390; Estate of Moses Townshend (1777), Probate No. 27941, Essex Probates (unpubl.).

51. Jack Cremer, *Ramblin' Jack: The Journal of Captain John Cremer, 1700–1774*, ed. R. Reynall Bellamy (London, 1936), 39. Note, however, that "Ramblin'"

Jack Cremer was not in reality quite the inveterate failed drifter he presented in his memoirs. In fact, he rose to become a shipmaster and married a young woman from his hometown of Plymouth in Devon, to which he retired after his sailing days were over. Ibid., 255–256.

52. The strongest statement of this can be found in Rediker, *Between the Devil and the Deep Blue Sea*.

53. See "List of Salem Vessels in 1765"; Massachusetts Archives, 7:87–209.

54. See the depositions of seventy-eight mariners in Peter Wilson Coldham, ed., *English Adventurers and Emigrants, 1609–1660: Abstracts of Examinations in the High Court of Admiralty with Reference to Colonial America* (Baltimore, 1984); Peter Wilson Coldham, ed., *English Adventurers and Emigrants, 1661–1733: Abstracts of Examinations in the High Court of Admiralty with Reference to Colonial America* (Baltimore, 1985). On Spanish and Dutch sailors see Pablo E. Pérez-Mallaína, *Spain's Men of the Sea: Daily Life on the Indies Fleet in the Sixteenth Century*, trans. Carla Rahn Phillips (Baltimore, 1998), 54–62; P. C. van Royen, "Manning the Merchant Marine: The Dutch Labour Market about 1700," *International Journal of Maritime History*, I, no. 1 (1989), 14–18. For a similar pattern in the smaller ports of nineteenth-century England see Greenhill, *The Merchant Schooners*, 1:210–211.

55. Judging from depositions, 28 percent of those seamen who embarked from London on transatlantic voyages, 1609–1733 ($n = 86$), were thirty years of age or older, compared with 13 percent of those who shipped out of Salem. Of those specialist career mariners such as gunners, boatswains, carpenters, and surgeons (common on larger vessels based in London but rare on Salem schooners) a full 45 percent ($n = 133$) were thirty or older. See Coldham, *English Adventurers and Emigrants, 1609–1660*; Coldham, *English Adventurers and Emigrants, 1661–1733*.

5. THE EIGHTEENTH CENTURY: MARITIME SOCIETY ASHORE

1. For the Thames-side sailortowns of eighteenth-century London, see Marcus Rediker, *Between the Devil and the Deep Blue Sea: Merchant Seamen, Pirates, and the Anglo-American Maritime World, 1700–1750* (Cambridge, 1987), 24–27; for Triana in sixteenth-century Seville see Pablo E. Pérez-Mallaína, *Spain's Men of the Sea: Daily Life on the Indies Fleet in the Sixteenth Century*, trans. Carla Rahn Phillips (Baltimore, 1998), 4–5, 15–17; for nineteenth-century Halifax, St. John, and Quebec in Canada, see Judith Fingard, *Jack in Port: Sailortowns of Eastern Canada* (Toronto, 1982).

2. Francis Goelet, *The Voyages and Travels of Francis Goelet, 1746–1758*, ed. Kenneth Scott (Flushing, N.Y., 1970), entry for Oct. 21, 1750; Alexander Hamilton, *Gentleman's Progress: The Itinerarium of Dr. Alexander Hamilton, 1744*, ed. Carl Bridenbaugh (Chapel Hill, N.C., 1948), 122; J. P. Brissot de Warville, *New Travels in the United States of America, 1788*, ed. Durand Echeverria (Cambridge, Mass., 1964), 362; Donard Jackson and Dorothy Twohig, eds., *The Diaries of George Washington*, 6 vols. (Charlottesville, Va., 1976–1979), 5:483; Francisco de Miranda, *The New Democracy in America: Travels of*

Francisco de Miranda in the United States, 1783–84, ed. John S. Ezell (Norman, Okla., 1963), 176; Luigi Castiglione, *Viaggio: Travels in the United States of North America*, trans. Antonio Pace (Syracuse, N.Y., 1983), 26; John Adams, *Diary and Autobiography of John Adams*, 4 vols., ed. L. H. Butterfield (Cambridge, Mass., 1961), 1:318; James Birket, *Some Cursory Remarks Made by James Birket in His Voyage to North America, 1750–1751* (n.p., 1916; rpt. Freeport, N.Y., 1970), 15–16. See Persons Licenced for Innholders and Retailers for the Town of Salem, 1750, Essex County Court of General Sessions, Miscellany, 1692–1833, James Duncan Phillips Library, Peabody-Essex Museum, Salem, Mass.; Tax List of 1750, Salem Tax and Valuation Lists, 1689–, microfilm copy in possession of James Duncan Phillips Library, Peabody-Essex Museum, Salem, Mass., hereafter cited as Salem Tax Lists, 1689–; James Duncan Phillips, *Salem in the Eighteenth Century* (Boston, 1937), 168, 252, 431.

3. Salem Tax Valuation List of 1761, Salem Tax Lists, 1689–.

4. Hamilton, *Gentleman's Progress*, 122; Goelet, *Voyages*, Oct. 21; Miranda, *New Democracy*, 190; George R. Loring, ed., "Some Account of Houses and Other Buildings in Salem from a Manuscript of the Late Col. Benj. Pickman," *Essex Institute Historical Collections*, 6 (1864), 93–109. Note that this street was not called Essex Street in the eighteenth century. We have employed this anachronism so that readers may situate the street today.

5. Adams, *Diary and Autobiography*, 1:318.

6. Sidney Perley, "Salem in 1700. No. 22," *Essex Antiquarian*, 10 (1906), 24. Seventy-eight percent of Salem taxpayers in 1800 ($n=1,641$) were assessed for some real estate. See Salem Tax List, 1800, Salem Tax Lists, 1689–.

7. Samuel Eliot Morison, *The Maritime History of Massachusetts, 1783–1860* (Boston, 1924; rpt. Boston, 1989), 23.

8. J. Ross Browne, *Etchings of a Whaling Cruise*, ed. John Seelye (Cambridge, Mass., 1968), 1; Margaret S. Creighton, *Rites and Passages: The Experience of American Whaling, 1830–1870* (Cambridge, 1995), 46–57; John Samson, "Personal Narratives, Journals, and Diaries," in *America and the Sea: A Literary History*, ed. Haskell Springer (Athens, Ga., 1995), 95–97.

9. Philip Chadwick Foster Smith, ed., *The Journals of Ashley Bowen (1728–1813) of Marblehead*, 2 vols. (Colonial Society of Massachusetts, *Publications*, 44–45 [Boston, 1973]), 44:6–7, hereafter cited as Bowen, *Journal;* Jack Cremer, *Ramblin' Jack: The Journal of Captain John Cremer, 1700–1774*, ed. R. Reynall Bellamy (London, 1936), 31–40; Samuel Kelly, *Samuel Kelly: An Eighteenth-Century Seaman*, ed. Crosbie Garstin (London, 1925), 17–19; Edward Coxere, *Adventures by Sea of Edward Coxere*, ed. E. H. W. Meyerstein (New York, 1946), 5; Gorham P. Low, *The Sea Made Men: The Story of a Gloucester Lad*, ed. Elizabeth L. Alling and Roger W. Babson (New York, 1937), 14; Edward Beck, *The Sea Voyages of Edward Beck in the 1820s*, ed. Michael Hay and Joy Roberts (Edinburgh, 1996), 9.

10. Hector St. John de Crèvecoeur, *Letters from an American Farmer and Sketches of Eighteenth-Century America*, ed. Albert E. Stone (Harmondsworth, 1981), 144–145.

11. Edward Barlow, *Barlow's Journal of His Life at Sea in King's Ships, East and West Indiamen, and Other Merchantmen, 1659–1703*, ed. Basil Lubbock, 2 vols. (London, 1934), 1:23, 31, 32.

12. Jacob Nagle, *The Nagle Journal: A Diary of the Life of Jacob Nagle, Sailor, from the Year, 1775 to 1841*, ed. John C. Dann (New York, 1988), xvii, 5–6, 14, 17.

13. Peter Wilson Coldham, ed., *English Adventurers and Emigrants, 1609–1660: Abstracts of Examinations in the High Court of Admiralty with Reference to Colonial America* (Baltimore, 1984); Peter Wilson Coldham, ed., *English Adventurers and Emigrants, 1661–1733: Abstracts of Examinations in the High Court of Admiralty with Reference to Colonial America* (Baltimore, 1985). There were a further seventeen mariners in Coldham who gave birthplaces that were either too general to allow for any coastal or inland identification (e.g., Cornwall, Scotland) or too obscure to find (e.g., West Deepen, Lincs.). See also T. J. A. Le Goff, "The Labor Market for Sailors in France," in *"The Emblems of Hell"? European Sailors and the Maritime Labour Market, 1570–1780*, ed. Paul C. Van Royen, Jaap R. Bruijn, and Jan Lucassen (St. John's, Nfld., 1997), 300–305; Paul Van Royen, "Manning the Merchant Marine: The Dutch Labour Market About 1700," *International Journal of Maritime History*, I, no. 2 (1989), 16–18.

14. Bowen, *Journal*, 44:9; Barlow, *Journal*, 1:27–28; Cremer, *Ramblin' Jack*, 69, 70; Coxere, *Adventures by Sea*, 6.

15. Kelly, *Samuel Kelly*, 19–20, 40–41, 75, 123, 125, 226.

16. Low, *The Sea Made Men*, 19–20; Coxere, *Adventures by Sea*, 6, 10, 30–32; Bowen, *Journal*, 44:14–19; Cremer, *Ramblin' Jack*, 41–45, 47–48, 73, 102.

17. Cremer, *Ramblin' Jack*, 46–48, 61–62, 91; Low, *The Sea Made Men*, 24–25; Coxere, *Adventures by Sea*, 34–35; Bowen, *Journal*, 44:10.

18. Barlow, *Journal*, 1:28; Low, *The Sea Made Men*, 28; Kelly, *Samuel Kelly*, 20, 24, 27; Cremer, *Ramblin' Jack*, 62, 64; Bowen, *Journal*, 44:24; Coxere, *Adventures by Sea*, 32.

19. Richard Henry Dana, Jr., *Two Years Before the Mast* (Harmondsworth, 1981), 330; Bowen, *Journal*, 44:26–28; Barlow, *Journal*, 1:60–61.

20. Dr. G. Paul, High Court of Admiralty, London (1751), quoted in Peter Pope, "The Practice of Portage in the Early Modern North Atlantic: Introduction to an Issue in Maritime Historical Anthropology," *Journal of the Canadian Historical Association*, 6 (1995), 20.

21. On the problem of the so-called invisibility of women in colonial seaport society, see Elaine Forman Crane, *Ebb Tide in New England: Women, Seaports, and Social Change, 1630–1800* (Boston, 1998), 121–124.

22. On Mary Bates see Account of Benjamin Bates, Jr., in Richard Derby, Account Book, 1756–1790, Derby Family Papers, 1716–1921, James Duncan Phillips Library, Peabody-Essex Museum, Salem, Mass.; Harriet Silvester Tapley, ed., *Early Coastwise and Foreign Shipping of Salem: A Record of the Entrances and Clearances of the Port of Salem, 1750–1769* (Salem, Mass., 1934), 153. On Mary Coxere see Coxere, *Adventures by Sea*, 76. On John and Martha Beal, see "Essex County Notarial Records, 1697–1768," Essex County Notarial

Records, 1697–1768, hereafter cited as Essex Notarial Recs., Essex Institute, *Historical Collections* 41 (1905), 191, 382, hereafter cited as *EIHC*; Sidney Perley, *The History of Salem, Massachusetts*, 3 vols. (Salem, 1924–1928), 3:307, 312, 320; Estate of John Beal (1699), Probate No. 2192, in Probate Records of Essex County, Massachusetts, Massachusetts Archives, Boston, hereafter cited as Essex Probates (unpubl.). See also Laurel Thatcher Ulrich, *Good Wives: Image and Reality in the Lives of Women in Northern New England, 1650–1750* (New York, 1980), 35–50; Jeanne Boydston, *Home and Work: Housework, Wages, and the Ideology of Labor in the Early Republic* (New York, 1990), 11–18; Lisa Norling, *Captain Ahab Had a Wife: New England Women and the Whale-fishery, 1720–1870* (Chapel Hill, N.C., 2000), 29–50; Crane, *Ebb Tide in New England*, 125–132.

23. Quotation from Bowen, *Journal*, 45:594. See also Crèvecoeur, *Letters from an American Farmer*, 157.

24. Accounts of William Abbott, Timothy Orne, Account Book, 1762–1767, Orne Family Papers, 1719–1899, James Duncan Phillips Library, Peabody-Essex Museum, Salem, Mass.; Tapley, *Early Coastwise and Foreign Shipping*, 131, 132, 141. Ulrich carefully qualifies her assertion of the significance of the deputy husband role in precisely this way in *Good Wives*, 47–48.

25. Ulrich, *Good Wives*, 44–47.

26. Accounts of Samuel Carrel, Miles Ward, Account Books, 1745–1753, Ward Family Papers, 1718–1945, James Duncan Phillips Library, Peabody-Essex Museum, Salem, Mass. Abigail died sometime before 1762, when Carrel married a second time, to Mehitabel Williams. See *Vital Records of Salem, Massachusetts, to the End of the Year, 1849*, 6 vols. (Salem, Mass., 1916–1925), 3:191, 193, hereafter cited as *Salem Vital Records*. See also Boydston, *Home and Work*, 11–16; Ulrich, *Good Wives*, 15–18.

27. Bettye Hobbs Pruitt, ed., *The Massachusetts Tax Valuation List of 1771* (Boston, 1978); United States Bureau of the Census, *Heads of Families at the First Census of the United States Taken in the Year 1790: Massachusetts.* (Washington, D.C., 1908). In the 1790 sample, $n=1,137$; in the 1771 sample, $n=1,942$. See also Vince Walsh, "'Up Through the Hawse Hole': The Social Origins and Lives of Salem Shipmasters, 1640 to 1720," M.A. thesis, Memorial University of Newfoundland, 1995, 150; Crane, *Ebb Tide in New England*, 14–15. See sources in Appendix A.

28. Estate of Lewis Hunt (1715), Probate No. 14257, Essex Probates (unpubl.); Perley, *History of Salem*, 3:182; Estate of Thomas Elkins (1764), Probate No. 8667, Essex Probates (unpubl.); *Salem Vital Records*, 3:330, 5:227.

29. Evidence based on thirty-nine Salem wives who were widowed under the age of thirty-five or less than thirteen years into their first marriage and whose subsequent marital histories (or lack thereof) are known. Note that there were twenty-two additional widows (mainly born outside Salem) who disappeared from local records and probably returned home (where they may well have married again). See sources in Appendix A. See also Daniel Vickers, "An Honest Tar: Ashley Bowen of Marblehead," *New England Quar-*

terly, 69 (1996), 531–553; Alexander Keyssar, "Widowhood in Eighteenth-Century Massachusetts: A Problem in the History of the Family," *Perspectives in American History,* 8 (1974), 86–94.

30. On Abigail Pickman see Estate of Benjamin Pickman (1719), Probate No. 22031, Essex Probates (unpubl.); Essex Notarial Recs. *EIHC,* 44 (1908), 327; Accounts of Abigail Pickman, Joseph Orne, Account Book, 1719–1744, Orne Family Papers, 1719–1899, James Duncan Phillips Library, Peabody-Essex Museum, Salem, Mass.; *Salem Vital Records,* 2:174–176, 4:195, 6:143. A fuller treatment of the Pickman's family history can be found in Walsh, "'Up Through the Hawse-Hole,'" 159–163.

31. These percentages are proportionate to an estimate of the total number of widows living in Salem. Assuming a town population of 5,500 and a proportion of widows within that population of 0.06, we estimate a total of 330 widows. See Pruitt, *Massachusetts Tax Valuation List of 1771,* 130–155; Felt, *Annals of Salem,* 2:410–411.

32. Pruitt, *Massachusetts Tax Valuation List of 1771,* 130–155. On Mary Ashton see Pruitt, *Massachusetts Tax Valuation List of 1771,* 148–149; Perley, *History of Salem,* 1:342; Estate of Jacob Ashton (1770), Probate No. 917, Essex Probates (unpubl.). On Elizabeth Lee see Pruitt, *Massachusetts Tax Valuation List of 1771,* 140–141; Perley, *History of Salem,* 2:425; Estate of Richard Lee (1767), Probate No. 16644, Essex Probates (unpubl.). On Elizabeth Sanders see Pruitt, *Massachusetts Tax Valuation List of 1771,* 140–141; *Salem Vital Records,* 4:285; Estate of Philip Sanders (1770), Probate No. 24769, Essex Probates (unpubl.). On Mary Eden see Pruitt, *Massachusetts Tax Valuation List of 1771,* 144–145; Perley, *History of Salem,* 2:387; Estate of Thomas Eden (1768), Probate No. 8568, Essex Probates (unpubl.). On Mary Grafton see Pruitt, *Massachusetts Tax Valuation List of 1771,* 132–133; Perley, *History of Salem,* 1:435; Estate of Joseph Grafton (1767), Probate No. 11475, Essex Probates (unpubl.). On Elizabeth Higginson see Perley, *History of Salem,* 1:158, 3:365; Accounts of Elizabeth Higginson, Timothy Orne Account Book, 1762–1767. On Anstiss Crowninshield see Richard Derby, Account Book, 1756–1790; *Salem Vital Records,* 2:430, 3:262, 5:185.

33. Accounts of Sarah Mansfield, Timothy Orne Account Book, 1762–1767; Accounts of Ruth Tarrants, Miles Ward, Account Books, 1753–1764, 1765–1777. On Mary Glover and Benjamin Shaw see Accounts of Widow Mary Glover, Timothy Orne, Account Book, 1735–1753; Perley, *History of Salem,* 2:404, 3:19; Portledge Bill, schooner *Beaver* (1752), box 2, folder 2, Orne Family Papers. On Mary Elkins see Accounts of Mary Elkins, Henry Elkins, Richard Derby, Account Book, 1756–1790. Identifying Henry Elkins as Richard Derby's nephew hinges not on a provable genealogical link but on the facts that (*a*) Derby's sister, Martha, married a Thomas Elkins (who had a younger brother, Henry) in 1736; (*b*) a Thomas Elkins not conclusively connected to anyone other than Martha died in 1749; (*c*) both a Thomas and a Henry Elkins appear in the Salem records around 1760, just as (if they were Thomas and Martha's children) they were coming of age; and (*d*)

Derby was receiving Henry's wages until the latter was married in 1762. This admittedly circumstantial evidence suggests that Martha moved in with her brother Richard after her husband, Thomas, died, and Henry grew up in the Derby household. See Perley, *History of Salem*, 3:145; *Salem Vital Records*, 3:329, 5:227; Estate of Thomas Elkins (1749), Probate No. 8666, Essex Probates (unpubl.). For many other similar examples from other seaports, see Crane, *Ebb Tide in New England*, 125–130; Karin Wulf, *Not All Wives: Women of Colonial Philadelphia* (Ithaca, N.Y., 2000), 130–142.

34. Quotations from Nathaniel Hawthorne, *The House of the Seven Gables* (Harmondsworth, 1981), 34, 35; Benjamin F. Browne, "Youthful Recollections of Salem, Written by Benjamin F. Browne in 1869," *EIHC*, 50 (1914), 291. See also Bryant F. Tolles, Jr., *Architecture in Salem: An Illustrated Guide* (Salem, Mass., 1983), 41–42. On huxters in Philadelphia, see Wulf, *Not All Wives*, 144–145; Patricia Cleary, "'She Will Be in the Shop': Women's Sphere of Trade in Eighteenth-Century Philadelphia and New York," *Pennsylvania Magazine of History and Biography*, 119 (1995), 181–202.

35. Accounts of Sarah Adams, Abigail Browne, Elizabeth Herrick, Elizabeth Elkins, Elizabeth Bowditch, and Mary Bowditch, Richard Derby, Account Book, 1756–1790; *Salem Vital Records*, 3:42, 5:42; Browne, "Youthful Recollections," Essex Institute, *Historical Collections*, 49 (1913), 291, 300; Persons Licenced for Innholders and Retailers for the Town of Salem, 1750, Essex County Court of General Sessions, Miscellany, 1692–1833. Out of nine licensed innholders in 1750, two (including Hannah Pratt) were women, and out of forty-five licensed retailers, eight were women. Of the ten licensed women, six were not taxed at all; three were taxed but ranked only in the poorer deciles; and one, Hannah Pratt, ranked in the second decile. See also David W. Conroy, *In Public Houses: Drink and the Revolution of Authority in Colonial Massachusetts* (Chapel Hill, N.C., 1995), 99–156; Crane, *Ebb Tide in New England*, 177–183.

36. This percentage was based on twenty-seven mariners whose names appeared on portledge bills, 1690–1775, and who had fathers for whom death dates are known. Out of those aged twenty to twenty-nine ($n=98$), the proportion was only 22 percent. We conclude that boys with fathers did not have to go to sea so young. See sources in Appendix A.

37. Accounts of Sarah Adams, Mercy Beadle, Richard Derby, Account Book, 1756–1790; Accounts of Widow Coffin, Widow Corning, Mary Glover, Susanna Glover, Ruth Tarrants, Eunice Stevens, Widow Symes, Widow Gotty, Widow Valpy, and Widow Waters, Miles Ward, Account Book, 1745–1753, 1753–1764; Accounts of Mary Millett, Elizabeth Valpy, Timothy Orne, Account Book, 1735–1753. On the widow Goutier (or Gotty) see also *Salem Vital Records*, 5:290. On Mercy Beadle see also Perley, *History of Salem*, 2:387.

38. Of all locally born seamen and boys who are recorded as having shipped out of Salem, 1690–1775, and survived their seafaring careers to become taxpaying residents of the town (hereafter cited as the Retired Mariner Sample, $n=45$), 9 percent climbed into the highest wealth decile and stayed there for

ten or more years—a predictable indication that the householder in question belonged to the town's merchant elite. See sources in Appendix A.

39. In addition to the four merchants in the Retired Mariner Sample, a further sixteen rose beyond the fourth decile but not permanently into the first, suggesting the possession of some assessable productive wealth. On the seafaring activities of Philip English see George Francis Dow and Mary G. Thresher, eds., *Records and Files of the Quarterly Courts of Essex County, Massachusetts, 1636–1686*, 9 vols. (Salem, 1911–1975), 6:392. For Benjamin Pickman see Registry of Massachusetts Shipping, Massachusetts Archives, Boston, 7:109, 199, 209, 221, 295. For Richard Derby see Essex Notarial Recs., *EIHC*, 41 (1905), 383–384, 394–395. For Orne see Naval Officer Shipping Lists for Barbados, C.O. 33/15. On Benjamin and George West, see Portledge Bills, schooner *Sea Flower* (1751), box 10, folder 3, schooner *Fisher* (1752, 1754), box 6, folder 1, Orne Family Papers; Tapley, *Early Coastwise Shipping*, 10, 100, 106, 119, 125, 126; Perley, *History of Salem*, 2:305; Pruitt, *Massachusetts Tax Valuation List of 1771*, 136–137, 154–155; "Map of Salem about 1780" in Phillips, *Salem in the Eighteenth Century;* Estate of Benjamin West (1809) Probate No. 29330, Essex Probates (unpubl.).

40. For George Peele see Bentley, *Diary,* 2:366. For David Felt see Portledge Bills, schooner *Molly* (1753, 1754, 1755, 1757, 1759), box 7, folder 10; schooner *Louisa* (1760), box 7, folder 6; schooner *Eunice* (1762, 1763, 1764, 1766), box 5, folders 4, 5; Orne Family Papers; Tapley, *Early Coastwise Shipping*, 61; Bentley, *Diary*, 4:484–485; Perley, *History of Salem*, 3:226, 227; Pruitt, *Massachusetts Tax Valuation List of 1771*, 144–145. For Thomas Ellis see Essex Notarial Recs., *EIHC*, 44 (1908), 91–92; Account of Thomas Ellis, William Pickering Account Book, 1695–1718, James Duncan Phillips Library, Salem, Mass.; Perley, *History of Salem*, 3:243, 310; *Salem Vital Records*, 1:276; Estate of Thomas Ellis (1743), Probate No. 8804, Essex Probates (unpubl.). See also Bentley, *Diary*, 4:424; Estate of John Touzell (1737), Probate No. 27950, Essex Probates (unpubl.); *Essex Antiquarian*, 7:182; Account of Jonathan Gardner, Jr., Richard Derby Account Book, 1756–1790; Estate of Nathaniel Andrew (1762), Probate No. 694, Essex Probates (unpubl.).

41. In the Retired Mariner Sample (*n*=45), twenty-five never climbed into the top three deciles that defined most assessable productive property in Salem at any time in their lives. Of all men who went to sea between 1690 and 1775 and were designated in a deed, probated inventory, or other death notice by occupation in the year they died, 68 percent (*n*=74) were termed mariners, and almost all the rest were either merchants, esquires, or yeomen. Virtually none of these retired seamen were identified by an artisanal calling. See sources in Appendix A. For Ashley Bowen see Vickers, "An Honest Tar," 543–545. For William Peele see Portledge Bill, schooner *Molly* (1759), box 7, folder 11, Orne Family Papers; Portledge Bill, schooner *Hitty* (1763), box 1, folder 1, Ward Family Papers; Perley, *History of Salem*, 3:386; Bentley, *Diary*, 1:13, 226. For John Scollay see Tapley, *Early Coastwise Shipping*, 134, 155; Essex Deeds, 125:115. For Samuel Swasey see Portledge Bills, schooner *Beaver* (1753, 1754,

1757, 1758), box 2, folders 3, 5, and 6, Orne Family Papers; *Salem Vital Records*, 4:362, 6:259; Bentley, *Diary*, 1:15, 337, 2:32, 174, 4:137.

42. Analysis of taxpayers in 1786 is based on the eighteen colonial mariners who were forty-five years of age or older in that year (and so assumed retired). Even those assessed for faculty were generally rated at the lowest possible levels—£10 or £15. See Assessment List of 1786, Salem Tax Lists, 1689–. Age of retirement from physical labor is a subject that could use more research, but various age distributions of work being performed in the colonial period suggest that by age fifty, participation in visible work outside the home was quite rare for New England males. For agriculture see Daniel Vickers, *Farmers and Fishermen: Two Centuries of Work in Essex County, Massachusetts, 1630–1850* (Chapel Hill, N.C., 1994), 70, 74–75; for the cod fishery, see ibid., 184–185; for the whale fishery see Vickers, "Nantucket Whalemen in the Deep-Sea Fishery: The Changing Anatomy of an Early American Labor Force," *Journal of American History*, 72 (1985), 285. For Benjamin Abbott see Account of Benjamin Abbott, Timothy Orne, Account Book, 1735–1753, Miles Ward, Account Book, 1745–1753; *Salem Vital Records*, 4:37. For John Muckford see Account of John Muckford, Timothy Orne, Account Book, 1735–1753, Miles Ward, Account Book, 1753–1764, Richard Derby, Account Book, 1756–1790; *Salem Vital Records*, 4:106.

43. *Essex Gazette*, June 19–26, 1770. On the delivery of wages to parents and guardians, see Barlow, *Journal*, 1:91; Coxere, *Adventures by Sea*, 35; Kelly, *Samuel Kelly*, 30–31.

44. Very few of those 225 locally born foremast hands under the age of twenty-one were either married or counted by the town as independent household-ers for taxation purposes, and when reference to the wages they earned crops up in merchant's books, the sums were invariably posted to their mothers' or fathers' accounts. Quotation from Christopher Prince, *The Autobiography of a Yankee Mariner: Christopher and the American Revolution*, ed. Michael J. Crawford (Washington, D.C., 2002), 13. Note however, that Prince kept the profits from his adventures as his own; ibid., 20.

45. Bowen, *Journal*, 45:555, 558, 560, 561, 563, 565, 569, 574, 578, 579, 582–591, 595, 599, 604, 605.

6. THE NINETEENTH CENTURY

1. Ship's Journals, sloop *Adventure*, June 1, 1774, Marine Logs and Journals Collection, James Duncan Phillips Library, Peabody-Essex Museum, Salem, Mass.; *The Journals of Ashley Bowen (1728–1813) of Marblehead*, ed. Philip Chadwick Foster Smith, Colonial Society of Massachusetts, *Publications*, 2 vols. (Boston, 1973), 45:394–397, hereafter cited as Bowen, *Journal*.

2. James Duncan Phillips, *Salem in the Eighteenth Century* (Boston, 1937), 396–397, 406, 432, 440–442.

3. Phillips, *Salem in the Eighteenth Century*, 468; James Duncan Phillips, *Salem and the Indies: The Story of the Great Commercial Era of the City* (Boston, 1947), 9–16; Bettye Hobbs Pruitt, *Massachusetts Tax Valuation List of 1771* (Boston,

1978), 130–154; William Bentley, *The Diary of William Bentley, D.D.: Pastor of the East Church, Salem, Massachusetts,* 4 vols. (Salem, 1905–14; rpt. Gloucester, Mass., 1962), 1:7; Evarts B. Breene and Virginia D. Harrington, *American Population Before the Federal Census of 1790* (New York, 1932), 31.

4. Harold A. Innis, *The Cod Fisheries: The History of an International Economy* (Toronto, 1940; rpt. 1978), 220.

5. Naval Officer Shipping Lists for Salem and Marblehead, Massachusetts, 1753, 1756, C.O. 5/849, 850; James Duncan Phillips, "Salem Ocean-borne Commerce from the Close of the Revolution to the Establishment of the Constitution," Essex Institute, *Historical Collections,* 75 (1939), 135–158, 249–274, 358–381; 76 (1940), 68–88, hereafter cited as *EIHC*. On the postwar depression in New England generally, see Samuel Eliot Morison, *The Maritime History of Massachusetts* (Boston, 1921; rpt. Boston, 1979), 30–40.

6. Phillips, *Salem in the Eighteenth Century,* 468; Phillips, *Salem and the Indies,* 92–128, 166–190, 222–248; James Duncan Phillips, "Who Owned the Salem Vessels in 1810?" *EIHC,* 83 (1947), 1–13; Morison, *Maritime History of Massachusetts,* 79–95.

7. Phillips, *Salem and the Indies,* 180.

8. U.S. Bureau of the Census, *Heads of Families at the First Census of the United States Taken in the Year, 1790: Massachusetts* (Washington, D.C., 1908), 9; U.S. Department of State, *Aggregate Amount of Each Description of Persons Within the United States of America, and the Territories Thereof: Agreeably to Actual Enumeration Made According to Law, in the Year 1810.* (Washington, D.C., 1811; rpt. New York, 1990), 10a; Timothy Dwight, *Travels in New England and New York,* ed., Barbara Miller Solomon, 4 vols. (Cambridge, Mass., 1969), 1:323; Bentley, *Diary,* 2:84.

9. Bentley, *Diary,* 2:88; Phillips, *Salem and the Indies,* 179–180; Charles Tyng, *Before the Wind: The Memoir of an American Sea Captain, 1808–1833,* ed. Susan Fels (New York, 1999), 100–101, 136–146; Gorham Low, *The Sea Made Men: The Story of a Gloucester Lad,* ed. Elizabeth L. Alling (New York, 1937), 80–84, 150–151, 255–267; Frederic W. Howay, *Voyages of the "Columbia" to the Northwest Coast, 1787–1790 and 1790–1793,* Massachusetts Historical Society, *Collections,* 79 (1941, rpt. 1990), 37–40, 188, 240–241, 310–313; Richard J. Cleveland, *In the Forecastle, or Twenty-Five Years a Sailor* (1842; rpt. New York, ca. 1870), 163–176, 194–198, 284–327.

10. Bentley, *Diary,* 2:84, 145; 3:258, 280, 282; Phillips, *Salem and the Indies,* 101–105, 244–245; Tyng, *Before the Wind,* 56–57, 68–69, 97–98, 146–148, 164–165, 254–255; Low, *The Sea Made Men,* 78–79; Richard Henry Dana, Jr., *Two Years Before the Mast: A Personal Narrative of Life at Sea* (Harmondsworth, 1981), 58–59; Benjamin W. Labaree et al., *America and the Sea: A Maritime History* (Mystic, Conn., 1998), 190–191.

11. Bentley, *Diary,* 2:84; Phillips, *Salem and the Indies,* 101–147, 239–241, 262–281, 308–328, 372–422.

12. Shipping News, *Salem Gazette,* Jan. 4–Dec. 29, 1820; Bentley, *Diary,* 4, 382; Nathaniel Hawthorne, *The Scarlet Letter,* ed. Ross C. Murfin (Boston, 1991), 24.

13. Morison, *Maritime History of Massachusetts*, 90–91, 219–223; John H. Galey, "Salem's Trade with Brazil, 1801–1970," *EIHC*, 107 (1971), 198–219; Richard H. Gates-Hunt, "Salem and Zanzibar: A Special Relationship," *EIHC*, 117 (1981), 1–26; Edward Randolph, "Report to the Committee for Trade and Plantations," Oct. 12, 1676, in *Edward Randolph Papers*, ed. Robert Noxon Toppan, *Publication of the Prince Society* (Boston, 1898; rpt. New York, 1967), 25:249.

14. Low, *The Sea Made Men*, 14, 31, 59, 75, 110; Tyng, *Before the Wind*, 14, 64, 78, 86–88, 118; Hawthorne, *The Scarlet Letter*, 28. The proportion of locally born masters is harder to determine, since they filled out the crew list forms and seldom recorded this information for themselves. Of those who did, in 1805, 1815, 1825, and 1835, 79 percent were born in Salem ($n=216$), but the many missing cases render these data less dependable than one would wish.

15. The absolute number of locally born mariners population is calculated for 1765 and 1800 by estimating the number of mariners needed to man the Salem-owned vessels in each year (1765: 575; 1800: 1,325) and multiplying this number by the proportion of mariners shipping out of Salem who had been born in Salem (1765: 60 percent; 1805: 33 percent), as estimated from portledge bill crew lists, supplemented by the genealogical sources listed in Appendix A. The number of locally born mariners in 1850 represents all mariners, aged fifteen to fifty, listed in the manuscript census of 1850 as having been born in Massachusetts (478), multiplied by 0.57 (the proportion of all Massachusetts-born mariners in the 1850 Salem Crew Lists who were born in Salem). See Salem Crew Lists, 1803–1850, Crew Lists, 1805, 1850, Massachusetts, Records of the U.S. Customs Service, National Archives Northeast Region, Waltham, Mass.; United States Census Office, *The Seventh Census of the United States, 1850* (Washington, D.C., 1853; rpt. New York, 1976), 50; Joseph B. Felt, *Annals of Salem*, 2 vols. (Boston, 1845–1849), 2:410. The assumption that the number of Salem-born mariners serving in the Salem fleet did not exceed the numbers serving in 1805 is based on the fact that the total of 456 Salem-born mariners clearing port in 1805 was not exceeded in any of the other years (1815: 339 mariners; 1825: 422 mariners; 1835: 323). See Salem Crew Lists, 1805, 1815, 1825, and 1835.

16. Percentages are based on aggregate number of seamen ($n=2,269$) who signed articles in the sample years, 1805, 1815, 1825, and 1835. The proportion of African-American seamen is estimated following the standards of identification described in W. Jeffrey Bolster, *Black Jacks: African American Seamen in the Age of Sail* (Cambridge, Mass., 1997), 234. Bolster found that in Providence, New York, Philadelphia, Baltimore, Savannah, and New Orleans, African Americans usually constituted anywhere from 10 percent to 20 percent of crews in the first half of the nineteenth century, although, especially in the South, they declined in number as the Civil War approached. Ibid., 235–237.

17. See Nathaniel Bowditch to Timothy Pickering, Dec. 29, 1815, reel 30:415, Timothy Pickering Papers, Massachusetts Historical Society, Boston;

William McNally, *Evils and Abuses in the Naval and Merchant Services Exposed; With Proposals for Their Remedy and Redress* (Boston, 1839), 44–47. Thanks to Rachel Wheeler for drawing our attention to the Bowditch letter.

18. Data on Salem wages were culled from the portledge bills and shipping agreements described in Appendix A. Comparative wage data come from Winifred Barr Rothenberg, *From Market-Places to a Market Economy: The Transformation of Rural Massachusetts, 1750–1850* (Chicago, 1992), 203; Donald R. Adams, Jr., "Wage Rates in the Early National Period: Philadelphia, 1785–1830," *Journal of Economic History*, 28 (1968), 406, 424; Donald R. Adams, Jr., "Some Evidence on English and American Wage Rates, 1790–1830," *Journal of Economic History*, 30 (1970), 512. On Daniel Perkins see Crew List, ship *Exeter* (1805), Salem Crew Lists; Portledge Bill, ship *Exeter* (1805), box 2, folder 2, Benjamin Pickman Papers, 1763–1843, James Duncan Phillips Library, Peabody-Essex Museum, Salem, Mass.

19. Ship's Accounts, ship *St. Paul* (1839–1840), box 3, folder 2, Phillips Family Papers, 1636–1897, James Duncan Phillips Library, Peabody-Essex Museum, Salem, Mass. See also Shipping Accounts, ship *Malabar* (1821–1822), box 25, folder 6, Orne Family Papers, 1719–1899, James Duncan Phillips Library, Peabody-Essex Museum, Salem, Mass.; ship *Eliza* (1833–1834), ship *Brookline* (1836–1837, 1837–1839), ship *St. Paul* (1840–1841), box 2, folder 1; box 3, folder 2, Phillips Family Papers.

20. Out of 312 seamen listed on seventy-five shipping agreements, 1793–1824, 146 had privileges added to their wages. See sources in Appendix A. See also Allan A. Arnold, "Merchants in the Forecastle: The Private Ventures of New England Mariners," *American Neptune*, 41 (1981), 165–187.

21. Phillips, *Salem and the Indies*, 116; Arnold, "Merchants in the Forecastle," 177–183; shipping agreements, schooner *Rajah* (1795), box 1, folder 3 (oversize), ship *Rachel*, box 1, folder 2 (oversize), Peele Family Papers, 1753–1871, James Duncan Phillips Library, Peabody-Essex Museum, Salem, Mass. All the ship's accounts cited earlier in this chapter mention advances to seamen in foreign ports.

22. Low, *The Sea Made Men*, 14; "Boardman Genealogy," *Essex Antiquarian*, 9 (1905), 150, 151.

23. Cleveland, *In the Forecastle*, 48, 49, 75; Tyng, *Before the Wind*, 105, 151, 158; Low, *The Sea Made Men*, 176. See also Jacob Nagle, *The Nagle Journal: A Diary of the Life of Jacob Nagle, Sailor, from the Year, 1775 to 1841*, ed. John C. Dann (New York, 1988), 296; Samuel Kelly, *Samuel Kelly: An Eighteenth Century Seaman*, ed. Crosbie Garstin (New York, 1925), 187, 223.

24. Bentley, *Diary*, vols. 1–4; Benjamin F. Browne, "Youthful Recollections of Salem," *EIHC*, 49 (1913), 193–209, 289–304; 50 (1914), 6–16, 289–296; 51 (1915), 53–56, 297–305. On sailortown institutions elsewhere see Judith Fingard, *Jack in Port: Sailortowns of Eastern Canada* (Toronto, 1982), 216–220, 229–232, 234–241; Glenn Gordinier, "Faith, Sailortowns, and the Character of Seaman's Benevolence in Nineteenth-Century America," in Labaree et al., *America and the Sea*, 252–255.

25. Data on seamen's privileges are based on 312 cases, 1792–1824, and 311 cases, 1825–1850. See the sources in Appendix A. On the growth in real wages and labor productivity in the United States over the period, see Stanley Lebergott, *Manpower in Economic Growth: The American Record Since 1800* (New York, 1964), 154–158; Robert A. Margo, "The Labor Force in the Nineteenth Century," in *Cambridge Economic History of the United States*, 3 vols., ed. Stanley L. Engerman and Robert E. Gallman (Cambridge, 1996–2000), 2:221–222. On New England, see Rothenberg, *Market-Places to a Market Economy*, 167–174. On total factor productivity in shipping and other sectors of the United States economy, see Douglass C. North, "Sources of Productivity Change in Ocean Shipping, 1600–1850," *Journal of Political Economy*, 76 (1968), 953–970; C. Knick Harley, "Ocean Freight Rates and Productivity, 1740–1913: The Primacy of Mechanical Invention Reaffirmed," *Journal of Economic History* 48 (1988), 860–862, 867–870; Stanley L. Engerman and Kenneth L. Sokoloff, "Technology and Industrialization, 1790–1914," in Engerman and Gallman, *Cambridge Economic History of the United States*, 2:370–377; Jeremy Atack, Fred Bateman, and William N. Parker, "The Farm, The Farmer, and the Market," ibid., 2:259.

26. *The Salem Directory and City Register* (Salem, Mass., 1837); Shipping Agreements, ship *St. Paul* (1849), BR 656–669 1949, Broadside Collection; schooner *Erie* (1841), box 2, folder 9, Gregory Family Papers, 1807–1873, both in James Duncan Phillips Library, Peabody-Essex Museum, Salem, Mass.; Shipping Agreement, brigs *Cherokee* (1841, 1843, 1845) and *Star* (1844), box 2, folders 1, 2, box 3, folder 1, box 9, folder 8, Michael Shepherd Papers, 1809–1893, James Duncan Phillips Library, Peabody-Essex Museum, Salem, Mass. On Eben Griffin, see entries for Ebenezer Griffin, Salem, Mass., 1850 Manuscript Census for Massachusetts, using Family Tree Maker, *Massachusetts, 1850 from the National Archives of the United States* (Novato, Calif., 1998), a searchable CD-ROM version of that census; entries for Eben Griffin, Sr., on Salem Tax and Valuation Lists, 1829, 1834, 1840, 1845, 1850, Salem Tax and Valuation Lists, 1689–, microfilm copy in possession of James Duncan Phillips Library, Peabody-Essex Museum, Salem, Mass., hereafter cited as Salem Tax Lists, 1689–; 1850 Census: Instructions to Marshals and Assistant Marshals, IPUMS website (http://www.ipums.umn.edu). On shipping agents and crimps in the nineteenth century, see Fingard, *Jack in Port*, esp. 194–199.

27. Ship's Journal, ship *Janus*, Sept. 29, 1825, Marine Logs and Journals Collection, James Duncan Phillips Library, Peabody-Essex Museum, Salem, Mass.; A. Frank Hitchins and Stephen W. Phillips, ed., *Ship Registers of Salem and Beverly, 1780–1900* (Salem, Mass., 1906), 95; Crew List, ship *Janus* (1825), Salem Crew Lists. For the Boardman family see "Boardman Genealogy," *Essex Antiquarian*, 9 (1905), 150, and sources in Appendix A.

28. Ship's Journal, ship *Janus*, Sept. 29, 1825–June 19, 1827. For U.S. trade to the Pacific coast of South America, see Paul Gootenberg, *Between Silver and Guano: Commercial Policy and the State in Postindependence Peru* (Princeton, 1989), 36, 164.

29. Crew List, ship *Janus* (1825), Salem Crew Lists.

30. Ship's Journal, ship *Janus* May 13, June 11, 1827; Crew List, ship *Janus* (1825), Salem Crew Lists.

31. Richard J. Cleveland, *In the Forecastle, or Twenty-Five Years a Sailor* (1842; rpt. New York, ca. 1870), 14, 26, 27. Dana, *Two Years Before the Mast*, 98–362. On adventure seeking as one motive for going to sea in nineteenth-century New England, see Morison, *Maritime History of Massachusetts*, esp. 109–110; Margaret S. Creighton, *Rites and Passages: The Experience of American Whaling, 1830–1870* (Cambridge, 1995), 46–57. Tyng, *Before the Wind*; Low, *The Sea Made Men*; and Nagle, *Journal*, are as much travelogues as maritime memoirs.

32. Cleveland, *In the Forecastle*, 13. On the emergence of the seaman's narrative genre, see John Samson, "Personal Narratives, Journals, and Diaries," in *America and the Sea: A Literary History*, ed. Haskell Springer (Athens, Ga., 1995), 83–98; Thomas Philbrick, Introduction to Dana, *Two Years Before the Mast*, 21–24.

33. Low, *The Sea Made Men*, 143–144; Edward Beck, *The Sea Voyages of Edward Beck in the 1820s*, ed. Michael Hay and Joy Roberts (Edinburgh, 1996), 166; *The Moslem* (1846), *Federal Cases, Comprising Cases Argued and Determined in the Circuit and District Courts of the United States . . .*, 30 vols., 17:894–895, hereafter cited as *Federal Cases*. See also *The William Harris* (1837), *Federal Cases*, 29:1305.

34. Quotation from *Foster et al. v. Sampson* (1849), *Federal Cases*, 9:573. On regular fare see also *The Mary* (1838), *Federal Cases*, 16:946–949; *Healey v. Martin* (1823), *Federal Cases*, 11:958; *Martin et al. v. The William* (1819), *Federal Cases*, 16:917; *Marder et al. v. Boynton et al.* (1843), *Federal Cases*, 16:1001–1002.

35. *Collins et al. v. Wheeler et al.*, 31:724 (U.S., 1st Dist., March 1850); *Collins et al. v. Wheeler et al.* (1850), *Federal Cases*, 6:134–136. For other cases see *The Childe Harold* (1846), *Federal Cases*, 5:619–622; *Foster et al. v. Sampson* (1849), *Federal Cases*, 9:572–573; *Healey v. Martin* (1823), *Federal Cases*, 11:958; *Mariners v. The Washington* (1840), *Federal Cases*, 16:750–751; *Martin et al. v. The William* (1819), *Federal Cases*, 16:917; *The Mary* (1838), *Federal Cases*, 16:946–949; *Marder et al. v. Boynton* (1843), *Federal Cases*, 16:1000–1001; *Wilson v. Schooner, Favorite*, 4:171 (U.S., 1st Dist., 1810). Quotation on Boston Indiaman from Nathaniel Ames, *A Mariner's Sketches, Originally Published in the Manufacturers and Farmers Journal* (Providence, R.I., 1830), 190.

36. *The Brookline* (1845), *Federal Cases*, 4:236–238.

37. Dana, *Two Years Before the Mast*, 239–240, 348–352.

38. Tyng, *Before the Wind*, 208–209; *Farwell v. Jenks*, 20:491, file papers (U.S., 1st Dist., 1836); Deposition of James Walker, Aug. 29, 1823, box 1, folder 2, Andrew Dunlap Papers, 1754–1847, James Duncan Phillips Library, Peabody-Essex Museum, Salem, Mass.; Dana, *Two Years Before the Mast*, 261.

39. Dana, *Two Years Before the Mast*, 143–144, 254–255. See also *Thompson v. Busch* (1822), *Federal Cases*, 23:1024–1027.

40. Thomas H. Gregory to John H. Gregory, Mar. 22, 1818, box 2, folder 7, Gregory Family Papers.

41. Beck, *Sea Voyages*, 52; Eric Sager, *Seafaring Labor: The Merchant Marine of Atlantic Canada, 1820–1914* (Kingston, 1989), 113–114.

42. Sources for the 194 shipping agreements and portledge bills consulted can be found in Appendix A.

43. The practice of deserting for higher wages is described in Kelly, *Samuel Kelly*, 304; Tyng, *Before the Wind*, 158, 178; and in excellent detail in Fingard, *Jack in Port*, 16–18, 68–71, 90–92, 141–153. Lawsuits in which American sailors defended their decision to desert include *Douglass v. Eyre* (1830), *Federal Cases*, 7:975–978; *Magee et al. v. the Moss* (1831), *Federal Cases*, 16:384–390; *The Rovena* (1836), *Federal Cases*, 20:1271–1277; *Sherwood v. McIntosh* (1826), *Federal Cases*, 21:1294–1298.

44. The annual number of recorded deaths of mariners of known rank, aged twenty to twenty-nine, numbered 1.8 between 1785 and 1794 (or 0.023 percent of Salem's total population at that time) compared to an average of 2.6 (or 0.022 percent of the town's population for the entire period, 1795–1824). These deaths were culled from *Salem Vital Records*, vols. 5, 6. For the population of Salem see Joseph B. Felt, *Annals of Salem*, 2 vols. (Boston, 1845–1849), 2:411. See also Maris A. Vinovskis, "Mortality Rates and Trends in Massachusetts Before 1860," *Journal of Economic History*, 32 (1972), 206–207.

45. "Journal of Captain John Crowninshield at Calcutta, 1797–1798, When Master of the Ship, *Bellisarius*," *EIHC*, 81 (1940), 354–382; 82 (1942), 26–41, 122–134.

46. See sources in Appendix A. On Nathaniel Hathorne, see Perley, *History of Salem*, 1:285–286; Edwin Haviland Miller, *Salem Is My Dwelling Place: A Life of Nathaniel Hawthorne* (Iowa City, 1991), 23–25, 27; and sources in Appendix A. The author added the *w* to his surname to make the spelling match the pronunciation.

47. Cleveland, *In the Forecastle*, 26–27.

48. There were forty seamen in this sample drawn from the Salem Crew Lists, 1803–1813, and traced through the same lists as far as 1840.

49. This is based on an analysis of 89 shipping agreements with masters, 1793–1850. An analysis of 465 seamen over the same period reveals that the difference in wages between those with and without privileges was statistically insignificant, suggesting that their value to the sailor was insignificant as well. See sources in Appendix A.

50. For Charles Atkinson see Crew Lists, schooner *Fame* (1804), brig *Catherine* (1806), ship *Alexander Hodgdon* (1806, 1808), schooner *Two Sisters* (1809), brig *Eliza and Mary* (1810), ship *Rambler* (1811), and bark *Patriot* (1815), Salem Crew Lists; *Salem Vital Records*, 3:63, 5:58; *Salem Directory* (1837); and sources in Appendix A.

51. On taxable wealth, see Salem Tax Lists, 1800–1850, in Salem Tax Lists, 1689–; and sources in Appendix A. Probated estates included Estate of William Moulton (1828), Probate No. 19054 (the poorest); Estate of John C. Callum (1820), Probate No. 4561 (the wealthiest); and Estate of William Babbage (1828), Probate No. 1163 (the median), all in Probate Records of

Essex County, Mass., Massachusetts Archives, Boston, hereafter cited as Essex Probates (unpubl.).

52. Of 1,472 mariners on the Salem Crew Lists, 1825, a total of 140 could be traced with confidence to the 1850 Manuscript Census for Massachusetts, using Family Tree Maker, *Massachusetts, 1850 from the National Archives of the United States* (Novato, Calif., 1998), a searchable CD-ROM version of that census. The proportion of mariners from the 1825 crew lists who were termed masters on the 1850 census was 33 percent (*n*=46) among locally born mariners, but only 11 percent (*n*=19) among in-migrant mariners.

53. On Jehiel Hard see *Salem Vital Records*, 3:465, 5:309; Crew List, schooner *Havanna* (1825), brig *Saucy Jack* (1825), Salem Crew Lists; Estate of Jehiel Hard (1826), Probate No. 12329, Essex Probates (unpubl.).

54. Dwight, *Travels*, 1:322–326.

55. Bentley, *Diary*, 2:440, 3:291; Phillips, *Salem and the Indies*, 13–15.

56. Phillips, *Salem and the Indies*, 148–165.

57. Benjamin Browne, "Youthful Recollections of Salem," *EIHC*, 49 (1913), 206–207, 289; Bentley, *Diary*, 2:75, 298, 4:350; Phillips, *Salem and the Indies*, 158–159, 161–165.

58. Felt, *Annals*, 2:164, 183–184; Louis McLane, *Documents Relative to the Manufactures in the United States: Collected and transmitted to the House of Representatives, in compliance with a resolution of Jan. 19, 1832*, 2 vols. (Washington, D.C., 1833), 1:251–252; Bentley, *Diary*, 2:28, 174, 4:362.

59. Phillips, *Salem and the Indies*, 158–159; Bentley, *Diary*, 2:236, 298, 4:262, 276, 362, 415, 514, 564, 599, 709–710; Felt, *Annals*, 2:157, 168; McLane, *Documents Relative to Manufactures*, 1:251–252; *Salem Directory* (1837).

60. Phillips, *Salem and the Indies*, 290–292; Susan Geib, "Landscape and Faction: Spatial Transformation in William Bentley's Salem," *EIHC*, 113 (1977), 163–180. Between 1760 and 1810, most of the wealthiest householders in town (meaning the top 5 percent of all taxpayers) lived in the easternmost wards of the town; after 1820 the majority of this group lived in the westernmost wards. See Salem Tax Lists, 1760–1850, in Salem Tax Lists, 1689–.

61. Salem Tax Lists, 1785–1850, in Salem Tax Lists, 1689–; Manuscript Census for Massachusetts, Salem (1850), *Salem Directory* (1837).

62. Browne, "Youthful Recollections," 54; Hawthorne, *Scarlet Letter*, 25; Caroline Howard King, *When I Lived in Salem, 1822–1866* (Brattleboro, Vt., 1937), 36–37.

63. Perley, *History of Salem*, 1:375; Phillips, *Salem in the Eighteenth Century*, 151–154, 276; J. Foster Smith, "Stage Point and Thereabouts," *EIHC*, 66 (1930), 2–3, 6.

64. Smith, "Stage Point," 7, McLane, *Documents Relative to Manufactures*, 1:251–252.

65. Smith, "Stage Point," 14–15.

66. C. H. Webber and W. S. Nevins, *Old Naumkeag: An Historical Sketch of the City of Salem, and the Towns of Marblehead, Peabody, Beverly, Danvers, Wenham, Manchester, Topsfield, and Middleton* (Boston, 1877), 205; Charles S.

Osgood and H. M. Batchelder, *Historical Sketch of Salem, 1826–1879* (Salem, Mass., 1879), 230; Smith, "Stage Point," 15–16.

67. Ralph D. Paine, *The Ships and Sailors of Old Salem: The Record of a Brilliant Era of American Achievement* (New York, 1909), 639–640, 642.

68. On the Peabodys, see *History of Essex County, Massachusetts: With Biographical Sketches of Many of Its Pioneers and Prominent Men*, comp. D. Hamilton Hurd, 2 vols. (Philadelphia, 1888), 1:228–231; Osgood and Batchelder, *Sketch of Salem*, 235. For the changing occupational and ethnic structure of Salem, see the United States, Federal Census, 1850, 1860, and 1870 for Salem, Massachusetts, HeritageQuest Online version.

7. MASTERY AND THE MARITIME LAW

1. Richard Henry Dana, Jr., *Two Years Before the Mast: A Personal Narrative of Life at Sea* (Harmondsworth, 1981), 463–464.

2. Nathaniel B. Shurtleff, ed., *Records of the Governor and Company of the Massachusetts Bay in New England*, 6 vols. in 5 (Boston, 1853–1854), 4 (1):10, 4 (2):345, 389, 575, hereafter cited as *Mass. Recs.*; Richard B. Morris, *Government and Labor in Early America* (1946; rpt. New York, 1965), 228; L. Kinvin Wroth, "The Massachusetts Vice-Admiralty Court," in *Law and Authority in Colonial America: Selected Essays* (Barre, N.H., 1965), 35–36. The first case heard by the Court of Assistants can be found in *Records of the Court of Assistants of the Colony of the Massachusetts Bay, 1630–1692*, 3 vols., ed. John Noble and John F. Cronin (Boston, 1901–1928), 3:23. The remainder of the volume is filled with scores of other cases.

3. Morris, *Government and Labor*, 228–229. It should be noted that the Massachusetts Code contained fewer rules than the European codes and skipped certain subjects entirely. Compare its 27 articles in *Mass. Recs.*, 4 (2):388–393, with those of the Rolls of Oléron (47 articles), in *Monumenta Juridica: The Black Book of the Admiralty*, 4 vols., ed. Sir Travers Twiss (London, 1871–1876), 2:433–481; Laws of Wisbuy (70 articles), ibid., 4:265–284; Consulate of the Sea (252 articles), ibid., 3:37–657; and the Marine Ordinances of Louis XIV (247 articles), in *Federal Cases, Comprising Cases Argued and Determined in the Circuit and District Courts of the United States . . .*, 30 vols., 30:1203–1216, hereafter cited as *Federal Cases*. Gerard Malynes, *Consuetudo, vel, Lex Mercatoria: or, The Ancient Law-Merchant* (London, 1686), 97–140, takes about 25,000 words to summarize what the Massachusetts Code dealt with in about 2,500 words. Among the topics that the Massachusetts Code failed to mention were marine insurance, loans on bottomry, wreckers and pirates, and the thorny problems surrounding the obligations of masters toward ill seamen or the payment of wages to the widows of those who had died abroad.

4. Charles Molloy, *De Jure Maritimo et Navale or A Treatise of Affaires Maritime and of Commerce in Three Books*, 2d. ed. (London, 1677), 177.

5. Ralph Davis, *Rise of the English Shipping Industry in the Seventeenth and Eighteenth Centuries* (London, 1962), 159–174; Rolls of Oléron, Articles 1, 3, 8, 9,

22, Laws of Wisbuy, Articles 15, 38–40, 45, in Twiss, *Black Book of the Admiralty*, 2:433–437, 441–445, 457, 4:269, 276–277, 282; Laws of the Hanse Towns, Articles 37, 44, 45, 60, in *Federal Cases*, 30:1199–1201; Marine Ordinances of Louis XIV, Title Fifth, Title Eighth, in *Federal Cases*, 30:1210–1211, 1215.

6. Massachusetts Code of 1668, Articles 11, 14, 16, 17, in *Mass. Recs.*, 4 (2):391–392.

7. Laws of Wisbuy, Article 45, in Twiss, *Black Book of the Admiralty*, 4:278; Laws of the Hanse Towns, Article 9, in *Federal Cases*, 30:1198; Massachusetts Code of 1668, Article 8, in *Mass. Recs.*, 4 (2):390–391.

8. Massachusetts Code of 1668, Articles 4, 8, 26, 27, in *Mass. Recs.*, 4 (2):390–391, 393. For a broad, compelling treatment of the shipmaster's ambiguous position, see Margaret Creighton, *Rites and Passages: The Experience of American Whaling, 1830–1870* (Cambridge, 1995), 87–99.

9. Richard B. Morris, the modern authority on maritime labor law argued that it was "largely determined by a venerable tradition," the essence of which "was the principle of obedience." See Morris, *Government and Labor*, 262–278; Judith Fingard, *Jack in Port: Sailortowns of Eastern Canada* (Toronto, 1982), chap. 4; Marcus Rediker, *Between the Devil and the Deep Blue Sea: Merchant Seamen, Pirates, and the Anglo-American Maritime World, 1700–1750* (Cambridge, 1987), 120–121; and Dana, *Two Years Before the Mast*, 463–464.

10. Robert J. Steinfeld, *The Invention of Free Labor: The Employment Relation in English and American Law and Culture, 1350–1870* (Chapel Hill, N.C., 1991), 25–34, 40. On the variety of forms around the Anglo-American world, see Christopher L. Tomlins, *Law, Labor, and Ideology in the Early American Republic* (Cambridge, 1993), 239–258; Paul Craven and Douglas Hay, "The Criminalization of 'Free' Labor: Master and Servant in Comparative Perspective," *Slavery and Abolition* 15 (1994), 82–90.

11. Charles Abbott, *A Treatise of the Law Relative to Merchant Ships and Seamen in Four Parts; Enlarged With an Addenda Relative to Some Laws and Customs of the United States* (Philadelphia, 1802), 107; Massachusetts Code of 1668, Articles 4, 6, 18, 19, 22, 23, in *Mass. Recs.*, 4 (2):390–393. For a full description of these powers in the nineteenth century, see Richard Henry Dana, Jr., *The Seaman's Friend: A Treatise on Practical Seamanship* (Boston, 1879; rpt., Mineola, N.Y., 1997), 134–138.

12. Malynes, *Lex Mercatoria*, 104; Rolls of Oléron, Articles 12, 13; Laws of Wisbuy, Articles 24, 25, in Twiss, *Black Book of the Admiralty*, 2:447–449, 4:272; Abbott, *Treatise*, 108; Richard B. Morris, ed., *Select Cases of the Mayor's Court of New York City, 1674–1784* (Washington, D.C., 1935; rpt., Millwood, N.Y., 1975), 661; Myra Glenn, *Campaigns Against Corporal Punishment: Prisoners, Sailors, Women, and Children in Antebellum America* (Albany, N.Y., 1984), 8–9; Steinfeld, *Invention of Free Labor*, 25–26, 31. For the distinction between "chastise" and "beat," see *OED Online* (2d ed., 1989).

13. Morris, *Government and Labor*, 247, 256–260; Good Customs of the Sea (otherwise known as the Catalan Consulate of the Sea), Chapter 223, Amalphitan Table, Article 14, Gotland Sea-Laws, Article 66, Laws of Wisbuy,

Article 61, in Twiss, *Black Book of the Admiralty*, 2:511, 4:13, 127, 282; Massachusetts Code of 1668, Articles 7, 22, *Mass. Recs.*, 4 (2):390, 392–393; Act for the Better Regulation and Government of Seamen in the Merchants Service, 1729, 2 George 2, ch. 36; Act for the Government and Regulation of Seamen in the Merchant Service, 1st Congress, 2d Sess. ch. 29 (1790).

14. Steinfeld, *Invention of Free Labor*, 26, 27–33; Tomlins, *Law, Labor, and Ideology*, 241–249; Morris, *Government and Labor*, 434–43. For an argument emphasizing the unusual character of laws regarding maritime desertion see Rediker, *Between the Devil and the Deep Blue Sea*, 121.

15. Robert C. Ritchie, *Captain Kidd and the War Against the Pirates* (Cambridge, Mass., 1986), 141–154; Abbott, *Treatise*, 111–116. On the suppression of piracy see Rediker, *Between the Devil and the Deep Blue Sea*, 281–285.

16. Morris, *Government and Labor*, 268–272, 461–470; Abbott, *Treatise*, 108.

17. Abbott, *Treatise*, 109.

18. *Elwell v. Martin* (1824), *Federal Cases*, 8:587; *Sheridan v. Furber et al.* (1834), *Federal Cases*, 21:1267.

19. Daniel Vickers, *Farmers and Fishermen: Two Centuries of Work in Essex County, Massachusetts, 1630–1850* (Chapel Hill, N.C., 1994), 151–152.

20. *The Mentor* (1825), *Federal Cases*, 17:16; Rediker, *Between the Devil and the Deep Blue Sea*, 77–115. On medieval restraints on masters' authority see Rolls of Oléron, Article 2, 12, The Good Customs of the Sea, Chapter 120, Laws of Wisbuy, Articles 14, 21, 24, in Twiss, *Black Book of the Admiralty*, 2:435, 447, 3:229, 4:268–269, 271, 272.

21. *Sellman v. Gardner* (1727/8), *Spencer v. Gardner* (1727/8), in Dorothy S. Towle, ed., *Records of the Vice-Admiralty Court of Rhode Island, 1716–1752* (Washington, D.C., 1936), 123–125.

22. *Hooper v. Harris*, 1:198 (Mass. Vice-Admiralty, 1725); *Broughton v. Atkins*, 2:25 (Mass. Vice-Admiralty, 1727); *Wills v. Segall*, 2:36 (Mass. Vice-Admiralty, 1727); *Rex v. Owen*, 1:187 (Mass. Vice-Admiralty, 1724); *Hopkins v. Fennel*, 3:97–124 (S. Carolina Vice-Admiralty, 1737); *Fry v. Beekman* (1728), in Morris, *Cases of the Mayor's Court*, 660–662; Libel, *Collis v. Smith* (n.d.), in *Reports of Cases in the Vice Admiralty of Province of New York, 1715–1788*, ed. Charles Merrill Hough (New Haven, 1925), 262–264.

23. *Benton v. Whitney* (1841), *Federal Cases*, 3:258.

24. *Sellman v. Gardner* (1727/8), *Spencer v. Gardner* (1727/8), in Towle, *Records of the Vice-Admiralty Court of Rhode Island*, 123–125.

25. Lawrence William Towner, *A Good Master Well Served: Masters and Servants in Colonial Massachusetts, 1620–1750* (New York, 1998), 168–169; George Francis Dow and Mary G. Thresher, eds., *Records and Files of the Quarterly Courts of Essex County, Massachusetts, 1636–1686*, 9 vols. (Salem, Mass., 1911–1975), 8:91–92, hereafter cited as *Essex Co. Court Recs.*

26. *Essex Co. Court Recs.*, 8:91–92.

27. Paul Griffiths, *Youth and Authority: Formative Experiences in England, 1560–1640* (Oxford, 1996), 313–347; Towner, *A Good Master Well Served*, 184–185; Edmund Morgan, *The Puritan Family, Religion and Domestic Relations in*

Seventeenth-Century New England (Boston, 1944; rpt., New York, 1966), 116; Morris, *Government and Labor*, 470–500; Terri L. Snyder, "'As if There was not Master or Woman in the Land': Gender, Dependency, and Household Violence in Virginia, 1646–1720," in *Over the Threshold: Intimate Violence in Early America*, ed. Christine Daniels and Michael V. Kennedy (New York, 1999), 219–236.

28. Douglas Hay, "Patronage, Paternalism, and Welfare: Masters, Workers, and Magistrates in Eighteenth-Century England," *International Labor and Working-Class History*, 53 (1998), 27–48; Douglas Hay, "Master and Servant in England: Using the Law in the Eighteenth and Nineteenth Centuries," in *Private Law and Social Inequality in the Industrial Age: Comparing Legal Cultures in Britain, France, Germany, and the United States*, ed. Willibald Steinmetz (Oxford, 2000), 232–239. Of all wage cases against masters before the Massachusetts Vice-Admiralty Court, 1718–1747, plaintiffs won 80 percent of the time (*n*=386). Of all desertion cases against mariners, masters won 90 percent of the time. See *Records of the Court of Admiralty of the Province of Massachusetts Bay, 1718–1747*, 3 vols., Massachusetts Supreme Judicial Court Archives, Suffolk County Court House, Boston. See also Morris, *Government and Labor*, 232–233; Fingard, *Jack in Port*, 187–188; Jerry Bannister, *The Rule of the Admirals: Law, Custom, and Naval Government in Newfoundland, 1699–1832* (Toronto, 2003), 242–245.

29. *Saunders v. Buckup* (1831), *Federal Cases*, 21:528; *Gould v. Christianson* (1836), *Federal Cases*, 10:858, 860. On similar issues, see Deposition of Henry Burns, July 29, 1827, box 1, folder 2, Andrew Dunlap Papers, 1754–1847, James Duncan Phillips Library, Peabody-Essex Museum, Salem, Mass.; *Elwell v. Martin* (1824), *Federal Cases*, 8:584–588; *Forbes v. Parsons* (1839), *Federal Cases*, 9:419; *Jarvis v. the Claiborne* (1808), *Federal Cases*, 13:373; *Magee v. the Moss* (1831), *Federal Cases*, 16:388; *Ringgold v. Crocker* (1848), *Federal Cases*, 20:814; *Carleton v. Davis* (1844), *Federal Cases*, 5:68; *Forbes v. Parsons* (1839), *Federal Cases*, 9:419; *Mitchell v. Pratt* (1841), *Federal Cases*, 17:516. On the campaign against and abolition of flogging see Glenn, *Campaigns Against Corporal Punishment*, 43–44, 85–101, 112–121, 128–132; Harold D. Langley, *Social Reform in the United States Navy* (Urbana, Ill., 1967), 139–206.

30. *Dean v. Huffington*, 21:177 (U.S., 1st Dist., 1837).

31. Ibid.

32. Tomlins, *Law, Labor, and Ideology*, 259–292; Steinfeld, *Invention of Free Labor*, 147–172; quotation from Michel Foucault, "Two Lectures," in *Power/Knowledge: Selected Interviews and Other Writings, 1972–1977*, ed. Colin Gordon (New York, 1980), 104.

33. *Butler v. McClellan et al.* (1831), *Federal Cases*, 4:907; *Elwell v. Martin et al.* (1824), *Federal Cases*, 8:587–588; *Sheridan v. Furber* (1834), *Federal Cases*, 21:1267–1268; *The William Harris* (1837), *Federal Cases*, 29:1307.

34. *Wood et al. v. the Nimrod* (1829), *Federal Cases*, 30:471; *Butler v. McClellan et al.* (1831), *Federal Cases*, 4:909; *The Rovena* (1836), *Federal Cases*, 20:1277; *Sheridan v. Furber et al.* (1834), *Federal Cases*, 21:1268; *The Mentor* (1825),

Federal Cases, 17:16. See also *Cloutman v. Tunison* (1833), *Federal Cases*, 5:1093; *Elwell v. Martin et al.* (1824), *Federal Cases*, 8:588; *The Moslem* (1846), *Federal Cases*, 17:896; *Snell et al. v. the Independence* (1830), *Federal Cases*, 22:718; *Smith v. Treat* (1845), *Federal Cases*, 22:688.

35. Molloy, *De Jure Maritimo*, 209; Malynes, *Lex Mercatoria*, 102. Other early modern works on maritime law that assert the authority of the shipmaster but see no need to justify its personal character include William Falconer, *An Universal Dictionary of the Marine* (London, 1769; new ed. London, 1780), 191; René-Josué Valin, *Nouveau Commentaire sur l'Ordonnance de la marine de mois d'Août, 1681*, 2 vols. (La Rochelle, 1776), 1:509–560.

36. One of the best recent historians of seafaring life in the age of sail, Pablo E. Pérez-Mallaína, has suggested that in the eighteenth century "authority sustained by the lash converted many decks into authentic slaughterhouses." Pérez-Mallaína borrows the term "slaughterhouse" from Marcus Rediker, who used it in specific reference to vessels of the East India Company. If Pérez-Mallaína's construction of Rediker's point is broadly correct, however, the argument made here that the labor regime at sea resembled that on shore cannot hold. See Pérez-Mallaína, *Spain's Men of the Sea: Daily Life on the Indies Fleets in the Sixteenth Century*, trans. Carla Rahn Phillips (Baltimore, 1998), 192; Rediker, *Between the Devil and the Deep Blue Sea*, 213.

37. Quotation from Sir W. S. Gilbert and Sir Arthur Sullivan, *H.M.S. Pinafore*, act 1. Marcus Rediker deals with some of these issues in *Between the Devil and the Deep Blue Sea*, 219, 315–316; Rediker, "The Common Seaman in the Histories of Capitalism and the Working Class," *International Journal of Maritime History*, 1, no. 2 (1989), 342–343. See also Greg Dening, *Mr. Bligh's Bad Language: Passion, Power, and Theatre on the Bounty* (Cambridge, 1992), 113–132; Bannister, *Rule of the Admirals*, 229–231. The Massachusetts Vice-Admiralty Court heard 478 cases between 1717 and 1733 that may have been connected to issues of discipline and treatment. Over that same period, Massachusetts customshouses probably cleared between 6,000 and 7,000 vessels. See Massachusetts Vice-Admiralty Recs., vols. 1–3; Gary B. Nash, *The Urban Crucible: Social Change, Political Consciousness, and the Origins of the American Revolution* (Cambridge, Mass., 1979), 410; James B. Lydon, "North Shore Trade in the Early Eighteenth Century," *American Neptune*, 28 (1968), 264–265.

38. Edward Barlow, *Barlow's Journal of His Life at Sea in King's Ships, East and West Indiamen, and Other Merchantmen, 1659–1703*, ed. Basil Lubbock, 2 vols. (London, 1934), 2:451–453. See also the remarks of Capt. John Higgins cited in Peter Earle, "English Sailors, 1570–1775," in *"The Emblems of Hell"? European Sailors and the Maritime Labour Market, 1570–1780*, ed. Paul C. Van Royen, Jaap R. Bruijn, and Jan Lucassen (St. John's, Nfld., 1997), 90.

39. John Cremer, *Ramblin' Jack: The Journal of Captain John Cremer, 1700–1774*, ed. R. Reynell Bellamy (London, 1936), 138. Pierre-Sébastien Boulay Paty, *Cours de Droit Maritime*, cited in *Butler v. McClellan et al.* (1831), *Federal Cases*, 4:909.

40. *Mahoney v. Nickerson,* 17:70–71 (U.S., 1st Dist., 1829); *Williams v. Crosby,* 17:172 (U.S., 1st Dist., 1829); *Stanley v. Lincoln,* 12:424 (U.S., 1st Dist., 1821); *Parker v. Bursley* 17:215 (U.S., 1st Dist., 1829); *Rex v. Harrison,* 4 (part 2):49–50 (S. Carolina Vice-Admiralty, 1758).

41. See the marine logbooks describing seventy-six voyages listed in Appendix A.

42. Cremer, *Ramblin' Jack,* 124, 138, 157–158, 224–225, 227; Jacob Nagle, *The Nagle Journal: A Diary of the Life of Jacob Nagle, Sailor, from the Year, 1775 to 1841,* ed. John C. Dann (New York, 1988), 177–178; Charles Tyng, *Before the Wind: The Memoir of an American Sea Captain, 1808–1833,* ed. Susan Fels (New York, 1999), 18, 22–23, 89, 133, 135–136, 152, 177, 179, 225; Gorham Low, *The Sea Made Men: The Story of a Gloucester Lad,* ed. Elizabeth L. Alling (New York, 1937), 125–126.

43. Samuel Kelly, *Samuel Kelly: An Eighteenth Century Seaman,* ed. Crosbie Garstin (New York, 1925), 27; William McNally, *Evils and Abuses in the Merchant Service Exposed; With Proposals for their Remedy and Redress* (Boston, 1839), 62–79, 180.

44. Edward Coxere, *Adventures by Sea,* ed. E. H. W. Meyerstein (New York, 1946), 6; Cremer, *Ramblin' Jack,* 50; Kelly, *Samuel Kelly,* 74, 226. See also Coxere, *Adventures by Sea,* 4, 10, 29; Cremer, *Ramblin' Jack,* 45; Kelly, *Samuel Kelly,* 23–24, 40, 41, 75, 152. See also Philip Chadwick Foster Smith, ed., *The Journals of Ashley Bowen (1728–1813) of Marblehead,* 2 vols. (Colonial Society of Massachusetts, *Publications,* 44–45 [Boston, 1973]), 44:14–18; Tyng, *Before the Wind,* 19, 22–23.

45. Nagle, *Journal,* 288.

46. The best treatments of African-American sailors in the antebellum and colonial periods are Bolster, *Black Jacks;* and David Cecelski, *The Waterman's Song: Slavery and Freedom in Maritime North Carolina* (Chapel Hill, N.C., 2001). The proportion of cooks and stewards who were victims of discipline is based on thirty-four incidents drawn from Salem Marine Log Collection, 1807–1849, James Duncan Phillips Library, Peabody-Essex Museum (using the library's subject index), and a sampling of cases before the United States First District Court, Massachusetts, 1820–1850, National Archives Northeast Region, Waltham, Mass. Of all cooks and stewards on board Salem vessels, 1805–1850 (n=91), 86 percent were black. Cooks and stewards composed 14 percent of all nonofficers aboard Salem vessels in both 1805 (n=1,168) and 1825 (n=280). See sources in Appendix A. For evidence that seacooks in Providence, R.I., were almost all black as well, see Bolster, *Black Jacks,* 235, 279 [n27].

47. *Dobbins v. Low,* 11:547–548, 550, 554, 556, 559 (U.S., 1st Dist., 1820); *Parker v. Burseley,* 17:214–216 (U.S., 1st Dist., 1829). See also *Williams v. Crosby,* 17:172 (U.S., 1st Dist., 1829); *Mahoney v. Nickerson,* 17:68 (U.S., 1st Dist., 1829); *Carleton v. Davis* (1844), *Federal Cases,* 5:68; Ship's Journals, ship *St. Paul,* Aug. 16, 1837; bark *Ezpeleta,* Mar. 30, 1846; brig *Sciot,* May 7, 8, 1831, all in Marine Logs and Journals Collection, James Duncan Phillips Library, Peabody-Essex Museum, Salem, Mass.

48. Rediker, *Between the Devil and the Deep Blue Sea*, 209n. Out of twenty wage, assault, or negligence cases heard by the Essex County Courts between 1653 and 1683, only two arose on coastwise voyages to North American destinations. See *Essex Co. Court Recs.*, 1:391, 9:397–398. For the few domestic voyages that generated disciplinary cases before the United States' First District Court, Massachusetts, see *U.S. v. Peterson et al.* (1846), *Federal Cases*, 27:515–520; *Harkell v. Wortman*, 17:132 (U.S., 1st Dist., 1829). Sailors' memoirs relating to coastwise voyages include Benjamin Bangs, Diary, vol. 1, 1742–1749, Massachusetts Historical Society, Boston; Edward Beck, *The Sea Voyages of Edward Beck in the 1820s*, ed. Michael Hay and Joy Roberts (Edinburgh, 1996), 5–37. On the North Sea, see Janet Kinloch, "Working Conditions of Scottish East Coast Seamen," *International Journal of Maritime History*, 9, no. 2 (1997), 161–163, 165; Paul Van Royen, "Personnel of the Dutch and English Mercantile Marine (1700–1850): An Introductory Paper," in *Anglo-Dutch Mercantile Marine Relations, 1700–1850*, ed. J. R. Bruijn and W. F. J. Mörzer Bruyns (Leiden, 1991), 105.

49. The most thorough study of mistreatment at sea is Rediker, *Between the Devil and the Deep Blue Sea*, 213–243, and although home port and destination are not his categories of analysis, most of the incidents where these *are* mentioned in his text pertain to lengthy overseas voyages that concluded in London. On conditions aboard East India voyages, see A. J. R. Russell-Wood, "Seamen Ashore and Afloat: The Social Environment of the *Carreira da India*, 1550–1750," *Mariners' Mirror*, 69 (1983): 35–52; F. S. Gaastra and J. R. Bruijn, "The Dutch East India Company's Shipping, 1602–1795, in a Comparative Perspective," in *Ships, Sailors, and Spices: East India Companies and Their Shipping in the 16th, 17th, and 18th Centuries*, ed. J. R. Bruijn and F. S. Gaastra (Amsterdam, 1993), 202; Sir Evan Cotton, *East Indiamen: The East India Company's Maritime Service*, ed. Sir Charles Fawcett (London, 1949), 60–61, 93–94.

50. Nathaniel Ames, *Nautical Reminiscences* (Providence, R.I., 1832), 35; Nathaniel Ames, *A Mariner's Sketches, Originally Published in the Manufacturers and Farmers Journal* (Providence, R.I., 1830), 102; Richard Henry Dana, Jr., *Cruelty to Seamen, being the Case of Nichols & Couch* (1839; rpt. Berkeley, Calif., 1937), 6, 9.

51. *Healey v. Martin* (1823), *Federal Cases*, 11:957–960. On the rise of "naval discipline" in the merchant services generally, see Yrjö Kaukiainen, "Finnish Sailors, 1750–1870" in Van Royen, Bruijn, and Lucassen, *"The Emblems of Hell"?* 227; Heide Gerstenberger, "The Disciplining of German Seamen," *International Journal of Maritime History*, 13, no. 2 (2001), 47–48.

52. Nathaniel Ames, *An Old Sailor's Yarns* (New York, 1835), 53; Herman Melville, *Moby-Dick; or, The Whale* (Harmondsworth, 1972), 246, 259; Dana, *Two Years Before the Mast*, 382.

53. *OED Online* (2d ed., 1989).

INDEX